What do men and women really want from each other in marriage today? Who controls money, children, careers, sex? The facts are in. The truth is out. HUSBANDS AND WIVES is the first complete nationwide survey to ask the frank questions, to present the frank answers...

HUSBANDS AND WIVES

* * *

ANTHONY PIETROPINTO, M.D., is the Director of the Mental Health Clinic of Brooklyn's Lutheran Medical Center; he lives in New York with his family.

JACQUELINE SIMENAUER is a psychiatric editor, syndicated columnist and writer who lives with her family in New Jersey.

* * *

THE NEW YORK TIMES called their previous book, BEYOND THE MALE MYTH, *"the most extensive look taken at the sexual attitudes and practices of American men since Dr. Kinsey's famous study in 1948."*

A NATIONWIDE SURVEY OF MARRIAGE

HUSBANDS AND WIVES

Anthony Pietropinto, M.D. & Jacqueline Simenauer

BERKLEY BOOKS, NEW YORK

This Berkley book contains the complete
text of the original hardcover edition.
It has been completely reset in a type face
designed for easy reading, and was printed
from new film.

HUSBANDS AND WIVES:
A Nationwide Survey of Marriage

A Berkley Book / published by arrangement with
Times Books

PRINTING HISTORY
Times Books edition / January 1979
Berkley edition / January 1981

ISBN: 0-425-04701-6

A BERKLEY BOOK ® TM 757,375
Berkley Books are published by Berkley Publishing Corporation,
200 Madison Avenue, New York, New York 10016.
PRINTED IN THE UNITED STATES OF AMERICA

Acknowledgments

A personal tribute to Tillie and Harry Himelstein for their contribution of love and devotion, and whose memories will be forever cherished by all.

To Arnold L. Lyslo, A.C.S.W., Director of the Talbot Perkins Children's Services in New York City, a man of great wisdom and sensitivity.

For Sarah M. Holbrook, A.C.S.W. for her insight, kindness and generosity.

To Talbot Perkins Children's Services, a 50-year-old agency that provides adoption, family day care, foster care and preventive services to families for their guidance and help.

With appreciation to Lisa and Lothar Simenauer for the time they extended, and Mildred Roberta Hunter for her dedication and care.

A special note of thanks to Doris Walfield, Bert Himelstein, Helena De Paola and Judy Voccola for their assistance.

Last but not least to Roger Jellinek and the staff at Times Books for their determination and persistence.

TO OUR OWN HUSBANDS AND WIVES
AND OUR CHILDREN

Joy Ann, Rita Diana, and Laura Joy Pietropinto
and
Peter and Tara Heidi Simenauer

A deep acknowledgment is made to George Bernard Shaw, playwright, philosopher, and social activist, whose observations on marriage and the family seventy years ago are as progressive and valid today as ever and whose wit and insight has been a source of inspiration throughout this book. As Don Juan in Hell served as allegorical guide for our previous book, *Beyond the Male Myth*, Bishop Bridgenorth and the members of the wedding raise their irreverent voices throughout the ensuing chapters, to be joined occasionally by Henry Higgins, Eliza Doolittle, John Tanner, and his ancestor Don Juan, and the other Shavian saints and supermen, devils and devils' advocates who for nearly a century have bemused their audiences into daring to question our traditions and conventions, and to carry visions of a better world as far as thought can reach.

Contents

Introduction:

A State of Revolution

> There is no subject on which more dangerous nonsense is talked and thought than marriage.

—*George Bernard Shaw*

The play is called *Getting Married*. In the course of its action, the prospective bride and groom decide that, rather than submit to the injustices and follies of marital law, they will simply draw up and live according to their own private contract. The bride demands a salary for housekeeping. Another young woman in the play wishes to enter into a group marriage with two men, especially since the men enjoy each other's company more than hers. An older spinster, named Lesbia, wants to have a child but cannot bear the presence of men; she resents the attitudes of a society that loses the superior offspring of intelligent, independent women who will not endure the restrictions of marriage. A wife who constantly seeks extramarital romance is said to be a more stimulating companion and better wife because of her proclivities. And a clergyman states that the only grounds for a divorce should be the wish of either party without forcing a spouse to charge the other with one sort of heinous behavior or another.

It is a most appropriate play for our modern times, dealing as it does with the outdated attitudes of society towards marriage and coming to grips with the novel, unconventional remedies now being proposed. It is a play written and first performed in 1908.

When one encounters a 70-year-old popular drama that, save for its setting in early post-Victorian England, appears to have been written yesterday—and reads its preface in which playwright Shaw speaks of the young women who seek his advice on whether they should consent to marry the men they have chosen to live with—one is bound to experience a feeling akin to that of a novice air-traveller who shuts his eyes and grips his chair as the plane starts its engines and is dismayed to discover 30 minutes later that the plane is only at the runway. To say that society is changing and that its institutions must change with it is no more debatable than to say the universe is moving and aging; we are most easily misled by our experts not in their contention that marriage is undergoing crisis and change but in the impression that our age is witnessing startlingly new crises and breathtakingly rapid changes.

Sociologist Ira Reiss quotes the statement: "The last fifty years have apparently changed the marriage relation from a permanent and lifelong state to a union existing for the pleasure of the parties. The change thus swiftly wrought is so revolutionary, involving the very foundations of human society, that we must believe it to be the result not of any temporary conditions." This statement, so descriptive of the current state of affairs, was written in 1887. Despite the warnings of history, social scientists like Watson predicted in 1927 that marriage would not survive the next fifty years and Sorokin, two decades later, predicted that divorce would reduce the family to incidental cohabitation of male and female and the home to "an overnight parking place mainly for sex-relationship." In retrospect, these doomsayers seem as ludicrous as the ancient Greeks who moaned that the world was going to pot because the youth did not respect their elders.

The problem with marriage today is not a matter of its continued existence—that seems assured, with over 95 per cent of the population still marrying at some point in their lives—but the quality of its existence. The old comparison of marriage to a besieged city, with all those outside wanting to get in and those inside wanting out, was never more valid, with the national divorce rate having increased fifteen-fold in the past century and doubled in the past decade. More than half of divorced couples have children under 18, and at least 40 per cent of schoolchildren will live part of their lives in a single-parent household. The fact that four out of five divorced people do remarry, half within a year, is enough to convince us that the abolition of marriage is not imminent. But it is this dramatic escalation in the number of disrupted marriages that compels us to examine the health of an age-old, indestructible institution, to apprehend it in the midst of its unimpeded growth and try to analyze and diagnose the nature of its ailments. Granted, we may argue that more divorces simply mean fewer bad marriages and that the rising divorce rate merely means that relaxation of civil laws and social sanctions have permitted couples to avail themselves of release from unhappy unions which would have been just as unhappy, though undissolved, decades ago. Nevertheless, it is reasonable to assume that virtually all couples enter a marriage wanting it to be permanent and successful and a divorce, which now terminates nearly one in three marriages, often represents a failure of the most important endeavor in one's life. It has become fashionable to extol divorce in terms of personal growth and liberation, but, like the cigarette advertiser who came up with the slogan "cancer is good for you," proponents of this optimistic philosophy rarely convince the losers that they would have been worse off not having loved at all. Divorce generally hurts and when that pain affects more than 15 million Americans, we are justified in regarding the situation as something of a national health emergency.

Social problems and social changes can have significance only in proportion to the number of people affected by them. In any effort at social change, it is always the radicals and the most unconventional solutions that attract and occupy our interest, but the population at large moves much more slowly, if at all. It takes thousands of revolutionaries to effect a revolution; fewer may constitute an underground movement at best and a lunatic fringe or simple lunatics at worst. Thus, the living-togethers, the commune-ists, the swingers, the radical feminists, and certainly the divorcees have always been among us; it is not their presence, but their number that we must now reckon with. And in so reckoning we must never lose the count and forget which problems and viewpoints are representative of large segments of society and which are concerns and solutions that affect vociferous and often worthy small minorities but are never incorporated or even perceived by the mainstream. Since all innovations begin in the minds of a few and are tested initially by the most radical, the secret in understanding the ways of a society lies not in detecting new crises and coping methods, but more in perceiving when such issues become relevent to large numbers of average people.

Unfortunately, most of the writing is done, not by average people, but by those who are most disenchanted with the status quo and most disposed to sweeping reforms and highly unconventional solutions. A fair amount of our current ideas about relationships and marriage has been shaped by militant feminists, homosexuals, and others who have neither experience in nor the inclination for marriage. While we should not disparage such people's intellects or opinions, we should regard their writings as we might *Joe DiMaggio's Book of Football*, respecting the author's achievements and abilities, but wishing he had remained in his spheres of expertise, such as baseball, banking, and coffee. Psychotherapists and marriage counsellors are acknowledged to have a higher divorce rate than those in most other occupations; while divorce does not necessarily impugn their clinical abilities, a troubled spouse who consults them with the firm intention of saving a marriage might well react upon learning of the therapists' personal track record as though he had unwittingly enrolled in the Don Rickles charm school or the Phyllis Diller beauty program.

Again, the problem is not that we are learning from and being guided by gifted individuals who are outside of marriage, either because they have never entered or have exited through the door of divorce, which, in view of the high remarriage rate has apparently become a revolving door. The problem is that we hear far too little from people currently involved in marriages—not ideal marriages, not extraordinary unions and exceptional partnerships, but ordinary, functional relationships which somehow manage to survive the pressures of environment, family, mate, and one's own person. We have had far too much information from the routed troops who have disengaged themselves from the struggle and from the chart-consulting intelligence corps who have never known combat; it's time we heard more from the blighters in the trenches, those who are holding their positions under fire while all around them are in retreat.

The aim of this book is to survey the experiences, feelings, and attitudes of married men and women throughout America, people of all ages, social backgrounds, and income levels. Some are in their second or even later marriages; some have lived with partners prior to marriage; some are even in the process of divorce—but all are currently married, giving us the benefit, not of hindsight or speculation, but of a perception of marriage as they are living the experience. These people are the heart and substance of this book. The statistics culled from the survey are here for those who want them and we can use such numbers as roadmarkers indicating where married America is at and in which direction it is going, but ultimately it is our subjective hearing of individual voices rather than our objective viewing of collective figures that will guide our understanding of contemporary marriage, with its diversity of aims, needs, satisfactions, and problems.

The community mental health clinic offers us a better vantage point than does the office of the marriage counsellor or the private psychiatrist, for we can trace the progress and effects of marriages long before their deterioration becomes so severe that the patient identifies them as a problem requiring special counselling. While the lower socioeconomic classes still divorce or separate more readily than their more affluent counterparts, they less frequently seek professional counselling, unless the economic hardships, the emotionally determined physical ailments, and the turmoil wreaked on the children have already led the family to the mental health clinic in the phase of turbulence that invariably precedes the capsize of the marriage. For every patient who has the money, time, and sophistication for private psychotherapy, there are countless troubled spouses who suffer alone and in silence. Fear of social stigma, ignorance, mistrust, or pessimism keep most of them from getting professional aid even in the few neighborhoods where it is available at low or no cost to them, but thousands do find their own way or are fortuitiously netted through referrals from physicians, welfare agencies, or school guidance counsellors. Our expertise, such as it is, comes from daily contact with large numbers of married men and women from all social strata whose marriages play a key role in their emotional well-being, often in a destructive, painful way, frequently as the only positive source of support, but usually in a complex interaction of positive and negative vectors resulting in forces that may not control, but certainly influence, the direction of their lives. Our studies of marriage should not be based primarily on autopsies of unions already given up as dead or treated only after having been diagnosed as critical. We must examine the healthy and those enduring the inevitable, commonplace ailments that are as prevalent and untreatable as the common cold.

We must be like the diner who was served a one-clawed lobster and told by the waiter, "He must have lost it in a fight"; the customer thereupon demanded, "Then take it back and bring me the winner." In surveying thousands of individuals actively involved in marriages, we will encounter few non-combatants and many who would not classify themselves as winners, but nearly always we will be dealing with unions where there is some measure of hope, concern and viability. These are living marriages, those possessing potential, future, and actual existence. All else is mere hope and history.

Search and Research

In surveying married Americans, we began our study with a set of basic goals. First we needed a large enough sample to insure statistical significance, with equal numbers of men and women; we set our goal at at least 3,500 individuals (ultimately winding up with 3,880), since a sample of that size, provided it is balanced to be representative of all types of people, will give proportionately the same result as a sample ten or a hundred times that number. Next, we wanted a sample that would include percentages of subgroups compatible with U.S. census figures on such parameters as income level, education level, type of occupation, region of the country, age group, ethnic group, and parenthood.

We employed two forms of questions to be asked each participant. One type required the respondent to check off one or more listed responses to a question, often offering the option of writing in his own brief response instead. There were 50 of these multiple-choice questions and the responses could be computer-tabulated to indicate what percentages of the total sample and each of the subgroups chose that reply. All 3,880 respondents completed this form. The other type of question required a personal handwritten reply. These answers were subjective and individualistic, and could not lend themselves to computer analysis. There were 32 of these questions, dealing with all aspects of married life, from courtship and reasons for marrying to divorce, remarriage and opinions on the rising divorce rate. Because of the amount of time these lengthier answers required, each respondent answered 2 to 4 questions. Since the 32 questions were distributed randomly on a rotating basis, we received, on the average, about 300 replies to each.

The survey was conducted by Crossley Surveys, Inc., in New

York City, a firm founded over 50 years ago for private marketing research and public research polling. It was this firm that had assisted us in compiling the data received from 4,000 American men as the basis for the book *Beyond the Male Myth: What Women Want to Know about Men's Sexuality*. The research firm conducted interviews in 19 states and the District of Columbia, involving 41 cities or areas, in some of which as many as ten different testing locales were employed. These locales encompassed shopping centers, hotel lobbies, air and railroad terminals, universities, and office buildings, preselected from past experience to yield a valid cross-section of the population with regard to age, race and socioeconomic status.

At the testing sites, field agents approached men and women at random to enlist their participation. If the person did not decline, he was presented with the following statement on a Crossley Surveys letterhead explaining the nature of the survey:

Your Opinion Is Important

Dear Married Person:
This survey is an important and serious professional effort to gather information on current attitudes toward marriage. The questions on the survey are for married people between the ages of 18 and 65 years of age. "Why ask me" you might say. Your participation is needed so that your anonymous opinion can be included with the opinions of several thousand others across the United States.
You are being asked to take this questionnaire and fill it out in privacy. When you have checked all the answers place the questionnaire in the sealed box located by our representative. Your answers will be confidential and since you are not asked to sign anything there will be no way to identify the responses with you.
In the past, surveys have been done on this subject but there has never been a survey like this one which will cover several thousand married individuals across the country, from all walks of life. It is important that you participate so that the final results include people like yourself. It will only take a few minutes of your time. Why not have your opinion counted?

Thank you!

P.S. We have included essay questions so that you can fully express your ideas without being limited to pre-established categories. Feel free to answer fully. If you need more space, please write on the back of the paper. If you need more time to consider your answer you may take them home to fill out and mail back your reply in the postage-paid envelope.

Couples who were approached were given a statement addressed "Dear Couple," identical with the above except for the added sentence. "Don't consult your spouse; we want your personal opinions."

Respondents who were not with spouses at the time they were approached were given a similar questionnaire to take home to their husband or wife, who could then complete it and mail it back in a postage-paid envelope. By the use of this method, we were able to include both halves of a married pair in the study more often; since the essay questions were color-coded to indicate the sex of the respondent and bore the same identifying number for each husband/wife pair we attempted to engage, we were able, where both participated, to compare the responses of both parties to the same questions.

Of the people approached by the survey representatives, 57 per cent, or nearly three out of five initially agreed to participate. The low rate of refusals may seem strange to people who reside in large cities where any approach by a stranger is tantamount to assault, but a cordial approach to people not currently involved in their own work and the total anonymity offered in the study, whereby not even the "interviewer" would see the responses to the questions, encouraged cooperation. Of course, nearly half of those approached who were receptive had to be eliminated because they were not currently married. Finally, a total of 3,563 questionnaires were completed at the testing sites. Including the questionnaires that were mailed in by spouses not directly contacted, 3,880 married people ultimately participated. There were 869 couples in that total; that is, both husband and wife took part.

This book will present many of these responses and use them in an attempt to analyze the status and trends of contemporary American marriage. Admittedly, each answer represents the experience and viewpoint of a single individual, and the variation in aims, needs, satisfactions and problems makes each marriage a unique entity, transcending the attempts of religious dogma, civil law, social morality, romantic convention, and ethnic tradition to define exactly what a marriage is and should be. While our statistical tables enable us to generalize and speculate about majorities and pluralities, it is the range and subjectivity of individual experience that determine the protean essence of marriage, and it is hoped that exposure to a variety of such experience will give the reader a greater intuitive understanding of this way of life than any number of cold statistics could possibly convey.

This is the first large-scale nationwide survey on the subject of marriage ever conducted, based exclusively on responses of people currently married, equally balanced to represent both husbands and wives. Our professional research corporation took care to insure that these spouses would be drawn from all age groups, income levels, occupational groups, and racial backgrounds, with representation proportional to that in the general population, according to census figures. We were able to document many trends in contemporary marriage, some representing striking differences or even complete reversals of traditional marital patterns, the implications of which will be explored and analyzed with particular reference to the experiences and viewpoints of our 3,800 husbands and wives.

Why People Marry

We find, in sharp contrast to previous studies, that less than half of married people wed for love. While love was the most frequently given reason, there is a definite break with the old ideals of romanticism, and a more pragmatic approach to selection of partners. Home-life is a less important concept among the youngest spouses, where the employment of wives and the deferment of childbearing have erased the hallowed images of domesticity, while companionship on an egalitarian basis is replacing the old practice of husbands' and wives' adopting male and female roles and duties. Whereas in the past romantic infatuation mellowed over the course of years into a partnership based more on affection and respect than passion, couples today seem to begin the marriage on the type of footing that would have previously taken considerable time to evolve.

Mate Selection

We found that spouses select each other on the basis of their individuality rather than their promise of meeting traditional role expectations for husbands, wives, and parents. Personality has become the most important factor in mate selection. Men still rely on sexual attractiveness and physical beauty to a greater degree than women in choosing a partner, but these attributes are secondary to personality traits. Wives are abandoning the old criteria of being in love as the basis for marriage, making what seems to be a more deliberate rational choice. While marriages between people who are alike predominate over matches between opposites, the similarities seem to lie more in the sharing of common goals and ideals, rather than similar backgrounds.

Sex in Marriage

While most couples reported their sex lives to be satisfactory, there was a notable drop in the number who rated it very good, compared to responses in previous studies. Sex is no longer tailored to meet the needs and demands of men, since husbands and wives were virtually identical in their assessment of marital gratification. The growing discontent may be a reflection of unreasonable expectations based on the proliferation of literature promising zeniths of sexual fulfillment through a variety of physical techniques and psychological interactions, for the biggest sexual problem these days seems to be not in the area of performance, but in sexual desire. While oral sex has received wide acceptance, some of the even more unconventional variations are practiced by surprisingly small numbers of couples, indicating that our highly popular sex-oriented magazines have perhaps given us an unrealistic picture of the extent of the Sexual Revolution.

The Marriage Relationship

In surveying spouses' ideas of those elements most essential for a good marriage, we find a premium placed on good communication, as well as emphasis on similar ideas and interests and concern for one another's needs. While these are indisputably assets, it was striking to find them rated so far ahead of the traditional goals of marriage, such as mutual sexual satisfaction, having children, and financial security. In other words, we find an emphasis on the process through which goals are achieved superseding the goals themselves—the communication and concern that enable the achievement of mutual aims becoming aims in themselves. Stability rather than love was determined to be the satisfactory equilibrium point in a marriage, again reflecting an attitude of pragmatism replacing romantic ideals. We find that, despite increasing egalitarianism between the sexes, there is still a sex-based division of responsibility in many marriages, the husbands controlling business interests, automobiles, and, to a lesser extent, sexual activity, while the home remains a woman's province. Money is not as strictly relegated according to gender, but tends to fall into the control of one spouse or the other, rather than becoming subject to joint governing procedures.

Marriage and the Self

As in the way they tended to view their mates, most married people see and value themselves as being considerate, indicating that they are willing to consider a viewpoint that may be markedly different from their own and modify their goals accordingly. Although the vast majority felt that marriage had changed them for the better in some way, one-third also felt they had been changed, in other ways, for the worse, and one-third also felt that their mates did not appreciate them fully as people and/or lovers. Marriage is seen as improving people by giving purpose and meaning to their lives and increasing the capacity to handle responsibility—more so than through the more passive satisfactions of emotional security and alleviation of loneliness.

Children in Marriage

Children were once conceived out of a sense of moral obligation, to provide financial security for parents in old age, and to perpetuate the family name; today, they are viewed by just about half the parents as a source of love. As givers of affection, more than recipients, the children are assuming a more personal and dominant role in the family structure, and the diminishing family size further underscores each child's individuality. A significant number of both husbands and wives see children as essential to the fulfillment of one's destiny as a man or woman, and far more parents regard their children as having brought them closer together than as exerting disruptive forces in the marriage. The husband's role apparently poses many problems in child-rearing, since the male no longer exercises unquestioned authority as law-giver and disciplinarian, and has yet to find a new role despite feminists' clamor for more nurturing behavior by men toward their children.

Fighting in Marriage

Our society may be moving away from the materialism that characterized the industrial revolution, but money is still the major source of disputes in marriages and debts constitute the worst crises in more marriages than any other trauma. Personal habits and conflicts over relatives are bigger problem sources than the vital areas of child-raising and sexual relations. Violence is a prominent part of American marital battles, with one-quarter of our sample admitting to physical abuse by one or both spouses during fights, with the husband becoming the sole victim in a significant number of cases. Illness is an inevitable crisis that strikes older couples and its effects, virtually never experienced in youth, tend to dwarf all previous crises.

Infidelity

Even among a sample of couples all of whom were currently in viable marriages, we found a quarter who admitted to cheating on their current spouses, with husbands outnumbering wives nearly 2-to-1. We find a double standard still prevailing, not only in the incidence of actual infidelity, but in the predominance of men who saw themselves as vulnerable to temptation. The percentage of couples who openly condone extramarital relationships is still miniscule, but there is a wide acceptance of calm and rational discussion as the proper way to deal with infidelity, though some of the lower socioeconomic groups cling to old standards of non-negotiable demands or immediate separation. Affairs tend to be brief and infrequent, rather than reflections of prolonged emotional involvements or consistent promiscuity.

Divorce

Although one in three American marriages now ends in divorce, our survey indicates that most married people basically are opposed to the concept, only one spouse in five expressing the view that a marriage should be readily dissolved at the mere wish of either partner. There is no substantial difference between men and women, despite the traditional belief that women have a stronger vested interest in the institution of marriage. One-third of couples believe that marriages should never be dissolved, and this includes an identical percentage of those who have already remarried. In spite of the prevalent feeling that divorce is an extreme measure, one-third of those we surveyed admitted to considering divorce at some point. Yet, people envision divorce not as a positive, liberating factor, but as a step that will consign them to loneliness, financial insecurity, and alienation from children and former friends. In an era of ever-increasing divorce rates, emotional and intellectual acceptance of divorce lags far behind its practice.

Remarriages

Although census figures indicate that people in remarriages have a slightly poorer chance of remaining together for life, our survey indicates that they seem to be enjoying some distinct advantages over those in first marriages: they less often feel taken for granted, less often feel that marriage has changed them for the worse in some way, and more often claim they would definitely marry the same spouse again. They have a higher rate of reported sexual satisfaction and this is reflected by a higher frequency of marital intercourse. Remarriages appear to be more carefully planned, with over twice as many couples in second marriages having lived with their spouse prior to marriage as those married for the first time. Having cited immaturity as the major cause of previous marital failure, they less often marry "for love" and marry more often for companionship or economic security. While they are far more likely to tolerate extramarital affairs with open knowledge and consent of one another, they are even more likely than the first-wed to seek immediate divorce on learning of infidelity.

Lifestyles and the Future of Marriage

Including a statistical look at the living-together phenomenon where we find that a quarter of couples have lived together prior to marriage with a five-fold difference between the youngest and oldest groups, we find that despite the acknowledged increase in premarital sexual experience and the apparent increase in extramarital affairs, modern couples are still overwhelmingly opposed to the idea of outside partners. Married couples discuss what they would ask for in a formal contract with their present spouse and we found considerable disagreement over the assumption of roles and the division of labor between husband and wife, as well as emphasis on respect, consideration, and emancipation from relatives. Married couples generally blame the rising divorce rate on a shift in marital goals from shared effort and compromise to egocentric growth and individual pursuit of happiness without regard for the feelings and well-being of the spouse.

The questions we have posed to the married people of America and their answers should interest not only those involved in marriages of their own, but also single people who are or will be contemplating marriage, as well as those who have lost spouses through divorce, separation, or death, marriage having been an important part of their past and a potential part of their future.

In presenting the thoughts of today's couples, we have often been able, through comparison with the data supplied on the objective portion of the questionnaire, to tell you a little about the person who gave the response, not only his or her history, but some of their other views as well. The reader will often encounter some surprising contradictions; for example, a respondent who describes her husband in only positive terms on an essay question may have, on the objective questions, admitted considering divorce or having a poor sex life. Such examples indicate how complex marital relationships are and how few unions can be characterized as unequivocally good or bad. We were also struck by the frequency with which a husband and wife indicated by their corresponding answers to the same question vastly differing perceptions of some aspect of their marriage. Thus, not only is every marriage different but even one marriage has two different existences, depending on which partner is experiencing it.

Marriage has been praised as a divinely ordained road to personal joy and fulfillment, and damned as a means of enslavement and source of intense misery. Given these extremes, there can obviously be no one statement that will be valid for all marriages. To comprehend modern marriage one must turn not to one expert, not to one typical or ideal couple, but to as many people as possible whose aspirations, conflicts, and experiences contribute equally to that polymorphous hybrid, a blend of culture, religion, society, instinct, and romance, called the American marriage.

A Nationwide Survey of Marriage

Please indicate your answers to each question by circling the number to the right of the statement that comes closest to your thinking.

1. **How would you describe your marriage?**
   a. Always stable 6–1
   b. Generally stable .... –2
   c. Fairly stable .... –3
   d. In constant turmoil .... –4
   e. Always loving .... –5
   f. Generally loving .... –6
   g. Fairly loving .... –7
   h. Generally hostile .... –8
   i. Alternating periods of closeness and remoteness –9
   j. A failure .... –0

2. **Which two of these do you think is important for a good marriage?**
   a. Similar ideas or interests 7–1
   b. Strong affection .... –2
   c. Mutual sexual satisfaction .... –3
   d. Individual freedom .... –4
   e. Having children .... –5
   f. Financial security .... –6
   g. Good communication .... –7
   h. Concern for one another's needs .... –8

3. **Over which decisions does your spouse have principal control?**
   a. Raising the children 8–1
   b. Handling the money .... –2
   c. Sexual activity .... –3
   d. Business and career choices .... –4
   e. Home and furnishings .... –5
   f. Vacation arrangements .... –6
   g. Friends and social life .... –7
   h. Car and other transportation .... –8
   i. Involvement in local politics, civil organizations –9

4. **What is the major problem in your marriage?**
   a. Money 9–1
   b. Lack of communication ....–2
   c. Sexual dissatisfaction ....–3
   d. Conflicts over relatives ....–4
   e. Disagreements about the children ....–5
   f. Problems involving jobs ....–6
   g. Cheating ....–7
   h. Alcohol ....–8
   i. Difference in personal interest ....–9
   j. Other *(SPECIFY):*   –0

5. **How would you describe your spouse?**
   a. Considerate 10–1
   b. Dominant ....–2
   c. Passive ....–3
   d. Emotional ....–4
   e. Mature ....–5
   f. Irresponsible ....–6
   g. Reserved ....–7
   h. Anxious ....–8
   i. Possessive ....–9
   j. Affectionate ....–0
   k. Warm ....–x
   l. Inconsiderate ....–y
   m. Impetuous 11–1
   n. Methodical ....–2

6. **How would you describe yourself as a spouse?**
   a. Considerate 12–1
   b. Dominant ....–2
   c. Passive ....–3
   d. Emotional ....–4
   e. Mature ....–5
   f. Irresponsible ....–6
   g. Reserved ....–7
   h. Anxious ....–8
   i. Possessive ....–9
   j. Affectionate ....–0
   k. Warm ....–x
   l. Inconsiderate ....–y
   m. Impetuous 13–1
   n. Methodical ....–2

7. How do you think your spouse views you?
    a. Loves and appreciates me fully 14–1
    b. Appreciates me as a spouse, but not as a lover ..–2
    c. Thinks I am a good lover, but need improvement in other ways ....–3
    d. Appreciates me, but doesn't really love me ......–4
    e. Takes me for granted ....–5
    f. Wishes we had never gotten married ....–6

8. How has marriage changed you for the *better*?
    a. Have become calmer and more emotionally stable 15–1
    b. Have become better at handling responsibility ...–2
    c. Have become a more considerate person ....–3
    d. Have become a better lover ....–4
    e. Have a feeling of emotional security and of being loved ....–5
    f. Feel I am no longer alone in times of crisis ......–6
    g. Feel my life has more purpose and meaning .....–7
    h. Have more confidence in myself ....–8
    i. Have not changed for the better ....–9

9. How has marriage changed you for the *worse*?
    a. Feel tied down and trapped 16–1
    b. Feel overwhelmed by responsibility ....–2
    c. Feel unloved and unappreciated ....–3
    d. Feel I live for my children ....–4
    e. Have become disillusioned about romance and love ....–5
    f. Feel sexually unsatisfied ....–6
    g. Feel more nervous and irritable ....–7
    h. Feel dominated by my spouse ....–8
    i. Have not changed for the worse ....–9

10. What influenced you the most in your choice of your present spouse?
    a. Good looks 17–1
    b. Personality ....–2
    c. Financial or social status ....–3
    d. Similar backgrounds or interests ....–4
    e. Ability to communicate ....–5
    f. Intelligence ....–6
    g. Sexual attraction ....–7
    h. Career achievement ....–8
    i. Pressure from parents or peers ....–9
    j. Other *(SPECIFY):*   –0

11. Would you marry the same person again today?
   a. Definitely would 18–1
   b. Probably would ....–2
   c. Unsure—might or might not ....–3
   d. Probably not ....–4
   e. Definitely not ....–5

12. How old were you when you got married for the first time?
   a. Under 18 19–1
   b. 18–20 ....–2
   c. 21–24 ....–3
   d. 25–29 ....–4
   e. 30–34 ....–5
   f. 35–39 ....–6
   g. Over 40 ....–7

13. What was the most important reason for your marrying?
   a. Having a companion 20–1
   b. Having children ....–2
   c. Having regular sex ....–3
   d. Pressure from partner ....–4
   e. Pressure from parents, peers or others ....–5
   f. Having a homelife ....–6
   g. For love ....–7
   h. For economic security ....–8
   i. For support in a time of crisis ....–9
   j. Because of pregnancy ....–0

14. Based on your experience, if you were single now, would you marry?
   a. Definitely would 21–1
   b. Probably would ....–2
   c. Not sure—might or might not ....–3
   d. Probably not ....–4
   e. Definitely not ....–5

15. What do you feel is the worst crisis your marriage has faced?

   a. Spouse leaving home 22–1
   b. Extramarital affair ....–2
   c. Relative living with you ....–3
   d. Illness ....–4
   e. Unemployment ....–5
   f. Debts ....–6
   g. Alcohol ....–7
   h. Moving ....–8
   i. Birth of or actions of children ....–9
   j. Other *(SPECIFY):*   –0

16. What is your attitude towards spouse's job?

   a. Very happy with it 23–1
   b. Does not pay enough ....–2
   c. Takes up too much time ....–3
   d. Involves too much travel ....–4
   e. Dislike co-workers ....–5
   f. Dislike boss ....–6
   g. No opportunity for advancement ....–7
   h. Don't understand it ....–8
   i. Too dangerous ....–9
   j. Spouse is unemployed ....–0

17. What do you and your spouse argue about the most?

   a. Money 24–1
   b. Sexual problems ....–2
   c. Children ....–3
   d. Job and career ....–4
   e. Relatives ....–5
   f. Friends ....–6
   g. Attention to members of opposite sex ....–7
   h. Alcohol ....–8
   i. Social activities ....–9
   j. Personal appearance ....–0
   k. Politics ....–x
   l. Religion ....–y
   m. Personal habits 25–1
   n. Never argue ....–2

> SKIP TO Q.19
> IF NEVER ARGUE

18. **Have your arguments ever resulted in physical attacks?**
    a. Have struck or otherwise assaulted one another 26–1
    b. Husband has struck wife only ....–2
    c. Wife has struck husband only ....–3
    d. Fights never involve physical attacks ....–4

19. **If remarried, why do you believe this marriage will be successful? If this is your first marriage, what has increased its chances for success?**
    a. Increased maturity 27–1
    b. Financial security ....–2
    c. Stronger sense of commitment ....–3
    d. Development of similar interests ....–4
    e. Better sexual compatibility ....–5
    f. Better communication ....–6
    g. More love ....–7
    h. More cooperation ....–8
    i. More easy going partner ....–9
    j. More responsible partner ....–0

20. **If you have remarried, was your new spouse similar to or different from your former partner? If you were to remarry, what type of person would you choose?**
    a. Very similar to ex-spouse in most ways 28–1
    b. Similar in appearance, but different type of personality ....–2
    c. Similar in personality, but different in appearance ....–3
    d. Quite different in most ways ....–4
    e. Unsure ....–5

21. **If remarried, why did your last marriage fail? What would be most likely to cause your first marriage to fail?**
    a. Sexual dissatisfaction 29–1
    b. Money problems ....–2
    c. Disagreement over children ....–3
    d. Extramarital affair ....–4
    e. Immaturity ....–5
    f. Poor choice of spouse ....–6
    g. In-law problems ....–7
    h. Job interference ....–8
    i. Dissimilar interests ....–9
    j. Inconsiderate partner ....–0

22. **How would you describe your sex life with your spouse?**
    a. Very good 30–1
    b. Good ....–2
    c. Variable ....–3
    d. Satisfactory ....–4
    e. Generally dull ....–5
    f. Unsatisfying ....–6
    g. Never or very rarely have sex ....–7

23. **How often do you usually have intercourse with your spouse?**
    a. More than once a day 31–1
    b. Once a day ....–2
    c. Five or six times a week ....–3
    d. Three or four times a week ....–4
    e. Twice a week ....–5
    f. Once a week ....–6
    g. Two or three times a month ....–7
    h. Once a month ....–8
    i. Less then once a month ....–9
    j. No longer have intercourse ....–0

24. **How often do you reach orgasm during intercourse with your spouse?**
    a. 90% or more of the time 32–1
    b. 60 to 89% of the time ....–2
    c. 40 to 59% of the time ....–3
    d. 10 to 39% of the time ....–4
    e. 0 to 9% of the time ....–5

25. **How often do you usually masturbate alone?**
    a. More than once a day 33–1
    b. Once a day ....–2
    c. Five or six times a week ....–3
    d. Three or four times a week ....–4
    e. Twice a week ....–5
    f. Once a week ....–6
    g. Two or three times a month ....–7
    h. Once a month ....–8
    i. Less than once a month ....–9
    j. Never ....–0

26. How often do you usually have fellatio (sexual contact between mouth and penis) with your spouse?

a. More than once a day 34–1
b. Once a day ....–2
c. Five or six times a week ....–3
d. Three or four times a week ....–4
e. Twice a week ....–5
f. Once a week ....–6
g. Two or three times a month ....–7
h. Once a month ....–8
i. Less than once a month ....–9
j. Never ....–0

27. How often do you usually have cunnilingus (sexual contact between mouth and female sexual organs) with your spouse?

a. More than once a day 35–1
b. Once a day ....–2
c. Five or six times a week ....–3
d. Three or four times a week ....–4
e. Twice a week ....–5
f. Once a week ....–6
g. Two or three times a month ....–7
h. Once a month ....–8
i. Less than once a month ....–9
j. Never ....–0

28. Which, if any, of these sexual variations do you and your spouse engage in?

a. Group sex 36–1
b. Mechanical aids ....–2
c. Anal sex ....–3
d. Bondage ....–4
e. Inflicting or receiving pain ....–5
f. Mate swapping ....–6
g. Homosexual activity ....–7
h. Use of clothes or objects to enhance fantasies ...–8
i. Drugs to enhance pleasure ....–9
j. None ....–0

29. **Which, if any, of the following ways do you use when you want to avoid sex with your spouse?**
    a. Simply decline advances 37–1
    b. Pretend sleep ....–2
    c. Say you're not feeling well ....–3
    d. Say that you're tired ....–4
    e. Watch television ....–5
    f. Act disagreeable ....–6
    g. Pick a quarrel ....–7
    h. Get involved with work ....–8
    i. Other *(SPECIFY):*   –9

30. **What is your general attitude towards marriage?**
    a. It is a lifelong commitment never to be broken 38–1
    b. It is a strong commitment, to be broken only under exceptional circumstances ....–2
    c. It should be ended whenever it proves unsatisfactory to either partner ....–3
    d. It should be entered with the expectation that it might be temporary ....–4

31. **What is your attitude towards extramarital sexual activity?**
    a. Both spouses should be free to have outside affairs, with each other's knowledge 39–1
    b. Both partners should have outside affairs, but should not reveal them to one another ....–2
    c. Husband only should be permitted outside sexual activity ....–3
    d. Faithfulness is preferable, but extramarital affairs should be tolerated ....–4
    e. Faithfulness is important, and extramarital affairs should be regarded as serious threats to the marriage ....–5
    f. Extramarital affairs almost inevitably lead to separation and divorce ....–6

32. **Did you live with your spouse prior to marriage?**
    a. No 40–1
    b. Less than three months ....–2
    c. Three to six months ....–3
    d. Six months to a year ....–4
    e. Over a year ....–5

33. Have you ever cheated on your spouse?
a. Never 41–1
b. Have been involved, but with partner's knowledge and consent ....–2
c. Yes, with one other person, briefly ....–3
d. Yes, with one other person, over more than a year ....–4
e. Yes, with two or three others, briefly ....–5
f. Yes, with two or three others, at least one for over a year ....–6
g. Yes, more than three others, none for over a year ....–7
h. Yes, more than three others, at least one for over a year ....–8

34. What would tempt you to cheat?
a. Poor sex at home 42–1
b. Constant fighting at home ....–2
c. Exceptionally attractive new partner ....–3
d. Being away from home ....–4
e. Person who understands me better than spouse ..–5
f. Chance of brief, casual affair ....–6
g. Finding true love ....–7
h. Chance for job advancement ....–8
i. Money or gifts ....–9
j. Boredom ....–0
k. Would never be tempted ....–x

35. What keeps you faithful?
a. Love for spouse 43–1
b. Moral beliefs ....–2
c. Fear of spouse ....–3
d. Lack of outside opportunity ....–4
e. Fear of losing children ....–5
f. Loyalty to spouse ....–6
g. Fear of social censure ....–7
h. Shyness ....–8
i. Fear of hurting career ....–9
j. Other *(SPECIFY):*   –0
k. Not faithful ....–x

36. **How would you react to your partner's cheating?**
   a. Ignore it 44–1
   b. Seek professional counseling, if spouse agreed ..–2
   c. Seek professional counselling, with or without spouse's cooperation .... –3
   d. Seek divorce immediately .... –4
   e. Have an affair yourself .... –5
   f. Harm partner physically .... –6
   g. Confront spouse's lover .... –7
   h. Withhold sex from partner .... –8
   i. Discuss situation calmly with spouse .... –9
   j. Demand spouse give up lover .... –0

37. **Have you ever considered divorcing your present spouse?**
   a. No 45–1
   b. Have thought about it, but never discussed it ....–2
   c. Have both considered it, but taken no action ....–3
   d. Have consulted lawyer about divorce .... –4
   e. Have had a period of separation .... –5
   f. Definitely plan to divorce .... –6

38. **If you would ever consider divorce, what would be the biggest obstacle?**
   a. Money problems 46–1
   b. Custody of children .... –2
   c. Moral or religious considerations .... –3
   d. Fear of loneliness .... –4
   e. Disapproval of others .... –5
   f. Loss of spouse's services .... –6

39. **What would be the major effect of a divorce on your life?**
   a. Would give me the freedom to fulfill myself .47–1
   b. Would alienate me from my children ....–2
   c. Would leave me alone in the world ....–3
   d. Would force me to lower my standard of living .–4
   e. Would enable me to find true love ....–5
   f. Would leave me depressed ....–6
   g. Would lower my self esteem considerably ....–7

40. How many children do you have?

One 48–1
Two .... –2
Three .... –3
Four .... –4
More than four .... –5
No children .... –6

> SKIP TO Q.43
> IF NO CHILDREN

41. How have your children affected your marriage?

a. Have drawn us closer together 49–1
b. Have driven us further apart .... –2
c. Have led to many quarrels .... –3
d. Have not changed our relationship .... –4
e. Have added a new and positive dimension to our relationship .... –5

42. Why did you want children?

a. As an additonal source of love 50–1
b. To have someone to care for .... –2
c. To perpetuate family name .... –3
d. To fulfill myself as a woman or a man .... –4
e. To insure a stable marriage .... –5
f. Sense of moral obligation .... –6
g. Security in old age .... –7
h. To please spouse .... –8

DEMOGRAPHIC DATA

43. What is your sex?

a. Male 51–1
b. Female .... –2

44. Including your present marriage, how many times have you been married?

a. Once 52–1
b. Twice .... –2
c. Three times .... –3
d. Four times .... –4
e. More than four times .... –5

45. What is your racial background?
    a. White 53–1
    b. Black ....–2
    c. Hispanic ....–3
    d. Oriental ....–4
    e. Filippino ....–5
    f. American Indian ....–6
    g. Other *(SPECIFY):*   –7

46. What was your family's total income before taxes in 1977?
    a. Less than $8,000 54–1
    b. $8,000–$9,999 ....–2
    c. $10,000–$14,999 ....–3
    d. $15,000–$24,999 ....–4
    e. $25,000–$49,999 ....–5
    f. $50,000 or more ....–6

47. What is the highest level of education you have completed?
    a. Did not complete high school 55–1
    b. High school graduate ....–2
    c. Some college education ....–3
    d. College graduate ....–4
    e. Post graduate education ....–5

48. Would you describe yourself as a person with firm religious beliefs?
    a. Yes 56–1
    b. No ....–2

49. What is your age?
    a. 18–30 57–1
    b. 31–40 ....–2
    c. 41–50 ....–3
    d. 51 or over ....–4

50. What is your occupation?
    a. Professional, technical, management 58–1
    b. White collar worker ....–2
    c. Blue collar ....–3
    d. Student ....–4
    e. Homemaker ....–5
    f. Retired, unemployed ....–6
                                              59–
                                            60–
                                            61–

Each person who completed the questionnaire was requested to answer several of the following essay questions:

Why did you decide to marry? What were your expectations, and were they fulfilled?

How old were you when you decided to marry, and what factors in your life influenced that decision?

Why did you happen to choose your particular spouse?

Describe your present spouse. Are the two of you more alike or different in your personalities, and in what ways?

Describe your father and mother. Does your spouse resemble either of them in appearance or personality? Describe the main differences and similarities.

What is your biggest sexual difficulty? How does your spouse deal with it? How do you try to cope with it?

What is your spouse's biggest sexual difficulty? How do you deal with it?

Do you or your spouse ever deliberately withhold sex from one another? For what reasons? How do you deal with it?

Do you ever masturbate alone? What advantages or purpose does this have, compared to sexual activity with your partner? Do you have any particular erotic fantasies, and if so describe them.

How have you and your spouse attempted to improve your sex life since marriage? Are there any techniques or new experiences you have found particularly gratifying? What would you like to try that you have not, or do more often?

If you consider your marriage successful, what are the reasons for its success? If not, what has prevented its success?

Are you more or less in love with your spouse compared to when you were first married? What are the reasons for any changes?

What are the strongest reasons for you and your spouse staying together?

How has your marriage changed you as a person?

How would you describe your emotional temperament? How would you compare it with your spouse's?

How would your life be different if you had remained single?

How have your children affected your relationship with your spouse and your marriage in general?

What are the main problems you've faced as a parent, and how have you handled them?

Describe the worst fight you and your spouse ever had.

What is the worst crisis that you have had to face—and how was it resolved?

How do you conduct yourself during a fight? Do you yell, remain silent and cold, walk out, break things, etc.? How does your partner's style of fighting differ from your own?

How do you usually make peace after a quarrel?

What would you do if you discovered your spouse was having an extramarital affair?

Have you ever had an affair or affairs? How did it happen, and how do you feel about it? Did your spouse find out? What did your spouse do about it? If you've been faithful, what has been your biggest source of or reason for temptation?

What prevents you or inhibits you from extramarital affairs?

If you have been divorced, why did that marriage fail? If not, what dangers and strengths do you see in your marriage's stability?

What obstacles would prevent or inhibit you from getting a divorce if your marriage was bad?

If you remarried—or were to remarry—what did or would you look for in your new spouse, and how would this compare to your former spouse?

If you have—or were to remarry—what steps would you take to insure its success, and what mistakes, based on past experience, would you avoid making?

If you and your spouse were to renew your marriage vows and wanted to draw up a contract stating what you expected from one another, what provisions would you include in that contract?

Do you believe in extramarital sexual activity for yourself and/or your spouse? What allowances and limits would you recommend? How would you deal with infidelity?

Why do you think the divorce rate is so high today? What would you advise newly married couples to do to prevent ultimate divorce?

HUSBANDS AND WIVES

1

On Purpose:

Why People Marry

Marriage is tolerable enough in its way if you're easygoing and don't expect too much from it. But it doesn't bear thinking about.

—*George Bernard Shaw*, GETTING MARRIED

If a foreigner were to try to estimate the trend of the marriage rate in the United States based solely on his reading of current magazines and books, he would be bound to conclude that there had been a sharp decline in the percentage of people entering that beleaguered state. Our hypothetical well-informed foreigner would probably cite the following reasons why people are not getting married:

More than one million couples are living together without being married. This may involve as many as 10 per cent of adult males under the age of 30. Moreover, the living-together phenomenon is no longer the exclusive province of the poor and the blue-collar classes; we find just as many high-income and professional people, in proportion, engaging in this lifestyle. On some college campuses, one-quarter of the students have lived with a partner at some time. Clearly, what was once called "living in sin" has received the blessing of the American public and is slowly replacing conventional marriage.

Only 40 per cent of Americans are living in a typical nuclear family, consisting of a husband and wife. This obviously indicates that traditional marriage is on the wane.

Fewer than 60 per cent of families have children under 18, and the national birth rate continues to decline. Since having children is one of the prime purposes of marriage, the marriage rate is bound to decline with the birth rate.

People no longer require marriage as a condition for sexual intercourse. Since at least 90 per cent of people in their mid-twenties engage in premarital sex and, under the liberating effects of the sexual revolution, are interested in a varied sex life, more people are bound to opt for the sexual bounty offered by the single life.

The Women's Liberation Movement has made women career-conscious and led them to believe that marriage is a form of enslavement whereby women are reduced to performing unpaid domestic labors, expected to supply sex on demand for insensitive husbands who are usually unfaithful, and deprived of any control over the major decisions that affect their lives. With a world of new opportunities ahead and the freedom to pursue sexual pleasure without guilt, modern women will shun marriage and settle into less restrictive lifestyles.

With the divorce rate climbing to nearly one-third of all marriages. Americans are becoming disenchanted with marriage and will progressively give up on it.

Americans are concerned as never before with self-fulfillment. Call it actualization, reaching full potential, becoming your own person, doing your own thing—whatever name you use, it means a life of liberty and the pursuit of happiness, and, frankly, marriage demands too many compromises and imposes too many restrictions for people imbued with this philosophy.

We could go on providing good reasons for not getting married, but, contrary to expectations, people *are* getting married. More than 95 per cent of our population marries at least once—and since the homosexual/bisexual runs close to 5 per cent, that leaves precious few heterosexuals who don't get involved. The American marriage rate, at 10 per 1,000 population, is one of the highest among the industrialized nations and only slightly below its 1972 level when it led those nations.

Statistics are misleading. While the birth rate is declining, the number of childless wives between the ages of 30 and 40 is also declining, so women are having fewer children, but only in less than 10 per cent of marriages none at all. The high rate of childless families reflects only the young couples who are postponing but not eschewing pregnancy and the older couples whose progeny have reached adulthood. The average wife will have two children and that number is unlikely to change over the coming years.

New trends are also misleading, for the living-together rage appears to be a prelude to, not a replacement for, marriage. Surveys have shown that couples who live together are just as determined to marry ultimately as those who never become involved in premarital cohabitation. And divorced people at any given age level are more likely to remarry than their inexperienced counterparts.

So, while the marriage rate is not as high as during the post-World War II boom, neither is it as low as it was during the Depression years; our present rate has nested snugly midway between those two extremes, just about where it has usually been during the past century.

Despite an abundance of apparent reasons why people should not be getting married, the fact is they continue to do so. While people's desire for marriage never changes, their reasons for marrying do. We asked our subjects what they expected of marriage and whether these expectations were met.

High Hopes

If there is one single question about marriage where the answer should be predictable nearly all the time, it would be "Why did you marry?" The expected answer is, of course, "for love." In our society, that response is practically a reflex. Exactly what people mean by love is not so predictable. It can mean anything from kindness to sexual appetite. But because love covers a multitude of sins and virtues, it can be cited as a rationale with little fear of contradiction. Lewis Carroll's Humpty Dumpty told Alice that when he used a word, it meant precisely what he chose it to mean, neither more nor less, since he was its master; being a fair master, however, he paid extra wages when a word worked overtime. By those standards, "love" would be the richest word in the dictionary.

A Roper poll in 1974 showed that 83 per cent of women and 77 per cent of men cited love as their main reason for getting married. In preparing the questionnaire for our survey on male sexuality, we avoided an anticipated dilemma by asking men, "What else *besides love* would be your main reason for getting married?"

In view of the preoccupation with love, it is surprising that the majority of our respondents did *not* give love as the most important reason for their marrying. Forty-eight per cent of them gave this answer, by far the most frequently chosen response, but still less than half. Women gave this reply significantly more often than men—56 per cent versus only 39 per cent. The other most commonly given reasons were having a homelife (26 per cent) and having a companion (25 per cent). Since some respondents chose more than one answer, this makes the unexpectedly low number mentioning love even more remarkable.

In our subgroup of 869 matched coupes, both spouses replied that they had married for love in one-third of the cases. When each partner is presented with 10 possible answers, there are 100 different combinations of answers, so it is not surprising that this was the only answer combination which more than 15 per cent of the couples gave.

Why did you decide to marry? What were your expectations, and were they fulfilled?

WIFE: "I married for love and companionship. I expected the same thing in return. They have been fulfilled."

HUSBAND: "I decided to marry because I loved my wife and wanted to spend the rest of my life with her. To have children and a good career. Some were fulfilled, others were not."

WIFE: "We fell in love, we wanted to be together. After 31 years of marriage my heart still skips a beat when he enters the room. There is no other person I would rather spend my life with than him."

HUSBAND: "I guess we were getting sexually involved and before anything happened I thought we should get married. She was everything I thought a wife should be. I was in love with her and I am sure that my expectations were fulfilled."

WIFE: "My expectations were love, understanding, happiness, some fights, good lover, beautiful in-laws, for more love than I could imagine—a good listener to my problems and *yes* they were all fulfilled to the fullest and this is only the beginning of many, many, many years to come."

HUSBAND: "I married for love of my spouse. My expectations were to have a successful job that I enjoyed with good income. To give my spouse what she wanted, to have children."

WIFE: "I decided to marry when I realized what life would be like if I didn't marry the man I loved. I was full of romantic ideas, some of which have not been fulfilled. I just assumed we would have a wonderful sexual relationship: however, that has not happened yet."

HUSBAND: "Nothing but love. Full of love."

Perhaps one of the reasons that love and companionship are so prominent among reasons for marrying is because the other traditional functions of marriage have been eroded by the changing times. One concept that has been thoroughly annihilated is that of the family as a unit of economic productivity. The family business, particularly where skilled craftsmanship was involved, has given way to the factory and large retail store, and except for the occasional successful business whose management is handed from father to children, there is almost complete separation of family from industry. Farms were once entirely self-sustaining, with specific vital chores delegated to various family members. The family supplied its own food, clothing, and necessities, and the children who provided labor were welcome and indispensable additions to the unit. Our culture today is too specialized for any family to become self-sustaining, and since the modern child is more of a consumer than a producer, children are economic liabilities rather than assets.

The traditional family was not only a producer of children, but also the sole agent for their care, rearing, and education. The state now has assumed almost all the function of education and monitors their health care through the schools. With television taking over most of children's recreation time, the Federal Communications Commission takes over where the Board of Education leaves off. With the growth of well-baby clinics, adolescent health programs, Head Start programs, day nurseries, summer recreational and employment programs, and school guidance offices, the state and the parents are reversing their old roles, so that the state assumes direct responsibility for the child's education, health care, and socialization, while the parents can be little more than monitors of the system.

Since the small number of children in the average family means fewer years spent taking care of small children, reproduction and its consequences seldom emerges as the dominant activity in a marriage. So, virtually by a process of elimination, the emphasis is shifted from the family to the couple, and companionship and affection become the prime motivation for marriage. Affection can be extended to the children, and where there are fewer of them, the affection can be spread thicker. While the home may not be essential for survival, its conveniences and comforts provide the chief attraction to marriage for many, men more so than women.

WIFE: "To have a home and children. To live a happy life—with children and a nice home to live and relax in. Yes, to a point my expectations were fulfilled. We have a comfortable home and a beautiful, bright outgoing daughter."

HUSBAND: "Because of love, be happy; have children. Yes they have been fulfilled."

She's between 18 and 30 and a homemaker. They have one child. She feels their marriage is in constant turmoil and says she is overwhelmed by responsibility. He's between 31 and 40, and works in management. Earns between $15–25,000 a year. He rates his marriage as generally stable.

WIFE: "To have a mate—to be a family, to have children and someone to share my life. ALL and *more* of my expectations have been filled."

HUSBAND: "I married because I found someone who was decent and honest and I loved her. I had a bad first marriage with a woman who was neither honest nor decent. You can bet my expectations were fulfilled. Best thing ever happened to me. Shortly after marriage I received Christ in my heart."

She's between 31 and 40. They have two children. He's 51 or over, retired or unemployed. He's never cheated on his wife, and was most influenced by her good looks when he married her. Says he married for regular sex.

Since historian John Demos tells us that at least a third of eighteenth-century Puritan brides were pregnant at the time of marriage, we might say that premarital pregnancy is part of our Puritan heritage. In spite of improvements in contraception, increased sex education, and, in many regions, liberal abortion laws, it is estimated that one in three women is still pregnant on her wedding day. Only 4 per cent of our sample gave pregnancy as their reason for getting married. Since we know that as many as eight times that number were probably pregnant, we can conclude that such couples prefer to think they married for other reasons. Indeed, commitment to marry often results in beginning of premarital relations, more frequent and casual relations, and conscious or subconscious lapses in contraception to insure the ceremony. As in the case below, pregnancy usually affects the time rather than the act of marriage.

WIFE: "We were planning to marry, our marriage date was set ahead because of pregnancy. My expectations of marriage were to be with my husband more and share our life, ideas and interest."

HUSBAND: "We married due to pregnancy. I met my Janet at 14, we got married when I was 20. We planned this wedding one year after meeting each other and after 15 years of marriage I would not change anything and thank God for bringing us together."

She's between 31 and 40, and didn't complete high school. They have three children. She says they generally have a loving marriage, and when they do fight it's mostly over their children. He's also in the same age range, is blue collar. He says he's passive, and feels that the major problem in their marriage is over relatives.

If one's expectations are based on the partner's behavior during the courtship period, disappointment can result, even if the partner is handsome, successful, and faithful, as was the husband of this respondent:

WIFE: "He was good-looking, rich, with promise of a good future. He would be able to give me all the advantages in life that I never had as a child.

"I have a good life now. Secure and well taken care of. My husband's lack of interest in sex and his highly motivated interest in his job lead me to my extramarital affairs.

"I am sure things would not have turned out this way if he had given me the same attention he did when we were dating."

She's between 18 and 30. Has one child. Admits that she cheated on husband briefly with two or three other men. Feels that spouse appreciates her as a wife, but not as a lover.

Among the women who married for love, even those who found happiness often experienced hardship along the way:

WIFE: "I married because I felt that was the right thing to do. I thought I loved this man totally and wanted to spend all my time with him. I wanted a home and children. I wanted to make him happy and comfortable and proud. I pictured us working together, playing together, worshipping together. The expectation of worshipping together went by the wayside. My husband became very possessive and did not want to share me with anyone, church, kids or friends. Time and trials have matured both of us. Prayer again has brought us a long way. Most of the expectations have been fulfilled."

She's a professional, with some college background. Between the ages of 31 and 40. At this point she's unsure whether she'd marry the same person again.

WIFE: "I married because I was in love. I was 22 and had gone with my husband for 4 years. I started going with him when he came home from World War II. He fought in the South Pacific.

"My main idea was to be his wife and help him in his profession. My expectations were fulfilled and we have been very happy. This does not mean we always agree. Money has never been a problem because neither of us has money wants. We both want to invest in farming, etc. One year we tried out farming and our income was $400.00, but all went okay. We lived on savings."

She's a college graduate between the ages of 41 and 50. Says their social life is their biggest problem.

WIFE: "I was very much in love but was not mature enough at 18 to realize the responsibilities ahead of me. I did have a loving husband and together we came through a rough two years of losing our first child, unemployment, etc."

She's now 51 or over, and a homemaker. A high school graduate. Though alcohol is their major problem she feels their marriage is a loving one.

Other wives sought love and found mainly disappointment:

WIFE: "I guess it was mainly sex drive. I was raised an orphan (practically). All my life, I wanted someone to love *me*. The first two years of our marriage (we were job-transferred away from his family) I really felt he loved *me*. Then when the babies started coming and demanding more and more of my time (I was 30 when the first was born and 38 when the last was born—no help at any time) I was constantly exhausted. This contributed to our drifting apart. We are only together now because his church (Catholic) frowns on a divorce. He lets me know that I'm not what he wants—but he won't make a move. I guess I am guilty of the same thing. Our youngest has a learning disability—we feel we need to give him the best start possible."

She's 51 or over, a white collar worker with 4 children. Feels that spouse wishes they'd never gotten married. Says that their children have pushed them further apart.

WIFE: "Love and consideration. Marriage to me has had many problems that were my own mistakes. If I had to do it over again I would wait until I had reached my 30's instead of when I was 19."

A high school graduate working in a white collar job, she's between 41 and 50. Feels that their major problem is lack of communication. Says she's cheated with another man for over a year.

In America, two of our most deeply ingrained values are personal liberty and true love. Now that women are free to live alone, pursue careers, and engage in sexual relations without marriage, it seems inconceivable that anyone would marry without wholeheartedly wanting to. Yet, 1 in 20 of our respondents gave pressure from parents, partner, or peers as their main reason for getting married. Women tended to feel pressure more from parents and peers, while men felt it more often from eager fiancées. The youngest genration of married people succumbed to pressure from partners three times as often as the oldest group. This means that although young people today are far more likely to enter into a "no-strings" intimate relationship than their parents were, one of the partners may later agitate for a permanent legal bond.

In the cases below, wives gave in to pressure from mother, husband, or the internal compulsion of tradition:

WIFE: "Actually could have gone the rest of our lives going (living) together. Pressure from Mother made me want marriage."

A homemaker, between the ages of 18 and 30, with some college education.

WIFE: "Pressure from spouse. He couldn't stand leaving me at night. It was just time. I think everything I expected out of marriage has been fulfilled but sometimes it could be a little easier."

A high school graduate and homemaker between the ages of 18 and 30. She feels taken for granted. Their biggest problem is over conflicts involving relatives.

Pregnancy can also be considered a form of internal pressure.

WIFE: "I married because I was in love but at the time pregnant so we were married at an earlier age than had been planned.

I thought marriage was going to be a 50-year honeymoon. I learned the true meaning of love, commitment, responsibility toward another person."

A homemaker between the ages of 41 and 50. High school graduate. Though she says the children are their major problem, and she's more nervous and irritable these days, she would still marry the same person again.

As might be expected, higher percentages of those who did not complete high school or were in blue collar occupations gave pregnancy as the reason for marriage. People who described themselves as non-religious gave pregnancy as their reason more than twice as often as those with firm religious belief, reflecting, to some extent, a higher incidence of premarital sexual activity. We can also speculate, however, that among the lesser educated and those less bound by traditional religious conventions there is less of a tendency to rationalize or romanticize the motive of a marriage, thus calling a spade a pregnancy.

According to our survey, pregnancy motivates more remarriages than first marriages. It is not a major reason, and people remarry for the same reasons they married the first time. Love still ranks number one, but it is more than 10 percentage points below the figure for first marriages. Companionship and homelife are slightly higher than in the case of first marriages.

WIFE: "Lonely—widowed at twenty with a son to raise. Sexual fulfillment, happiness, yes—but my last husband is thirteen years older than I am and that is too much age difference to continue sexual fulfillment and other interests for someone almost fourteen years younger than her husband."

A homemaker 51 or over. Says they never or rarely ever have sex because of ill health of spouse, and illness has become a major crisis. Feels sexually unsatisfied.

WIFE: "I decided to marry because I needed security. I was raising two children alone and I got tired. I didn't love my husband then, but he satisfied me completely. I never knew what real love was until my present husband. He satisfies me in every way. I needed satisfaction in sex. I was frustrated when I married, and he changed all that."

A homemaker between 31 and 40. This is her second marriage.

To some, the reasons for a marriage are sacred:

WIFE: "I thought it was God's will. Expectations—to have a Christian home, which I do, and to have children, which I do.
   "I want to have more outside interests besides our common one, the church."

She's between 18 and 30, with one child, and a homemaker.
Says she's reserved. Their major arguments are usually about sexual problems.

To a few, motives are less sacred—if not profane, at least carnal:

WIFE: "He was so handsome, a big stud, and he wanted me of all the girls he could have had. He's a fantastic lover."

A homemaker with two children. They have sex five or six times a week. She considers her spouse to be dominant.

Men who married for love generally found their expectations fulfilled:

HUSBAND: "I wanted a companion to share my life with. We loved each other and have grown closer together. We wanted a stable home, children, and a decent standard of living. Above all we wanted to please Christ."

He's a professional, between 31 and 40, with a postgraduate education. Describes himself as religious. Says they don't have any major problems, but their worst crisis is not being able to have children. Rates his marriage as always being stable.

HUSBAND: "I was in love and wanted to live with my spouse. Marriage was the acceptable arrangement. I expected my wife to be loving, faithful, considerate, and a good mother/parent. I expected to be a good provider, a good parent, and a good mate.
   "My expectations have been fulfilled through this point in the marriage."

HUSBAND: "Because I loved her and the two children. She caters to me and has complete trust in me and our sex life is fantastic."

HUSBAND: "We were always together anyway. To have her around when I needed her the most. Yes."

A young blue collar worker between 18 and 30, with some college education. He feels overwhelmed by the responsibility of marriage.

Men who married because of sexual desire or its consequences were more likely to be disillusioned, though even conservative, work-oriented types may find that security does not insure contentment.

HUSBAND: "Sexual reasons. I like to fuck a lot. The only expectations I had were for sex and they were fulfilled most of the time."

He's a college graduate and works in the professional field. Between the ages of 18 and 30. Describes his sex life as variable, has intercourse five or six times a week, cunnilingus twice, masturbates twice, and is involved in group sex, sadmasochism and takes drugs. He would not marry if he was single again.

HUSBAND: "I married because I was young and stupid. My expectations were the achievement of the American dream My expectations were not fulfilled."

A blue collar worker with some college between the ages of 31 and 40. He married between the ages of 18 and 20 for regular sex (he has intercourse twice a week). They argue about money, and have struck each other.

HUSBAND: "When I was younger, I was drinking too much, but not an alcoholic. Got sick and tired going out drinking every night. Also did it because I had to get married."

A high school graduate working in the white collar field. Between 31 and 40, he would not get married again if he became single.

HUSBAND: "Love, I suppose. It was thing to do in those days. Work hard raise a small family. Buy a home, save a little for retirement. I accomplished all objectives very well. Only this was too tame for the other half."

He's 51 or over. Didn't complete high school. A blue collar worker. If he ever remarried he would choose a different type of personality. He says his wife is dominant and has struck him during arguments.

HUSBAND: "I thought I was lonely. My first wife had left me. And all my friends were married and I just felt lonely."

A blue collar worker, between 18 and 30 who didn't complete high school. He says his wife loves him and appreciates him fully, but he feels overwhelmed by responsibility. Feels that marriage has not changed him for the better.

There have been many poetic analogies to matrimony as a sea and marriage as a ship, but most ocean voyages have a destination which is the purpose of sailing off in the first place. If we persist in nautical metaphors, marriage must be regarded as a cruise in which the voyage itself is the *raison d'être*, not some distant port. While some of the goals, such as households with several children and economic security may take a while to reach, so, too, must the New Yorker on a mid-winter cruise to the tropics defer plunging into the ship's outdoor pool for a day or so and savor instead some of the other shipboard pleasures. A queen who married a prince from another land might have given a distant goal, the union of two nations, as her reason for marriage, and an Asiatic woman entering a parentally arranged marriage might express the hope to find love developing some day, but when Americans wed, their reasons lie in the present, not in the future.

Reasons vary with generations and ethnic groups. Couples currently over 50, our survey showed, married primarily for a home-life more often than our youngest group, where career-minded, educated wives are less likely to provide exclusive domestic services. Pregnancy was more often a factor of the marriages of people still under 40 than in people who married when premarital sex was less common. Blacks gave, not love, but companionship as the main reason for marrying, indicating less preoccupation with romantic concepts; Hispanics were far more interested in love, though not as much as the white population.

Blue collar workers were less motivated by love than white collar groups, and more likely to marry for regular sex. The more religious were more likely to marry for love.

Students showed a very low interest in marrying for a homelife. While they still believed strongly in marrying for love, they showed a high incidence of marrying because of pressure from parents or partners, about a quarter of our small subsample giving this response. Ironically, this segment of our population that we would expect to show the most independent thinking is the one that most often winds up marrying (if they do so while still in school) under pressure from other parties.

Nature's Way

We still have, despite critics in abundance, plenty of marriages and even more reasons for marriage. Still, people *could* find love, companionship, and sex without marriage—and even homelife and child-rearing could be provided in communes or similar lifestyles without resorting to marriage, the bonding of one man to one woman. There are probably fewer than 2,000 rural communes in the United States today, but almost all of these have sprung up within the past decade and represent only the most radical fringe of a great back-to-nature movement.

In Marin County, California, couples often marry outdoors, the sky being the vault of their cathedral, the trees their pillars of the church, and the grass their pews. Couples write their own vows to replace the archaic stipulations of traditional ceremonies, speaking them to the accompaniment of guitars and birdsong. And, in Marin County, the divorce rate is well over 50 per cent, climbing steadily toward a 70 per cent fatality. It just seems to show that marriage is the artificial product of society, which must impede the liberty of man and subjugate his natural urges to some vague common good. While the newest therapies encourage clients to shed clothing and inhibitions, to relive their births and recry their primal screams, people continue to go against their natural inclinations by getting married.

Imagine how early man must have lived. It might be supposed that he mated indiscriminately with any woman who attracted him and casually moved on, as did his partner; while people might have banded together for protection against the saber-toothed tiger, the hunting of the mastodon, and preventing the usurpation of their belongings by neighboring club-owners, would they subject themselves to restrictions on their sexual activity and form stable pairs, prior to the invention of morality?

If you do suppose that primitive men lived in a happy and innocent state of promiscuity, you are wrong, but don't feel bad.

In the nineteenth century that theory found great favor with the prominent social scientists and was even more popular with the Victorian people who read their learned texts. The myth of the happy savage appeals to the adult as much as it does to the child who plays at being a wild Indian. Certainly, the sex-obsessed and sex-repressed Victorians were delighted to contemplate the lascivious delights of primitive life.

Once the anthropologists left their library to venture out into the bush, the findings did not meet the expectations. There are hundreds of primitive people still on earth, untainted by contact with industrialization and organized religion, and in every single group we find some form of marriage, along with restriction of sexual freedom. The unattached generally have more freedom than the married, and even total sexual monogamy is rare, but the illusion of societies where men and women do not form exclusive conjugal bonds has been shattered. Just as men isolated from civilization always manage to develop language and tools, so, too, do they develop marriage. If marriage is ever abolished, it will not be because we have managed to return to life as nature intended us, but because we have managed to rebel against one of our most deeply ingrained natural proclivities—dare we say instincts—and adopted a basically inhuman existence.

God's Way

We live in a predominantly Christian society and tend to pronounce every ethic a Christian one. Almost as fallacious as the contention that marriage violates unspoiled nature's plan for us is the conviction of many Christians that marriage has firm roots in the teachings of Christ and that the early church influenced western society to make marriage its keystone. Christian supporters of marriage are likely to extol it as a sacrament divinely instituted by Christ and a pathway to salvation (forgetting that the world and marriage went on for millenia before Christ), while critics bitterly contend that the church is to blame for the continuation of a way of life that has outlived its usefulness. Needless to say, civil marriages have largely replaced religious rites and the state, through licensing and registration, intrudes on every marriage, adding to the increasing secularization of what was formerly the province of the temples even before the churches. The sphere of religion has waned, but marriage has become no less popular.

Among the hazards of modern authorship is the need to consort with fellow guests of TV talk shows; one of the most curious people thus encountered was a formerly successful airline executive who had proclaimed himself a witch and set up his own church to counter the evils of Christianity. Happy to be freed of his previous drive for material success, he snarled, "Christ is to be blamed for it all, with His damned Christian work ethic." His indignation was tempered when he was reminded that not only did Christ never hold the sort of job that would have enabled Him to file a W-2 form, but His most memorable pronouncement on the subject was praise for the birds of the air and lilies of the field who neither sowed nor reaped.

Back in television's earliest days, when Milton Berle was undisputed king of the ratings, he drew some unexpectedly heavy competition in New York from Bishop Fulton J. Sheen. The rivalry was a good-natured one and the clergyman, playing on the tradename of Texaco's gasoline, would say, "We have the same sponsor—Sky Chief." And Berle would grunt, "After all, he's got better writers." Christ was apparently a powerful speaker, but never wrote anything down, so the holy word came down indirectly through the authors of the gospels and epistles. Since the four evangelists were primarily concerned with narrative reporting, the moral guidelines that survived in written form came from the epistles, letters to the faithful in converted areas from missionaries who wanted to make sure they did not lose previously won territory while on the road acquiring new followers. And the most gifted, most zealous, most articulate of these leaders was Saul of Tarsus, a citizen of Rome and former soldier, who became St. Paul after he was struck down from his horse on his way to wage a persecution against the Christians.

What sort of man was St. Paul? To put it bluntly, a misogynist and a misogamist—a hater of women and marriage. He proudly admitted having nothing to do with women and advised the unmarried to stay that way, conceding only that for those with no self-control, "it is better to marry than to burn." Thus, Christianity began with an attack on marriage, not a defense of it. The antihedonistic, anti-sexual bias, even basis, of the church came, not from Christ, but from St. Paul, yet its influence persists to the present time, where priests of the Roman Catholic and other sects do not marry in spite of the Reformation that took over 1,500 years to free a segment of the clergy from celibacy. Marriage remains for the traditional priest incompatible with higher spiritual attainment.

St. Paul's dream of an unmarried, sexually abstemious congregation was never realized and one may wonder how a practical organizer like himself coped with the problem of replenishing the faithful in generations to come. The answer lies partly in the belief, that the second coming promised by Christ, the end of the world, was imminent and sure to occur within the lifetimes of the newly converted. Even before the realization sank in that God was not eager to reclaim the world, the clergy had to contend with man's flesh, which was not as amenable to asexuality as his will might have been; the church decided to take things in hand, as best it could, by declaring the sanctity of marriage, rather than letting the flocks lie indiscriminately in pastures green and anywhere else they chose. This 180-degree turn left the church encumbered with two conflicting ideologies that exist side by side, pro-marriage and anti-sex, which is almost as confusing as the co-existing dogmas of heaven after death and a Last Judgment Day.

If we are to understand modern marriage and its trends, we must not overestimate the role of religion (and, by extension, conventional morality) in its existence and preservation. Christianity was more shaped by the pre-existing institution of marriage than vice versa and morality is more its servant than its master. Let us heed Don Juan's admonition that "the confusion of marriage with morality has done more to destroy the conscience of the human race than any other single error," and give the devil his due throughout our examination of marriage without worrying about outraging public morals. The devil is in nature's service as much of the rest of us, and thus far marriage seems to be part of nature's way at least as much as it belongs to the system of moral codes and traditions we often refer to as God.

The Beginnings of Love

Our survey confirms that people marry primarily for love, but that there seems to have been a recent shift away from a romanticized ideal toward the more prosaic goal of companionship. It is difficult to arrive at a concrete definition for either term, but we should assume they are not the same thing. Companions are those who are with us, who keep us from being alone; while we usually love, or at least have genuine liking for, companions, business or other necessity may throw us into close association with and even make us dependent on people we actually dislike. Poeple who hate to be alone will seek out a companion of any sort just to avoid loneliness. On the other hand, when we love someone, we generally desire their companionship, and this is chiefly true for peers. Most people would say they love their parents, but few adults seek out their parents as companions. We can love people through our knowledge of them though circumstances prevent actual companionship; Dante certainly loved Beatrice, the inspiration of his greatest poetry, but their one chance meeting scarcely qualified her as a companion. And absence may make the heart grow fonder, but it precludes companionship.

Companionship between men and women seems to be a later ideal than love. St. Augustine exemplified early Christian philosophy when he declared that the only conceivable reason God created woman was for sexual reproduction, and for friendship a man should turn to other men. Nor was this devaluation of the companionship of women a particular quirk of Christianity, the legacy of the contemptuous St. Paul. It is true that, although Christ, an apparent celibate, seemed as wont to open his thoughts to women as to men, the church persisted in its chauvinistic discrimination through Aquinas, who declared that man was form containing the divine spark of will and reason whereas woman was mere matter, through the present papacy which continues to exclude women from the priesthood. Yet, this attitude did not originate with the Pauline church, but was merely carried over from the pre-existing Greek civilizations. The Greeks went to prostitutes and concubines for sexual amusement, wives for procreation and domestic services, and men for companionship. Love for women, certainly in its purely erotic aspects and undoubtedly on some higher levels, existed and the evidence survives in classical poetry. Companionship is another matter. Homer describes how Ulysses gave up not only carnal delights but the promise of immortality from a beautiful nymph to return to his aging wife, Penelope. This story still touches us 3,000 years after its writing, but we know that in spite of a love for his wife that transcends a sexual relationship Ulysses will find his true companionship, not in the bedroom with Penelope, but around the banquet table and on the docks with his noblemen, shipmates, and male comrades as he did during his long absence from home.

If it seems paradoxical that there has always been a substantial number of faithful daughters of the church, even to the extent that women adhere to orthodox rites more than men, despite their treatment as "weaker vessels," it should be recalled that the treatment they received from the church fathers was no worse than the routine scorn accorded them in centuries past, and, at least, the church was woman's ally in keeping home and family together. If we have St. Paul to blame for the church's bias against women as sexual beings, we have to go back an additional 500 years before Paul and blame Aristotle for the biases against women as companions. Lest the reader feels we are beleaguering the matter of religion too much, remember that for at least 1,500 years the church controlled not only man's religion, but also his education. The aristocracy was far too busy with property, politics, and war and having a difficult time keeping the church from controlling those venerable concerns without bothering to secularize education. The philosophers, teachers, copiers, and preservers of manuscripts were clergymen. Yet with the coming of the Renaissance and the rise of humanism, the beginning of a movement that would enable man to see himself as having value on earth as something more than a soul waiting to be harvested for heaven, the first source that newly enlightened thinkers turned to was the ancient Greeks, notably Aristotle, the man who had influenced the thinking about woman's relationship to man through the Dark Ages.

We turn to Aristotle not as a musty, 2,500-year-old relic, but as a writer who profoundly influenced western civilization throughout most of its existence. To win an argument several centuries ago, one merely had to know Aristotle's opinion on the subject and pronounce, "according to Aristotle..." That automatically ended the matter, Aristotle being sort of an ancient forerunner of the *Guinness Book of World Records*. To hold that kind of authority two thousand years after his death, Aristotle's thoughts must have contained considerable timeless truths, even if certain male chauvinistic attitudes of his would not find favor in today's time.

What did this man have to say about love and companionship so very long ago, and how much is still relevant today? In his *Nicomachean Ethics,* he discourses at length about love, but says little about the husband-wife relationship. What he does say is: "The association of man and and wife seems to be aristocratic; for the man rules in accordance with his worth, and in those matters in which a man should rule, but the matters that befit a woman he hands over to her. If the man rules in everything the relation passes over into oligarchy; for in doing so he is not acting in accordance with their respective worth, and not ruling in virtue of his superiority." Aristotle even speaks of the marital relationship in terms of friendship: "The friendship of man and wife, again, is the same that is found in an aristocracy; for it is in accordance with virtue—the better gets more of what is good, and each gets what befits him; and so, too, with the justice in these relations."

We can see that Aristotle did not regard wives as mere domestic servants or as being subject to their husbands in all things. He even speaks of cases where the wives rule by reason of inherited wealth, though such rule is "not in virtue of excellence but due to wealth and power." But while there is a degree of democracy in his concept of ruling according to worth (and we may well question how much worth Greek women could hope to acquire given their educational and social limitations), he writes earlier of friendship, which seeks other aims than justice: "But equality does not seem to take the same form in acts of justice and in friendship; for in acts of justice what is equal in the primary sense is that which is in proportion to merit, while quantitative equality is secondary, but in friendship quantitative equality is primary and proportion to merit secondary."

Our modern trend toward equality in all aspects of marriage is more in accordance with this latter definition of friendship than with the earlier formulation of the husband-wife relationship. Many couples feel that both partners should be able to pursue careers, even if one partner is better educated or has more earning potential; that both should share in housekeeping and child-raising equally, regardless of either partner's affinity or ability. This is not in keeping with the Aristotelian concept of a marital relationship, but it *does* conform to his definition of the highest form of friendship.

For Aristotle, a friend is a love object, so he uses friendship and love as interchangeable terms. However, he does describe three distinct types of love objects: those whom we seek because they give us pleasure; those who are useful to us; and those whom we truly admire and perceive as good and virtuous. "Nature seems above all to avoid the painful and aim at the pleasant," he declared, a couple of thousand years before Sigmund Freud founded a theory of psychoanalysis on his "discovery" of the pleasure principle. The search for pleasure leads many young people to one another for erotic enjoyment, and though this is an inferior form of friendship, it is valid, for each gives the same as he gets over an equal duration of time. Moreover, he noted, after youth has faded and desire become less intense, the lovers' familiarity with one another often leads them to appreciate one another's virtues, especially if they were similar types of people to begin with, and this moves the friendship to a higher plane. (Bear in mind that the Greeks, who described sexual unions that developed into deep friendships, probably had homosexual relationships in mind, as in Plato's *Symposium*, although Plato also speaks of man and woman needing each other for physical completion.) In friendships based on utility, each serves the other, as in business partnerships. Unlike the amorous relationship, the utilitarian relationship rarely becomes permanent, for such people do not necessarily find each other pleasant and are more interested in some profit than in one another.

In the highest form of love, one esteems the partner, but since absolute equality (as opposed to that imposed by justice where each gets in accordance with relative merit) is essential, the two parties must be relatively similar. Flattery and honor, which many people prefer to love, is esteem accorded from those who are or pretend to be inferior, but love is shared between equals. Thus, while friends wish good for one another, if one's accomplishments raise him too far above the other, the friendship must fail, for a friend is loved for what he is and, therefore, cannot change too much.

On reflection, love really has not changed much since Aristotle's time. Most relationships start with the pleasure phase, the promise of or actual sexual gratification, the delight in a partner's physical attractiveness, enjoyable social times, and the mutual attention paid. If this atraction falls short of a genuine knowledge and appreciation of the other's qualities, it is understandable, given the time required to become truly familiar with a person; it is the pleasure bond that keeps a couple together long enough for this to develop. While Aristotle tended to exclude sweethearts from the utilitarian relationship, it seems to have been a basis for many marriages in history; in marriages arranged by parents or governments for purposes of political or social advantage, such is obviously the basis. The same can be said of frontier cultures where a strong, healthy wife was valued beyond any irrelevant considerations, such as physical beauty, education, or sexual responsiveness; we can say the same of cultures where women's total economic dependence on men made them look for nothing more than a good provider. Unlike Aristotle's examples of business partnerships (here, again, the problem is his thinking exclusively in terms of males), such marriages would not be likely to outlive their usefulness since the utility was required for a lifetime. Recently, psychologists have been telling us what we know from direct observation and experience without even having read Aristotle, that the relationship in marriage changes after a couple of years from one of romantic infatuation and sexual excitement to a more stable, caring, and warmer one, more akin to companionship than romantic love.

But if many aspects of love have not changed since Aristotle's time, there seems to be one profound change that has occurred. The thinkers of ancient Greece and the philosophers they in turn influenced through the centuries could not accept the notion of a basic equality between the sexes, the very equality that Aristotle deemed a *sine qua non* for the highest love and friendship. To be sure, there have been marriages which defied the prevailing thought, especially those where great adversity was overcome in the only possible way, by a couple sharing effort and communication in an atmosphere of equality, as a team in harness must work equally or not at all. Many women feel that our Aristotelian heritage has not been basically altered; we have not been able to dent the concepts of male-female relationships that have governed the thinking of western civilization since its inception. Perhaps their pessimism is justified; however, even if much of the professed new equality of sexes is lip service, even if corrective legislation is slow to develop, and chauvinistic prejudices die hard, the very idea of a world where men and women can be true equals and true companions is revolutionary. And once the basic relationship between men and women has changed, marriage is bound to change as well.

What I Did for Love

If, as our survey seems to show, couples seem to be valuing companionship more and love less, should we regard this as a positive or negative phenomenon? Should we regard companionship as a more realistic and truly egalitarian goal, or as evidence that we have become so alienated from our fellow-creatures that love is beyond reach and we settle for relief from loneliness?

One clue is the lack of consistent differences in reasons for marrying among the different age groups, which would indicate that we are not witnessing a dramatic change in the attitudes of those marrying within the past decade or two. Any changes being wrought seem to be affecting all married people, not just the youngest generation.

But the question, you may argue, was "What *was* your reason for marrying?" and how can a decision already made in the past be affected by later developments? The probable answer is that we all marry for several reasons, both love and companionship bound to be among them. Looking back, we are likely to state as our most important reason the one which we *now* consider to be the most important. Since romantic love is most highly valued in the earliest years of marriage and quickly cedes ground to companionship, persons married for several years will often pick companionship as their most important reason, though the majority will still select love. To some extent, this explanation is borne out by our student subgroup, one which we know to be, in virtually all cases, recently married; here we find a high valuation for love, as in other groups, but a low estimation of companionship.

True companionship, the genuine regard for one another as friends and equals, takes time to develop, even in the most liberal and well-educated of youngsters, who are still primarily drawn together by those sexual and emotional needs we call falling in love. Can older couples achieve the same degree of friendship, even where the woman is less educated than the man and has been passive in decision-making? If both partners are receptive to new ideas, they can benefit even if they were not raised in an atmosphere that encouraged equality and free communication between the sexes. Certainly, many older couples have benefited by the new sexual freedom, adding new information and techniques to their sexual relations after years of ignorance and conservatism. Likewise, an awareness of the expanded potential and growing achievements of women can enhance a wife's self-esteem and encourage her own self-development, provided her husband is supportive to her personal growth and its beneficial effects on their relationship.

Only in America could love take on negative connotations and come under attack as a basis for marriage. Our national ambivalence is reflected in the advice Dr. Albert Ellis claims he frequently gives his clients: "You had better not marry anybody you don't love, but you also had better not marry everybody you do love." The confusion stems from our using the term "love" to describe the intense physical and emotional attraction we feel for someone of the opposite sex with its corresponding view of that person as unrealistically perfect, as well as to describe a genuine regard for someone we truly know and understand, which generates a commitment to their welfare, which we value at least as highly as our own. We may call the first feeling infatuation and the other genuine love, but this is misleading, for infatuation means literally a state of foolishness and, since this state is invariably a requisite to deeper love, it is not fair to denigrate it. It can certainly make us feel foolish, and we can empathize with the lovesick aristocrat in Shaw's *Getting Married* who shamefully confesses, "I felt in her presence an extraordinary sensation of unrest, of emotion, of unsatisfied need. I'll not disgust you with details of the madness and folly that actually followed that meeting. But it went as far as this: That I actually found myself prowling past the shop at night under a sort of desperate necessity to be near some place where she had been. A hideous temptation to kiss the doorstep because her foot has pressed it made me realize how mad I was."

Love, American style, becomes malignant when the songwriters, magazine publishers, novelists, television producers, and advertisers lead us to become infatuated with infatuation, preventing us from exercising the healthy skepticism and realistic critical faculties we need to supplant that intoxicated feeling with a realistic appreciation of and commitment to the loved one. One expert has stated that modern urban America is in the grip of a peculiar romantic complex known in the entire history of civilization only to Northwestern Europe, Polynesia, and the aristocracy of eleventh and twelfth century Europe. If half our sample does not give love as its most important reason for marrying, it is obvious that some are not victims of this malady; but what are the symptoms by which we can identify those affected by it? If infatuation is characterized by over-idealization and unrealistic expectations of a partner, a problem develops when the same attitudes are held toward love itself. The incurable romantic believes that there is one right person for him, that he will know that person instantly, and fall in love without being able to help himself. Since this is true love, it will last forever and the lovers will have no problem adjusting to marriage, since happiness is inevitable. He and his beloved will live solely for one another and freely reveal their most intimate thoughts, without fear of hurting or offending one another. Love is an unequivocally positive feeling and is reserved entirely for the spouse.

What is too silly to be said may be sung, it has been said, and some believe the songs. Since we are all subject to infatuation, all of us believe, to some degree, in unrealistic romantic ideals early in life, just as we all believed in Santa Claus. We lose our faith in St. Nick gradually; it's not a matter of someone brusquely telling us he's not real, for kids are subjected to the taunts of unbelievers from the start, but don't accept it until the evidence accumulates. And we still celebrate Christmas. So, too, we lose faith in romantic perfection, but don't give up on love. Our American romantic tradition is harmful only to those who never give up the nagging belief that there is a form of trouble-free, selfless, unwavering devotion that they have missed out on. They flee their marriages to look for it, or, worse, feel trapped and discontented, but stay on, hating their partners for robbing them of their dream.

Most Americans, despite growing up in a popular culture of romantic fantasy, ultimately exchange their dreams for a more mature form of love and companionship without undue trauma, just as they learned that the gifts from a loving mother and father were not such a bad substitute to accept even for the likes of Santa Claus.

The Age of Consent

"The great thing," advised Shaw's Alderman Collins, "is to get the young people tied up before they know what they're letting themselves in for."

While there has been a small increase in the percentage of men and women who defer marriage until after age 30, most couples still marry well before the age of 25. In 1976, the median age for brides was 21 and for grooms 24. Since 1900, the age has fluctuated between 20 and 22 for women and 23 and 26 for men. Men are marrying younger than they did at the turn of the century, possibly due to better starting salaries and working conditions, though the median age for grooms in 1960 was a full year younger than in 1976.

The median age is that above and below which equal numbers appear, so fully half of American brides are under 21. But if we wish to blame their eagerness for marriage on not knowing what they're letting themselves in for, how are we to account for the 80 per cent of divorced people who remarry, obviously knowing what they're in for?

Our own survey confirms that over the past half-century, which would encompass the first-wedding dates of our entire sample, the median age for brides is approximately 20, and 23 for grooms.

The most striking finding is that nearly twice as many people who have remarried were younger than 18 at the time of their first marriage, compared with those still married to their first spouse. This indicates a higher divorce rate among couples who marry very young. Members of minority groups marry more often while still under 18.

How old were you when you decided to marry, and what factors in your life influenced that decision?

Perhaps they are victims of the all-American romantic complex, but for some young people, the right age was when they met the one right person:

WIFE: "I was 23, met the right man, fell in love, we are like *one* person, we are so much alike, it's *scarey* sometimes, but he makes me feel beautiful and loves me and gives me all I need, and he is someone I thought was only in a dream. But I found the perfect mate—that is the factor that made my decision. *I met the perfect man and fell in love.*"

HUSBAND: "I was 20 years old. Love for my spouse was the most important factor. Compatibility, personality, personal appearance."

They have no children. She's a white collar worker between 18 and 30. Though she calls her husband the "perfect man" she admits to striking him during arguments. He's a college student of the same age. Says they argue mostly about attention to members of the opposite sex.

WIFE: "I was 13 years old when I began praying to God that he would prepare me for the person of His Divine choice, and that God would prepare and protect that 'Special One' for me. God answered my prayer. We met in college and were married two years later when I was 24 years old and he was 26 years old.
 "My mother married the wrong person and my childhood was miserable. This is the very opposite of what my marriage has been."

HUSBAND: "After World War II, more mature; then a Christian 'born again' experience brought real purpose to my life. I was 25."

She's a retired schoolteacher between the ages of 41 and 50. Has 3 children. Says she feels overwhelmed by responsibility, and is tied down and trapped. He's 51 or over. In technical work. Believes his wife takes him for granted, and that his job interferes with his sex life.

For some, they reached the age when they felt ready to settle down, an age that ranged between 21 and 58:

WIFE: "18 years. Getting away from home. Wanting freedom to live my own life."

HUSBAND: "21 years. Wanted to settle down and raise a family. Also have a reliable sex partner."

She's a young homemaker between the ages of 18 and 30, with 2 children. She was influenced mostly by spouse's good looks when deciding to marry. He's a white collar worker, between 31 and 40. He says their sex life is variable.

WIFE: "I was 20 the first time and madly, blindly in love! So I thought. *Bah!* Better to marry someone, as I did the second time (I was widowed at 42) for companionship. We get along great. Married four years and never argue. *Better this way.*"

HUSBAND: "58 years. Needed a companion, tired of living alone, preferred being married to being a bachelor."

She's 51 or over. Retired or unemployed. Feels their sex life is satisfactory and says their marriage is stable. He feels their marriage is generally loving, says they have no major problems, and considers their sex life to be very good.

WIFE: "26. We'd lived together three years and had no intention of parting."

HUSBAND: "Age 33. Stable relationship, decided to make it legal."

She has a postgraduate education. They have one child. Her big problem is lack of time together with spouse. However she's sure they have a loving marriage. This is his second marriage. Also has a postgraduate education. He thinks they have a communication problem.

If people barely old enough to consider themselves adults feel too young to make their own decisions about marriage, they can usually find people around them to make the decision for them— often with unfortunate results:

WIFE: "I was nineteen when I married. I was very much in love. Nevertheless, I would have gone on to college before marriage had my father and mother not refused to send me. There was a lot of parental pressure about how evil the world was for an unmarried female. I had been taught since childhood that the ultimate for a woman was marriage, that a woman simply couldn't cope with the world alone. Therefore, I married earlier than I personally would have chosen to do."

HUSBAND: "20. Peers."

She's between the ages of 31 and 40, with 3 children. Feels unloved and unappreciated. He's in the professional field, making $15-$25,000 a year. Feels the major problem in their marriage is communication, and admits that during arguments they've both struck each other.

WIFE: "19. My friends thought it would be a better arrangement."

HUSBAND: "20 years old. Spouse pregnant but miscarried."

She's a homemaker, between 18 and 30. No children. She says she married because of pressure from others, and that her marriage alternates between periods of closeness and remoteness. He's in management, between 41 and 50. Admits to engaging with spouse in group sex and mate-swapping.

Sometimes one's marital history depends on geography, such as moving to where the groom happens to be or moving with him where he happens to go:

WIFE: "I was 17. We loved each other very much and still do."

HUSBAND: "I was 22 years old. Factors influencing my decision were love for my future spouse, the fact that I was soon moving to Memphis, and the fact that I knew together our immediate financial future would be more stable."

She's a blue collar worker, 18 to 30, no children. Was attracted to spouse's intelligence, and would definitely marry the same type again. He's a college student. Says the worst crisis their marriage has faced was their moving. He considers the marriage to be a very loving one.

Among the wives who responded, it seems that those who married under the age of 21, regardless of their motive, more often were dissatisifed with their unions:

WIFE: "I was 19½ years old when I married.
     "Factors at that time: Depression (economic); wanted to leave small town where I lived; thought I was in love; and wanted to be independent."

She's retired, 51 or over. Has some college education. Married to have children. Says their major problem is lack of communication, and would definitely not marry the same type of person again, or marry at all.

WIFE: "The first time I married I was 18. My life was very confused at the time. I married a man 12 years my senior. I was so immature, I think now, that I believed marriage would be the answer to my problems. That it would provide security— both emotional and financial. I sort of gave up my father for a father image. Through marriage I thought I could trade fathers and come up with a good one more to my liking.
     "This is my third and last marriage. I married this time because I have found someone to share my life with. He doesn't have to fulfill any father role."

She's now between 41 and 50, with some college education. Believes that her husband appreciates her, but doesn't love her. She married for economic security and stability. The worst crisis in their marriage was interference by husband's friends.

WIFE: "First marriage, age 19, probably affected by peers—first husband was 'hero' type at school. I didn't know or think of how responsible he would be as a husband and father. I was very infatuated with him and thought he was a 'great catch.'

"Second marriage, age 33, my present husband is the most considerate and affectionate person I have ever met. He makes me feel wanted and loved; I could not be more fortunate than to have found him."

She's in the management field, and has some college education. Married this time for love. Personality and career achievement influenced her the most in her choice of spouse.

WIFE: "I had just turned 20 years of age and a tragic happening happened. I was suddenly separated from my lover, who is now my spouse. For three months we communicated by letters and phone calls, and then we decided our love couldn't survive without each other. So I moved to where he was and we were married."

A high school graduate, working in technical field. Married for love. Spouse is now in prison and she's not sure whether she'd marry the same type of person again.

WIFE: "I was young and I wanted sex with him all the time but felt guilty outside of marriage."

A white collar worker, between 41 and 50 with some college education. Describes her marriage as a failure. Says their sex life is variable, and admits to cheating with more than 3 men, with one affair lasting over a year.

WIFE: "Age 18. All my friends were going to college; I couldn't afford it and wanted to get away from home."

She has some college education, is between 18 and 30, and works in the professional field. She admits now she would not marry the same type of person again. Money and conflicts over relatives are her major problems.

Wives who married after their teen years seemed more satisfied with their decisions:

WIFE: "I was 23 years old. We went together for two years. We did not live together, did not believe in it, because it is a sin. After the marriage we've been living together for 24 years.

"For your children you should wait two years before a

couple raises children. This way you know your spouse—his or her interests. We have a 21-year-old son and 16-year-old daughter.

"You know I am glad they are getting our opinion why we *got married*—the *time* we *got married*. Because I believe a girl or man should get married after 21 years of age. You are stable in your everyday life, ready to settle down. And too, you should see the country and travel."

WIFE: "I was 23 years old. As I said before, I had reached a stage in life where I was ready to settle down.

"I was tired of 'the dating game' and felt that with someone who was reasonably attractive, kind, considerate, intelligent and had a sense of humor, I could make a good life. I found him—or I should say I believe God led me to him—and we did.

"Not without *many* problems I must add—but *with* a commitment and determination, we've grown together and we are happier today than ever. Praise the Lord!"

A college graduate, working in the professional field, between the ages of 41 and 50.

WIFE: "I was 20 when I got married because I was afraid if I waited no one would want me. I was very insuecrue. But we grew together and so far have a good life and marriage."

A homemaker, between the ages of 31 and 40. High school graduate. Married for economic security. Would probably marry the same type of person again, but does have a feeling of being taken for granted.

WIFE: "I was 22. We married because of strong religious beliefs about birth control. We wanted to take the responsibility for having children."

One child. Working in technical field. Has some college education. Says she married also for companionship. Sex life is very good—they have sex more than once a day.

Among husbands, there are a few whose entire lives seem to lead up to the moment when they make a careful and conscientious choice of a bride, as in the case of this devout gentleman:

HUSBAND: "We met in January 1940; at that time I was 25. In June 1942 we were married. I had asked the Lord to give me a Christian wife. He began the work in our lives—a love for each other that has become stronger day by day! I was influenced to make a wise choice by Christian parents, and dedicated teachers at Bible College and Seminary."

He's 51 or over, has some college education. Works in management. His worst problem was unemployment. They never argue; have a good marriage.

Such cases are exceptional. Many marry under a sense of pressure rather than volition:

HUSBAND: "I was 28 and not looking to get married. I decided to marry when I was given an ultimatum and decided I did not want to lose my wife."

A professional, between the ages of 31 and 40. Has a postgraduate education.

HUSBAND: "18. I wanted to get married, at 20 I had to get married."

For some men, the pressure is not external, but internal and libidinal:

HUSBAND: "Must have been sex. Had nothing in common with spouse. Different interests entirely."

He's 51 or over. Has some college education, and is a blue collar worker. He married between the ages of 21 and 24. Based on his experience, if he became single again he probably wouldn't marry, or would marry someone quite different in most ways.

HUSBAND: "We met in high school and went together through college. When I was sent to Germany I knew I did not want to be away from her. We married after she graduated from college. I suppose it was sex that we looked forward to—and it is sex that has kept our marriage alive."

He's in management, between 41 and 50, and has some college background. Says he keeps faithful to wife out of love, fear, and loyalty.

But for many men, it was neither a matter of falling deeply in love nor succumbing to pressure. For them, there was just a sense that the time had come to get married—and they did.

HUSBAND: "I was 28 years old. Parents were same approximate age at time of their marriage. It took that long to do the things that I wanted to do as a single person."

He's a college graduate, between the ages of 31 and 40. In the management field. His marriage gives him a feeling of emotional security and of being loved.

HUSBAND: "I had done everything there was to do."

Now between the ages of 41 and 50. Retired or unemployed, earned less than $8,000 last year. He and his wife have considered divorce, but rejected it because of moral and religious considerations, and because it would alienate him from his children.

HUSBAND: "I was 23. She was the same age. All our friends were marrying. The single world was disappearing and it seemed time to become part of the new life of people in their 20s."

A blue collar worker, high school graduate, now between the ages of 41 and 50. Says money is their biggest problem, and he's become disillusioned about romance and love. Both he and his wife have considered divorce.

HUSBAND: "About 25. Was engaged at 30 but broke up before marriage. Dated frequently but did not get serious again for years. Married at 42. Always felt I would eventually marry."

Because of his marriage, he now feels he is no longer alone in times of crisis, and says his life has more purpose and meaning. He believes he is a good lover, but feels that his wife thinks he needs improvements in other ways. Now between 41 and

50, he works in management. Has one child. Says the most important reason for him marrying was to have children.

HUSBAND: "40. I found the right girl for me."

"It's mean to let poor young things in for so much while they're in that state," laments Shaw's Mrs. George, referring to the state of wild infatuation in which most young people—and a good portion of the older ones—marry. Let us not even consider the most tragic cases, the nearly 300,000 teen-aged mothers who marry each year, often dropping out of high school and rendering themselves unemployable for life because of their lack of education or job skills. Women who marry before the age of 18 are three times as likely to divorce as those who marry later.

Even those who marry between the ages of 18 and 20 face hazards related to our peculiar culture, and significant numbers do marry at that vulnerable time of life. In our survey, 42 per cent of the women had married between 18 and 20, in addition to the 16 per cent who had been 17 or younger. Among the men, 28 per cent were under 21 at the time of their first marriage. In our subsample of matched couples, nearly a quarter had wed when both partners were under 21. Legally, people over 18 are adults in most jurisdictions; they can vote, drink, fight wars, and marry without parental consent. There are many cultures where a person of 18 would be regarded as well into adulthood, with full economic, marital, and even parental responsibility, no different from someone twice that age. In America, however, adolescence seems to be prolonged more than anywhere else. High school students rarely have any responsibilities beyond attending classes and a third of the men, and nearly as many women, continue this academic existence into college, delaying their entrance into the work force for even more years. With the trend toward smaller families, few adults have had experience caring for younger siblings or even had much exposure to small children except for their childhood peers. Not only do young adults lack practical experience in coping with the world of the breadwinner and the homemaker, but they get much of their impressions of the real world from television, movies, and advertising, all of which convey the message that love and happiness are based on sexual attractiveness and romance.

The consequences of entering a marriage with expectations based on the glorification of the most mind-befogging of human instincts are often unpleasant. As in the case of the fellow who bought a copy of the classic *David Harum* thinking the title was *David's Harem*, the problem is not the nature of what you wind up with, but its failure to be anything at all like you anticipated.

2

A Matter of Choice:

Mate Selection

Why, you would not make a man your lawyer or your family doctor on so slight an acquaintance as you would fall in love with and marry him!

—*George Bernard Shaw*, MAN AND SUPERMAN

Her problem, she explains to the psychiatrist, is that she is getting married in five weeks and is dubious about going through with it.

She is a 33-year-old social worker employed by a child guidance agency. She is a slim, neat, articulate woman, not outstandingly beautiful, but neither would you object to encountering her on a blind date. She has never been married, and until last year lived with her European-born parents, getting her own apartment over their strenuous objections. Her fiance is a doctor, American-born but trained in Mexico, currently completing a pathology residency and trying to pass his state license exam. He is her age, having worked for several years prior to medical school; he was fired from job after job because of "personality problems." She describes him as moody, pessimistic, and critical of everyone. He

37

seems guilt-ridden about their sex life, which is not very satisfying. He speaks often about homosexuality and when she recently asked him if he was homosexual, he said cryptically, "Maybe." He does not seem very interested in his career; his chief interest in life seems to be a book he is writing based on his professional experiences. She finds it childishly written and boring; he tells her she has no appreciation of good literature. He has dated other women, but none stay with him very long; he admits, "I don't have much to choose from."

The next question for the therapist to ask is not why she wants to call off the wedding, but why she ever agreed to it. She shrugs. It just snowballed. A vague proposal two months ago, an arbitrary wedding date, pressure from her parents to look at wedding gowns, pressure from him to select a reception hall. And the void in her life. Before she met him a year ago, she had dated another doctor for two years. In the beginning there were statements of love and implications of marriage. Then, objections from his mother and the realization there would be no wedding. The worst blow was his marriage to someone else just a month after the breakup. She was rebounding and knew it. A married sister with a hospital job arranged the introduction to doctor number two. She instantly disliked him, but accepted a date. They broke up once, but a chance meeting led to a reconciliation.

"I tell my parents there's not going to be a wedding," she sighs, "but I can't tell him."

You can ask for time, the therapist suggests. A two-month engagement is not a very long one. If the decision to marry is the correct one now, it will still be valid six months from now. He points out what she already knows well: that she's just begun to live independently, that she has a good career, that she has said nothing positive about her fiance in the past hour.

She leaves, agreeing to return in a week. But when she cancels the appointment the therapist is not surprised.

The one word that comes to mind in such a case is "un-American." In America, we are supposed to marry because we are in love with someone. Well-educated women with careers do not feel compelled to marry a man simply because he makes a good living; they do not panic because they have reached the age of 30 and find the thought of a lifetime of spinsterhood intolerable. We do not let our parents select our mates or make us feel like failures because we are single. In short, the American ideal is one of freedom, free choice of marrying, and free choice of partners.

But then there are the pressures that impinge upon that freedom, external ones from parents wishing to be grandparents and lovers wishing to be spouses, and internal ones, from our inability to bear loneliness and our need to be accepted in a society where marriage is the norm. Pressure, according to the laws of physics, involves two variable factors. One is force and the other is area. A force applied in a small enclosed container will result in a greater pressure than that same force dissipated across a wide space. Similarly, people experience more pressure when they feel they have little maneuvering room, fewer life options. The confining space may be one of actual area, as for the small-town spinster who knows exactly how many eligible men there are or the clerk whose existence seems limited to an office which new faces never enter. The narrowed space may be chronological, as for the aging person who feels "I haven't too many good years left." The limits may be cultural, such as restricting prospects to one's own ethnic group or religious sect, or psychological, such as avoiding people whose lifestyles differ from our own.

Very few people seriously consider the option of not marrying at all, and when one is governed by the unspoken assumption that one must marry, one's orientation really changes at some point from a passive hope that love will come along to an active search for an acceptable partner, the chief of whose criteria is a reciprocal desire to marry. Despite the American tradition of romantic love and the national ideal of freedom, we are often more pragmatic than idealistic in our choices. Still, we have some measure of freedom in when to discard ideals and when to yield to pressures, a liberty that newlyweds in other times and other climes have never known.

The American Way

They tell the story of a network executive who, in the early days of radio, was aghast when it was suggested that a program be aired on a Sunday afternoon. "But who would listen at that hour?" he objected. "That's when everyone plays polo!"

It is human nature to become so involved with our own lifestyles that we assume the rest of the world lives as we do. The concept of marrying for love and choosing one's own spouse is so ingrained in us that we never stop to think that the greater part of the world for the greater part of history has relied on marriages arranged by families, not by the involved spouses. In most of Asia and the Arab nations, the non-romantic marriage was the rule for centuries, and while modern laws generally now permit personal choice, the old traditions still prevail in many regions.

In India, for example, parents not only arrange marriages between youngsters of similar social status, but as the children marry they move in with the groom's parents and turn all earnings over to the control of the parents. The eldest son assumes control upon the parents' death and his wife becomes the new matriarch for the younger married siblings as well as the families of their own sons. This system is perpetuated on the grounds that young people are too immature to make sound choices with regard to mates. Marriage pacts between families are often sealed while the prospective spouses are mere toddlers. Advocates of this sytem point out that divorce in India is practically unknown. Obviously, the fault with that argument is that divorce is no more a free choice than marriage; few would contend that orthodox Catholic marriages are invariably happy simply because the parties never divorce one another.

While it would be impossible for Americans to adopt Asiatic customs so contrary to our own traditions, the alarming fatality rate of teen-aged marriages forces us to concede that young people make poorer marital choices than those only a few years older. Brides of 17 or younger are three times more likely to divorce than women who marry in their twenties. Paradoxically, girls who marry under 18 and boys under 21 require parental consent in most states. How can we advocate more parental involvement in the selection of mates if the marriages they now have some legal voice in turn out so badly? To be fair, we have to admit that many, if not most, parents giving consent for marriages of minors are doing so with less than whole-hearted enthusiasm, often in the face of a premarital pregnancy or a headstrong youngster whom they have long ago given up on controlling. But, on the other hand, very young brides and grooms are often fleeing households made intolerable by ineffectual, if not abusive, parents. The cases that could have most benefitted by the intervention of a mature parent are most often the ones that lacked a mature parent from the beginning.

Arranged marriages found favor during the course of European civilization chiefly among the aristocracy and propertied classes. Their main interest was not the mature selection of compatible partners by concerned parents, but the preservation and augmentation of wealth and power. The nobility did not rebel at the idea of marrying someone they had no personal attraction to, provided the price was right, but neither did they forego romance. An ideal of courtly love—the politest term ever coined for adultery—sprang up, whereby every knight paid court, not to a maiden, but to some languishing married lady. The inherent conflicts in such a system, which could have catastrophic results if the stakes were high as when kings and kingdoms were involved, have been immortalized in the legends of classic triangles, such as Arthur-Guinevere-Lancelot or Tristan-Iseult-Mark, wherein king, queen, and knave are bound to one another by ties of loyal devotion as strong as those of the opposing passionate love. The system was terrible as a means of obtaining romantic love through marriage, but very effective in centralizing political power and consolidating lines of succession and inheritance. In short, marriage had nothing whatever to do with personal happiness, other than that acquired from a sense of security and of having done the right thing. Human nature being what it is and royal wealth not being what it used to, we can trace the erosion of this self-sacrificing spirit from the sixteenth-century aristocracy, when Don Juan's peers disgusted the traditionalists by courting each other like common peasants, through twentieth-century monarchy, with the abdication of Edward VIII and the wedding of Caroline of Monaco.

To assume that marriage changed dramatically from an institution concerned with property to one whose prime interest was romantic love with the advent of industrialized democracy is unrealistic; rather we can say that the economic concerns pressed romantic traditions into service to insure the survival of women who had neither independent wealth nor employability. While the laboring classes were free to marry as they chose—within their own class, of course—English and American society was saddled with genteel ladies who, because of their sex, were denied training for entrance into the more lucrative professions and who, if their families let them pursue menial trades, could never maintain their accustomed standards of living. In short, they were fit to be nothing but wives for husbands with sufficient earning power to maintain them in their usual style. Thus, it became the overriding concern of these young women and their families to arrange suitable marriages as quickly as possible. Parental involvement was more subtle than in the days of open contract negotiations between families, but any mother worth that name would school her daughters in the arts of grooming and dress, send them to the best

schools she could afford and add extras such as French and music
lessons, build a circle of friends that would give the daughters
access to the company of eligible young men, and, by an endless
series of stratagems, convert the girls into the sort of delicate,
attractive, and non-utilitarian sexual beings that any red-blooded
male would covet. If a planned exchange of sexual charms for
monetary gain sounds uncomfortably like the sort of trade that a
less discreet girl could get arrested for, one can only protest that
until our society manages to extend economic independence to all
women, such situations are bound to exist.

Are we finally beyond the old bargaining, at last free to follow
our hearts? Surely, educational opportunities for women and the
passage of equal rights laws have finally given them the economic
independence required for truly democratic mate selection. But,
of course, there will be the child-raising years. And the doors to
top-level positions are opening ever so slowly. And how many
first-rate husbands are available to a single woman over 30?

And one thinks of the reluctant bride who somehow cannot
bring herself to reject the doctor she does not love and one wonders
how far, in this Land of the Free, we have really come.

Mr. and Mrs. Right

In one of the vintage television situation comedies, the hapless
Chester A. Riley had a houseguest with a fearsome reputation as
a troublemaker. He was a poker-faced, laconic, bespectacled man
who seemed incapable of stirring up a puddle—until Riley's neighbor dropped by and introduced his wife.

Neighbor: Glad to meet ya. And this is my wife, Madge.
Guest *(morosely):* Why?
Neighbor *(perplexed):* Why? Well . . . because I married her.
Guest *(as before):* Why? *(Long silence.)*
Wife: Jim, he asked why you married me.
Neighbor: I know, I know. I'm thinking. *(More silence.)*
Wife *(desperately):* I know why I married *you!*
Neighbor *(with exasperation):* But that's not the question! The
question is why I married you! *(Wife exits in tears and neighbor
follows, trying to make amends.)*

The memory of that scene makes one hesitant. One would
certainly think twice about asking an acquaintance why he or she
married their particular spouse, lest it appear that you could not

see a likely reason—or they could not recall one. But our questionnaires give one the opportunity to ask all manner of troublesome questions.

Why did you happen to choose your particular spouse?

Personality was the trait named most often by both sexes as that which influenced them most in selecting their future spouse. But husbands more often than wives mentioned good looks or sexual attractiveness as important, and this was reflected in the answers we received from couples, where wives tended to stress being in love and husbands spoke more in terms of attraction:

WIFE: "We were in love. I was totally attracted to him in every way. We got along well and enjoyed doing different things together. I was the center of his life. He went out of his way to make me happy. I felt he could be a good provider and give me financial security."

HUSBAND: "She was attractive, vivacious and interesting. I thought she would prove to be a loving companion, a wonderful wife and mother."

She's a homemaker between the ages of 18 and 30, with a postgraduate education. He's professional, with the same educational background and age range.

WIFE: "I enjoy being with my husband. We enjoy camping, 4-wheeling, and just having a good time. We're able to communicate and enjoy doing so. I love him because he's kind, considerate, and affectionate—also conservative in thoughts on marriage and children. He also shows a lot of respect for me as a *woman*, and that means a lot to me. He treats me as his equal."

HUSBAND: "A very beautiful person.
 1. Personality
 2. Looks
 3. Etc."

They are both between the ages of 18 and 30. She's a home-maker with some college education. He's a college graduate, working in management. They lived together for 3 to 6 months before marriage. This is his second marriage, her first. He married for a homelife; she for love.

Sometimes, people start out with specifications, as in a help-wanted ad, and wait until someone comes along who fits them:

WIFE: "He did not drink, smoke or swear, and is a Christian. He's nice looking, taller than me and not overweight. He had a good job and earned a decent living, and I loved him for his *goodness.*"

HUSBAND: "Love her, she is pleasant to be around and we hit it off together—also she met my predetermined requirements for a wife, such as non-smoker, non-drinker and a virgin."

She's a high school graduate between the ages of 31 and 40. Says their only major problem is difference in religion. He's between 41 and 50, has some college education and is a white collar worker.

Some women wanted financial security and they saw it in their husbands—and there was little more they wanted to say:

WIFE: "Financial security, companionship."

HUSBAND: "Personality and looks."

She has no children, and is between the ages of 18 and 30. She says her husband is dominant. He's a high school graduate making between $15-$25,000 a year. 18 to 30. He believes that lack of communication is the major problem in their marriage.

In some states, the presence of an irresistible urge leading to a crime can result in acquittal on the grounds of insanity. Here's a response from someone married more than four times whose irresistible urge led him into another marriage:

WIFE: "Aggressiveness and his love for me."

HUSBAND: "Once I had seen her I had no other choice. I was irresistibly drawn to her. For the first time in my life I chased a woman in spite of what she said."

The wives who were satisfied with their marriages often indicated that they considered their prospective husbands good friends, as well as lovers:

WIFE: "I was always a close friend and physically attracted to him and fell in love with him. He is really my best friend and always has been and always will be. I chased him till he fell in love with me and wanted to marry me."

A homemaker, with some college education (18 to 30). She would definitely marry the same person again.

WIFE: "I knew and dated my husband a few times a year for *13 years*. No matter how long it had been since the last time we had been together we were very close. I completely trusted him as to being sincere towards me. We have the same ideas on how to bring up children, lifestyles and character."

She then lived together with her spouse for 3 months before finally marrying him. 31 to 40, works in the professional field, with some college background.

WIFE: "He was a widower for eleven years. I knew he had a happy marriage and raised a family of children himself. He was well liked and respected by friends and employees, had over twenty years on the same job and I also thought he was very handsome and had a marvelous personality. I looked forward to having a big family as his children were still at home. He is a very fun-loving person and brought the best out in me."

WIFE: "In retrospect I'm not quite sure. We just sort of happened. The qualities which I now like were not that evident to me at the time. I've learned what to look for if ever there were another marriage. Personality and similar interests are now very important."

She married for companionship at the time. She's 31 to 40, a homemaker with some college background. Her major problem she feels is different socioeconomic backgrounds, but she would still definitely marry the same person again.

WIFE: "Love. Common interests and he showed love and concern for his mother. I was told one time to watch how a fellow treats his mother and that's how he'll treat his wife. Passed this information on to our daughter now."

We hope when the lady above passes that information on to her daughter she adds a few notes of caution. If the man treats his mother as though she were the only woman in the world, that opinion might not be altered by marriage. And it's fine to treat his wife like he treats his mother, provided he doesn't act as if she *were* his mother. We'll have more to say about mothers and spouses who resemble them later.

Where the wives responded more in terms of circumstances that led them into marriage rather than some quality in the man, the marriage rarely worked out satisfactorily:

WIFE: "Death of only parent at age 18 and my husband was 23. He seemed my light in the storm. I was never forced to be independent."

A high school graduate, now between the ages of 31 and 40. White collar. She feels taken for granted, and probably would not marry the same person again. Admits to cheating on spouse with one person briefly. Feels she lives only for her children. Her main temptation to cheat is boredom.

WIFE: "When the guy I was dating left for college I needed companionship. I met my spouse and we enjoyed each other. He had money and took me out to fancy places."

This high school graduate, between 18 and 30, feels tied down and trapped, and probably would not marry the same person again. She's been involved with 2 or 3 other men in affairs, and with one of them for over a year. She's considered divorce, but taken no action.

WIFE: "I got pregnant and thought it best to get married."

A young homemaker between 18 and 30, who didn't complete high school. Though she believes her marriage is generally loving, she admits to cheating on spouse with one other man, briefly.

WIFE: "The only one my parents liked."

She married because of pressure from her partner. They never or rarely ever have sex, and she's cheated on her husband with one person for over a year. She feels that lack of communication is their biggest problem. She has some college education, is between 41 and 50, and works in management.

Among the responses from husbands, there were several who wanted a wife who would accept them just the way they were and not try to change them or divert them from doing things their own way:

HUSBAND: "My wife attracted me as a quiet, natural, very un-affected person. I could (and still do) feel very comfortable with her. She accepts me as I am, does not expect me to be something artificial and is not artificial herself."

He's a professional, between 31 and 40, with a postgraduate education. Has 3 children. He married mainly for companion-ship and love, and was most influenced by his wife's good looks and personality. Believes his marriage is always stable, with a very good sex life. Yet with all this he still feels tied down and trapped.

HUSBAND: "Personality.
"Acceptance of me as I was.
"Loneliness."

And, finally, there are men like the one on the television comedy show who seem to have trouble explaining why they ever did get married:

HUSBAND: "High school sweetheart. Only had one other girl friend. We both wish we would have lived together as well as had more experience with other people and life.
    "I don't know why I married her. I wanted to. I was pretty sure I loved her. I wanted to give her a good life. We got along well. I enjoyed her company."

At this point in his life, this young man (18 to 30) would probably not marry the same person again. He admits to cheat-ing on his wife with 2 or 3 other women, briefly, and feels sexually unsatisfied. Says he's appreciated, but not really loved. He's got a postgraduate education, and is a professional.

Woman's Way

Shaw's Jack Tanner explains, "It is a woman's business to get married as soon as possible, and a man's to keep unmarried as long as he can."

This cynical viewpoint is bound to be vociferously opposed by radical feminists who will claim that marriage meets all of men's needs and very few of women's. This argument has a great deal of validity and we will even defend it in forthcoming chapters, but it is quite irrelevant. The one need that marriage undoubtedly fills is the provision of a home and its maintenance for the raising of children. Whether women desire to bear children because nature so dictates, or out of a personal conviction, or because society has conned them into something opposing their personal interests, most women do want children at some point in their lives and make it their business to insure that goal.

Consider the responses you have been reading. Can you honestly imagine a woman saying she didn't know why she married her husband or that it wasn't really a choice? Compare these vacillating replies with the simple answer of the pregnant bride who tells us, "I thought it best to get married"—not "I had no choice" or some equally passive evasion. The men in our sample are better educated—one-third having had some college courses, compared with a quarter of women—and yet the women consistently give answers that are lengthier, more articulate, and more carefully thought out. Certainly, you can argue that women have more patience with questionnaires than men and even a questionnaire on politics or business might have given us the same sort of female-dominated pattern. Perhaps, but women will often give succinct answers that reflect as much appropriate insight into the matter as their more detailed responses, whereas a man's answer, whether brief or (infrequently) long betrays that he has never thought much about the topic before and isn't doing very well at it now. There are exceptions, the introspective men and impulsive women, just as there are male domestics and female mathematicians, and we will encounter a few, but when we talk of mate selection, we may as well focus on the women as the selectors.

The fact that 80 per cent of women work prior to marriage and 40 per cent hold jobs after marriage, without one bit of difference in the average age at which women marry or the percentage who ultimately marry compared with 50 years ago, indicates how futile it is to try to make something as paramount to women as marriage dependent on such extraneous factors as employment or education. Women marry early not to avoid work (since they have jobs) or get out of school (the number of married women between 25 and 34 attending college has practically doubled since 1970) or to escape their parents' households (since single adult women can live independently with society's sanction now); they marry early because marriage is a goal they actively pursue and generally achieve by the time they are 22. If men actively pursued marriage as women do, there would be no reason to suppose they, too, would not marry early; instead they pursue education and careers until they are deemed ripe for the plucking, upon which they offer such bewildered rationales as "I guess I was just ready for marriage," meaning some woman felt he was worth the effort.

Men have defended themselves from too much overt aggression by setting up polite ground rules that declare men must initiate romantic liaisons, but this has merely obliged women to develop a set of subtle territorial encroachments and preliminary signals that entice the man to make his perfunctory overture. Our honest female respondent above informs us, "I chased him till he fell in love with me and wanted to marry me"; do we dare accuse her of unconventionality or do we acknowledge that she is merely playing in real life the role of the pursuing female that has endured through every great comedy from Shakespeare's time to the latest TV sitcom, a role that endures because of its basic veracity?

The spider is as much a predator as the lioness, though the former must spin her intricate web and wait rather than race after her prey and drag it struggling to its doom. Nor should women be condemned for practicing the guile and devious allurement that man's turpitude and squeamish conventionality consign them to, anymore than one society can in good conscience malign those we herd into squalid ghettos by denouncing them as slum dwellers.

Just as we, for all our years of civilization, wind up with a system of marriage only a stone's throw from that of the most primitive bushman, so too will we wind up reproducing our kind in accordance with irrevocable natural laws, despite our hollow cants about personal goals. Woman is nature's instrument for childbearing and man is woman's instrument for sustenance and, regardless of how much love, respect, and intellectualizing goes on between man and woman, it is doubtful they will ever alter their basic roles in nature's master plan.

Likings and Likenesses

The debate about whether stronger loves exist between those who are opposite or those who are similar in personality goes back to ancient times. Aristotle says, "Many lovers on the other hand are constant, if familiarity has led them to love each other's characters, these being alike." Heraclitus said, however, "From different tones comes the fairest tune."

Sexual attraction, we must admit, is indiscriminate. People from different races and cultures who cannot even speak the same language may feel a profound inclination toward one another, engage in passionate lovemaking, and even fall in love. Soldiers have returned with warbrides who had to rely more on sign language than verbal communication and who had no concept of their husbands' social culture, much less personal history. Wars in Japan, Korea, and Viet Nam produced unions that had to transcend not only racial and language barriers, but cultural gaps so extreme that Kipling's admonitions about a non-merging twain seemed to rumble a prophecy of doom across the decades. Yet, many of these unions not only survived, but developed as deep an understanding and concern between the partners as marriages between childhood sweethearts.

But how do people tend to view their spouses? Asked to describe their mates, what characteristics do they focus on? And do they feel that they are basically alike or different as people?

The one word that married people selected most often to describe spouses on the objective portion of the questionnaire was "considerate," a term chosen by just about half (each respondent selected an average of 1.7 adjectives), with "affectionate" and "mature" picked about half that often. Consideration means a concern for someone else's feelings and desires, and this implies that, at least some of the time, those person's inclinations are different from our own. Offering a cigarette to another when lighting up is considerate (the National Lung Association's opinion notwithstanding), though here the act is based on the assumption the person shares your taste and urges. Ultimately, the considerate person is one who can empathize, put himself in the other's place, and remember that where the other person is coming from is not necessarily where the considerate person is at.

But while considerateness is a keystone to marital harmony, it would seem that the more similarities that exist between partners, the less conscious considerateness will be necessary, since so many of the partners' wants and goals will naturally coincide.

Describe your present spouse. Are the two of you more alike or different in your personalities, and in what ways?

According to some theories of attraction, we see the partner as possessing the shortcomings that we ourselves lack. Depending on our degree of satisfaction with ourselves, we can either select people who are very like us but perceived as possessing our best qualities to a greater extent, or who are totally dissimilar. Hence, a shy person who feels that an outgoing personality is the truly desirable one will marry an uninhibited gregarious partner. The very sociable person may secretly envy the person who seems to be comfortable alone and not under constant pressure to have people like him. Many marriages between introverts and extroverts develop for these reasons:

WIFE: "My present spouse is a good husband and lover to me, and generally a good parent. He is irreplaceable to me.

"He is very emotional, very religious, has set ways, is generally stable but likes excitement. He has always had nervous energy.

"We are quite different in personality. This is what attracts us.

"I am generally more stable, less religious, less energetic, and need less excitement than my husband to be happy.

"We are both emotional and have many interests in common."

HUSBAND: "She is a caring and loving spouse. She is quite good at raising our children. She is a good homemaker and helps with the bills by working and also taking care of the children. My personality is more outgoing than my wife's. She is quiet and quite shy. I like to be on the go more than my wife."

Both are blue collar workers. She's between 31 and 40, with a high school education. He's younger, between 18 and 30, and a college graduate. She is quite sure she would marry the same person again. He was most influenced in his choice of spouse by her intelligence, and her ability to communicate, even though she has a lesser education and is older.

WIFE: "My husband is more personable and dominant. I am more passive and shy."

HUSBAND: "She is a patient woman who puts up with a lot from me and the kids. We are more alike in that our personal tastes in most things coincide. The only differences stem from the fact that I tend toward freer thinking in most areas, while she tends to react in more conventional ways."

She's religious, he isn't. A young homemaker between 18 and 30, with some college background. He's in the similar age range and educational level. She feels their biggest problem is money—they are heavily in debt.

The wife is not always the quiet one in such unions. Sometimes she is the extrovert:

WIFE: "We are more alike than different, but there are differences.

Husband	Wife
Reserved	Outgoing
Shy	Extroverted
Frugal	Less frugal
Neat	Less neat
Loves the children	Loves the children
Moderately religious	Moderately religious
Involved with children	Involved with children"

HUSBAND: "Present spouse is emotional, carefree and outgoing. We are more different in personalities. I am unemotional, conservative and somewhat of an introvert."

Both are college graduates; she's a homemaker; he's a professional, with an income between $25-$49,999 a year. She's 31 to 40; he's 41 to 50.

WIFE: "He is affectionate, intelligent and easygoing. We are different in that he is more easygoing than I am and more patient. In most other ways we are alike."

HUSBAND: "More alike now. She is aggressive and doesn't give up or forget. I am getting that way too."

This young couple, both between 18 and 30, say their major problem is sexual dissatisfaction, yet they would still remarry each other. Both graduated college.

Some couples see themselves as basically alike and view what differences there are as positive factors:

WIFE: "Affectionate person who tries very hard to be thoughtful and understanding. Has a good sense of humor and is considerate of others. Difference in personality involves handling day to day problems. I worry over little things that do not bother my husband. He offsets my 'worry wart' tendency. I tend to place much importance on communication between spouses; he tends to 'clam up' when things bother him."

HUSBAND: "Attractive, stubborn, affectionate, emotional, smart, considerate, warm, reserved. Probably more alike in personalties. Spouse is occasionally more reserved in money matters, which is a good thing. Other than that both of us can be stubborn at times, but talking always settles things."

She's between 31 and 40, working in the white collar field, and has some college background. This is her first marriage. He's a college graduate, white collar worker, same age range. This is his second marriage and he feels his present spouse is quite different from the first.

WIFE: "I would say we are more alike than different, but that our few differences can be a complement to the other person's weaknesses."

HUSBAND: "She is darn near perfect . . . more calm than I in most circumstances. Strong where I am weak."

Both are 51 or over. He's a professional with a postgraduate education. She has some college background. Both feel they have no major problem in their marriage.

WIFE: "We are pretty much alike. We both can go our separate ways and not get mad at each other. Most people want to stay stuck in each other's faces."

HUSBAND: "Alike and she's beautiful."

Both are 18 to 30. She's a high school graduate; he has some college. She works at home; he's in the blue collar field.

Some couples don't agree that similarity is unequivocally good:

WIFE: "Alike. We get along and like to do things with each other and care for each other."

HUSBAND: "We are almost exactly alike—so much so that it sometimes causes conflicts."

Both work in the professional field, both are 18 to 30, and both are college graduates.

Others can't decide whether they're basically alike or different:

WIFE: "We are very different. He is friendly and outgoing to others, but is anxious and has a temper."

HUSBAND: "More alike; we like a lot of the same things. Spouse is independent which I like all right. When we first got married she could hardly do anything without me (which I didn't like). She is stubborn; hard for her to admit she's wrong. (I am also.)"

Both in the same age range (31 to 40). She didn't finish high school, he did. She's a homemaker; he's a blue collar worker. Both feel taken for granted, and unsure whether they would marry each other again. They've had a separation.

WIFE: "A lot alike. Same religious preference. Very faithful, committed, a minister, good provider, Christian, good husband, good father, understanding, dedicated.
"We are alike in most of these qualities above."

HUSBAND: "Alike in religious faith, love of sports, travel, spending habits. Different in attitude toward people who disagree with us."

Wife says she's dominant; husband is not happy with that role. She's 41 to 50, high school graduate. He's in the same age bracket, but has a superior education—a postgraduate degree. Works in the professional field.

Not all characteristics attributed to spouses were positive ones. While "dominant" is not necessarily a bad trait, in our present climate of sexual equality many would consider it so. It led potentially negative responses, with 11 per cent of married people using it to describe spouses, women seeing men as dominant twice as often as the reverse. Possessiveness is generally considered undesirable and one in ten respondents found this in spouses, possessive husbands being cited slightly more frequently than wives, and higher frequencies of possessiveness occurring among non-whites.

Spouses who are highly critical of one another expectedly see themselves as dissimilar:

WIFE: "Immature, but very loving. Very different from each other. He lives for the day. I for the future. I am thinking of children, he is not."

HUSBAND: "My spouse is a very childish person. We are very different in that I live in the world of reality and she lives in a fantasy world."

WIFE: "A. Handsome   B. Pretty much alike
       Lovable   We like the same
       Likable   things just about
       Funny   and have same
       Serious   beliefs."

HUSBAND: "Very jealous and dominant. Different because I don't act very responsible according to my wife."

This is her second marriage, his first. Both are blue collar workers, 18 to 30. She didn't complete high school; he did.

Judging from the answers we received from wives, there are more differences than similarities in the personalities of spouses. A few saw their characteristics as very much alike, but note in the response of the woman given directly below that the similarities are really common goals and ideals, not really common traits:

WIFE: "We are alike and different at the same time. We both believe in the traditional roles of male and female. We are both willing to sacrifice for our children and each other. We wanted to give our children everything important for life and feel we have succeeded. We have never had much money because we gave of our time to other activities than moneymaking. We value our home life and family far above affluence. Our children have always had love and emotional security and they are mature, responsible, outgoing, self-confident and capable and very different in their interests and accomplishments. My husband and I share recreation interests and home projects. He is loving and helpful and fun and has never been angry at me in 26 years. I started our marriage with a vicious temper and was angry many times. Over the years I have learned to be much calmer.

"Our major difference has always been his employment and financial problems. He has changed jobs at least fifteen times and has been self-employed twice—neither time with great success. He recently started a new job as a sales representative at which he excels. (Proved by all the things he has sold me on!) I think he has made up his mind to stay in the company permanently."

She's between 41 and 50, a homemaker with some college education.

WIFE: "We are very much alike. Both of us like people. We try not to make the relationship overdominating. He is very friendly, very versatile—gets along with everyone. Very intelligent and quick-witted."

She's married for the second time; they lived together for 3 to 6 months before doing so. Her spouse is unemployed, and she says their major problem is money.

In most cases of marked personality differences, the wife perceived the husband as more outgoing, sociable, aggressive, and active; these traits were considered praiseworthy even to the point of constituting a "better personality." Women whose development of such extroverted traits was inhibited in childhood by imposed cultural norms of "feminine" behavior may gravitate to men who display the desired attributes.

WIFE: "He is 2″ taller, in good physical condition, intelligent, gets along well with peers and most people his age. Is usually considerate, not too well organized at times, good sense of humor, tends to be late for social events involving our presence, but is punctual for work appointments, etc.

"Our personalities are quite different. I'm conservative and fairly shy—he is outgoing and doesn't mind being in front of a lot of people. He is much more aggressive and a perfectionist, where I settle for less."

For a shy gal, this woman admits to cheating on her husband with 2 or 3 other men, briefly. She married for companionship. Says their biggest crisis was a year's separation when he went away to school. She works in the professional field, has a postgraduate education, is between 18 and 30.

WIFE: "We are alike morally. We believe in faithfulness. He has a more outgoing fun personality. I can't seem to show my fun times; or laugh easy even when I find something funny, whereas he can. He is narrow-minded without realizing it, but I admire him for this sometimes. We both like to dance, watch TV and enjoy being together. He likes to *hang out with male friends at local pub. I am more a homebody* but have a good time once we're out. I worry about everything, our grown children, etc., and show it. He worries but doesn't like to show it. He definitely has a better personality than I do."

Alcohol is their major problem, but she admits she would marry the same person again. A high school graduate, she works in the technical field.

WIFE: "He is a big man—6′2″ and 275 lbs.—and his very presence is intimidating. He is an aggressive and dominant person. People look to him as a knowledgeable and authoritative source for personal problems. We are both Christians and are surrounded by a vast spectrum of people with varied occupations and personalities.

"We are different in the fact that we are direct opposites.

"I am not aggressive or dominating, except with our children. I am only 5 feet tall and that also adds to our contrasting differences. But he is openly loving and affectionate. I am not. He is not as secure about my feelings for him as I am about

his for me. Our tastes are different and have always struggled
to find the halfway point acceptable to each other. But we have
been through a great deal in 6 years of marriage and I think
we are both content to stay together. It is a challenge."

This homemaker is a high school graduate, 18 to 30. She says
her husband is dominant.

WIFE: "My present spouse is a considerate man, has many guilt
feelings regarding two previous marriages that were not successful, has a volatile personality. I put most situations into
perspective and do not let myself get upset by things that I
can't change.
"We are different in many ways, but agree politically and
our ethical and moral values are similar."

This is her second marriage. They lived together for 3 to 6
months before marrying. Children from previous marriage constitute their biggest crises. She's 51 or over, has a postgraduate
education, and works as a professional.

Sometimes this pattern is reversed, and the husband is the
partner seen as more passive, reserved, or calmer:

WIFE: "Very much the same interests. However, his personality
is too *passive* at times for my liking. All too often I *wear the
pants* in the family."

She definitely would not marry the same person again. She's
sexually unsatisfied, feels unloved, disillusioned, and has the
feeling of living only for her children. They never or rarely
ever have sex. Works at home, is between 41 and 50, and a
high school graduate.

WIFE: "He is a loving, understanding, compassionate man. I
consider it a privilege to be his wife. We are similar in that
we are both flexible and like to do things together and yet we
have our times to ourselves. Perhaps he is a more reserved
individual than I am. I am more impulsive at times."

Works at home, between 31 and 40, has some college education,
and is very religious.

WIFE: "He is tall, well-built and good-looking. He is intelligent
and a hard worker, thoughtful, loving, kind and gentle.

"We agree on most subjects but are different in some ways.
He is very calm and I tend to panic to crises. I'm lazy at times
and have to watch my temper. He seldom gets mad at anyone.
We are both Christians and believe strongly in a Christian home
life.

"He is also a fantastic father. Is very helpful in raising our
little girl.

"I'd like to say I love my husband very much!"

This homemaker has considered divorce, describes her husband
as passive, and admits to cheating on him with more than 3
men, one for over a year. With all this she still describes her
marriage as stable and loving. She has some college background
and is between 18 and 30.

The great secret of Burger King's popularity is that it is the
only place in the world where you can always have it *your* way.
Not so in the American household. Some husbands who wish they
lived at Burger King are obsessive-compulsive personalities: hard-
driving, meticulous perfectionists; others are strong types with
equally strong opinions; and some just can never admit to being
wrong. In marriage, you have to accept an occasional Big Mac,
even if you don't particularly like lettuce, cheese, pickles, onions,
or special sauce.

WIFE: "Different and alike. My husband is a driving business
person. And he has to be perfect, wants everyone around him
to be perfect. Demands a lot of everyone. But we both want
a good marriage. Work hard for it. I am more relaxed about
things than he."

Her second marriage. Children from previous marriage have
led to many quarrels. They lived together for over a year before
they decided to marry. Though she says the sex is very good,
she feels her marriage alternates between periods of remoteness
and closeness. A high school graduate between the ages of 31
and 40, she works in the technical field.

WIFE: "He is exciting and keeps me on my toes. He has strength
and a dominance that I feel I need to a certain degree. He has

emotional stability that I like. He has definite opinions and I do too but we can agree or disagree regardless in a way that doesn't cause hard feelings."

Though this wife says her marriage is "always stable," they no longer have intercourse. Yet she still would marry the same person again. She's a homemaker between 41 and 50, a high school graduate.

WIFE: "He is all for himself. We are different in a lot of ways. He is very difficult to live with. He is never wrong. I try to get along with everybody. I like lots of friends. He wants to be alone all the time. Wants everything his way."

She's considered divorce, but taken no action. Says her husband is inconsiderate, dominant, and possessive. Describes her marriage as a failure; they hardly ever have sex, and she definitely would not marry the same man again. A homemaker, 41 to 50, she did not complete high school.

When couples differ in their orientation to life, the presence or absence of a loving, caring attitude may determine whether the relationship is deemed a raving success or a dismal failure.

WIFE: "Super! Kind, considerate, devoted; has a sense of humor. Different—he is a convergent thinker; I am divergent. Similar in that we are both warm, loving and caring."

Not all husbands are considerate all the time. Some are considerate only around certain times and others only around certain people—other than their wives:

WIFE: "My spouse, when he is *not drinking* is the most tender, gentle man I know. Very much opposite. When he drinks I sometimes just tolerate him. Other times I scream at him or just plain walk out for a while until he is his old self again. He's usually very confident.

"We are a lot alike. We both come from broken homes; and now no matter how hard things are and what went wrong, we work it out somehow. Even when we feel we almost hate each other; somehow we work it out. Sometimes right then and sometimes later.

"One way we are different is he likes to drink and he gets

carried away. I don't like to drink. I'd rather make a fool of it, rather than it of me."

She describes her husband as reserved, and herself as emotional and warm. Even with the drinking problem, she would still marry the same man again. She works in the blue collar field, is between 41 and 50 a high school graduate. The worst crisis they've faced is the death of their two children.

WIFE: "He is big—289 lbs. and losing right now—and Italian (and they are not lovers). He is a Democrat and I am a Republican, which causes arguments. He is Catholic and I am Presbyterian, which causes more trouble. He has learned to dislike everything about me. I feel sorry for him for his insecurities.

"He is nice around others (his friends) but my friends are not to be entertained or even associated with. When we are by ourselves he acts ugly, sarcastic and avoids me—no kissing, no goodbye or hello or good night. He has an insecure idea that I am cheating on him everyday all the time—meeting men everywhere. I have never stepped out on him or cheated on him.

"I am quiet and easygoing, too easygoing. I do my own thing—ceramics, organ, knitting, crocheting, American Legion and church circle. I belong to the Legion. He joined but hates them all down there. I go anyway. I read religious books and live around my children and my grandchildren. I am very nice to his kids (5) and make things for them and his 12 grandchildren.

"In other words I just *take* it all—sarcasm and hate—and ignore his suggestions of a divorce. I am looking now for security in my old age."

This is her second marriage. She consulted a lawyer about divorce, but then gave up the idea. They no longer have sex, and says spouse wishes they'd never gotten married. Marriage is generally hostile for this homemaker who is 51 or over, and a high school graduate.

WIFE: "He loves to party—I want him home with me. He has a girl friend and if I say anything about it he hits me."

This homemaker (31 to 40) didn't complete high school. She feels tied down and trapped, and says marriage hasn't changed her for the better. Describes her husband as being irresponsible, and says she's a "maid" and is being taken for granted. With all this she indicates that her sex life is still very good!

WIFE: "We are not alike in any way. Divorce is what we need. It seems the only way since I married an s.o.b."

This wife is planning a divorce. Says alcohol is their major problem, and an extramarital affair was their biggest crisis. This is her second marriage, and she's between 41 and 50. She has no children, and works in the white collar field. They lived together for over a year before she finally married him.

Husbands were far more likely to term their wives "emotional." This designation has both positive and negative connotations. Emotional people are more likely to be able to show affection, to have more stimulating personalities, and to experience the highs and lows of life to a greater degree. On the other hand, we tend to think of emotional people as impulsive, irrational, and not very reliable in times of crisis. This correlation between emotionality and maturity was reflected in the higher percentages of young marrieds and in first marriages who used the term, whereas "mature" was used to describe the partner more often in remarriages, where partners are older on the average. Students, whose spouses were generally young, used the term "emotional" more than any other occupational group.

Husbands, like wives, tended to stress differences rather than similarities, even though most were content with the marriages. The few who saw themselves as similar were not very specific or made reference to common values and enjoyments, rather than personality traits:

HUSBAND: "My wife is a very loving and considerate person; she is very beautiful and is a wonderful mother.

"We are quite a bit alike in our personalities. We like the same activities. We like the same vacation ideas. We like the same kind of home and its furnishings. We both love children."

HUSBAND: "My wife is an intelligent, attractive 33-year-old adult female standing approximately 5'2" tall and weighing 137 lbs. Shapely figure, pleasant features. College educated—French and English—mother of one daughter, age one year.

"Our personalities quite similar also in mood and temperament; ranging to a variety of different circumstances and situations."

He married to have children, yet he feels tied down and trapped, but admits his marriage is a generally loving one. He's between 31 and 40, has some college background and is in the technical field.

The introvert-extrovert dichotomy was the most prevalent, usually with one partner being more sociable than the other. Sometimes it was the wife who was more content to sit home at the hearth:

HUSBAND: "An old-fashioned type of girl who has a mind of her own, very religious and family oriented. Her main love is the children, myself, and her parents. She is very concerned with money matters and 'what the neighbors think.' She has few close friends who are not relatives. A very intelligent woman who is satisfied taking care of the house and working part time although she is capable of a career of her own."

He married because of pressure from others, and now feels tied down. He has cheated with 2 or 3 other women, briefly. He's a college graduate, between 41 and 50, working in management.

HUSBAND: "We both enjoy being home together in the evenings, she more than I. She takes more interest in the house, yard and garden. We both take interest in our daughters. She has a better communication with them and other people than I. Spouse is more friendly and can meet strangers more than I. I handle the finances, she almost dominates all of our other affairs."

HUSBAND: "She is beautiful, intelligent although not an intellectual, practical, responsible, follows through. On the other hand, my interests are scholarly, and I am somewhat bolder and more socially aggressive, tenacious once I have committed myself to a course of action, not methodical with regard to my papers and effects, and require some goading to follow through expeditiously. While our personalities and backgrounds are quite different—my wife is English while I am American—we complement each other."

He married when he was over 40—for the first time. He's now 51 or over, has a postgraduate degree, and works in the professional field. Believes his marriage is generally stable, and always loving.

In fewer cases, the husband was less drawn to people than was the wife:

HUSBAND: "Different:——
   I: Scientist, graduate education, prefer 'things' to people.
   She: Business woman (secretary, etc.), prefers people to things.
   Both: Enjoy travel, home, being together.
      "I'm lucky!!!"

He's 51 or over, works in management, has a postgraduate degree. Feels their marriage is always stable, and the sex is very good.

HUSBAND: "Different personalities. She tends to rush into things where I am more methodical and a planner.
      "We're both outgoing, although I have my periods of reticence when I wish to be alone.
      "She is more concerned with my wants and needs than I am hers."

This is his second marriage, yet he definitely would not remarry the same person again. The sex is bad, has intercourse less than once a month, and because of this he has cheated on his wife with another woman, briefly. Their children have led to many quarrels. He's a professional, 41 to 50, and a college graduate.

And the most irreconcilable differences for husbands were often those leading to sexual dissatisfaction:

HUSBAND: "Our interests are similar but morals are different. I am liberal minded; she's prudish."

Retired, 51 or over, with some college background. He has had a period of separation, and admits to cheating with 2 or 3 women, briefly. According to him, the sex is unsatisfying—they have sex maybe once a month, even though he married for regular sex. He describes his wife as being dominant, emotional, and possessive.

HUSBAND: "Always on the make. Different—in all ways."

This husband feels his marriage is a failure, and says his spouse wishes they'd never gotten married. The sex is generally dull, and they argue about his attention to other women. An extramarital affair was his worst crisis. He feels unloved and unappreciated. A professional, 41 to 50, with a postgraduate education.

A Touch of Class

We tend to idealize America as a classless society, ignoring the fact that underlying our social mobility and struggle to abolish discrimination is a foundation of a multitude of ethnic groups, each of which has contributed elements of its own traditions to the common culture. Our coins remind us that our national motto is *e pluribus unum,* but we embrace the *unum* and forget the *pluribus,* the "many" which compose the "one." Yet, studies of the American marriage have led some investigators to the undemocratic conclusion that marriages between partners of the same religion and ethnic group have a better chance of success than those where the backgrounds are disparate. The underlying assumption is that there are basic values inherent in such groups, and couples who agree on the importance of various goals and the methods of reaching them will gain more satisfaction with a minimum of disharmony. We have seen, in the answers above, that happy couples are not necessarily similar in temperament, but generally do agree on aims and values. Shared religious affiliations and beliefs are often mentioned, though couples can share moral attitudes without subscribing to a formal religion. The magic in marriages that don't cross ethnic lines has nothing to do with native soil or skin coloration but with the likelihood that both parties grew up with similar experiences, tastes, and ideals. The commercials reassure us that you don't have to be Italian to cook Italian; but though you don't have to be Italian to think like one, values do not come in cans like spaghetti sauce and do have to be acquired. Similarly, the value in belonging to the same socioeconomic class has nothing to do with bank balances; a jackpot lottery ticket may vault its lucky owner into a distant tax bracket but cannot endow him with the ideas and tastes it has taken someone born into wealth decades to cultivate.

It is quite possible to find, through diligent search, an ideal partner closer to your own value system than anyone you could possibly find in your own socioreligioeconomic group, coming from a vastly different background. However, since people acquire mates, not by rational, intensive search and inquiry, but by falling in love in a virtually random way, the person who seeks his companions more or less among those of the same educational and social level is more likely to draw an intellectually compatible mate.

In our own subsample of matched couples, we found that people with firm religious beliefs tended to marry spouses of similar persuasion, whereas those who were not formally religious were about as likely to wind up with a religious as a non-religious partner.

Advocates of marriages limited, as much as is possible in these days of frequent geographic relocation and eradication of stable neighborhoods, to people who share a common heritage stress the duties of parents to familiarize children with ancestral traditions and to encourage their children to cultivate friends of similar backgrounds. It sounds like a radical idea in a land where "all men are created equal," but until the improbable day when young people are coolheaded enough to make objective judgments about the ideas in the heads of those whose hands they seek, an adoption of a "separate but equal" philosophy may be the most prudent course.

My Mother, My Spouse

"Every man marries his mother," it has been said. How much of that statement is valid and how much of it was influenced by the national passion for psychoanalysis, which is based on Freud's discovery of the Oedipus complex? And does every woman marry her father?

Disregarding Freudian theory, there are other reasons we could supply for suspecting this hypothesis to be true. To some extent, every man expects to get from a wife the same domestic services he obtained from his mother: preparation of meals, cleaning the house, doing the laundry, etc. On a less concrete level, he expects similar spiritual nurturance—seeing to his ease after a day at work, nursing him through sickness, consoling him in times of difficulty, and increasing his sense of self-esteem. In short, he is looking for *a* mother, though not necessarily one like his own.

Women might like to acquire a mother through marriage, but the case is rather hopeless. The liberated woman might insist on some sharing of housekeeping chores, but she could never hope to find a man to provide such services unilaterally, even though many women do so for men. With the slow breakdown of male-female role barriers, men are becoming somewhat better at expressing tenderness and providing emotional support, but they are still not very good at mothering. Some women are willing to settle for a father, one who will provide financial support and handle some of the heavier chores, such as home repairs and snow shoveling, and take charge in times of situational and emotional crisis by virtue of his alleged broader experience and emotionally stable temperament. How much a person will expect a spouse to be exactly like a parent, even to the extent of physical and personality traits depends on how the seeker perceives himself as a full adult rather than a child in a grown-up body.

We have just discussed the benefits of marrying partners from similar backgrounds, and people who feel secure in their roots will often seek to recreate households resembling the ones in which they were raised. They may unconsciously model themselves on the parent of their sex and seek out a mate who appears to be a replica of the other parent.

Finally, we are raised to regard sex in a very ambivalent manner. Children are given the idea that sex is dirty, repulsive, and undesirable. Adolescents come to believe that sex is delightful and exciting, but nevertheless evil and forbidden. Finally, young adults are supposed to accept the awkward stance that sex is good and beautiful, as well as exciting, but should be enjoyed only within the context of marriage or a deep love relationship. Thus, one's parents are good sexual beings, but people who tempt us to have sex before marriage, our peers, are bad. The person one ultimately chooses to marry becomes the good sex partner, like the parent, regardless of whether or not there have been premarital encounters with other bad partners. There is a countertendency in operation, that of avoiding someone too much like the parent because of the incest taboo, a more primitive and repressed factor than the societal pressure to keep sex within marriage.

While we can advance all these theories as to why people will marry spouses like their parents, all the current trends seem to be away from the motivating forces we have just described. Increased employment of wives and the women's liberation movement are leading to the demise of the restricted roles of wife and husband (or mother and father); women are no longer held solely responsible for housework and mothering, or men for breadwinning and decision-making. People are less preoccupied with ethnic heritage and formal religion, and mingle freely with people of all national and religious backgrounds. Finally, the sexual revolution has made us more accepting of premarital sex, sex with a variety of partners, and guilt-free experiences, so that far fewer people feel compelled to limit themselves to one virtuous partner during the course of a lifetime.

One can argue it either way—or simply ask:

Describe your father and mother. Does your spouse resemble either of them in appearance or personality? Describe the main differences and similarities.

Since the concept of the ideal woman seems to be changing far more rapidly than that of the ideal man, we would expect women who admired their fathers to seek similar husbands, but not necessarily vice versa. The father who was a good provider, loving, firm, and understanding would be just as valued today. But a mother who was an excellent housekeeper, devoted to her children, passive, puritanical, and poorly educated would not win as much approval today as a well-educated, sexually uninhibited, career-minded and independent type. Thus, we often see a wife identifying husband with father but not the reverse, though both appreciated the parent of the opposite sex:

WIFE: "Mother and father very happy. Father died when I was sixteen; mother died after I married. I had very happy life and I knew I was loved. Husband is a family man and a good father. *Both father and husband excellent cooks.* Husband is thoughtful of family and is generous with all his talents."

HUSBAND: "Never knew father. Mother raised brother and me. She remarried when we were in high school. She was then a housewife, excellent cook, etc.

"Wife does not resemble her in any way, except being female. Wife only average cook and housekeeper, but No. 1 in bed."

Wife is 41 to 50, a white collar worker, with some college education. Husband is 51 or over, works in management, and is a college graudate.

WIFE: "Had a devoted marriage, but mother would have been happier if father was less dominant.
   "Spouse resembles my father in his love for sports and faithfulness and love for spouse."

HUSBAND: "Father: hard worker, liked fun, friendly. Mother: hard worker, liked family life and children, liked friends.
   "Spouse has no resemblance to father or mother. Spouse is woman's libber, inquisitive, egotistic, charming, pretty, capable worker and smart. Extrovert, but insecure."

She's 51 or over, has some college background and works in the technical field. He's in the same age range, a professional, and a college graduate. Their total family income is over $50,000 a year.

Sometimes similarities between father and husband led to recurrences of unpleasant situations experienced in childhood:

WIFE: "My husband resembles my father in being firm and not ever giving financial aid to children or spouse when in college or for clothes. My mother provided the finances. The same cycle is repeating itself in my own family. The demands are there when the children are in their teens. My husband is short, tough and a civil engineer. My dad was tall and slim and a pharmacist. Both are the quiet type, but carry a big stick."

HUSBAND: "Wife resembles her mother in personality."

She is 41 to 50, a college graduate, working in the professional field. The husband is also a professional, in the same age range, with a postgraduate degree. Neither feels the marriage has changed them for the better, and admit that their children have led to many quarrels.

WIFE: "Father works hard, has periods of feeling good, has periods of feeling low, doesn't express his troubles sometimes, religious, old-fashioned, caring, tries to understand.
   "Mother set in ways, caring, tries to understand and help, old-fashioned, religious, works, likes to work with people.

"Spouse resembles father in periods of depression and feeling good. He resembles mother in liking to work with people. Spouse has tendency to be set in attitudes."

HUSBAND: "My mother is domineering in the family; having control over money and family life. She is considerate and generous to her children—works for their happiness. Father is passive yet understanding. Doesn't lose temper unless provoked. Very patient.

"Spouse is understanding, patient, but somewhat emotional. Difficult for her to break a habit."

He's in technical work; she's blue collar. Both have some college background. She feels that spouse wishes that he would never have gotten married.

While neurotics are said to marry people like troublesome parents so they can vicariously try to resolve the old conflicts, most people who experienced some difficulty with a parent avoid similar characteristics in prospective spouses:

WIFE: "*Father:* short, intelligent, smart, heavy drinker and gambler, not a family man, man of the world, handsome. *Mother:* beautiful, caring, hard working, considerate, loving, giving, compassionate. *Husband:* dedicated family man, hard worker, loving, considerate, good provider. Does not resemble my father physically or personalitywise. Does not drink (excessively) or gamble. He loves his home and children and is totally involved with their development."

HUSBAND: "Father was strong, silent type, very conservative. Mother was very responsible and loving, hard working. Spouse does not resemble either. Main difference is lack of conservatism. Spouse *is* similar to mother from emotional aspects."

Wife is between 31 and 40, homemaker and college graduate. Husband is 41 to 50, also a college graduate working in management. Family income is between $25-$50,000 a year.

WIFE: "My father is a 'depression' era man. A good provider, not demonstrative concerning emotions or affections. I consider him stubborn and tactless concerning others. He is short and bald. My mother is intelligent, sensible and sensitive. She is grey-haired, short and slightly overweight.

"My spouse does not resemble either one in appearance. My husband has a good sense of humor like my parents. He is very organized like them. He has concern for details and efficiency like them. One difference is his open display of affection and his open-minded attitude to new people and new ideas."

HUSBAND: "Father kind and loving—strong commitment to responsibility. Mother hard working and honest—fun loving. No, wife has commitment, love; honest and fun loving."

Both are between 18 and 30, he has a postgraduate degree; she did not finish college. Both feel that they are fully loved and appreciated.

Sometimes the parents are vastly different in background and temperament. This makes it difficult for the child to identify with both, and may cause difficulties in future mate selection:

WIFE: "To describe my father I would say kind, gentle, loving and passive. His role in the family was subject to being dominated by my mother. Mother was a professional medical person who gave up many things (career) to marry him, a farmer, and live on an Iowa farm. I feel this frustrated her personally and was therefore a dominating 'smothering' mother to my brother and myself. Therefore when choosing a mate I found someone in college with the same profession and degree."

HUSBAND: "*Father:* college educated, large ego, kind, loving, older parent, reasonable, outgoing, artistic. *Mother:* college educated, artistic, kind, quiet, brave, loving. *Wife* resembles mother's characteristics."

Both are professionals with postgraduate degrees, between 18 and 30. Both agree that he is dominant, yet he still feels taken for granted.

WIFE: "Mother blond and beautiful. Father Jewish. Mother Gentile. Lot of confusion and drama and lots of laughs. No resemblance."

HUSBAND: "No, my mother was reserved and religious. She cut my father off sex in her 40s. She adored me and my sister."

She's between 18 and 30, works in the professional field, is a college graduate. He's in the same age range, but did not complete college. They are into group sex, mate swapping, and affairs with others.

Wives were more likely to compare their husbands to their fathers in terms of emotional characteristics and personality, rather than physical appearance or occupation. Where the father was loved, she was usually able to find similar traits in the man she married.

WIFE: "My father was one of the nicest men I have ever known. He was kind, generous, and always had time for me. Any time I needed anything he was always there to give it. My mother was always working around the house and yard. I had one of the cleanest houses to live in as I was growing up. She was always a wonderful cook. My father did the scrubbing of the floors, walls, and windows. He did the painting. He cut the grass and shoveled the snow. He felt that it was a man's work not a woman's. My husband is the same. My life is now very similar to the way I lived as I was growing up."

She married for a homelife, and believes she has a generally stable marriage. She's a homemaker, 51 or over, and has had some college education.

Sometimes the common traits in father and husband were not strictly desirable ones:

WIFE: "Father: small, quiet man yet strong will. Mother: was determined to make life better for her offspring. My spouse doesn't resemble either of my parents in appearance, but he does have the determination and strong will of my parents. He is much more dominant than my parents were to each other. A very demanding personality."

This young homemaker, who is between 18 and 30, has more than 4 children. Though she feels marriage has given her life more purpose and meaning, she's thought about divorce. Says her husband is dominant, and during arguments they've both assaulted or struck each other. The major problem in marriage is about the children, and worst crisis was alcohol.

WIFE: "My father handled the money in our family, as my husband does. My mother had a hard time whenever she tried to talk about budgeting, etc., as I have in my marriage. My husband even decided how much I needed for groceries when he never even went shopping with me. In the past ten years or so I have asserted myself more and feel better about the money situation even though now I work and earn money myself. When we were engaged I can remember making a list of how much we needed for various expenses and of how he just ignored it. He was brought up to believe the man handled the money alone in a family."

This wife feels unloved and unappreciated, and is disillusioned about romance and love. She says her spouse is inconsiderate, but still feels they have a fairly stable marriage. Her major problem was her obligation to her sick, poor parents. She's 51 or over, works in the professional field.

WIFE: "My father was very domineering and demanding. We were raised in fear of him, yet he would give us children the shirt off his back. He was a very giving and loving father, but not considerate. My husband is a little like him. My mother was afraid, loving, understanding, dutiful and shy."

She describes her husband as considerate and methodical. This homemaker is 51 or over, a high school graduate.

Sometimes the wife said her husband reminded her more of her mother than her father:

WIFE: "My father is a short heavy man who is fun, but has a hard time showing love or saying 'I love you.' He was always closed-minded about sex. My husband doesn't remind me of my father in any way except for teasing. My father teases and jokes a lot and every once in a while it gets to me.
   "My mother is tall and slender and completely opposite of my father. She has a very bad inferiority complex, brought on by my father's teasing. She is very loving, sensitive and emotional. I think sometimes though, that she takes things a little too seriously. My parents are divorced. My husband reminds me more of my mother because of his loving personality."

WIFE: "My father is an easygoing man, very giving of himself and yet a little selfish maternalwise. My mother was a very strong-willed, domineering, loving person with very strong beliefs. My husband doesn't resemble either in appearance to me or personality yet he is similar to my mother as being domineering and strong-willed, but very opposite to both my parents who were in marriage very easygoing with each other (my mother passed away). My husband is a very active person, sometimes very moody and sometimes very quiet and not affectionate. Yet at other times he's extremely affectionate, and it makes me know he loves me dearly. My parents always babied me and my husband doesn't."

She describes herself and her spouse as dominant and possessive, and admits to cheating with her husband's consent and knowledge. A young homemaker between 18 and 30, with some college education.

WIFE: "My mother is very possessive and dominant. My father is very religious and unselfish. My husband is more like my mother, possessive and dominant."

She feels dominated by her husband, but says their marriage is fairly loving. An extramarital affair was her worst crisis. Married to have kids. Didn't complete high school, she's a blue collar worker between 41 and 50.

Some who saw their fathers as ineffectual, overly inhibited, or otherwise restricted in their potential avoided picking spouses with similar problems:

WIFE: "My father was very small—about 5'6" and maybe 110 lbs. *Very* skinny. Dark hair, dark eyes. Very witty. Very intelligent. He had a zest for the simpler things in life—hunting, fishing. But he never quite learned how to be a real part of life. He surrounded himself with people of lesser intelligence and social station. That way he was sure to be 'looked up to,' liked and respected. He would rather do less than he was capable of and be an outstanding success, than to live up to his potential and maybe be a failure.

"My mother is short, 5'7" she's rather plump, about 150 lbs. Salt and pepper hair, blue eyes. She was raised to be a gentlewoman. A lady in every sense of the word. I have *never* seen her consume alcohol or tobacco. I have *never* heard her say or do anything crude or vulgar. She is a kind, loving person.

"My husband does resemble my father in his physical appearance. He is short, though well built. Has dark hair and eyes.

"There the resemblance ends. My husband isn't an intellectual as my father was. But he will go farther in life and find greater happiness because he doesn't let the fear of failure keep him back.

"He is a warm sensitive person. He has learned to roll with the punches in life. He also knows his limits, but sets high goals for himself, which he strives to attain. He loves life and people. He doesn't even have the ability to be cruel, or calculating, as my father often was."

WIFE: "Parents—old world people—straight-laced. Spouse doesn't resemble them. Modern and up-to-date."

A young homemaker (18 to 30) with a high school education, she says her marriage is always loving, but unsure at this point whether she'd marry the same person again today.

WIFE: "My husband has absolutely no traits resembling my parents. My father was always late in paying bills and also in business for himself. My husband is just the opposite."

There were the wives who had felt unloved in childhood but came to find love in the arms of their husbands:

WIFE: "My mother is very domineering. She is also very assertive (by this I mean she makes herself happy and consequently the rest of the family)—she won't take any guff. She is not affectionate. My father is affectionate, passive and a considerate, loving, kind man.

"Differences are height, weight, skin color, hair color; my husband and my father have brown eyes. My husband is a listener, but also a talker; my father is also. My mother is a talker. The main difference between my husband and parents is that I feel loved and valued by my husband and worth not much by my parents."

A young homemaker (18 to 20) with 2 children. She believes that her husband appreciates her as a wife, but not as a lover. Says he's affectionate, while she feels she is emotional and anxious. The major problem in marriage is lack of communication and sexual dissatisfaction. She is also unsure at this point whether she'd marry the same man again. Marriage, though, has given her more confidence in herself.

WIFE: "My father was intelligent and quiet. My mother is cold and self-centered. My spouse isn't like either of them. He's easygoing and loving. I feel no similarities and the main difference I would say that in his life I come first and with my parents I come last."

She says she's cheated on her husband with 2 or 3 other men, and one affair lasted more than a year. The problem is sex; it is unsatisfying for her. A homemaker, high school graduate, 41 to 50.

WIFE: "My father was old enough to be my grandfather; he was a retired Colonel and a retired schoolteacher. He was very strict and did not know how to show love and substituted money.

"My mother was almost 30 years younger than my father. When I was younger I only remember my mother as being sick. My mother was and is loving, but more interested in herself, maybe that explains her three marriages. My husband is nothing like either of my parents."

A homemaker with 2 children, between 31 and 40. She married between the ages of 18 and 20 for companionship. Says she was most influenced in her choice of spouse because of emotional security, and that marriage has given her life more purpose and meaning, has become better at handling responsibility, and has become a more considerate person. Only major problem—money.

WIFE: "My father was a small man with blond hair. My husband has the same build and coloring, although their personalities are different. My parents never showed any affection in front of others. Therefore it was never easy for me to show any kind of affection. It is getting easier for me the older I get."

A homemaker between 41 and 50, with a high school education.

It didn't happen often, but once in a while the husbands compared unfavorably to the parents:

WIFE: "My spouse is completely different from my parents, both in appearance and personality. My parents are kind and loving and considerate. My husband is a nag."

She has consulted a lawyer about a divorce, and they have been separated. She admits to cheating with 2 or 3 other men, and one of them was for over a year. She says they never or rarely ever have sex, and her husband is inconsiderate and irresponsible. A homemaker, between 41 and 50, with some college background.

WIFE: "My father and mother both worked for as long as I can remember. My husband doesn't work any more than he has to."

Whereas wives often provided colorful portraits of their fathers, husbands tended to portray their mothers in a flattering, conventional way, depicted in typical domestic roles:

HUSBAND: "I am a country boy. My Dad was a good, honest, hard-working rancher cattleman and farmer. My mother lived on a farm most of her life. They were both quite modest. Dad was even shy and had very high morals. He blushed easily. My wife is like them in ways, but she is also very outgoing and loves to work with people."

He's more nervous and irritable than ever since his marriage, feels overwhelmed by responsibility. A white collar worker, 41 to 50, with some college background.

HUSBAND: "My mother died when I was rather young but what I do remember is that she was a good wife and mother providing the homelife that I feel is necessary. In this my wife and my mother are similar because she also is a good wife and mother, providing a good homelife."

He feels their marriage has no major problems and is generally stable but he does admit to cheating on his wife with one other woman, briefly. A blue collar worker, 51 or over, and a high school graduate.

Wives were often compared to mothers in terms of their roles as homemakers, though husbands made allowances for the changing times:

HUSBAND: "My father is a very kind, ambitious, and considerate man. He worships my mother. My mother is a very independent and devoted wife. She is a good cook and housekeeper and is easy to talk to. She gave up her life for her children. My wife is also a devoted wife and mother but realizes that she must have interests of her own even though she spends a great deal of time with the children."

The mother of a generation ago was likely to be homebound, frugal, and passive. Most men do not expect their wives to be that way, but a few chauvinistic stragglers seemed to feel that mother knew best:

HUSBAND: "Sex life between parents practically nothing.

"*Father:* Quiet man, prone to letting off steam by yelling or going off by self or not talking to wife for long periods of time. Hard working and sometimes very sensitive. On occasion to have affair without spouse's knowledge.

"*Mother:* Home type, whole world revolves around house. Doesn't go out except when husband threatens to go somewhere without her. Picks on people if she doesn't get own way.

"*Wife:* Has only one thing in common with parents—is hard-working when she does a job appointed to her. Parents and wife are opposite ends of scale."

A blue collar worker, 31 to 40, with some college education. He says sex with wife is good, and their marriage is generally a stable one. Says his wife is considerate and warm, and loves him and appreciates him. Married mainly for companionship. Only major problem in marriage is money.

HUSBAND: "They were hard working and saving people. My wife does not resemble them in appearance or personality. She is hard working but doesn't believe in savings."

A blue collar worker, 51 or over, with a high school education who believes his marriage is always loving.

HUSBAND: "Conservative, working class, religious, reality-oriented, stable, hard working, supportive.

"No resemblance to parents. Differences include social class status (much higher in wife), better education."

He feels that his wife is passive and anxious, and that her leaving home was his worst crisis. They've had a period of separation, and they no longer have sex, yet he would marry the same person again today. Works in management, 41 to 50, has a postgraduate degree.

HUSBAND: "Mother knew her place. My wife does not."

Not all mothers, however, were quiet and passive; nor are all wives today aggressive and assertive:

HUSBAND: "Loving and dominant. *Father:* Loving; however, a pain in the ass at times. Kids too much. *Mother:* Loving, but too nosy and dominant. Spouse does not resemble them— the opposite—wife understanding and quiet."

A white collar worker, between 41 and 50, with 3 children. Describes his wife as mature, and himself as considerate. Says they have no major problems and marriage has changed him for the better. Though he rates his sex life as satisfactory, he feels that sexual dissatisfaction is the one thing that could cause his marriage to fail.

HUSBAND: "My dad is a soft, quiet, patient, wonderful guy. My mom is self-centered, strong headed. My wife is unlike either. She comes closer to my dad than my mom. I am more like my mom and would like to be more like my dad."

He feels that his wife appreciates him, but doesn't really love him; describes himself as dominant, and admits to cheating on wife with 2 or 3 other women, briefly. Says he's sexually unsatisfied.

HUSBAND: "My mother is hypochondriacal, but sweet; she is short and fat. My father is a very possessive man. He is tall and skinny. My spouse is a complainer, but no similarities in appearance."

The final question regarding mate selection is the most important of all: "Would you marry the same person again today?"

Four out of five married people that we surveyed said they definitely or probably would choose the same spouse again. The women said they definitely would slightly more often, but the "probablies" evened things out, and, as we have noted, men always seem to be treading unsure ground whenever they talk about marriage. Only one in ten, regardless of sex, said they definitely or probably would not make the same selection, leaving 10 per cent undecided.

There are probably a lot of things wrong with the way we go about finding mates in America, but at any given moment there are more spouses content with their choices than not. Why don't four out of five couples stay married? That remains to be answered.

3

Wedding and Bedding:

Sex in Marriage

Do my sex the justice to admit, Senora, that we have always recognized that the sex relation is not a personal or friendly relation at all. . . . In the sex relation the universal creative energy, of which the parties are both the helpless agents, overrides and sweeps away all personal considerations, and dispenses with all personal relations. The pair may be utter strangers to one another, speaking different languages, differing in race and color, in age and disposition, with no bond between them but a possibility of that fecundity for the sake of which the Life Force throws them into one another's arms at the exchange of a glance.

—*George Bernard Shaw,* MAN AND SUPERMAN

"We have a problem communicating sexually," Linda explains demurely. She has been married to Nick for three years, during most of which time they have been seen in therapy together. The fact that she has asked for this session to spend alone with the therapist confirms that there is, indeed, a communication problem in this particular marriage. They are not youngsters, both of them

81

approaching 30, but they speak often of seeing themselves as a couple of kids, admittedly overattached to their parents and overwhelmed at times by financial budgeting. Linda sees Nick as having an unusually strong sex drive—"He would like it 24 hours a day." In actuality, it is not unusual for them to go two months without relations. She is tense during intercourse, often to the point of his being unable to penetrate her. She generally finds intercourse painful and, asked if she ever has orgasms, she replies she is not sure what they are, which, according to the Masters and Johnson rule-of-thumb, means she does not have them. Linda has severe premenstrual pain for at least 10 days prior to her period; intercourse during menstruation is unthinkable. This eliminates 17 days out of every month for sexual activity, and, since her periods are irregular, the painful "premenstrual" period can last for weeks.

Linda understands that some of her problems are psychological. She received no sexual education at home and her mother spoke of sex as a rather onerous duty in marriage. Linda was sexually involved with a boy friend in her late teens. Once they had begun having sexual relations, he coerced her into variations she found revolting by threatening to tell her parents she had lost her virginity. "Every time I had oral sex, I would puke out afterward," she says. She will not engage in similar activities with her husband or even touch his genitals.

Several weeks and joint sessions together, both seem more satisfied. Linda had suggested a "separation," since she was a failure at meeting Nick's needs and he had lovingly ridiculed the notion. Still, he says, "Marriage is 90 per cent sex. Why else would a man get married? Men cheat because they don't get good sex at home." The therapist openly confronts Nick, asking how sex can be "90 per cent of marriage" when theirs has survived three years in a generally positive atmosphere despite periods of abstinence lasting, literally, months. Linda says her sexual interest runs in "spurts." Nick laughs and asks, "When? Every three years?" Looking back on their premarital sex life, Nick reminisces, "She was a terror!" Then, he laments, "How come it's so easy before you're married and so hard afterward?"

The question Nick poses is one that applies to most marriages, for, in truth, marital sex is far more complex than sex between less-committed partners. Dr. Natalie Shainess holds a viewpoint subscribed to by many marital therapists, that a good sex life does not develop immediately, and takes about two years to evolve.

This obviously does not mean that sexual encounters between partners who have been intimate for far shorter periods of time are generally unsatisfying; in fact, people are likely to recall isolated, spur-of-the-moment experiences as among the most exciting and physically gratifying they have ever known. It depends on one's definition of satisfaction and how much of the pleasure, even the orgasm, depends on psychological perceptions (where a sense of adventure and romance are powerful stimulants) and how much on physical components (where a long association should bring partners mutual knowledge of each other's particular pleasures, but only if they are insightful and caring enough to seek out and use that knowledge). While a knowledge of basic techniques, now available in paperback form at every dimestore, and a modicum of direct experience with a particular partner should be enough to insure a reasonably adequate sex life, problems tend to accumulate rather than diminish in marriage as factors extraneous to sexual gratification get drawn in. For example, if Nick really believes that he has a higher-than-normal sex drive and that sex is 90 per cent of marriage, why is he so nonchalant and understanding, while Linda obsesses about what a poor partner she is? To make some sense of this, you would have to know that Linda has the role of the mature, competent partner; she is the one whose checkbook is always balanced and whose debts are paid, whereas Nick is constantly overdrawn and over his head in bills. Linda, despite her psychosomatic symptoms, takes charge in every crisis. Nick was never much of an aggressive lover; in fact, after a long period of avoiding men, Linda was drawn to him because he acted like a gentleman and did not make her feel like a slut. In their present sexual equilibrium, however, Nick tries to emerge as the indefatigable lovemaker whose extraordinary potential is thwarted by the incredibly bad luck of having an asexual wife.

Can sex therapy help this couple? The therapist certainly does not ignore the sexual aspects of their relationship, and his participation has ranged from encouraging frank discussions of hangups to showing them what a tube of K-Y jelly looks like; however, to take their complaints and wishes at face value and attack the sexual problems without regarding the complex underlying motivation for the behavior patterns would be naive. After a few sessions devoted mostly to sexual discussion, both recently reported a week of very satisfactory sexual activity—Linda had had intercourse twice and Nick four times! They bantered back and forth as to how many times they had relations, each insisting to have the correct count. The therapist silently noted that Nick was insisting they had engaged in intercourse more frequently than Linda contended; if his motivation were really to have sex more often, he probably would have accused Linda of not giving in as much, whereas she would have claimed she was more obliging than in actuality. The therapist ended the argument by stating that as long as both were in agreement that it had been a better week than usual, the actual number of times was irrelevant. A disquieting fact he did not mention is that each partner experiences his own reality, often far different from the spouse's, and, at that moment, Nick's four experiences were just as real as Linda's two. Getting a couple to live in the same world is usually an insurmountable goal; we settle for bringing those two worlds a little closer together.

Ways and Means

In the movie *Annie Hall*, two therapists on a split screen ask their respective patients, lovers Woody Allen and Diane Keaton, how often they have sex. "He wants sex all the time," she groans. "At least four times a week." Woody says sadly, "Practically never. Four times a week at most."

Unlike Nick and Linda who cannot agree on the frequency, we see a couple who can keep the count straight but are divergent in what the numbers mean. We laugh indulgently at the screen characters, for they appeal to our ironic inner conviction that no matter how much sexual freedom and sophistication we acquire, man and woman can never be sexually satisfied.

Few married people, we found, consider their sex life dull, unsatisfying, or non-existent—only 11 per cent, or roughly 1 in 9, was significantly unhappy. Nearly 40 per cent rated it a rousing "very good," and a similar number satisfactory-to-good, the rest (11 per cent) citing it as "variable." Even though over half of our subjects did not have spouses likewise answering questionnaires, percentages of males and females were in complete accord at every level, indicating that neither sex has a current advantage in the pursuit of sexual happiness. Younger people found sex "very good" progressively more often than each succeeding older group, but this may be a function of attitude more than aging, since people who had remarried gave the highest percentage of "very good" responses, despite being at least older than the very youngest subjects.

Now, the initial temptation, given our comic stereotypes of harried housewives and television-addicted husbands, is to proclaim "good news" and, indeed, a sample where 9 out of 10 report at least variable satisfaction and 4 out of 5 consider their sex lives at least satisfactory is not very discouraging. However, if we compare our findings with those of Morton Hunt's survey for the book *Sexual Behavior in the 1970's,* based on data gathered in 1972, there are indications that people are not quite so content as they've recently been. Among Hunt's husbands, two-thirds rated their sex life in the past year "very pleasurable," significantly higher than those of ours who replied "very good." Moreover, only 3 per cent gave their sex lives either a negative or even a neutral rating in Hunt's study, much lower than our findings, even if we eliminate those responding "variable." The wives in 1972 were less enthusiastic in their responses than the men, although still more satisfied than in our sample: 60 per cent of the wives then found their relations "very pleasurable" and 7 per cent were neutral-to-negative in their replies.

We should point out some differences in the questions and the way they were asked in the two studies. Hunt asked how pleasurable respondents found marital coitus, whereas we asked them to describe their sex lives with their spouses. Marital coitus could be highly pleasurable, but so infrequent as to render the couple's overall sex life unsatisfactory. Or, a man might feel that marital coitus was enjoyable for him, but since his wife did not have orgasms, their sex life was poor; or, a wife might enjoy coitus, but find that her husband's demands for other forms of sexual behavior were so revolting to her that their sex life was bad. Also, Hunt's subjects spoke personally to interviewers and thus had less anonymity than our sample, possibly making them more reluctant to indicate an unsatisfactory sex life.

Nevertheless, it is quite plausible to imagine that earlier phases of the sexual revolution greatly enriched people's satisfaction through new information and more permissiveness with regard to experimentation, whereas with the passage of time, people came to acquire unrealistic expectations from the plethora of books and articles written about ideal marriages and sexual relations, and became jaded with now-familiar sexual variations which were, after all, finite in number.

We asked our couples to tell us how they had gone about improving their sex lives after marriage and what they could share with us about techniques that were particularly gratifying:

How have you and your spouse attempted to improve your sex life since marriage? Are there any techniques or new experiences you have found particularly gratifying? What would you like to try that you have not, or do more often?

Eustace Chesser's classic marriage manual, *Love Without Fear*, published in 1947, made it clear that the bridegrooms had a responsibility to teach the brides: "Their husbands have to be their guides." Later works, such as one published 12 years later, tried to assist the husband in his difficult role of coital coordinator by providing anatomic roadmaps and directions: "It should be studied; on the bridal night . . . the husband should compare the diagram with his wife's genital region."

Nowadays, regarding her own anatomy, the average woman knows the territory better than the most well-read man, and every bedroom contains two potential teachers, as well as two students:

WIFE: "I believe my spouse was not aware of my needs when we were first married and also did not know how to arouse me. I slowly taught him this and also had him read books on the subject. Our sex life is fair now but still needs improvement. I would like to have sex standing up, also more with the lights on. Also more gentle touching. I would like to see him have an orgasm and also have him watch my orgasm."

HUSBAND: "I have learned to be more patient and take more time in arousing her before sex. Sometimes she responds but not always. We mutually agree that she will tell me if I do something that does not help or causes her discomfort. That way we can minimize our unpleasant activities or experiences."

Both say their sex life is good, having intercourse twice a week, and believe their marriage is stable. She's a white collar worker, between 31 and 40, a high school graduate. He's between 31 and 40, works in management, has a postgraduate education.

Not every newlywed is armed with an armful of the latest literature from the love laboratories; sometimes knowledge and discovery are slow in coming:

WIFE: "Never had orgasm (didn't realize it) till married ten years. Each time seems to bring something new so far."

HUSBAND: "Anything two people can do."

Sex in the seventies may include gadgets, such as vibrators and exotic condoms, drugs ranging from marijuana to amyl nitrite "poppers," or frequent use of oral sex, which was employed by less than half of the most educated men in Kinsey's time. The tongue can make all the difference in having a satisfactory sex life—especially if it's used to talk things over with one's partner:

WIFE: "Trying different positions but more importantly, talking to each other if anything goes wrong. Communication, in my opinion, is the key to a good marriage."

HUSBAND: "In actuality we are very compatible in our sex life. Both of us seem to be sexually satisfied, and while there may be room for improvement, neither of us has expressed that opinion."

Both feel that the other is affectionate, and both believe sex is good. She's a blue collar worker, he has a postgraduate education. They have no children.

WIFE: "We use grass—it's super for sex. We're not afraid to try something new. We use sex as a game. One of us gets to choose what and how we want it."

HUSBAND: "Besides explicit exploring of each other's bodies we also have used a vibrator. I get great satisfaction in teasing my wife. I cannot think of anything that I have not tried or that I haven't already done."

Five per cent of our sample used drugs to enhance sexual pleasure, with slightly over twice that amount in the 18 to 30 age bracket. For some young women, such as the one portrayed in *Annie Hall,* pot has become as indispensable as the diaphragm, leading men to wonder whether she's turning on more to her joint or his charms. Laurie, a divorcee, recently told her therapist about an encounter with a new man: "It was a great evening: we drank, listened to music, rapped a long time, smoked a lot of grass, went to bed...hmm, did we have sex?...we must have, but I can't remember much about going to bed.... yeah, I think we did and it was probably good...." The problem with drugs is that, for some, sex is often good, but rarely very memorable.

In our subsample of matched couples, virtually none agreed that their sex life was unsatisfactory (possibly indicating that taking questionnaires together is a sign of sexual compatibility); however, only in 27 per cent of the cases did both partners characterize their sex life as very good. Couples can always press on to new frontiers of sexual enjoyment—unless one is perfectly content to remain where he or she's at:

WIFE: "No, I am completely satisfied with my present sex life."

HUSBAND: "Would like wife to be more experimental."

She married because of pressure from others, and says she feels trapped and tied down. He also has the same feelings of being trapped. They have sex 3 or 4 times a week. He's in technical work; she's a high school graduate.

"The trouble with reality," said a character in the movie *Morgan,* "is that it doesn't live up to my best fantasies." The brain is the most important sex organ and new surroundings, whether in reality or fantasy, can make the sexual experience seem like a new one, even if the partner and the act remain the same. Not everyone is fortunate enough to live near the specialized motels with "afternoon rates" that offer options such as waterbeds, mirrored ceilings, and X-rated movies on closed-circuit television, but even a night at Howard Johnson's Motor Lodge is worth the effort in these changing times when couples who register as husband and wife for a few hours' stay are actually husband and wife. And the improbability of making love in an airplane or on a beach did not stop some of our wives from turning on to the very thought of it:

WIFE: "Have tried to learn more about what gratifies my husband or turns him on. The only 'technique' we have found that is gratifying is when two people care enough to respond in a loving way to the other partner's sexual desires. Would like to make love in more unusual surroundings, such as on an airplane."

WIFE: "Yes, different locations usually help. When pretending that you're a totally different person making love on the beach is usually my favorite."

WIFE: "We have just used our imagination and gone from there. My husband has great imagination and always has a new idea. All are gratifying. I can't think of what I'd like to try or do more often. I'm generally conservative or either shy and usually can't talk or write down what I would really like to try or do."

A high school graduate, 18 to 30. This is her third marriage, and they lived together less than 3 months before marrying. They have intercourse 3 or 4 times a week, and she says their sex life is good. She also says that the marriage is always stable and loving.

WIFE: "We have improved our love life by stopping smoking cigarettes. No new experiences.

"I would like to try out some various roles in lovemaking—Doctor/Nurse, tying up, or slave/master, etc. It would also be fun to try lovemaking outside sometime. I would very much like to use a vibrator during sex."

This homemaker has a postgraduate degree. Says sex is generally dull, but the marriage is a loving one. She lived with her husband for over a year prior to marriage.

WIFE: "Not much. Yes, a shower at mid-day. I fantasize having intercourse on a golf green at 4 A.M."

She is a professional, 18 to 30, and a college graduate. They use drugs in lovemaking, and she says she reaches orgasm only between 10 and 39 per cent of the time, but describes their sex life as good (they have intercourse 5 or 6 times a week). Nevertheless, she says the marriage is in constant turmoil, she feels tied down, overwhelmed by responsibility, and unloved and unappreciated.

WIFE: "Drugs (including alcohol), devices, group sex, clothing and movies. The best is when both really want a mutual encounter and are psyched up to it with no aids. Quality, not quantity is the key. There really isn't much more to try."

Whether one is a fantasizer, like the lady golfer who finds imaginary splendor in the grass, or a doer, like the drug-smoking wife who finds splendor on it, people with a sense of adventure have richer sex lives. Note that the respondent above described her sex life as "good," though she rarely, if ever, had orgasms, as indicated on her objective questionaire.

Just about half the people surveyed engage in oral sex at least occasionally, with three-fourths of those under 30 doing so. Twenty per cent engage in fellatio and cunnilingus at least once a week, with 37 per cent of the youngest group doing it that often. (Throughout, figures for fellatio and cunnilingus are virtually identical; like love and marriage, you can't have one without the other.) People with no children practice it more often, but this may be a reflection of the youth of childless newlyweds rather than the result of an effective oral contraceptive.

Oral sex has allowed many women who had never experienced orgasm through coitus to reach a climax and, thus, effect dramatic changes in their sexual gratification. For others, inhibitions make it little more than an unreachable fantasy:

WIFE: "For the longest time I never had an orgasm. My spouse doesn't even last but maybe one minute at the longest. So, we tried oral sex. That does the trick for me and then he has his orgasm by intercourse. I'm willing to try just about anything to get out of this rut we're into, but he doesn't want to cooperate with me on anything."

This wife is planning to divorce her husband, and says she's cheated with 2 or 3 other men, briefly, even though she still has sex with husband 3 or 4 times a week. They argue mostly about attention to members of the opposite sex. She says the marriage is a failure, she feels tied down, and unappreciated.

WIFE: "Some experimentation with things not formerly practiced. Nothing extramarital because of both trust and strong religious convictions. We like a moderate amount of oral sex. Do not care to try much else."

This homemaker says sex is very good, and she has intercourse 3 or 4 times a week. Has anal sex. Says marriage is stable and loving. Between 31 and 40, with some college education.

WIFE: "I would like to try oral sex once to see how it is."

To many wives, it was not so much what they did, but how they went about doing it. Communication, awareness, and sensitivity were more important than any particular techniques:

WIFE: "By enjoying it. Don't know but it gets better and better, just when you think it's tops it gets better. Try to keep him happy at home. If you want to feel like a queen, you have to make your man feel like a king."

Some wives did not try to make their men feel like kings, because they themselves were not very interested in sex. And, in a few cases where the wives were, the husbands weren't:

WIFE: "I haven't tried a thing nor do I care to. My husband has tried everything from the gentle, passionate, romantic lover to the rough, aggressive raper. I didn't like any of them. He just doesn't turn me on anymore."

She's already cheated, and says sex is unsatisfying. Has intercourse 2 or 3 times a month, and argues mostly about sexual problems. Says her husband appreciates her as a wife, but not as a lover, and at this point she probably wouldn't marry the same man again.

WIFE: "I was a widow for four years, but did not live with my second husband until we married. I would say sex was better while we were single because the kids weren't around. I would like to be freer in sex but husband is inhibited.
    "Just more foreplay, sexy talk, etc., would help, but he won't do it. Husband No. 1 was definitely better! I feel it's hopeless and I don't care anymore as I am on the medication for high blood pressure which lessens my desire anyway."

She's 41 to 50, a college graduate, and currently a student. They have had a period of separation, during which she was briefly involved with 2 or 3 others. She says they have sex 3 or 4 times a week, and their sex life is very good. Alcohol is the worst crisis they've faced. The marriage is fairly loving and stable.

WIFE: "There really hasn't been any attempt at improvement. My spouse really thinks sex is dirty. I'm rather cool-natured."

WIFE: "I guess we are old-fashioned; the old ways of sex are just fine with both of us. Too old to try anything new. I hate to admit that."

What's sauce for the goose is sauce for the gander, and the ingredients are much the same: personal attractiveness, privacy, relaxation, and occasional change of environment:

HUSBAND: "I always take a shower and she always takes a bath. Clean bodies, powdered, and smelling good enhance our sex. It usually happens after an evening out. Our best sexual experiences are away at conventions—no phone calls, no children. My wife has no work. We always eat out, always dressed up. Rested and at our best—relaxed."

The sexual revolution has not annihilated the conservative population. Four out of five married people do not employ objects or techniques that might be termed far-out, kinky, or unconventional—and that includes drugs to enhance sexual pleasure. Only 4 per cent indulged in use of clothes or objects to enhance fantasies, mechanical aids, and anal sex; 2 per cent indulged in group sex or mate-swapping, and fewer than 1 per cent in bondage, sado-masochism, and homosexuality. People under 40 were minimally higher in percentage, but none were over 7 per cent, except for drugs, as discussed previously. Thus, most husbands were rather conservative, whether by their own choice or that of their wives:

HUSBAND: "We are fairly straight compared to what I think contemporary standards are. I am satisfied with our relationship without getting into 'kinky' practices."
He does not engage in cunnilingus nor does his wife do fellatio. Has sex once a week which he says is very good, and has no major problems in his stable marriage. A professional, 41 to 50, with a postgraduate education.

HUSBAND: "We try to be more sexually active, we sleep naked to assure each other that we're there when we need each other. This gratifies and also satisfies. I would like to try oral sex."

He's a professional, 41 to 50, with some college education. Their sex life is very good, and they have intercourse 3 or 4 times a week. He feels loved and appreciated fully, and says their marriage is always stable.

HUSBAND: "Different positions. Would like to try anal inter-course. She won't do it."

HUSBAND: "My wife is not responsive to anything besides a missionary style. I'm willing to try anything but it totally turns my wife off."

HUSBAND: "There really isn't much to try, my wife is a very sickly woman and is ill most times or she's having surgery so there isn't much time to try things with her. That is why I have outside interests."

HUSBAND: "Sex life has improved because we now take pre-caution against pregnancy which our religious convictions pre-vented earlier. Therefore, we are more relaxed."

HUSBAND: "We just do the old-fashioned way, no kinky type action for a couple of old folks."

Sexual conservatism is characteristic of older people, those who never attended college, and low-income earners, especially blue collar workers and the retired/unemployed. This is indicated by the higher percentages in these groups answering that they never engaged in oral sex or uncommon sexual variations. Blacks less frequently engaged in oral sex, but were much higher in the practice of anal sex and inflicting or receiving pain as part of sexual activity. People with firm religious beliefs were more con-servative, yet more often rated their sex life as very good.

Some husbands seemed willing to experiment, yet gave the impression that their sex life was to some degree unsatisfying:

HUSBAND: "We have tried most positions, discussed our sexual activities, and planned some of our sexual encounters. I have found oral sex (both giving and receiving) to be exciting and gratifying and my wife now enjoys cunnilingus very much. However, she does not enjoy returning the sexual favor by performing fellatio, which discourages me."

This husband says he probably wouldn't marry the same person again. Feels sexually unsatisfied, unloved, and unappreciated, and believes the marriage is in constant turmoil. He works in the technical field, has had some college education.

HUSBAND: "We do whatever feels right at the time. Nothing particularly gratifying. Nothing I would like to try that we haven't tried."

HUSBAND: "Have more sex, but only when I ask for it, not when I am pushed into it. This looks too false to me and I like to be the aggressive one."

The more unconventional types, alas, were not very inclined to writing, and their terse answers didn't even indicate whether they were referring to actual experiences or merely things they would like to try. What kind of a man would give such answers? By comparing the essay sheets with the objective questionnaires, we were able to learn a little bit about them:

HUSBAND: "Some anal—69 is fine."

He's been separated from his wife, and cheated with more than 3 women, with one affair lasting over a year. Feels more nervous and irritable as a result of marriage, but still feels marriage is fairly stable. A blue collar worker, with some college background.

HUSBAND: "Have wife swapping."

He's a college graduate, between 31 and 40. Says he's been involved in cheating, but with his wife's knowledge and consent. He feels that both spouses should be free to have extramarital affairs with each other's knowledge. He's into group sex, mate-swapping, homosexual activity. Has sex 5 or 6 times a week. However, he feels dominated by spouse, and feels taken for granted.

HUSBAND: "Threesome."

A white collar worker, he says he's consulted a lawyer about divorce, and has cheated on wife. Believes that only husbands should be permitted outside sexual activity. Engages in bondage, and admits to striking wife during arguments. He married for regular sex which he says he has 3 or 4 times a week, but at this point feels he lives only for his children. Says his wife dominates him. Between 31 and 40, with some college background.

HUSBAND: "The mouth and penis thrill."

This blue collar worker, between 31 and 40, says his sex life is very good, and his marriage is stable and loving.

HUSBAND: "Smear peanut butter all over."

Perhaps the last husband would have been more appreciated as a lover if he had watched that TV commercial that tells you which brand of peanut butter more housewives prefer. Masters and Johnson don't tell you *everything*.

Paradise Lost

In a recent study of over a thousand letters received by the American Association of Marriage Counselors from spouses requesting help, 40 per cent of the husbands and 20 per cent of the wives said that sexual relations was the main problem. And, lest one think that wives are not as concerned about sex, it should be pointed out that there were five times as many letters received from wives as husbands; hence, more actual complaints from wives.

It is one of the chief ironies of human existence that a natural, instinctual phenomenon that should be a prime source of pleasure can be such a source of dissatisfaction to so many people. Part of the discomfort stems from the partners' knowledge of what heights, according to things they have read and heard, sexual satisfaction can reach. One female author, for example, describes orgasm as "the high mountaintop of love of which the poets sing, on which the two together become a full orchestra playing a fortissimo of a glorious symphony." Considering that the average orgasm lasts about 3.5 seconds, that's barely time enough for a chord or two, so how can you blame a couple for feeling that they're missing a piccolo or that the third oboe was a bit weak? Yet, in 95 per cent of the letters received by the American Association of Marriage Counselors, the writer requested the name of a book or manual to solve the problem.

People who live in glass houses shouldn't throw stones and authors should not disparage the reading of books; however, rather than telling you about the problems with marital sex in America, we'll begin by letting the married people themselves describe their difficulties.

What is your biggest sexual difficulty? How does your spouse deal with it? How do you try to cope with it?

With the proliferation of sex therapists and their emphasis of techniques to promote sexual satisfaction, we naturally tend to think of sexual difficulties as performance failures, such as the husband's inability to maintain an erection or delay ejaculation, or the wife's inability to achieve orgasm. We tend to overlook the large number of cases where lack or inhibition of desire prevents any sexual activity from occurring, where the problem is not how you play the game, but whether anyone is on the ballfield. Because the taboos against premarital sexual activity, especially in adolescence, are stronger for girls and because boys more universally accept their sexuality through teen-age masturbation, it is often wives who feel a lack of sexual desire; however, not all husbands are lascivious satyrs, and many a wife complains of sexual neglect:

WIFE: "I am more anxious to have sex than he. He is patient about it. I just tell him so when I'm in the mood or try hard to entice him."

HUSBAND: "I haven't the strong desire my wife has so I have to give of myself more."

She's a homemaker, and a college graduate. They have one child. Says their sex life is good, and they have sex once a week. He's in management, 18 to 30, and rates sex life as variable.

WIFE: "Physically, there's only 24 hours in a day and between ages 30 and 40, one can cope with only job, children and other responsibilities. The question is priority. The desire to get ahead in this world occurs in your 40s and believe now you need every ounce of energy to try to get there."

HUSBAND: "Not enough sex, and I have abstained because wife doesn't care for sex (though I consider this normal).
"Become interested in other things, sports, etc."

She's a mother of three children, 41 to 50, works in management. Feels she lives for her children, and is overwhelmed by responsibility. He's in the same age range, a professional, making between $25-$49,999 a year. Says that his wife appreciates him, but doesn't really love him. Describes her as dominant, and feels that their marriage is in constant turmoil.

WIFE: "Disinterest! Most of the time!"

HUSBAND: "Not having enough sex. She has no real sex drive. I just put up with it and don't argue about it anymore."

Where a husband claimed some difficulty, such as premature ejaculation or difficulty reaching orgasm, the wife usually felt she, too, had a problem, either in being unable to reach orgasm consistently or in being too conservative and unable to give her husband the variety he wanted:

WIFE: "Myself reaching climax.
    "He is very calm, considerate about it. He tries to help out all he can.
    "Just try to do better the next time."

HUSBAND: "My biggest sexual difficulty is climaxing too quickly, not allowing my wife to reach orgasm with penile penetration. My spouse feels it is her fault because she's 'messed up down there.' I try to console her and say that it's no one's fault, besides we have only been married one year. With my wife having no previous sexual experience it will take time for me to learn our best ways of being sexually compatible."

A white collar worker. No children. Says she reaches orgasm from 0 to 9 per cent of the time. Describes sex life as variable. He's a blue collar worker, 18 to 30. Rates sex life as good, has sex once a week, but believes major problem is sexual dissatisfaction.

WIFE: "I find it repulsive to do other than to have a natural intercourse. Any other sex act is very revolting to me, and I cannot respond in any way. He has given up trying to force such acts on me and any sexual action that we might have are natural ones.

"I tried to comply but after several attempts and becoming violently ill I gave up trying."

HUSBAND: "Trying to reach climax after consuming enough alcohol to be competely drunk and incapable of anything except the desire for intercourse.

"She is very patient and does everything she knows how to help me—even to the point of exhaustion for herself."

A homemaker, 51 or over. One child. She believes her husband wishes that they would have never gotten married. They no longer have sex. He's a professional, same age range. Earns between $15-$25,000 a year.

WIFE: "Reaching orgasm.
"Tries new approaches.
"Masturbate."

HUSBAND: "The fact that I am attracted to men and women as they *are* attracted to ME. Maybe because bi-sexuality is chic these days."

In many cases, however, where the wife expressed feelings of being unattractive or too conservative for her husband, or just of not having sex very often, the husband did not feel he had a problem:

WIFE: "Fellatio and anal sex. He copes well with both my problems. I try to accept it and please him at the same time."

HUSBAND: "None that I know of, but I may be surprised."

She's a young professional, between 18 and 30. She says their sex life is variable, but rates her marriage as always being stable. She feels, however, that she is irresponsible. This is his second marriage. He's between 31 and 40. He claims that their sex life is very good.

WIFE: "Not enough.
"Spouse says we have to live with situation.
"Have learned to cope by understanding problem."

HUSBAND: "None."

How much is "enough" sex? On the average, couples in our sample had intercourse twice a week (22 per cent), but an equal percentage had sex three or four times weekly, the ones with frequencies of once a week or less pulling down the general average. Five per cent no longer have intercourse at all, and while this is true of one in ten couples over 50, 3 per cent of those between 40 and 50 are also celibate. But "enough" can be described only as that which both partners find satisfactory; in our couples under 30, one-third were having relations five or more times a week (more than one-sixth at least once a day), but the number having sex at least five times a week was only half as much in the 31 to 40 group. Even where a wife expresses satisfaction in their sex life, the husband may feel he is not up to her demands:

WIFE: "Sex 5 to 6 times weekly."

HUSBAND: "Making love more than 4 times a day is a little difficult. Cope with it by cuddling and not having actual intercourse."

She does professional-level work. Has no children. Says their sex life is very good, and feels her spouse is mature. He's a white collar worker, 18 to 30. He says they have sex once a day, and feels the marriage is stable. Engages in anal sex.

WIFE: "None."

HUSBAND: "Infrequency type.
    "Tries to help me.
    "Tries to get more."

She's a professional. No children. Says her marriage is stable and sex is good. He's a college student, rates sex life as very good. Says they have sex 5 or 6 times a week. Believes his wife is affectionate, but possessive.

Whereas there was not much disagreement between males and females in our total sample regarding the average weekly frequency of intercourse (3 per cent being the maximum variation for any one stated frequency), less than half of our subsample of matched couples agreed on their average frequency of intercourse. Since neither husbands nor wives consistently err on the side of estimating a higher frequency, the errors tend to average out over a large sample and give a false impression that there is almost unanimous agreement.

Morton Hunt, in commenting on the increase in frequency of marital coitus since Kinsey's time, says of his data, "Although the undersatisifed and the oversatisfied may distort their estimates somewhat, these people are in the minority; moreover, part of their distortions cancel each other out. The net result is that such distortions, though individually significant, have only a minor effect on the over-all averages for all males and all females." Whereas Hunt, as a statistical researcher, is interested in overall generalizations, we are just as concerned with the "individually significant" phenomena, for it becomes apparent in reading these responses that in many cases spouses are oblivious to each other's difficulties or strive to hide them from one another, and the sexual relationship becomes not a shared experience, but two different "realities."

WIFE: "Not being able to achieve orgasm each time we have intercourse."

HUSBAND: "My spouse is very much 'bed-oriented'; that is, she doesn't care for sex anywhere but in the bed. I don't make a big deal of it; I just enjoy sex with her in the bed."

Ten per cent of the women we sampled never or rarely have orgasms during intercourse, and 38 per cent (3 out of 8) had orgasms all or nearly all the time. Sixty per cent reached orgasm at least 60 per cent of the time.

Hunt regards the increased frequency of orgasm in married women compared with Kinsey's sample a generation ago as "a direct and precise measurement of the increase both in sexual pleasure and in the satisfactoriness of marital coitus for wives." While orgasm is pleasurable, not all women who fail to have orgasm regard their sex lives as unsatisfactory, and preoccupation with orgasm may cause more problems than accepting intercourse without it:

WIFE: "I have never had an orgasm and at first we coped great— we talked about it, but now I lead him to believe I do have one. I went to see a doctor and he told me to have him be patient, etc., but that's not the problem, he's very patient. I just don't understand why I don't. But I don't want to hurt him so I pretend I do."

This is her second marriage. They lived together for over a year before marrying. She's a white collar worker, between 18 and 30. While she believes her marriage to be a loving one, she feels that lack of communication is her biggest problem.

This woman had lived with her husband for a period prior to marriage, so she apparently did not feel that her inability to achieve orgasm was reason enough to seek a different husband in hope of a better sex life. Helen Singer Kaplan, author of *The New Sex Therapy,* says that 8 per cent of women are incapable of orgasm, regardless of how much therapy you give them; obviously, women should be encouraged to discover and develop orgasmic potential, but nearly one wife in ten will be doomed to a lifetime of guilt and frustration as long as they and their husbands are led to believe orgasm is *essential* for sexual and marital happiness. Many who cannot reach orgasm through intercourse may through masturbation or cunnilingus, but some are denied even this route through barriers of inhibition or yet unexplained physiological differences. Faking orgasm leads to problems such as experienced by one patient, a divorcee, whose lover accepted her explanation that she had never previously experienced orgasm until she lied to him on one occasion when he seemed particularly eager to please; thereafter, he obsessively persisted in his quest to recapture that one "success," until she fled the relationship.

For some wives, the inhibition was as much psychological as physical; for others, the inhibition rested in the husband:

WIFE: "Lack of desire. He tries to help me by working at arousing me. Sometimes it works, sometimes not. If there has been quite a bit of time since we last had intercourse I'll encourage him to try."

This homemaker, between 31 and 40, didn't complete high school. She says they have sex twice a week, and her husband is affectionate. Her major problem is difference in personal interests.

WIFE: "My biggest is not feeling that I can be as aggressive or different as I like to be without him reacting the way I'd like. I don't cope with it; just don't think about it."

This young homemaker is unsure at this time whether she'd marry the same man again. Feels her husband appreciates her as a wife, and not as a lover. Lack of communication is her biggest problem. Marriage alternates between remote and close periods.

WIFE: "Our biggest sexual difficulty took place about four years ago. My spouse was impotent for a short time. With a great deal of love and understanding we worked our problem out together. We now enjoy a very satisfying sexual relationship. I'm grateful for the experience we shared, it improved our relationship in many ways."

She's a homemaker, who has had some college education. Is between 31 and 40. She feels her marriage is stable and loving, and they have sex 2 or 3 times a week. Calls sex life very good.

WIFE: "Would like to have sex more often. Becomes defensive and angry. Use of vibrator to masturbate."

For women, problems relating to children—either in conceiving, bearing, or rearing them—affected their sex lives:

WIFE: "The fear of getting pregnant. Yes I deal with it by taking the Pill."

A blue collar worker and high school graduate who is between 18 and 30. Says her sex life is very good.

WIFE: "The biggest right now is that I'm pregnant! We switch positions and just try to be considerate of each other. Before, there were no difficulties—we both seem to have the same needs and feelings at the same time."

This homemaker says they have no major problem in their marriage. They have sex twice a week, and she says sex is very good. She's between 18 and 30, and has some college education.

WIFE: "No time for sex."

She works in the technical field, has two children, and is between 31 and 40. They have sex once a month. She feels tied down and trapped. Money is her biggest problem along with lack of communication.

Some women did not deal with sexual difficulties because they were insurmountable—or simply non-existent:

WIFE: "He is gay. I don't cope with it at all. We are getting divorced."

This homemaker who didn't complete high school has cheated on her husband with 2 or 3 others. One affair lasted at least a year. She says they no longer have sex. Married her spouse because of pregnancy. Says her husband is irresponsible, passive and anxious. She's between 18 and 30.

WIFE: "I am affectionate. Not into bondage or enemas. His idea of sex is to inflict pain. I can't understand this type of sex."

This is her second marriage. She's a white collar worker, between 41 and 50, and has some college background. She has sex less than once a month, and has orgasms from 0 to 9 per cent of the time. Says that her husband wishes that they would have never gotten married, and during arguments they have struck one another. She definitely would not marry the same person again today.

WIFE: "I really don't think I have any sexual difficulties. I am pretty loose, not uptight like my mother's generation."

Of course, many sexual difficulties are primarily reflections of tensions in the relationship that are not intrinsically sexual; in most of the cases, the involved parties may lack the insight acquired by this respondent:

WIFE: "My biggest difficulty is holding back on discussing the things which bother me and taking it out by no sex. In other words, by our not communicating our feelings about things, I feel resentment and take it out on my husband by not giving him sex. My husband has asked for sex instead of provoking me by physical stimulation. He has dealt with it by arguing with me to 'make' me feel guilty. I have been going through psychotherapy and am making very good progress by understanding myself."

We asked "What is *your* biggest sexual difficulty?" and many answered that it was the mate's inhibition or disinterest, which seems to be projecting the blame or, at least, evading the question. However, if the respondent had said "frustration" or "rejection," this would have been a personal answer though merely the result of the spouse's attitude, so perhaps we are overly preoccupied with semantics. Blushing brides still seem to outnumber shy bridegrooms regardless of the duration of marriage:

HUSBAND: "The biggest is wanting more sex than she is always able to give. Frequency seems to be the problem. Varying what we do is no problem. My spouse many times just refuses sex if she doesn't feel good, or if something is bothering her. At times she gives in to my desires and it becomes mechanical. I try to hurt her mentally at times to get my way, but, mostly, I completely avoid her—avoid her touch, avoid vocal contact, avoid kisses. At other times we both have complete understanding that one isn't interested in sex and we have no problem."

This husband married his wife because of pregnancy. He works in management, has a postgraudate education and is between 31 and 40. Though he says they have sex 2-3 times a week, and it's very good, he masturbates 2 or 3 times a month, and describes his wife as passive.

HUSBAND: "Mine is modesty; hesitancy to perform certain variations in technique. She is very understanding and I try to convince myself mentally not to be modest."

This young husband (between 18 and 30) is a college graduate and works in the professional field. Though he feels their sex life is very good, he feels dominated by his wife. Believes lack of communication is their major problem, and finds that his marriage alternates between remote and close periods.

HUSBAND: "My wife *never* takes the initative but almost always is understanding of my needs. I try then to be considerate of her wants sexually."

This technical worker between 41 and 50 believes he has a loving marriage, yet admits to cheating on his wife briefly with 2 or 3 other women. Says they have sex once a week, and it is good. Only major problem in marriage involves relatives.

HUSBAND: "Trying to make out early in the morning. She says that she's tired and wants to sleep.
      "I go out and get a little on the side."

Not all problems are related strictly to attitude. Men were often concerned about the sheer mechanics of sex, especially when critical parts were malfunctioning or inoperative:

HUSBAND: "Premature ejaculation. Most of foreplay done by me. Wife senses the amount of foreplay that can be tolerated. Experience has produced dual orgasm making for a desirable relationship."

He's 51 or over, retired or unemployed. This is his second marriage. Says he never or rarely ever has sex any more, and admits to cheating on wife with 2 or 3 other women, with one affair lasting over a year. He has never considered divorce, but believes one will enable him to find true love. Married for companionship and regular sex.

HUSBAND: "Can't get it up like I used to."

HUSBAND: "When we have sex, 85 per cent of the time she will bleed—I am 10¾ long and 3¼ round. Tries very hard to please me.

"Very gently because I might hurt spouse's feelings."

This husband lived with his wife between 6 months to a year before marrying. He feels that his wife appreciates him, but doesn't really love him. The main problem in the marriage is his wife's cheating on him, yet he rates their sex life as very good, though he admits that he has orgasms only 10 to 39 per cent of the time. He's a white collar worker, between 18 and 30, who didn't complete high school.

HUSBAND: "Fear of unwanted children, due to medical reasons wife couldn't take birth control pills. Tried IUD, but had problems, tried condoms also had problems, finally doctor O.K.'d pills and sex is returning to normal. Presently biggest difficulty is due to time difference in our jobs and not being able to be alone for spontaneous sex. Cope by doing without a lot of times and just putting up with it."

Ever since the first Thanksgiving Day, people of puritanical temperaments have been breaking bread with those of wilder proclivities; it's harder, however, to maintain harmony in the bedroom than at the dinner table:

HUSBAND: "Would like more anal sex. Until she enjoys it, it will remain a fantasy!"

He's between 41 and 50, works in technical field, with some college background. This is his second marriage. Says their sex life is very good, and marriage is stable and loving.

HUSBAND: "Want to make it with 2 women. Ignore it by not trying to bring it up too often."

This young management worker (between 18 and 30) says he has sex twice a week, and rates his sex life as variable. Calls his wife inconsiderate, and says that lack of communication is their biggest problem. An extramarital affair was his worst crisis, because his wife had cheated on him.

HUSBAND: "Boredom—wife doesn't know."

HUSBAND: "Being bisexual—(deals with it) by toleration. I don't."

HUSBAND: "I drink and my wife is a real churchgoer. She doesn't like me to drink and have sex with her."

The Trouble with Spouses

In a scene from *Annie Hall*, divorced swinger Woody Allen is lying disconsolately in bed beside his latest conquest. "I'm sorry I took so long to finish," she says unemotionally. Allen opens his mouth slowly and wiggles his jaw laboriously like the rusted Tin Woodman; "That's okay," he sighs, "I'm beginning to get sensation back in my jaw."

Doctors a generation ago would occasionally see someone with transient weakness of the arm and pain radiating down the length of the limb from the armpit; medical students called it "honeymooners' paralysis," since it occurred in newlyweds who had the romantic but impractical desire to sleep with their arms around each other. Now, with the universality of oral sex and the mandate for female orgasm in every encounter, we wonder how many cases of the new "honeymooners' paralysis," such as Woody's, wind up referred to oral surgeons.

When asked what was their spouses' main sexual difficulty,

a frequent answer from husbands was how much time it took their wives to get aroused in response to their advances; from the wives' point of view, it was often the infrequency of any advances to respond to. It is probable, however, that twenty years ago far fewer husbands would have taken the time to find out how much time it took for wives to experience arousal and satisfaction.

What is your spouse's biggest sexual difficulty? How do you deal with it?

WIFE: "My husband always wants and talks constantly of oral sex and unfortunately this is a turn-off for me. Sometimes I try for his sake and he in turn many times will *not* try to have oral sex since he realizes how against it I am."

HUSBAND: "She is very slow to be turned on. I live with it."

This mother of 3 feels she lives only for her children. A white collar worker between 41 and 50, she says they argue mostly about them. Has thought about divorce. Says sex life is "variable." He's in the white collar field also, and same age range. Total family income is between $25-$49,999 a year. Believes that his marriage is fairly stable. Describes his wife as "emotional."

WIFE: "Only the slowing of sexual activity that most men have after 60 or so. He just needs extra loving and attention and lots of encouragement."

HUSBAND: "Trying different ways—approach a new way slowly."

She's retired or unemployed and is 51 or over. Says they have sex once a week, and it is "variable." Feels that their marriage is generally loving. He's retired. Although he says their sex life is very good, he feels dominated by his wife.

WIFE: "Biggest sexual difficulty is with husband's depression. He doesn't require sex very often.

"Was a major problem early in marriage but have conditioned self to require sex less frequently.

"If in the mood and he refuses, usually read or do housework to use up excessive energy and help to sleep."

HUSBAND: "Not always inclined."

If the wives who complain that their husbands have low levels of sexual desire are wondering whatever became of all the sex-obsessed satyrs their mothers warned them about, we've found that they married women who have low levels of sexual interest:

WIFE: "Maybe he wants it more than I do.
"Tell him I'm tired."

HUSBAND: "She does not want to have intercourse as much as I do.
"I sometimes masturbate to compensate for her denials."

A homemaker, she's the mother of 4 children, and is between 41 and 50. Has sex twice a week. Feels that mutual sexual satisfaction is most important for a good marriage. He's 51 or over, works in management. This is his second marriage. Married for the first time over 40. Married to have regular sex.

WIFE: "Having to have it so often. I go along with it because I love him. This doesn't mean I don't enjoy it myself."

HUSBAND: "Having a climax.
"I try."

She says they have sex 5 or 6 times a week, and they engage in bondage. She also masturbates twice a week. Feels they have a good marriage. They have no children. She's between 18 and 30. He works in the technical field. Feels that his wife is very emotional, while he is passive. Smokes marijuana to enhance sexual act.

WIFE: "Sometimes too aggressive, too harsh, doesn't realize a soft touch is more pleasurable than harsh one.
"Try to guide him at the time."

HUSBAND: "Oral."

If marriages are made in heaven, the same perverse angel who sees to it that nymphs marry Galahads and satyrs marry Vestal Virgins likewise mates women who have difficulty reaching orgasm to the premature ejaculators:

WIFE: "Premature ejaculation. I don't deal with it."

HUSBAND: "Reaching orgasm."

This wife feels her marriage alternates between periods of closeness and remoteness, and feels overwhelmed by responsibility. She's a homemaker, between 41 and 50. He's a blue collar worker, in the same age range. He says they argue mostly about sexual problems.

WIFE: "Pre-ejaculation. Comfort him and instill confidence."

HUSBAND: "Decreasing sexual desire. We try various ways of stimulation."

Because marital coitus occurs less frequently than one or both partners would like, this does not always mean that the sex acts themselves are unsatisfactory. If they were, there would be less likelihood of wanting more of the same. Feelings of inadequacy and unattractiveness on the part of one spouse or anger over matters unrelated to sexual relations may be causes of avoiding or rejecting sexual activity, even though there is no inherent sexual problem.

HUSBAND: "Since she has gained weight, she feels unfeminine, unattractive and therefore asexual. If it can be called a sexual 'problem' she sometimes ignores sex for these reasons.

"In trying to deal with this I attempt to encourage her in her attempts to control her weight. I compliment her often to build her self-confidence and self-image."

This wife married for sexual attraction—that influenced her most in her choice of mate. Though she says their sex life is satisfactory, she feels tied down and trapped. They have no children. She's between 31 and 40, and works in professional field. He's in management, same age range. He says their sex life is generally dull, but feels their marriage is generally stable.

WIFE: "My spouse's biggest sexual difficulty is his need of sex isn't as often as I would like. He is terrific when we are making love but I would like quantity with quality. I deal with his lack of desire by substituting various activities and interest that we both like and share. Sex is important, but there are other ways to be fulfilled."

HUSBAND: "None."

This mother of 4 children is between 31 and 40, and is a homemaker. She says her husband is reserved, and he feels that she is a good lover, but needs improvement in other ways. He's between 41 and 50 and works in the technical field. He believes that their marriage is a stable one, and that his wife appreciates him fully.

WIFE: "The ability to turn me off by personal selfishness and rather than communicate he chooses to become more and more preoccupied with sports—his first love! I tell him a baseball, football can be hit or kicked but does not make good companion in bed or cook in kitchen!"

The seventies may not have witnessed a cure for the "tired" husband, but at least the more trendy among the wives can attribute periods of suboptimal sexual activity to the natural discrepancies in "biorhythms."

WIFE: "Different biorhythms or different libido periods, but close. Usually overlapping periods are satisfactory."

A professional, 18 to 30, with some college education. She describes their sex life as very good; they have intercourse 5 or 6 times per week. She says that their marriage is generally stable and always loving.

WIFE: "He is tired and would like to have sex more often but falls to sleep before I get to bed. We don't 'deal' with it, we just pretend it doesn't exist."

She's a high school graduate of 31 to 40. She says that their sex life is generally dull, and that they have sex once a week. She feels sexually unsatisfied, nervous and irritable, and disillusioned about romance and love, but she does describe the marriage as fairly stable.

WIFE: "Lack of urge. The only way to deal with it is to introduce variations to the act itself."

While modern husbands are becoming more aware of how women's bodies respond during lovemaking, some wives feel their husbands do not understand what goes on in the woman's mind and how important it is for sexual harmony:

WIFE: "My spouse's biggest sexual difficulty is not sharing my sexual fantasy. I have asked him to try and share, but as of now, he has not been able. I deal with it by fantasizing silently during lovemaking."

She's a homemaker, 31 to 40, with some college education. She describes their sex life as good; they engage in group sex. She feels appreciated as a spouse, but not as a lover, but describes the marriage as always stable and generally loving.

WIFE: "Not enough warmth and affection before the bedroom. I consider how good it is in the bedroom and seldom mention warmth or more affection beforehand."

While some wives complain that husbands cannot psychologically read their minds, other wives always know what's on their husbands' minds—it's sex and it's constant:

WIFE: "Wants sex constantly so he goes wherever and whenever."

This is her second marriage. She has cheated on her husband, but she says it is with his consent and knowledge. She's also into group sex. In view of all this, she still feels her sex life with her husband is satisfactory, but she's unsure whether she'd marry the same person again. A college graduate between 31 and 40.

WIFE: "When his children come to visit (4 children by previous marriage) he wants to play around in front of them, which I feel is not right."

People who have remarried apparently have more active sex lives than those in first marriages, according to our objective questionnaires—fortunately, not to the extent of its being a problem, as in the above cases. Not only did the remarrieds more frequently rate their sex lives as very good, but the percentage of remarried couples having intercourse three or more times a week was 47 per cent, as opposed to 36 per cent of those in their first marriages, despite the latter being younger.

Not all of men's sexual difficulties reside in the mind. Sometimes the spirit is willing, but the flesh is weak, aged, drugged, or excessive:

WIFE: "Has orgasms too fast. I don't."

This wife has already consulted a lawyer about a divorce. Says that sexual dissatisfaction, lack of communication and disagreements over their children are their major problems. They have sex 3 or 4 times a week. She's a homemaker between 31 and 40, with some college background.

WIFE: "Our ages."

She's 51 or over, and a homemaker. This is her second marriage. Says her sex life is unsatisfying, because they only have sex 2 or 3 times a month. In addition, she only has orgasm from 0 to 9 per cent of the time.

WIFE: "Spouse drinks too much—I don't enjoy sex with a drunk . . . spouse doesn't enjoy sex as much as I."

WIFE: "Position is difficult during intercourse as he is extremely overweight. I must always be on top and must insert his penis for him."

Orgasm is often the focal point of difficulty for a man. Not only is it a problem when his wife's failure to reach orgasm consistently makes him feel inadequate, but also when it is the husband himself who does not have orgasm:

WIFE: "Thinking that I must have orgasm in order for both to achieve satisfaction. He thinks that he can't turn me on."

WIFE: "Reaching a climax, also aching in prostate area so has not tried for 4 or 5 months. I try to be patient—undemanding—trying to get him to go to the doctor to get checked."

One of the most surprising findings in the study was the response to the question, "How often do you reach orgasm during intercourse with your spouse?" Eleven per cent of the husbands gave frequencies under 60 per cent and 4 per cent indicated rarely or never. We know that Hunt reported in 1972 that 8 per cent of men over 45 reported at least occasional ejaculatory failure and that for 15 per cent of men under 25 this happened at least a quarter of the time—a dramatic change since Kinsey's reference to ejaculatory failure as a very rare phenomenon with an incidence of about one man in a thousand. Our figures now show that failure to ejaculate during intercourse affects 20 per cent of husbands to some extent; incredible compared with Hunt's figures, but no more so than the discrepancy between the surveys of Kinsey and Hunt.

If the estimates are wrong, it could be because many men misread or misinterpreted the question to mean how often they brought their wife to orgasm. This, too, would be significant, because it indicates that contemporary husbands are more preoccupied with their wives' orgasms than their own, even to the point of defining "reaching orgasm" as female response. Probably this unexpected answer is a combination of the two factors, a redefinition of reaching orgasm and an actual decrease in ejaculatory frequency related to inhibition of spontaneous coital ejaculation because of attempts to delay until the wife has reached orgasm first.

Whereas wives often complained of husbands' lack of interest in sex, they did not attribute it to upbringing or deep-seated guilt feelings. Husbands, however, often blamed their spouses' inhibitions on an underlying conviction that sex is dirty:

HUSBAND: "She considers sex dirty. Attended group therapy, bought literature, discussed with her friends—wife understands it is a mental block but cannot overcome."

This husband feels his sex life is generally dull, and says he cheated briefly with 2 or 3 other women. They have sex 2 or 3 times a month, and argue mostly about her sexual problems. He married because his wife was pregnant. Says the major problem in the marriage is sexual dissatisfaction. A professional, 31 to 40, with some college background.

HUSBAND: "I think it is a mental block from childhood. I try to understand her better and put her in a playful mood."

This husband says he married to have children. Lived with his wife 3 to 6 months before marriage. Rates his sex life as "variable" and says he cheated on wife with more than 3 women, with one affair lasting over a year. He's in the technical field, 31 to 40, with some college education.

HUSBAND: "She does not think she is a female if she must be the aggressor. She is too quickly impressed by another man."

He admits to cheating briefly on his wife with one other woman. Says they have intercourse less than once a month, but when they do it is "good." He's a blue collar, 41 to 50, with a high school education.

HUSBAND: "Frequency. Discussion brought shorter periods of waiting but reduced quality and her apparent enjoyment. With 2 or 3 times a month quality is superior and self-satisfaction keeps me going between."

HUSBAND: "Reaching climax and not seeming to want it often enough. I've learned to live with it."

Alcohol is often used in cleaning fluids to dissolve grease, and it also does a fair job of dissolving inhibitions; however, the emotional and physical sequelae may lead to prohibition of its use for aphrodisiac purposes:

HUSBAND: "Unable to approach with affection, except under influence of alcohol and then this in late morning hours (2 to 4 AM) when temper of spouse may flare if protest made because of disturbing sleep."

He's a professional, 51 or over with a postgraduate education. Says they've had a period of separation, and admits to cheating on his wife with 2 or 3 other women, briefly. Feels sexually unsatisfied, terming his sex life "variable."

HUSBAND: "Three bottles of wine and she's just fine, but before that she's very inhibited."

If the lady discussed above is really consuming three bottles of wine a night, her mate may be confusing her convulsions with orgasms. Many wives appreciate men without the particular services of Johnny Walker or Jack Daniels, but for some husbands this interest in sexual gratification is too much of a good thing:

HUSBAND: "She can't be sexually satisfied by me. She continuously wants sex."

He has cheated with one other women, briefly. Says they have sex 2 or 3 times a month, which he terms "satisfactory." Yet because of his marriage, he feels more nervous and irritable, and believes that sexual dissatisfaction is their major problem. He still feels though that his marriage is generally a loving one. A professional, between 31 and 40, with some college background.

HUSBAND: "She would enjoy sex more often. Try to increase the frequency."

HUSBAND: "She wants oral sex and I don't want to give it."

HUSBAND: "Lack of willingness to continue variations in physically stimulating me. Not through actual objecting to such stimulation, but through her becoming so involved with my stimulating her that she neglects to do what I want unless reminded."

In the answers given above, the number of difficulties far outnumber attempted solutions, and the most common ways of dealing with problems are "learning to cope," "ignoring it," or other ways of expressing passive acceptance. The most successful outcomes apparently stemmed from communication and attempts at new lovemaking patterns, which, even if they resulted in compromises or a return to the old ways, often increased the spouses' love and appreciation for one another.

Bedroom Boycotts

> I will suffer no man, be he husband or lover,
> To approach me all hot and horny.
> I will remain at home unmated,
> Wearing my sheerest gown and carefully adorned,
> That my husband may burn with desire for me.
> And if he takes me by force against my will,
> I shall do it badly and keep from moving.

So pledged Lysistrata and the other Greek wives in Aristophanes' ancient comedy about how the women of Greece compelled their husbands to stop waging wars by withholding sex from them. The use—or, rather, non-use—of sex as a weapon in conflicts between husbands and wives, particularly in times of domestic rather than international warfare, probably pre-dates the stone axe. Eric Berne and the transactional analysts have distinguished these classic maneuvers by proclaiming them "games," with such contemporary titles as "Frigid Woman," "Corner," and "Women's Lib Trump," but they have been with us in one form or another since the days when a bunny club was used to kill rabbits.

Sometimes a spouse may rationalize withholding sex from the partner by claiming illness, fatigue, or emotional upset. In such cases the party begging off may not be consciously aware of the anger or resentment towards the mate that motivates the behavior. Often, however, there is premeditated hostility.

Do you or your spouse ever deliberately withhold sex from one another? For what reasons? How do you deal with it?

Only 10 percent of our sample denied ever avoiding sex with their partners, and the husbands surpassed the wives in being ever-ready by the barest of margins—11 to 9 per cent. Only a third of our married people said they directly declined advances; perhaps it was a matter of masculine pride, but husbands resorted to various deceptive stratagems more than wives. Using fatigue to beg off is a tired excuse, but still popular, leading all other strategems at 19 per cent. Feigning illness and watching television tied for distant second place at 7 per cent.

Not all cases of withholding sex are punitive. Sometimes physical conditions, such as vaginitis, prostatitis, and non-genital illnesses ranging from musculoskeletal problems to the common cold can render a normally pleasurable act painful or inadvisable. Some spouses, particularly women, usually find intercourse unpleasant, or, at best, neutral; unless they are in unusually good spirits, they will avoid activity, even though they are on good terms with their spouses. Some avoid sex for emotional reasons, but it is because they are preoccupied with personal stresses or demands, and, again, have no quarrel with their mates. Finally, there are those who are angry and withhold sex to punish and to emphasize their hostility. An example of each type of withholding is demonstrated by the couples below:

WIFE: "Never for retaliation only for medical problems that finally resulted in surgery. Any sexual problems we may have had were solved by this (hysterectomy for health reasons). Problems were caused by my hemorrhaging anytime we had intercourse."

HUSBAND: "Yes we both understand that in order to be good both must be ready."

WIFE: "Yes. Sex does not interest me that much—it's good when I want it but I'm frigid. It's not because I'm bored. When I don't want to I don't want it with anybody. I complain of illness, argue, just anything to get out of it. He never withholds sex—he wants it all the time."

HUSBAND: "Yes—don't want to—argue a lot."

WIFE: "Yes—if I'm upset with myself or very occupied with school, I find myself withholding from him. Sometimes I just don't feel attracted enough to my husband and won't make love only as my 'wifely' duty."

HUSBAND: "Yes, occasionally during times of emotional or physical distress. Mostly due to stress of graduate school for spouse and overinvolvement of myself in my work causing a few arguments."

She's a college student, and says sex in her marriage is good. She also believes her marriage alternates between close and remote periods. He feels their sex life is "variable." Says he feels tied down. He's a professional, with a postgraduate education, between 18 and 30. She's in the same age range.

WIFE: "No."

HUSBAND: "My wife has withheld sex from me after fighting to make me suffer."

In avoiding sex, for whatever reason, only 7 per cent would act disagreeable or pick a quarrel. Cold shoulders were most commonly encountered among students, blacks, people under 30, blue collar workers, and the low-income group. The highly educated and high income earners were least likely to avoid sex. Those with firm religious beliefs were slightly higher in never avoiding sex, and considerably higher in not using hostile behavior as a defense.

Nobody talks much about sin these days, even from the pulpit, and the confessional now resembles a psychiatrist's office where the parishioner sits and chats rather than kneeling and repenting, but any housewife over 30 with memories of a Catholic girlhood will recall having been instructed that to deny sex to one's spouse was a mortal sin, as serious as premarital sex or adultery. Men were technically bound by the same rule, but since impotence offered a natural and guilt-free escape for the reluctant husband, there was something of a double standard. In principle, most people would agree that sex should not be used as a weapon to blackmail the mate into giving in to some wish or to punish for some disagreement. On the other hand, if one party is realistically upset, is it reasonable to compel that person to engage in an act that should be loving and intimate, as the lady below explains?

WIFE: "I've never been faced with this question before. I suppose if I have deliberately (although I don't consider it deliberate) withheld sex from my husband it is because I've been upset with him about something and I just couldn't feel right about making love at that time when I had this mental or emotional, whatever, block to overcome. My frame of mind has to be right. I suppose when I feel resentment toward my spouse I haven't been in a loving mood. Thank goodness that hasn't been that often. Our marriage has had minor ups and downs but basically we are a loving couple, we are mentally and physically suited to one another, and have been able to provide good emotional and physical pleasure for one another."

Two ancient concepts seem to be undergoing slow erosion in our society, though they have been with us so long it is difficult to conceive their total abolition. They are the views of man as satyr and woman as chattel. One holds that men have a powerful need for regular sexual intercourse and any man who does not have constant access to his wife is, understandably and excusably, certain to find extramarital partners. (From our section on sexual difficulties, it seems men are more often afflicted by a shortage rather than an excess of libido.) The other venerable tradition is that of the wife's being subject to her husband in all things, with her self, body as well as soul, essentially his property. Few people today would outwardly agree with this view of woman, though inward attitudes die harder than outward credos. Thus, to some women, times when one is not in the mood for sex should be dealt with by the desirous mate's foregoing sexual experience, not by the reluctant mate's acquiescence. Others cling to the old values, often speaking of sex as a "need," as well as a desire:

WIFE: "We try to satisfy each other's needs and desires, denying sex only when there is a very good reason (pain, *extreme* fatigue)."

While this homemaker says her sex life is good, and they have sex 3 or 4 times a week, she also admits to infidelity, cheating briefly with one other man. However, she still feels that her marriage is stable and loving. She's between 31 and 40, with a postgraduate education.

WIFE: "Deliberate is not the word I use. If one partner feels this is not the time, he/she says so and that opinion is respected."

Ironically, just as one current in modern society, the Women's Liberation Movement, is convincing women that their bodies are their own exclusive property and need not be yielded on demand to any man, there is the more subtle countercurrent of the Sexual Revolution, whose message is that sex should be enjoyed as often as possible and disinterest in sex reflects a neurotic personality and a severely deprived lifestyle.

Some women—as well as their husbands—have no guilt about withholding sex, even out of anger; some may find reconciliation in each other's arms, but some evade negotiations via the arms of Morpheus:

WIFE: "My husband never does—he's always ready! I will at times if I'm angry with him—but never to get something I want. Usually, often when a disagreement has carried on most of a day, we'll go to bed and talk about the problem and many times have intercourse when things are O.K. between us again."

Though she believes her marriage is stable, and sex is good, she feels overwhelmed by responsibility. She's a homemaker, 31 to 40. Didn't complete high school.

WIFE: "He has and I have. Because of anger. I simply go to sleep. He says he'll never ask me again, but he does."

She's a blue collar worker, 41 to 50, and a high school graduate. She says that she has been involved with another man with her spouse's knowledge, and that she and her husband never or rarely have sex. She believes the marriage has alternating periods of closeness and remoteness.

WIFE: "After an argument. I don't go to bed the same time."

WIFE: "Yes—if he gets mad and loses his temper and raises his voice I withhold sex."

WIFE: "Yes. Don't like it. I haven't dealt with it yet."

Since husbands are traditionally the aggressors in marital relations, sexual avoidance patterns differ from those of the wives. We saw from the objective questionnaires that they "avoided" sex just about as universally as women, although frequency differences may be greater. The men, in essays, less often admitted to withholding sex deliberately, and this is probably because, in the waning but still predominating tradition of male initiative, failure to initiate sexual activity is a more passive maneuver than rejecting an advance, which is what the reluctant wife more often winds up doing.

In cases where husbands admitted to withholding sex, there were more often feelings of insecurity, and even allusions to impotence, than of anger:

HUSBAND: "I have done so on two occasions in our five years of sexual relations. Both occasions involved my feelings of being unable to deal with closeness at the time. I wanted distance from my wife. After much emotional upset on my part I was able to rise to the occasion within 24 hours. Usually enjoying a very exciting experience. My wife occasionally when tired will deny me sex but will always recoup within 24 hours."

He is a white collar worker with a postgraduate education, 18 to 30. He says they have sex twice a week, and their sex life is good. He describes the marriage as always loving, though he does feel overwhelmed by responsibility.

HUSBAND: "Yes—fear of not pleasing my wife and not knowing when she wants sex.
   "Deal with it by not doing anything about it."

He's a professional, 41 to 50, with a postgraduate education. He says their sex life is variable, he feels sexually unsatisfied, and they argue most about their sexual problems and the children. He describes the marriage as generally stable and loving, though.

HUSBAND: "At one time yes. Mainly I feel the fear of having another child. I also felt I would be doing my wife a disservice by having another child."

This husband feels he lives only for his children, and says that they have led to many quarrels. Though he believes his marriage to be stable, and says sex is "very good," he cheated with another woman, briefly. He's a professional, 41 to 50, with a postgraduate education.

HUSBAND: "I have withheld sex usually to serve my own needs; usually business reasons."

What possible "business reasons" could a man have for withholding sex, short of acting in an X-rated film? We suppose he meant spending time on work instead of in bed, although a few athletes or their coaches still subscribe to the Spartan theory that intercourse before a contest depletes masculine prowess. In recent years, some National Football League coaches have interdicted pre-game marital relations by keeping players in hotels even when the team was at home. The majority of coaches have disregarded such unscientific practices. Let's face it: six months in a monastery couldn't make winners of the Tampa Bay Buccaneers!

Most husbands responding to the question of withholding sex talked not about their own practices but about the treatment they received from their wives:

HUSBAND: "My wife used to sleep in another room to punish me. It used to hurt a lot. She moved to another bedroom permanently a few years ago because I 'snore.' Now we never sleep together. Occasionally we get together but usually my requests are ignored. It hardly matters any longer. I'm used to it."

He's between 41 and 50, works in the technical field. Says they've had a period of separation. Has sex 2 or 3 times a month, which he says is always unsatisfying. Feels both unloved and unappreciated. In view of all this he still rates his marriage as being a fairly stable one.

HUSBAND: "Yes—I think to make me feel more appreciative when it is offered. Wait—Wait—Wait."

He says that sex is very good, but at this point he feels he lives only for his children. The main problem in their marriage is lack of communication. He's a blue collar worker, between 41 and 50.

HUSBAND: "I feel that my wife has, however, I am sure she had good reasons. She had a long list. I suppose it's legitimate. I never have, and sure I never would. I let my wife have her way—she always wins."

This high school graduate, 51 or over, says their sex life is satisfactory, but also says he feels unloved and unappreciated. He describes the marriage as generally stable.

HUSBAND: "Yes. My wife withholds sex as a form of punishment for real and imagined slights."

He's a professional, a college graduate, 41 to 50. He has cheated with one person, briefly. He describes their sex life as unsatisfying, and says he feels more nervous and irritable since marriage.

HUSBAND: "Yes. It's hard to say—tolerate the old girl to say the least about it."

A professional between 41 and 50, this is his second marriage. Has sex less than once a month, and says it's unsatisfying. Says he feels overwhelmed by responsibility, and though he believes their marriage is generally stable, and he feels appreciated, he doesn't feel he is loved.

HUSBAND: "We do not relate anymore."

The one area in which husbands far surpassed wives in the art of sexual avoidance was the use of television watching. With the wives having sole access to the daytime serials and the children monopolizing the prime time viewing geared to their mentalities, the husbands can generally lay claim to the late hours and the traditional male provinces of news and sports. Television-watching is one of the few ways a man can claim to be "busy" with no expenditure of energy at all, and, unless he owns one of those incredibly expensive gadgets for taping programs, his wife cannot possibly ask him to defer watching a particular show until "later."

Not all husbands would sacrifice the pleasures of the night for the Game of the Week. Some say they never withhold sex, for reasons ethical or strictly recreational:

HUSBAND: "No. You might attain some short-term goal by doing this, but I think it would hurt your relationship severely in the long run. I think such an action demonstrates selfishness and a lack of maturity."

HUSBAND: "I or my spouse don't hold sex over each other's head, as a matter of fact. Half the fun of arguing is making up."

Withholding sex is like withholding tax—you should be happy with what you get, but you can't help missing and resenting what's withheld.

On Your Own

Effusion of semen represents the strength of the body and its life, and the light of the eyes. Whenever it is emitted to excess, the body becomes consumed, its strength terminates, and its life perishes.

—Maimonides

If the above quote sounds like an admonition to impressionable young boys against masturbation, be advised that the famous 12th-century physician meant it to apply to all sorts of sexual indulgence, and he went on to say that one in a thousand men dies from other illnesses, but the other 999 from excessive intercourse. However, his reference to "the light of the eyes" probably is the source of the once common belief that masturbation could lead to blindness, not to mention all other sorts of physical and mental illness. (*Playboy* magazine refutes the theory that masturbation can make you insane, but concedes it can make you "come unscrewed.")

Masturbation, which is the first sexual experience of virtually all adolescent males and a strong majority of females, was, in the previous century, regarded with such abhorrence that devices were sold to restrain sleeping children from getting their hands and genitals together. Masturbation has probably never in history been more respectable than it is today; sex therapists encourage women who have never been able to achieve orgasm to begin by practicing masturbation, and radical feminists who want personal, as well as economic, independence from men proclaim the superiority of masturbation over coitus as a source of satisfaction. The best-selling *Hite Report* presented us with a taxonomy of female masturbation, listing and graphically explaining six discrete types. And Masters and Johnson, the Pierre and Marie Curie of sex therapy, have been assailed by reactionaries for such statements as "Masturbating women concentrate on their own sexual demand without the distraction of a coital partner," reducing what was once called a "lover" to a now-extraneous potential hindrance in woman's systematic quest for orgasm.

For men, masturbation is not as likely to be an ecstatic, liberating discovery. They learned it long ago and practiced it in guilty secrecy; peers acknowledged it as the hallmark of boys, too young and insecure to acquire the female partners for which masturbation was a poor substitute. In the secret compartments of their wallets, in hope they encountered the wrong kind of girl, boys would cache a condom, much as Lewis Carroll's White Knight put anklets on his horse's feet to protect against shark bites and a mousetrap on its back, in a constant state of readiness for the most improbable happenings.

Masturbation among single men is not as respectable as among their female counterparts, who are as likely to own a vibrator as a diaphragm these days, but, in accordance with the new anything-goes, if-it-feels-good-do-it philosophy of the times, masturbation is more psychologically acceptable. Some of the more obsessive types use it for means other than pleasure, as with the fellow who wrote to the editors of a men's magazine saying that masturbation was as routine a part of his pre-date preparation as shaving and showering, to enable him to prolong intercourse with his partner.

Masturbation among the married is more controversial. Some believe that partners should rely solely on one another for any form of gratification and always make themselves available at the other's request, masturbation being tantamount to adultery. At the other extreme of opinion, it is held that masturbation enriches the sex life of the married by insuring that coitus occurs only when both partners are eager and willing; masturbation indicates consideration of the partner's individual desire level and avoids frustration and rancor.

Please note that in this discussion we are defining masturbation as an act committed alone. Some people regard manual stimulation of one partner's genitals by the other as masturbation. Some wives routinely stimulate their clitorises manually during intercourse to promote orgasm. To avoid confusion, we added the word "alone" to our questions.

Twenty-seven per cent of the wives we surveyed—roughly one in four—admitted to masturbating, although half of these did so once a month or less often. Not as many wives as husbands masturbate; 38 per cent of the men engaged in the practice, but only 20 per cent more than once a month. Masturbation seems to be not so much related to sexual dissatisfaction as to liberal views and the acceptance of a wider variety of sexual practices, including autoerotic activity; we found lower incidences of masturbation among the most poorly educated, the lowest income earners, nonworking women, and those with firm religious beliefs, all groups which we would associate with conservative attitudes.

Do you ever masturbate alone? What advantages or purpose does this have, compared to sexual activity with your partner? Do you have any particular erotic fantasies, and if so, describe them.

With couples who responded to this question, generally one or both said they masturbated in the absence or unavailability of their mate, thus making masturbation a definite secondary preference.

WIFE: "Yes, if he is not around, and I feel need, especially after reading erotic material."

HUSBAND: "Yes, if my spouse wasn't here, and I felt need for it. No advantage compared with a partner. Any erotic fantasies would have to include sex in a group."

This homemaker who is between 41 and 50 feels she has a stable marriage and a good sex life. Her husband, a blue collar worker in the same age range says they have sex 3 or 4 times a week, and he uses clothes or objects to enhance his fantasies.

WIFE: "Yes, releases tension. It is a natural feeling to masturbate. There is no comparison between the two. Masturbation is a temporary relief for the moment."

HUSBAND: "Yes, to relieve tension. When my spouse is not around.
"Yes. Three women and myself."

This mother of three children says he takes her for granted, and admits that they've both physically assaulted each other. She's between 31 and 40, and he's between 41 and 50. He's unemployed. Has some college background. Says he uses drugs to enhance sexual pleasure. Also feels tied down and trapped, thinks he lives only for his children.

WIFE: "I rarely masturbate—the only time I did was when my husband was gone for a long time. I much prefer my husband. I don't have any particular erotic fantasies."

HUSBAND: "Yes, the act releases me but is second best!"

He thinks his wife wishes that she would have never married him, whereas she says she'd definitely marry the same man again. Both are college graduates, between 31 and 40, and he has a postgraduate education.

Whereas men never seem to prefer masturbation to coitus, some wives indicated that it was physically more gratifying:

WIFE: "Yes, it is the only way I can achieve an orgasm."

HUSBAND: "Yes. It keeps me satisfied in between periods of lack of sex with partner. No fantasies."

Though they only have sex 2 or 3 times a month, both say sex is satisfactory. She works in the blue collar field, he's a white collar worker, with some college. Both between 18 and 30.

For men who find advantages in masturbation, they are more likely to be psychological than physical:

HUSBAND: "The main purpose of masturbation is to relieve sexual hangups. Most people live out their fantasies so they can remain emotionally stable. Since I find little sexual pleasure from my spouse, I must keep my sanity."

Couples who do not masturbate don't necessarily have harmonious marriages, as this pair indicated:

WIFE: "No. None."

HUSBAND: "Yes. Before marriage. More peace of mind. Yes, a pleasing, gentle woman who thinks of my needs, too."

This young wife (18 to 30) says she believes her husband wishes that they would have never gotten married, and she believes their marriage is in constant turmoil. He's a white collar worker in the same age range, and says his wife is inconsiderate, and has struck him during arguments.

Some couples feel masturbation enhances their sex lives together, either directly or as part of a highly diversified and liberal range of activities:

WIFE: "Sometimes. Sometimes to enhance sexual activity with partner by taking a little longer to reach climax.
"To be admired by someone famous."

HUSBAND: "Yes, to perform cunnilingus with one woman and intercourse with another."

HUSBAND: "Yes. Emotional, sexual relief. Wife engaged in sexual activities with animals."

This wife says her husband is irresponsible, takes her for granted, and has engaged in group sex, mate-swapping and homosexual activities. Says she has sex with him less than once a month. He says their marriage is a failure, and married only because his wife was pregnant. Feels sexually unsatisfied, and masturbates 5 or 6 times a week. Cheated with 3 other women, and claims that his wife has physically abused him. She's between 41 and 50, a homemaker. He's in same age range, in management. No children.

HUSBAND: "Yes. Thinking of Donald Duck walking in the nude in a tight jumpsuit while waiting for a bus (#B6)."

The gentleman who speaks of Donald Duck is obviously jesting, but one actually encounters weirder masturbatory fantasies than that in psychiatric practice. One psychotic young man went through a period of "piscatomania," in which thoughts and images of fish aroused him, and "marsupialomania," in which he found kangaroos, wombats, and other pouched creatures erotic. In healthier periods, his fantasies would shift toward human females, though usually ones who were considerably older than he, or of different races. He had never been involved with an actual woman, and his fantasies could not even deal with likely partners, becoming progressively closer to or removed from an appropriate object depending on his state of mental health. We see this tendency in the fetishists, the most bizarre of which is the small group that is "into rubber" and prefers images of women encased in bulky rubber outfits and hoods that completely disguise the body shape and features, even the gender, of the object; those who are turned on by leather again displace the soft, yielding flesh of a real woman to an unnatural substitute, and those who need nylon hose and silk lingerie are even more common and less bizarre, though still engaging in fantasies of displacement.

Female fantasies, whether or not associated with masturbation, deal not primarily with purely physical aspects of sex, but rather the personality of the partner, who is often a celebrity or some other distinguished person. The fantasy has a romantic quality, with strong Oedipal overtones, since the woman views herself as a passive object of desire, overwhelmed by this exceptional man:

WIFE: "Yes. My husband is away for two weeks at a time and this releases a good deal of tension. Woody Allen will sweep me away on a schooner to the South Pacific.

"Can you arrange it? I'll settle for Carl Sagan."

WIFE: "Yes. I only have an orgasm when I masturbate, but it is lacking in the loving closeness of sexual activity with my husband.

"Yes I have fantasies. Hundreds. Mostly I am in a passive position with some professional person and that I am still a virgin. (Sometimes homosexual fantasies.) Professional persons could be teachers, psychiatrists, doctors, nurses, etc."

While sex is generally dull, her marriage is a loving one, according to this homemaker, between 18 and 30, who has a postgraduate degree. She says she lived together with her husband for over a year before they married.

WIFE: "Very rarely. Almost none.

"Very rarely fantasize—used to fantasize about being 'helpless woman.' It wasn't a rape fantasy. More like 'swept off my feet' thing or 'I'm not responsible for having sex.' I guess it was in reaction to puritan or guilt feelings about sex."

Among the women who did not say they masturbated, some were satisfied, but others had unfulfilled longings:

WIFE: "Nope, I can't tickle myself either. May help others but there's no reason for me to. I'm not frustrated.

"Never had erotic fantasies. I'm a realist."

WIFE: "No I never have. My one sexual fantasy right now is making very tender love to my husband when he is released from prison."

WIFE: "The only fantasy I have is imagining that my husband is larger (has a larger erection) than he is. More sexually satisfying. And fantasies about oral sex and how it would feel."

She married for love—and regular sex, which she has once a week, and says it's "satisfactory." A homemaker between 41 and 50.

WIFE: "No. I sometimes fantasize about having an affair with another man or being with two men at the same time."

Not all housewives spend all their time doing housework and watching soap operas, as these ladies indicate. Some find gratification they rarely achieve with their husbands, but others feel they are constantly discovering new material they can bring to the marital act through their undress rehearsals.

WIFE: "Yes. I guess because I reach orgasm, and I don't usually during intercourse."

This wife is a blue collar worker (18 to 30) who feels that her sex life is good and her marriage is a loving one.

WIFE: "Yes, reduces sexual tensions I feel when he works long hours and is too exhausted. I get immediate satisfaction as opposed to intercourse when I do not always get it.
"None."

A homemaker, 18 to 30, with some college education. They lived together for 6 months to a year before marriage. They have intercourse twice a week, and she describes their sex life as variable, and the marriage as generally stable.

WIFE: "Yes. I am able to explore my body to discover places that feel good and then when we are together I can communicate these things to my husband during foreplay. Plus it feels so good and is a means of immediate gratification when my husband is not home."

She's a blue collar worker between 18 and 30, with a college education. They have no children, and lived together for over a year before getting married. They use mechanical aids in their lovemaking, and she says their sex life is very good (they have intercourse twice a week). Their major problem is conflicts over relatives.

WIFE: "Yes, I'm very horny. The afternoons I like to be alone and enjoy getting to know myself and what feels good to me. I think it's very important to know what turns you on. No erotic fantasies. Sometimes I enjoy thinking of other men."

She's a professional and a college graduate, 31 to 40. They have no children, and lived together over a year before marrying. She admits to having cheated briefly with one person. They have intercourse 3 or 4 times per week, and she says their sex life is good. They use drugs in their lovemaking. She says she masturbates alone once a month, approximately.

WIFE: "Sometimes. It is a purely selfish activity and makes it easier to be considerate of him when we are together. No particular fantasies, but would like to have sex in a pool which is strange because I'm afraid of water."

Men's sexual fantasies, unlike women's, are rarely romantic; they tend to be about unconventional or forbidden acts with highly attractive but impersonal women. Masturbation, like the fantasies, tends to be straightforward and devoid of complex motives. It's quick, easy, and unemotional.

HUSBAND: "Yes. I don't have to please anyone but myself—less work. I have a variety of fantasies. One of the main ones is imagining I am at a massage parlor. Others often take the form of my visualizing sexual opportunities (with others) I 'passed up' before my marriage, and going through with them. The lure of the 'massage parlor fantasy' is that it is purely sexual and involves no emotions or commitments; I don't feel very guilty."

Among the men who do not masturbate, not all were conservative in their sex lives; people with a variety of partners are rarely alone long enough to feel the need. And even those who do not masturbate can still have some highly unconventional fantasies:

HUSBAND: "I never masturbate alone anymore."

This college graduate who is a professional says he cheated—but with his wife's consent and knowledge. He's into homosexual activity, mate swapping and group sex. Yet he says his sex life with spouse is satisfying. However, he feels dominated by his wife, taken for granted, and says the marriage is in constant turmoil. He's between 31 and 40.

HUSBAND: "No. Spouse having cunnilingus and analingus (sic) performed on her by two (2) females."

Though he's only between 31 and 40, this college graduate says he only has sex once a month. Yet he's into using mechanical aids, and has anal sex. Describes his sex life as "very good," and himself as methodical, while he believes his wife is anxious. Works in management.

For some husbands, masturbation was the only sexual activity they were now engaging in:

HUSBAND: "Yes. Sexual outlet since there is no present sexual relationship with wife."

A professional (41 to 50) with a postgraduate degree, he says that mental illness is their main problem. Says they've been separated, and while his wife appreciates him, she doesn't really love him.

HUSBAND: "Masturbate in shower. Doesn't take as long as making love to my wife. No fantasies."

He's retired, 51 or over. This is his second marriage, and says they no longer have sex. Believes that his wife wishes that they'd never gotten married. He feels tied down and trapped.

HUSBAND: "Yes. It is a quick way of getting some physical satisfaction. I would love a woman who was totally interested in sex."

Some husbands masturbated because of dissatisfaction with their wives, and their fantasies often seemed an attempt to compensate for their wives' shortcomings:

HUSBAND: "Yes, sometimes just don't feel up to the effort needed to warm spouse and complete to her satisfaction. Too many fantasies to list."

He feels their marriage is a stable one, yet admits to feelings of being tied down—and trapped. Says he has sex 3 or 4 times a week, and he's between 41 and 50. While he says sex is very good at home, he admits to cheating with 2 or 3 other women, briefly. He works in the technical field, and has some college education.

HUSBAND: "Yes, since my wife had our child it's not as good with my partner. No, I don't have any fantasies."

HUSBAND: "Yes. Women with large breasts turn me on as my wife is of small size.

He's a professional, 51 or over, with a college education. They lived together for 6 months to a year before getting married. They have sex once a week, which he says is generally dull, though he has never cheated. He says their marriage is always stable.

HUSBAND: "Yes I masturbate alone; my most erotic fantasy is for a girl with medium size breasts; long brown hair; tall; large brown eyes to seduce me (behind my wife's back)."

The fact that a husband fantasizes about other women does not necessarily mean he considers his marital sex life unsatisfactory. Many are quick to admit that nothing compares with sex with their wives and some even include their wives in the fantasy world, a realm which is rarely monogamous:

HUSBAND: "Yes. It releases an overabundance of sexual desire. Yes, of my wife or any other attractive women performing fellatio on me."

This husband says he never has fellatio with wife, and describes his sex life as "variable," having sex twice a week. Feels trapped, and says they've been separated. Has cheated with another woman, briefly. Some college education, between 18 and 30, works in technical field.

HUSBAND: "Yes, relief from frustration.
"Yes, having a harem."

HUSBAND: "Yes, I do. It serves no purpose, I just do it when I feel like it. It definitely does not compare with sex with my wife. One fantasy—extremely large women—six feet tall at least."

How does a wife hope to measure up to a woman over six feet tall? Or a husband to a movie star on a schooner to the South Pacific? But what is the point of competing with these specters of childhood days, a time when heroes towered on a silver screen and the women who nurtured us beamed down on our upturned faces? "Can one love a god?" scoffed Shaw's Cleopatra, long after Aristotle had answered her question: "when one party is removed to a great distance, as God is, the friendship ceases. This is in fact the origin of the question whether friends really wish for their friends the greatest goods, e.g., that of being gods; since in that case their friends will no longer be friends to them." We fantasize about the ideal, but we love the real.

4

Two Are One:

The Marriage Relationship

> . . . when two people are under the influence of the most violent,
> most insane, most delusive, and most transient of passions,
> they are required to swear that they will remain in that excited,
> abnormal, and exhausting condition continuously until death
> do them part.

> —*George Bernard Shaw*, GETTING MARRIED, PREFACE

"We've made a drastic decision," she announces as they enter the therapist's office. "I want to move to New Jersey and get a job."

It's been almost a year since Barbara, a 29-year-old registered nurse, entered the office for the first time, opening the session with, "I have a sex problem." The decision she now refers to is "drastic" because she means that only she and their son are moving; it is an acknowledgment that the year-long efforts to save the marriage through therapy, communication, and trial separation have failed.

Her initial complaint was that the tenderness had gone out of their sex lives. He was more interested in sexual variations than coitus and love had been replaced by a *Playboy* philosophy of new techniques to heighten arousal and orgasm. Barbara admitted that his changes of pace often did fan her dying libidinal flames, but that didn't mean she wanted him to persist in them at the cost of the old warmth and gentleness. But the problems extended far behind the bedroom, as she herself was forced to concede when describing a recent lovemaking session during which she begged him to "just finish." When he protested, "But I want you to enjoy yourself, too," she snapped, "I don't want to enjoy myself!"

Gino, her husband, was 10 years older than she. Barbara had met him while still a teenager, a college drop-out trying to recover from a broken love affair. She had left the small town in Oklahoma where she had lived with her family all her life to spend several months in Italy, beguiled by her father's tales of the beauty of that land he had visited in the early 1940's, courtesy of the U.S. Army. Gino was as independent as she had been sheltered, a merchant seaman, shuttled from relative to relative in childhood, who had been on the seas from age 16. He was a tough, ambitious sailor, she an insecure drifter; they were fascinated by one another and the courtship spanned an ocean and most of continental United States, with frequent trysts in New York, the metropolis midway between their two worlds. He abandoned the seas for a job with a shipping company in the South and they were married. A few years later, they moved to New York where he acquired a maritime desk job, with rapid promotions.

But as Gino prospered, Barbara languished. She complained about their lack of friends and social life, and his preoccupation with business. She returned at every opportunity to the wheatfields and sunshine of Oklahoma and the town where every tradesman knew her by name, returning to New York with plaintive paeans that could have been orchestrated by Rodgers and Hammerstein. Gino urged her to return to college, then to get her R.N. degree and her first nursing job, and he shared the tasks with her of housework and childrearing. She became a competent though disenchanted nurse, but their relationship failed to improve. He protested that he had done everything for her except move to Oklahoma, which would be as appropriate a habitat for an Italian seaman as it would be for a tuna. "We have nothing in common," he sighs. "She's not interested in the world."

"I don't read newspapers," she concedes, testily.

"You wouldn't know if California falls into the sea," he persists. "You don't care about *anything*. Only the state of your mind."

Barbara feels he is worse; he is interested in world affairs and business, but no longer cares for love, family, and friendship. They have tried to seek out individual pastimes and friendships, and Barbara's most recent foray has directly led to the final split. She chose to visit a male acquaintance in Greenwich Village, an artist recently divorced. They listened to folk singers and drank wine, and the hours slipped pleasantly away; Gino was livid when she returned late and tipsy, accusing her of sexual involvement with the man.

And, in discussing this incident, the two finally come to grips with the unspoken conflict that doomed the relationship from the start, Gino's inability to accept Barbara's premarital involvement with other men. Now he throws up to her the philosophy of the Oklahoma college student: that it was wrong to lead a man on and not come across; her candid attitude toward sex in those courtship days; her bitter feeling that, once she had lost her virginity in a drunken, anesthetized state to a man she barely knew, there was nothing left to lose.

"It's not her fault," Gino says with a sneer. "How was she to know she'd meet a Neapolitan sailor who wanted a virgin?"

"Then why did you marry *her?*" the therapist asks.

He shrugs. "There are people who marry hookers from the street."

"Not many men would fall into *that* category," the therapist says.

"Well, I'm in that category," Gino states.

Turning to Barbara before they leave, he hurls a parting shot. "You went to Italy ten years ago to find yourself. What did you find?"

"She found you," the therapist interjects.

"And *that* was a failure!" he pronounces.

It was a marriage that had, on the surface, enough strengths to succeed. Gino was industrious at work and a devoted father at home; he was not only progressive enough to encourage his wife to pursue a career, he financed it and took over many of the domestic chores that were once Barbara's exclusive province. Barbara was conscientious, introspective, and reasonably liberal in seeking to augment their bedroom pleasure. Barbara, unfortunately, expected Gino to embody *all* the strengths which she lacked, not only stability, but also sociability and creative genius, the germs of which she was developing only very slowly within herself. He, on the other hand, rejected by his own mother when she remarried, really longed for a madonna-like model of domesticity and, despite his financial contributions, basically denigrated Barbara's attempts to expand her horizons. Thus, it was a marriage between two caring, intelligent mates who related to each other not in terms of what each other wanted for themselves, but what they *should* have been. Ultimately, she came to regard his independence and stability as aloofness and stagnation, and he to regard her youthfulness and introspection as immaturity and narcissism.

So do virtues become vices: Communication becomes intrusion, affection becomes lust, concern becomes smothering, and similar interests becomes sameness and boredom. We dare not be cynical about the qualities that underlie and regulate interpersonal relationships, however; such relationships are the very basis of marriage in the Seventies. A century ago, affection, a good sex life, children, and financial security were probably more than enough to ask from any marriage. Yet, none of these things rated among the top *three* when the married people we surveyed were asked to select *two* items that were important for a good marriage. Only one in four chose strong affection and one in five mutual sexual satisfaction. The top three, rated almost identically in importance, were good communication (selected by 38 per cent), similar ideas or interests (37 per cent), and concern for one another's needs (36 per cent). If we had asked for items important to a good friendship, we might have gotten the very same answers; marriage is defined today not in terms of a particular lifestyle or set of goals, but as a relationship between two people. We would thus expect the success or failure of a marriage to be based on the state of a relationship that exists not between two lovers, sexual partners or parents but between two individuals striving to share as much as possible while maintaining individual identities.

Win or Lose

Asked to describe their marriage on the objective questionnaire, most of our married people gave positive responses, less than 2 per cent picking the most negative answer, "a failure," and under 10 per cent choosing any negative answer. An additional 28 per cent selected such ambivalent answers as "alternating periods of closeness and remoteness," "fairly loving," and "fairly stable." Only one spouse in three could claim the marriage was "always stable" or "always loving," and far more cited stability than love as the distinguishing feature of their marriage, indicating a triumph of pragmatism over romanticism.

If you consider your marriage successful, what are the reasons for its success? If not, what has prevented its success?

Good communication was a far more pressing concern of wives than husbands, 46 per cent of women against 30 per cent for men, husbands giving a slight edge to concern for the spouse's needs. Perhaps this stems from the isolation of many housewives from the world at large, which compels a certain degree of vicarious living through the husband's broader range of experience. This is incomprehensible to many husbands, who find their daily occupation as humdrum as the discontented housewife's, and they are baffled by the frequently wailed "you never talk to me!" Successful husbands keep lines of communication open:

WIFE: "Love.
"Communication.
"Trust."

HUSBAND: "It is successful because we love each other, communicate very well and have a great sex life."

This young couple (18 to 30) say they would definitely marry each other again. They both agree that sex is very good, that marriage is a strong commitment, and have never considered divorce. He's a white collar worker, she's into technical work.

WIFE: "We talk about everything. Our friends we pick together so they're not his or mine to complain about. We've gotten away from our old friends who were a problem when we first married."

HUSBAND: "Very open communications.

"Lots of love.

"A mutual desire to make a good life and happy marriage for ourselves."

"A man's friendships are, like his will, invalidated by marriage," observed Samuel Butler. As the couple above indicates, the widely held ideal of similar ideas and interests is generally extended to the sharing of friends, which often means those who do not meet the spouse's tastes must be jettisoned. But what of individual freedom, including the choice of friends—is this also not a goal of modern marriage? Actually, throughout the sample, individual freedom does not rate very highly as important in a good marriage, only about one person in nine choosing it. Those under 30 picked it in 15 percent of the responses, more than twice as often as the oldest group, but the youngsters trailed the oldest respondents by only 5 per cent in the selection of similar ideas or interests. Loyalty to one another, doing everything together, and sacrifice in the name of love are the prevailing guidelines where you don't have to know how to be your own best friend when you have a spouse to be it for you.

WIFE: "It is successful because we share love for and loyalty to each other. Our goals are also the same. So our efforts to better ourselves are generally understood by both partners."

HUSBAND: "Social and religious background of spouse and myself. Common goals and ideals, children, security and financial stability have all contributed to my successful marriage."

This wife feels her husband is a workaholic, but both husband and wife describe their marriage as a loving one. She's religious, he isn't. Both married between 21 and 24. They have two children. He has a postgraduate education, and works in the professional field. Between 18 and 30.

WIFE: "I think that we both have matured over 25 years OF MARRIAGE. My husband is a very considerate person and he puts my welfare and that of our children above his own.

He depends on me for moral support and considers my opinions very important to him. We do share the same interests and have a strong religious-oriented family."

HUSBAND: "(a) We do everything together.
   "(b) We rely completely on each other.
   "(c) We love children and have six.
   "(d) We plan to do things as a family.
   "(e) We have similar education, background, interest and work together.
   "(f) We try to accommodate each other."

The wife is between 41 and 50, a college graduate and a home-maker. He's 51 or over, a professional with a postgraduate degree, earning between $25-$49,999 a year. She believes that sex is very good. They both feel that marriage is a lifelong commitment, and would definitely marry each other again. Both are religious.

For those willing to accept its authority, the Bible has settled more arguments than Aristotle and the *Guinness Book of World Records* combined:

WIFE: "I consider it successful. I would say it is because of an effort on the part of both of us to understand and meet the needs of each other. For the most part, we have both adhered to Biblical standards and teachings regarding marriage and this has helped very much."

HUSBAND: "Finding a person with the same religious commitments and goals as myself."

This couple believes that marriage is a lifetime commitment, and both agree that sex is good. They have more than 4 children. She's a homemaker, 31 to 40, and a college graduate. He's in the same age range, has a postgraduate education, and works as a professional.

WIFE: "Mutual love and concern and our religious beliefs help keep us in our respective places."

HUSBAND: "Successful—adhering to Bible standards concerning relative positions and duties."

"Let wives be subject to their husbands as to the Lord; because a husband is head of the wife, just as Christ is head of the Church, being himself savior of the body. But just as the Church is subject to Christ, so also let wives be to their husbands in all things."—Ephesians, ch. 5, v. 21-24.

This is the last word in the Bible on relative positions and duties of spouses, coming from the prolific and celibate apostle, St. Paul; he admonishes the husbands to love their wives, a relatively easy duty towards one who is subject to you in all things. Of course, many a modern woman will cite scripture to her own purpose and respond: "This is a hard saying. Who can listen to it?" (John, ch. 6, v. 61)

Twice as many of those with firm religious beliefs rated their marriages as "always stable," compared with the non-religious, though the percentages relating to the "loving" quality of the relationship were about the same for the two groups. The religious group gave a higher rating to similar ideas and interests, and placed less emphasis on individual freedom and mutual sexual satisfaction.

Not all successful marriages have been free from crises:

WIFE: "Generally yes, it is successful, but we have reached some mid-life problems which have been hard on both of us. We are in counseling and hope to overcome our problems."

HUSBAND: "Alcohol in recent years has affected us greatly. I feel she has a problem. If we can solve, a successful marriage should resume."

They've physically assaulted each other during arguments about alcohol. Both are 51 or over, and feel sex is still good. Family income is over $50,000 a year. He's a professional, college graduate. She has some college background.

WIFE: "Numerous problems have arisen—high and constant rise in cost of living (drastic financial problems in last seven years).
"Long sickness and death of mother was a real strain on everyone.
"Husband's affair and constant attention to other women."

HUSBAND: "Yes, love and children, home life, outside activities."

Some marriages survive crises better than others. The chronic shortages seem to plague unsuccessful marriages worse than acute traumas; among deficits cited were lack of communication, lack of attention, and lack of money:

WIFE: "(1) Lack of communication or the inability to verbalize hostilities.

"(2) Overdependent parents—the feeling that we must take care of our own folks.

"(3) The fear of overextending ourselves financially and therefore remaining stagnant. For example, not moving when you are not happy in your current apartment."

HUSBAND: "Not successful. Wife and I have seemed to grow apart. Differences of opinion on our future lifestyle seem to have taken over now."

She feels that sex is "variable" while he says they rarely ever engage in intercourse. Both husband and wife agree that their marriage alternates between very remote and very close periods.

WIFE: "I have mixed feelings. My husband was always shy with women and seems now to sort of be 'feeling his oats,' about sex. He could have sex every night or more, and is always staring at and saying things about other women's figures—usually lots younger women—which makes me feel that I'm not sexy or attractive or young enough to please him. And that's what we argue most about. So I don't know if I really feel it is successful. Maybe he will want to replace me with a new younger model. I guess I don't feel nearly as emotionally secure as I really would like to be."

HUSBAND: "I like my wife's affection—she is outgoing, too. Don't like it when she likes some guy making a play for her.

"Things would be better if she wanted sex as much as I do—I mean, as often. Also would like lots more fellatio."

This husband says he cheated—but with his wife's knowledge and consent. They've had a period of separation, and both say sex is "variable." This is her second marriage, his first. He's a white collar worker between 41 and 50, she's also in the same age range and same field.

WIFE: "In the beginning my frustrations were his not helping me around the house since I also hold a full-time job. He rarely helped. I felt more frustrated as time went on. I would initiate discussions about our problems, how I felt, but he did not want to discuss it. He did not want a marriage counselor because according to him we could work it out—but he still did not discuss things with me. Eventually I found my own friends, fun, etc."

HUSBAND: "Disinterest of spouse in my life."

Concern for one another's needs was a higher priority of women and of couples with children. Whereas deferring to husbands and children comes relatively easily, the individual needs and moods of wives may be neglected in the midst of their seemingly unwavering routine. Wives who considered their marriages successful often cited their mate's sensitivity as an important factor:

WIFE: "Understand each other's needs and their different moods, and adjusting to them. Also learning to give of yourself and your time to your spouse."

This is her second marriage, and she now feels appreciated and loved. Though she believes the marriage is a stable one, she said it does alternate between periods of remoteness and closeness. A homemaker, she's between 41 and 50.

WIFE: "My husband and I love each other, we respect each other's feelings and privacy. Neither of us is petty or jealous of time spent at our jobs. We believe our marriage to be a fifty-fifty partnership in all ways."

Respect for privacy, if only the acknowledgment that there will always be spheres of the spouse's existence with which the partner can never be familiar, can spare a marriage considerable strain. Our romantic idealism insists that husbands and wives share their lives, when most share little more than meals, beds, and children; as far as their work is concerned, a man's clerk or business associate, a woman's neighbor or car-pool sharer know more than the spouse. With more wives now employed in paid jobs, the private worlds of the married are expanding, not converging. Whereas the reproduction and raising of children was once tacitly accepted as the sole area shared by the intersecting household and business spheres, the new concepts of marriage seek to change mutually attracted strangers into companions by promoting togetherness to the maximum possible degree. Increased involvement by husbands in domestic chores and child-raising have diminished the isolation of the old "woman's world," but the attempt to recreate the important realm of one's work through verbal communication would tax the narrative powers of a Homer. Some successful couples maintain the illusion of "sharing everything," but a more realistic successful approach seems to be admitting that large portions of one another's existence will forever lie outside the direct experience of the spouse without adversely affecting the hours and experiences that can be truly shared.

In this age of television satellites, transoceanic conference calls, and telephones that can transmit printed documents, it is not surprising that communication should be deemed the most important factor in a successful marriage; however, there must be good feelings to communicate—otherwise, the marriage is nothing but bad news:

WIFE: "Communication, mutual physical attraction, mature attitude, honesty, love for our children, intelligence and I guess that old 'chemistry' we all talk about when we can't think of anything more explanatory."

She's a high school graduate, and works in the technical field. Believes her marriage is a stable one.

WIFE: "We loved each other enough to overcome a lot of problems this survey doesn't touch on; and the first years we fought a lot and I frequently felt trapped. Now we have grown much closer and have learned to lean on each other and face things together. Our troubles are from outside our marriage and we are slowly making progress on them."

When the lady above says that their troubles are from "outside our marriage," she may be referring to emotional problems that developed prior to or independently of the marriage, or to situations, such as with relatives, that have nothing to do with the spouses' interpersonal relationship. In any case, many couples tend to blame the marriage for problems that would have existed even if they had remained single. The psychological climate of our times preaches the doctrine of est: "You are responsible for everything that happens to you," and the message is echoed by best-sellers such as *Looking Out for Number One* and *Pulling Your Own Strings,* which imply that, with a little self-determination, you can shape your own destiny. The pleasant notion that all marriages have problems and successful marriages merely deal with them better has been disproven by sociological research studies which show, not surprisingly, that unhappy marriages have more and different problems compared with happy ones. Some of these problems do arise from poor mate selection, which might have once been under conscious control, but more, such as in-law relationships, financial hardships, and adverse working conditions, are externally imposed and are better endured than solved. Married couples would do well to recall the prayer recited by Alcoholics Anonymous members: "Lord, give me the grace to change the things I can, the patience to endure those I cannot, and the wisdom to know the difference."

Some couples are too dissimilar in their tastes and personalities, others are too much alike. Some wives want their husbands to change, some husbands want wives to change, and some want to try a change of partners:

WIFE: "In my situation, I seem to be the one who is the man of the house. I am a lady and wanted to be treated like one. I'm the one who is responsible for paying all the bills with my money. I'm responsible for keeping my husband's ego built up. I'm not saying I want to keep my paycheck to myself. I just want to at least be treated fair. I also don't want to be pushed into encouraging my husband. When I feel he's down I try my best to encourage him but he's spoiled rotten and doesn't want to encourage me when I'm down. He always wants to take and take but never give."

This white collar worker says her marriage is a failure, and her husband is irresponsible. Admits to cheating with 2 or 3 other men. She's between 18 and 30, and didn't complete high school.

WIFE: "My marriage is not a success because my husband would like for me to change my ways and that is very hard to do."

This homemaker believes that marriage hasn't changed her for the better—or worse. She does, however, consider the marriage to be a failure. Says they argue mostly over relatives. She's between 41 and 50.

WIFE: "We have a basic desire to keep the marriage together. We are seeing a therapist at this time. Our personalities are too similar—impatient = intolerant."

This homemaker says she got married because of pressure from others (parents or peers). While she believes her marriage is fairly stable she says sex is unsatisfying. Her worst crisis was the actions of her children. A college graduate, she's between 31 and 40.

WIFE: "Lack of communication biggest factor. I'm open, my husband isn't. For ten years I talked openly and hurt him—for ten years he withheld feelings of contempt or whatever until between me and the pressures of his job and problem with girls from his previous marriage he changed and began to prowl."

WIFE: "My husband's affair with another woman."

Alderman Collins says of his communication with his wife, "I'm that fond of my old Matilda that I never tell her anything at all for fear of hurting her feelings. You see, she's such an out-and-out wife and mother that she's hardly a responsible human being out of her house, except when she's marketing."

Some of our husbands, however, were not as guarded in their communication and found other ways of showing their fondness:

HUSBAND: "Ability to talk to spouse openly and honestly about any subject regardless of how intimate or potentially embarrassing. Very similar personalities. Enjoy being in her company and talking to her. Never allowing any argument to start."

He's a professional between 41 and 50. He says their sex life is very good, that they never argue, share all decisions, and have no major problems in their marriage.

HUSBAND: "Making your spouse Number 1 instead of yourself and receiving the same attitude from her."

This spouse says in-law interference was the worst crisis he's experienced to date. Between 31 and 40, with some college, he works in management.

HUSBAND: "Yes I consider my marriage successful. The reason for it is that we work together both for our financial security and we have give and take with our personal life habits. We have grown and matured together and we are considerate of each other's feelings."

Some husbands heeded the admonition of poet Kahlil Gibran, who exhorted, "Let there be spaces in your togetherness," and encouraged their wives' independence. Others saw the wives' total commitment to them and the family as the secret of success:

HUSBAND: "Basically we learned to respect each other's talents and interests, gave each other 'room to grow,' and encouraged excellence in whatever area of endeavor. Sensitivity to each other's deeper bond. In such freedom, we found strength in each other."

This husband has a postgraduate degree, works in the professional field, and is between 31 and 40. While he rates his marriage as being "always loving," he says sexual dissatisfaction is his major problem.

HUSBAND: "It is a successful marriage because my wife has committed herself to her family, home and husband."

Marriage alleviates hardship for some and brings it to others.

HUSBAND: "An old and wealthy bachelor marrying a lonely widow with three children and owing debts."

He's retired now, and is 51 or over. He married for the first time at 40. Says his wife has principal control of money matters, and his worst crisis was over alcohol. He's a college graduate.

HUSBAND: "Everything seems to have worked out OK. In-law problem (my mother) has been only real problem. It would be better if I made more money."

A professional, 41 to 50, he says their sex life is satisfactory and the marriage is generally stable.

HUSBAND: "We don't believe in divorce. We are stuck together because of our children."

HUSBAND: "We enjoy doing things together. We do things for and with each other even when it isn't what we would choose to do at the time.

"We love each other for what we are. We love God."

Under the Yoke

When speakers wish to wax poetic about marital happiness they are apt to invoke the overemployed term "conjugal bliss." "Conjugal" means "marital," and if we consider the origin of the word we are less likely to associate it automatically with bliss. It is derived from two Latin words, *con* (with) and *jugum* (yoke). Yokes are wooden devices used to join two draft animals, usually oxen, by the necks for the purpose of their working more effectively together. A yoke insured that each of the team was pulling in exactly the same direction rather than dissipating some of the joint energy in independent action. A yoke was a burdensome and unpleasant contraption, a symbol of domination often placed on the necks of vanquished enemies.

The yoke was a fitting image for marriage in times when the social institution was oriented towards achievement and production, rather than personal companionship and pleasure as now. Yet, consider the answer of the last respondent quoted—"We do things for and with each other even when it isn't what we would choose to do at the time"—and we see that the symbol is no less valid today. We somehow idealize marriage by believing that both spouses will be able to do and get what they want most of the time, when at best, each can get one's way half the time without undue advantage. The idea that two compatible people will have the same desires is a denial of human individuality; even Barnum's Siamese twins, possessing identical genetic makeups and having shared every moment of experience since birth, had to work out compromises whereby one would subjugate (another word derived from *jugum*) his will to the other.

Democracy may flourish under a two-party system, but it cannot work for a party of two. Democracy implies the will of the majority, but where two people are involved, there can be no majority unless one of two conditions prevail: the decision is unanimous, or one abstains in the voting. When parties pull in completely opposite directions, the net movement is not in a direction somewhere in the middle, but, as in a tug-o'-war, in either of the two directions; when a couple is faced with an either/or choice, such as "we're going there" versus "we're not going there," no compromise is possible regarding the visit's being made or not made. One spouse must give in—in effect, abstain from decision-making since a true change of heart is unlikely. Compromises, such as "next time, we'll do what *you* want," merely involve the other partner's waiving his vote on the next issue of contention. When choices are more complex and partners are less adamant on preferences, the forces incline away from one another, rather than being diametrically opposed. Hence, when the husband prefers the city and the wife prefers the country, they will invariably wind up in the suburbs, which has neither the cultural attractions of the city nor the natural purity of the country, so that no one is satisfied.

Professor Henry Higgins, Shaw's confirmed old bachelor, explains, ". . . the woman wants to live her own life; and the man wants to live his; and each tries to drag the other on to the wrong track. One wants to go north and the other south; and the result is that both have to go east, though they both hate the east wind." Lerner and Loewe's opinion notwithstanding, Higgins remains unmarried and doing just what he pleases, while Eliza Doolittle, having both the curbside toughness needed to survive the streets and the drawing-room *savoir faire* for the more challenging arena of high society, wisely elects to marry the spineless Freddie Eynesford-Hill who will always defer to her. The notion that two ambitious, determined people can actively pursue their goals in a common effort is a widespread fallacy devoutly espoused by both the unmarried and the married. Where such relationships work, it is because the partners have the good sense to keep out of one another's way when one of them has a strong need. No team in harness has ever surpassed an unencumbered creature running on its own as far as reaching an objective in the shortest possible time. Our concept of "similar ideas and interests" generally means no more than a taste for similar sorts of recreation or agreement on the spending of money (interest in which is so universal that it can scarcely be considered grounds for marriage).

One of the biggest problems in modern marital relationships is the couple's unrealistic notion that all decisions will be made together. At best, what will happen is that fewer decisions will be made without consulting the partner; but consultation can lead only to unanimous agreement, in which case no consultation was really necessary, or the discovery that the partner is in disagreement, in which case someone will be disappointed. When husband and wife had their own spheres to govern, there was greater harmony because there was far less opportunity for dissension. Granted, the modern way is more considerate and more democratic, but it is not smoother. Nothing runs more smoothly than an absolute dictatorship. The danger is in couples' perceiving that something is seriously wrong with their relationship because they are disagreeing with each other so often, when this dissension is merely a natural outcome of the communication we have lately been so highly extolling.

There remain, in the modern marriage, areas which tend to be delegated to the authority of one partner. Our survey showed that more than half of the men relegated principal control of the home and furnishings to the wife, whereas more than 40 per cent of the wives said the husband had principal control over business and career choices. Thirteen per cent of the wives felt their husbands essentially controlled sexual activity, although 6 per cent of the men said the wife was in charge. The family car was assumed to be the property of the husband in 30 per cent of the cases.

Note that where neither partner was said to have "principal control" it is likely that decisions are essentially shared on a daily or intermittent basis. Money was an interesting area because significant percentages of both sexes indicated that the spouse had principal control—wives ceding it to husbands in 37 per cent of the cases, but having control, according to husbands, in 27 per cent. Wives made the decisions more often in raising the children and had a slight advantage in controlling friends and social life. The only area where neither husbands nor wives tended to make decisions more often was in the scarcely crucial one of vacation arrangements.

In nearly all areas, we can conclude that in at least one-third of marriages one spouse or the other has principal control, and in the most vital areas of business, the home, and money management, one spouse has control in more than half the marriages. It seems reasonable, given this data, to suspect that in the remaining marriages decisions are not made with fifty-fifty equanimity, but that one spouse, sooner or later, adds that area of conflict to his fiefdom with a measure of advice and consent from the partner.

Marriage, perhaps, should not be thought of so much as one relationship, but a group of relationships around different spheres of interest, some harmonious and cordial, some strained and conflict-ridden. The complexity of the marital relationship was exemplified by the union of a Frenchman and an Italian woman living in America. Asked what language they spoke to one another, the wife replied, "We make love in French, we fight in Italian, and we discuss money in English."

Are you rejecting me sexually because you find me unattractive or are you angry that I bounced the check? Is the budget really that fouled up, or are you picking a fight because you're too tired to make love? Communication may not be enough, if the couple is not speaking the same language.

As Time Goes By

"I came to believe that in her voice was all the music of the song, in her face all the beauty of the painting, and in her soul all the emotion of the poem," said Shaw's Don Juan, referring not to any particular woman but to whichever one he happened to be in love with. Almost everyone has known the intoxicating feeling we call being in love, the conviction that someone of the opposite sex embodies everything we could possibly want in another and with whom a love relationship would convert our dull existence into an earthly paradise. What exactly is this phenomenon? Cynics will shrug it off as a purely sexual attraction, a natural phenomenon found in all species and perceived as something more esoteric by our overdeveloped brains. Yet, most people will admit that they find *many* others sexually attractive, and, even if they go so far as to consummate a sexual relationship, they usually do not fall in love with the partner. (We exclude, of course, those who would never have a sexual relationship unless they were in love to begin with.) To think of such a powerful feeling strictly in terms of a biological urge is misleading. Children "fall in love," and Charlie Brown's appetite-destroying infatuation with the little red-haired girl or Lucy's unrequited passion for Schroeder are not parodies of precocious children in adult situations, but accurate portrayals of the broken hearts that are strewn like candy wrappers across the playgrounds and recess-yards of America. Dr. Carlfred Broderick writes in Rubin Carson's *The National Love, Sex & Marriage Test* about his research on love among grammar school children; he found that about half of these children admitted to having been in love regardless of the grade they were in. As many seventh-graders as third-graders reported this phenomenon, instead of the expected increase with age, based on more years of life experience; and they usually said the first time they had been in love was during the past year. If pressed about former "love affairs," they would scoff that those were not the "real thing" and that the current heartthrob was their "true" love.

The most terminally incurable romantic would have difficulty discovering a case of true love in the third grade, but so would even the most orthodox Freudian be hard put to explain a 9-year-old boy's pursuit of a girl in strictly sexual terms. Like a dog chasing a car, the pursuer would not know what to do with his object if he ever caught it. Love is a blend of drives—and infatuation should not so much be thought of as lacking some of these components, but rather having some of them in short supply. Rollo May lists four components of love: *libido*, the sexual drive; *eros*, the romantic passion that promotes creativity; *philia*, friendship and respect for the other; and *caritas*, a strong concern for the other's welfare. While we can say that *libido* and *eros* predominate when people first fall in love, we can certainly see evidence of all four components even in the most puerile schoolyard romance.

What happens to love in the course of a marriage? Does it grow like a tree or wither like a blossom that has served its purpose as one element in the life of a more complex organism? Do the four components flourish or decay together, or do they pursue independent development, just as the roots, stems, leaves, and flowers of a plant are not equally hardy or perennial?

Are you more or less in love with your spouse compared to when you were first married? What are the reasons for any changes?

For couples who said they were more in love than when first married, they often regarded themselves or their feelings at the initial stage of the relationship as immature, and attributed their increased love to a more responsible attitude within themselves:

WIFE: "Every year I am more in love with him. First year of marriage we had poor communication and this led to all the other problems. Now we really communicate fully and are considerate and respectful of each other. We both agree. We fall in love more each year. We have been married 11 years."

HUSBAND: "Definitely more. I have learned to respect her judgment and developed a companionship with her. I treated her much worse while we were going together and I have learned that I was immature and selfish and I now respect her more than ever and would refrain from hurting her in any way."

Both are between 31 and 40. He's a professional, she's a white collar worker. They have no children. She's religious, he isn't.

WIFE: "I'm much more in love. A more grown-up love—a respect and trust that has come after twelve and a half years. I know that I want to be the best possible person for him and I think he feels the same for me. When I got married I only thought of me—now I think of both of us."

HUSBAND: "I am more in love with her. The tremendous respect I have for her. She has gone back to work in order to help us out of a financial bind."

Both husband and wife feel loved and appreciated fully, and agree that money is their major problem. They are both between 31 and 40; while he's a college graduate, she has some college background. Both are professionals.

Love is not blind, but infatuation is, to some extent. Infatuation involves an overidealization of the loved one, and this requires blindspots where faults are concerned. Respect, on the other hand, comes from the Latin word *respicere,* which means "to look at." When one can view the other partner objectively and still hold them in high regard (from the French *regarder,* again "to look at"), love is on a firmer footing than in the days when one worshiped dream-images on cloud nine.

WIFE: "My love for my husband grows more and more each day with all the problems we face. *He always includes me in his day's activities and I him.* We have respect for one another and we let it show to our friends, parents, and working companions. Respect means a lot to both of us."

HUSBAND: "*More.* Bearing our first child. Putting up with me."

He works in management, is a college graduate. She's a homemaker. They lived together for 3 to 6 months prior to marriage, and both say they would definitely marry each other again.

WIFE: "More in love. At the time of marriage, I was in love with the idea of being in love and getting married. Luckily, I found my husband filled most of my expectations, but even so, I have learned to love him for what he is. We have learned to accept each other's faults and a less-than-perfect marriage—as all must be."

HUSBAND: "More in love. Compared to then and now I was not in love then. The change is *open communication.*"

In some marriages, unfortunately, one spouse grows to love the partner as they become better acquainted, but the other becomes disenchanted:

WIFE: "More."

HUSBAND: "Less in love. I have become irritable at her actions as in housekeeping, cleanliness, sex, lack of mental awareness or intelligence."

WIFE: "I would say more in love. When we were first married our love was rather superficial and romantic. Now, it has deepened because of mutual sharing and caring and has been strengthened by some tests of it and facing problems together."

HUSBAND: "More—because of the children we are raising together. Less—because of unwillingness of both to change personal habits."

This couple has more than 4 children. Both are between 31 and 40, and while she's a homemaker, he works in a professional capacity, having a postgraduate education. They both believe that they are appreciated as lovers, but also believe that their respective spouse feels that they need improvement in other ways. They feel that marriage is a lifelong commitment, and would definitely marry each other again.

WIFE: "Less. He had an affair that caused me to lose faith in him for a while. We did work things out and now we are happy."

HUSBAND: "More—learned more about her."

At this point both are unsure whether they would marry each other again. She says their sex life is "variable." The wife is a blue collar worker, between 18 and 30, with a high school education. He's in the same age range, also a blue collar, but didn't finish high school.

HUSBAND: "At times less, especially at paydays and bank statement time."

The components of love that increase with a marriage are those of mutual respect and a feeling of true companionship *(philia)* and a valid concern for one another's welfare *(caritas)*. Whereas libidinal arousal and erotic passion will at very best remain constant, rarely if ever will they increase. Some couples accept this as inevitable, while those who marry primarily in hopes that the initial romance and sexual attraction will increase because of the marriage commitment are doomed to disappointment. Caesar's lieutenant warns Cleopatra that she is "a bad hand at a bargain" if she is willing to swap the mature and considerate Caesar for the youthful and passionate Antony, but not all would heed such a warning:

WIFE: "Yes, still in love . . . a bit more down to earth about it after the initial fever."

HUSBAND: "More or less."

This is the second marriage for each. She feels their sex life is very good, and he says their marriage is a loving one. Both agree that money is their major problem, along with his ex-wife. Neither one has cheated or considered divorce. He has a postgraduate education, she has some college. Both are between 31 and 40, with the wife working in the white collar field, he in the professional arena.

WIFE: "Definitely less. The changes in my attitude reflect the changes in his attitude. It is hard to deeply love someone who won't carry on a normal conversation, has no opinions, and doesn't care at all about me. Husband is very reserved and in general a bore."

"A man is like a phonograph with half-a-dozen records," Shaw's Bishop Bridgenorth warns a young woman who wants to change husbands. "You soon get tired of them all; and yet you have to sit at table whilst he reels them off to every new visitor." Boredom in marriage will depend on several factors. To follow the bishop's analogy, do the partners buy any new records; are they the sort of people who go on maturing and seeking new experiences? Do they play them for one another; do they communicate their thoughts to one another, so that the spouse benefits from an exciting, changing partner? Do they share the phonograph; will they let their spouses give play to some new releases of their own?

Eros is a curious aspect of love. While sexual interest, friendship, and concern are primarily directed toward the other person, though they give us gratification in fulfillment, *eros* is experienced mostly in the self. The man in love is preoccupied with his partner, but he senses that he himself is changed; all of his sensibilities are heightened, he enjoys life more, he dares to dream more, and he becomes a poet. He can say of love, as Alice said of the *Jabberwocky* poem, "Somehow it seems to fill my head with ideas—only I don't exactly know what they are!" The influx of another person's being sets off a series of chemical reactions within us catalyzing changes that are unpredictable and, therefore, as exciting as they are new. Many of the new experiences are sexual ones, but just as many involve other areas of our personalities and are nonetheless exciting. Thus, many wives consider themselves less in love when there are no more surprises and nothing seems to change.

WIFE: "No, passion is gone. I got used to my husband, there aren't any more surprises. Life gets kind of dull sometimes."

She's only between 18 and 30, and says her sex life is generally dull. Admits to cheating with one other man for a brief period. She and her husband argue mostly about sexual problems. A college graduate, she admits her extramarital affair was her worst crisis.

WIFE: "More in some ways and less in some. More because he has stood by me in some difficult times and hasn't given me reason to doubt that he loves me. Less sometimes because I wish there were more romance between us."

WIFE: "No. Sex life is not what I thought it would be."

Some wives welcome, or at least accept, the stability that comes with close familiarity with the partner's personality and needs:

WIFE: "After years of marriage it's a little hard to say if you're 'as in love.' It's companionship, habit, and knowing one another's needs."

A white collar worker 51 or over, she says she feels taken for granted. Married to have children.

WIFE: "Different degree and kind of love because of changes in age and subsequent growth and change in values, philosophy, etc."

While this college graduate feels tied down and trapped, she still believes her marriage is a fairly loving one, and generally stable. Now between 31 and 40, she admits that her worst crisis was learning to understand the need for individual freedom.

WIFE: "Less, physically, because of changes. More intellectually and emotionally because of years of closeness and common experiences."

Familiarity is said to breed emotions other than love, and even when there is change in one or both partners, the result may be divisive. Women's new desire for independence can put the relationship on a new and more slippery footing, and men may become less responsible as wives and children mature:

WIFE: "I'm less in love with him now than when we just married. I believe it has changed mostly due to our different schedules because we don't see each other that much. Then, when we do see each other it takes a while to get back into the love aspect of it and he seems in *my way a bit*."

WIFE: "Still in love with spouse, although my attitudes toward roles of husband and wife have changed. I don't feel particularly 'duty bound' to him. I do feel as though I could make it on my own."

While this wife is now working in the professional field, she has feelings of being overwhelmed by responsibility. She and her husband argue mostly about religion, but overall she believes her marriage is a stable and loving one.

WIFE: "We are *less* in love. Reasons: poor sex life and love me, love my kids. It is hard to let a man make love when he has just run down one kid or the other. Everyone was dumb or stupid except his kids (adults—what it boils down to was jealousy of my kids—I sent my kids to college—last one is there now). It wasn't easy. He doesn't talk to any of mine today and they like him less. I invite them to dinner when he travels. My girl just got home from college and they do not speak now.

"For security's sake at 59 I stay married as everything from my other home went into this one and I like this house. He stopped saying 'I love you' two months after we were married. Last six years no sex at all."

Aristotle said, "Those who quickly show the marks of friendship to each other wish to be friends, but are not friends unless they both are lovable and know the fact; for a wish for friendship may arise quickly, but friendship does not." The ancient sage cited a more ancient proverb, that people cannot know each other till they have "eaten salt together." Salt is not pleasant in large amounts, but couples who have tasted bitter experiences and made sacrifices gain a deeper appreciation and knowledge of one another. That knowledge can even augment the sex lives that mere familiarity often depreciates.

WIFE: "More in love. Because of the death of our third child we appreciated our other children more and ourselves were drawn closer together and we understood sex more."

She married because of pressure from others (either parents, peers or partner). Says her major problem is relatives, but feels their marriage is always stable. A homemaker, between 18 and 30, with a high school education.

WIFE: "More in love daily. We've gotten to know each other better and have learned to accept each other's faults *and* good qualities. Our commitment has grown stronger because we want it to, and we both recognize the sacrifices the other has made."

WIFE: "We are more in love. We have come to know each other. We have both mellowed in our ways. We are both more tolerant of each other.
   "With years of marriage, our sex life has improved. We are not quite as reserved as at first."

They say the Eskimos have 17 different words for snow, since it is so much a part of their world. Love must have been an important part of the world of the ancient Greeks and Romans—at least one to which they gave considerable thought—since there were several distinct words for it. The Greeks spoke of *eros*, *philia*, and *agape*, the last referring to an exclusive devotion to the beloved's needs, a more spiritual form than *eros* and a more intense feeling than *philia*. The Romans gave us *libido*, *amor*, and *caritas*. In St. Paul's best-known piece of writing, his preaching of charity to the Corinthians, we have difficulty translating the subject as "love," given Paul's aversion to anything remotely sexual. But we know he is speaking of something far beyond alms-giving when he says, "And if I distribute all my goods to feed the poor, and if I deliver my body to be burned, yet do not have charity, it profits me nothing." The Latin word, *caritas*, like the Greek *agape*, means a valid concern for the welfare of others that transcends any mechanical act of giving, regardless of its generosity.

When we consider our overworked word, "love," we might protest, as Alice did to Humpty, "the question is whether you *can* make words mean so many different things." And yet, as Lewis Carroll needed the word "slithy" to encompass both "lithe" and "slimy," so does "love" as we apply it to the marriage relationship comprise all the various emotions in the old Greek and Latin words. And if the mystery and passion of *eros* strengthens *libido* in the early stages of love, the regard of *philia* and the loyalty of *agape* may take over in service of physical desire later in the relationship.

Some of the husbands pointed out that there was a change in the quality of the love relationship, perhaps no more than a shift in emphasis, but their enjoyment of sex remained constant or actually improved:

HUSBAND: "More. The emphasis on a physical relationship has lessened because of an increase in the emotional understanding of our relationship.
    "We enjoy sex, but feel it is only a small part of our marriage."

This husband is between 31 and 40, works in management, and has some college background. He says that lack of communication is the biggest problem in their marriage.

HUSBAND: "I would have to say more in love now. Earlier our love was both physical and 'spiritual'—now it has moved to a mutual love and appreciation for each other as well as efforts to satisfy each other sexually. Our sex has more meaning to each of us now than it did at the first."

A professional with a postgraduate degree, he says his wife is passive, while he is emotional. He married her because she was pregnant. Between 31 and 40.

HUSBAND: "I don't feel that I am less in love but some of the very strong, highly emotional feelings have mellowed to a more steady state."

Fruits and wines ripen and mature with the mere passage of time, but a positive effect of aging on a wife generally involves some commitment and working towards mutual goals, her husband's career, and her own development:

HUSBAND: "1. More in love than when first married and it has grown and matured each year. 2. Total commitment to purpose and common goals and the desire to have a happy and fulfilled life."

What most influenced this husband to marry his wife was their similar backgrounds and interests. He's now between 41 and 50, works in the technical field, has a high school education.

HUSBAND: "More in love, due to her increasing support of my career objectives in both moral and financial means. Also due to her willingness to have my children."

He's a college graduate, and a professional. He says he would never be tempted to cheat, yet he and his wife argue mostly over his attention to other women. Between 18 and 30.

HUSBAND: "More—because the years have shown me the developing of what originally attracted me."

Once some bureaucratic city agency established to provide services for senior citizens placed an encouraging billboard in New York subway stations proclaiming: "At 50, Gauguin was a bank clerk." Underneath this hopeful message, some unfeeling cynic printed, "At 50, Mozart was dead." Thus, not everyone improves with age, and wives are no exception:

HUSBAND: "I am probably less in love with my wife now than when we were first married, if indeed I love her at all.
    "There are several reasons for my present feelings toward my wife, some of which are:
    "1. She is constantly in a state of emotional turmoil exhibited by extreme moodiness.

"2. Due to the above [statement #1] our sex life has suffered severely.

"3. She does not trust me or believe in me as a person, nor does she have faith in my judgment.

"4. We have very little in common (outside activities, music, general interest).

"5. My wife has had an affair."

He's a professional, 18 to 30, with some college education. He says that they argue most about money, and their major problem is lack of communication. They have both considered divorce, but taken no action.

HUSBAND: "Less. Lies, unfaithfulness, continuous bitching, nothing in common."

He's a blue collar worker, 51 or over, who didn't complete high school. He has cheated with one person briefly, and says that he and his wife never or rarely have sex. His wife has struck him in arguments. He describes their marriage as fairly stable.

HUSBAND: "Less in love—many social pressures."

He cheated on his wife, and said that caused the worst crisis of his marriage. However he said if his wife would do the same he would seek a divorce immediately. Married because he wanted a homelife. A blue collar worker, between 18 and 30, who has some college education.

HUSBAND: "No. I need more sex."

Sometimes, time brings not growth or deterioration, but a new love interest—perhaps the most disruptive change of all.

HUSBAND: "Less...I wish for the one I never had. Spouse doesn't know. Third party feels the same. Loyalty to spouse, inexperience, religious beliefs and respect of self all inhibit affair."

Of Human Bondage

The discontented gentleman above who craves an affair gives us several reasons which keep him from the other woman. Are these the same forces that bind him to his spouse? Why do most couples stay together? Does love continue to make their union one of choice, or do religious beliefs, dispassionate loyalty, and timidity ultimately convert a volunteer legion of lovers into a corps of conscripts?

What are the strongest reasons for you and your spouse staying together?

It's difficult to think of a better reason for staying with someone than because you genuinely like him. Virtually all couples will say they love one another, but occasionally you find a pair who clearly indicate that there is no one on earth they could possibly be more compatible with or consider a better friend:

WIFE: "I think we like each other as people. We are both considerate and kind people. We are interested in the same things and often think alike and when we don't we have some very intelligent and mentally challenging discourses. I think we are very proud of each other."

HUSBAND: "We are very devoted and loyal to each other. We both feel that we have made a tremendous 'investment' in each other and that we are extremely well suited for each other. Emotionally, my wife and I depend on each other. I look to her in times of crisis in my life and she does the same."

Both husband and wife are professionals, with postgraduate degrees. She says she married because of sexual attraction, but he says sex is now "dull," while she terms it "satisfactory." Both are between 31 and 40.

WIFE: "Strong love for each other and a real desire to make our marriage work."

HUSBAND: "Mostly and mainly my love for her. She has made my life worthwhile and meaningful. She has been open and honest in our communication and our marriage and I treasure this as one of her greatest gifts to me, by trying to be for me she makes her love alive for me and it makes me try a little harder to be more for her today than yesterday."

In Walt Disney's *Bambi*, there is a scene in which a bounding herd of young bucks, having startled the young fawn, freeze in their tracks to make way for a majestic stag. The Prince of the Forest interrupts his haughty march long enough to cast a look at Bambi, whose mother later murmurs deferentially, "He is your father." One modern child, unawed, turned indignantly to her mother after the stag departed and demanded, "And where is *he* going?"

Children may not be the main reason, but frequently one or both partners mentioned offspring prominently in their answers:

WIFE: "I feel having been married for five years and going through two separations—things are working out because we have grown closer together and the love for our child also keeps us together. We understand each other and have learned to sit down and talk things out and tell each other how we really feel about things instead of keeping it inside."

HUSBAND: "My son."

He's much older than she (41 to 50 to her 18 to 30). He says he would definitely marry her again. They lived together for less than 3 months before they married. He's a blue collar worker; she's a homemaker.

WIFE: "The strongest reason would be that we love each other. Also we have a family of six boys ranging in age from twenty-three down to seven years and they give us much pleasure as well as good hard work in bringing them up."

HUSBAND: "a. We love one another.
"b. We have a large family.

"c. We need each other.

"d. Our whole married life has been one of family togetherness.

"e. We have high ideals both for ourselves and our children.

"f. As Catholics we are morally dedicated to supporting and sustaining each other."

He's 51 or over and says they never or rarely ever have sex. She's between 41 and 50, and says sex between them is "very good." He feels that sexual dissatisfaction is their major problem, while she says it's disagreement over their children. Yet both still feel loved and appreciated. He has a postgraduate education, she's a college graduate.

WIFE: "We love each other. We understand each other. We both love our children."

HUSBAND: "We love each other very much. Good sex. Beautiful children."

Some, like the couple quoted directly below, believed they would be together for eternity. Others felt as if they had already experienced a taste of hell, and some, if they dared, would not keep the marriage going for another day.

WIFE: "Mostly because of our mutual love for each other that is so deep. Also because of our mutual religious beliefs that we will always be together through eternity along with our two lovely children."

HUSBAND: "Our common religious belief of Christianity, and the promise of a life forever together in the hereafter according to the teachings of The Church of Jesus Christ of the Latter Day Saints (Mormon)."

They married when both were under 18 because of her pregnancy. They've had a period of separation. At this point they both feel loved and appreciated, and agree that sex is very good between them. Husband and wife are between 31 and 40, he's a college graduate, and works in management. She had a high school education.

WIFE: "I love him—twenty-five years is impossible to forget, no matter what hassles we have. I think being without him would be unbearable although sometimes with him is hell. He has a temper."

HUSBAND: "1. Property
"2. Children and parents
"3. Money."

WIFE: "He wouldn't let me go. We do not argue or fight because of his attitude. So it is useless to do it. He can become violent and make threats."

HUSBAND: "Because I feel that we both do truly love each other, and our children also."

Occasionally, one encounters a couple who can't seem to decide whether they are kept together by love or the determination to win an argument that has been going on as long as the marriage:

WIFE: "I hate the thought of raising the children by myself. I also can't stand the thought of my husband being with someone else. I enjoy doing things with him on the weekends. I don't understand why, but I am just crazy about him and I have been ever since I was 14 or 15 years old."

HUSBAND: "I feel something for her. I guess it is love deep down inside of me. She says every time we fight that she will try and change. I am boss of the house and she can't get it through her head."

Byron said that love in women was a fearsome thing, for everything on that one die is thrown. At Cupid's dice table, some wives are big winners, some appear to have lost a little of what they once had, and some have the feeling they have crapped out, but keep rolling anyway.

WIFE: "I really adore him in a way I've never loved anyone else. For the first times in my life I understand 'worshipping the ground he walked on.' Were he to die or to leave me, there would never be anyone else in my life."

WIFE: "Because we had the kind of love affair that people dream about. The kind Kahlil Gibran knew about and Elizabeth Barrett Browning. It was so easy and beautiful and although we may never completely recapture it because of pressing problems, we can have something equally as good or better than it—if that's possible. I have never been loved so much by anyone ever or so completely and that keeps me from giving up!"

Her worst crisis was alcohol and mental illness, and she has cheated briefly on her husband with 1 other man. Now feels disillusioned about romance and love. Between 31 and 40, she works in her own business, and has some college education.

WIFE: "I'm brainwashed after thirty years. He is a heart attack tyrant and has not worked for six years. He plays golf twice a week and I encourage that as he gets very little exercise. I care for him and feel responsible. We've had a tumultuous love affair and he is still jealous. I have left him several times before his attack, but wanted to come back. Couldn't get very interested in others who claimed to love and want to marry me. Deep down we love each other and more or less deserve one another. In our earlier marriage he was *all* to me and hopefully I was to him. I made a vow to myself. I'd not be the cause of a second divorce. I'd let him go now if he really wanted to leave me."

"Go to the bee, thou poet: consider her ways and be wise," the cynical Jack Tanner chides the romantic Octavius in *Man and Superman*. "If women could do without our work, and we ate their children's bread instead of making it, they would kill us as the spider kills her mate or as the bees kill the drone. And they would be right if we were good for nothing but love."

Few wives would want to become black widows, but children certainly seemed to take precedence over love for some:

WIFE: "We have three young children who need our love and support. I feel that it is important for children to grow up in a traditional family, that is, with both parents livng in the home."

While this homemaker says her marriage is always stable, she feels she lives only for her children. She has a postgraduate education, and is between 31 and 40.

WIFE: "Kids, money and his threats."

WIFE: "We love and respect each other. I came from a broken home and realize the heartbreak and trauma it has on children; wouldn't want my children to go through same experience.... that's why I don't believe in fighting in front of children.... we go for a ride or to a restaurant or somewhere alone where we can discuss our differences."

Not all couples need to get away from the children in order to communicate, but communication is important enough for some to be their prime reason for staying together:

WIFE: "The strongest reason would be that we communicate well with each other. We're able to talk things out before they get out of hand!"

She is a homemaker, 18 to 30, a high school graduate. She says that their sex life is very good and the marriage is generally stable. Their major problem is money.

WIFE: "Probably the fact that we need and depend upon each other emotionally. We have a great deal of communication."

According to Rodgers and Hammerstein's paean to femininity, *I Enjoy Being a Girl,* the joys of womanhood include thrilling to a gift of flowers, drooling over lace dresses, and talking on the telephone for hours with a pound-and-a-half of cream upon one's face. After they have been married awhile, wives have less contact with flowers and lace, but communication never seems to lose its importance. But Ma Bell is a woman and husbands rarely stick with a wife primarily for reasons of communication. They can, and do, appreciate love as much as women, as their answers indicate:

HUSBAND: "Love! Mutual caring and affection. Sharing of words, responsibility and good times. Comforting each other in bad times. I feel happiest when we're doing things together."

He is a white collar worker with a postgraduate education, 18 to 30. He says he feels overwhelmed by responsibility, but describes his marriage as always loving. He says their major problems involve jobs.

HUSBAND: "We love one another and care for each other's welfare. We've been through many things together that would have separated the average couple. In the long run each of us comes first. Been married almost 30 years. She is pretty and works and keeps the house and she wouldn't if she didn't care. I need her. We are one life and one love."

HUSBAND: "She is my life, my love, my heart, my everything. I need her."

He works in management, between 31 and 40, with a postgraduate education. Says his worst crisis was his wife leaving home.

HUSBAND: "Love one another and she's to inherit large amounts of money."

The Laconians were an ancient group of Greeks who had a reputation for not wasting words. As legend has it, a messenger came from the enemy at the gates with a note: "Surrender. If we take your city by force, we will kill every man, enslave every woman and burn the city to the ground." The Laconian general replied: "If."

To this very day, answers just as the ones below are termed laconic:

HUSBAND: "Sex."

A white collar worker between 31 and 40, he says if he would become single again, he probably would not marry.

HUSBAND: "Sex."

While this husband describes his sex life as "very good," he has become disillusioned about romance and love, and would definitely not marry if he became single again. A high school graduate, between 18 and 30, he works in the technical field.

HUSBAND: "The kids."

This husband wanted children to ensure a stable marriage. He's between 41 and 50, a blue collar worker with some college education.

HUSBAND: "Children and sex."

Some husbands believe that marriage is a union for life. Others have been in it so long, it would seem foolish not to go the rest of the way:

HUSBAND: "We've been together through thick and thin for over 25 years now, and after that long it would seem strange not to have each other."

HUSBAND: "1. Because we believe marriages are made in heaven.
    "2. Because this union is for life. What God hath brought together let no man put asunder.
    "3. Because we believe it is God's work. He instituted marriage."

It would be practically blasphemous to presume that God would permit any man to put asunder what He hath brought together, yet devout people continually express concern in this area. Human effort seems required to keep even the happiest couples together, but if God does join husbands and wives, we should be grateful He organized the solar system in the days when His creations held together better.

5

Equal but Separate:

Marriage and the Self

Marriage is to me apostasy, profanation of the sanctuary of my soul, violation of my manhood, sale of my birthright, shameful surrender, ignominious capitulation, acceptance of defeat. I shall decay like a thing that has served its purpose and is done with; I shall change from a man with a future to a man with a past. . . .

—*George Bernard Shaw*, MAN AND SUPERMAN

Carlos is handsome, prosperous, dating and bedding pretty young women regularly, and sitting in the psychiatrist's office. He feels he should be married and fathering children. He was married briefly ten years ago when he was a struggling artist; she was an attractive, unsophisticated stewardess bred in the cornbelt; what Carlos enjoyed most about the marriage were the free flights to exotic places, thanks to his wife's profession, and the free access to pursue other women, thanks to that same profession. Now, the proprietor of a successful art gallery, he meets scores of liberal,

172

cultured beauties and doesn't have to worry about his plans being grounded because a snowstorm has cancelled his wife's trans-Atlantic flight from Kennedy International Airport. What he does have to worry about is the flight of time; people tell him he looks 35, but Carlos is over 40, and he knows how much work goes into the youthful, casual look he presents—the weight-watching, the efforts to catch the last rays of the summer sun to preserve his fading tan, the stylish shirts carefully unbuttoned to reveal an amorphous amulet on a field of pectoral hair, and the graying thatch that must be carefully arranged to cover as much of his balding scalp as possible. For the past six years, among the innumerable one-night stands, there had been one chaotic but consistent relationship with a divorcee; he had proposed marriage many times, but since they could never seem to remain together more than a month without a disruptive quarrel, she had always declined. The last time he proposed, she half-heartedly accepted—and now he has broken off the relationship. "I think the final straw was her getting silicone implants that made her chest like stone and a nose-job she didn't need," he complains. "I don't feel she's even the same girl."

Carlos breaks off his discussion of the latest woman in his life, a 23-year-old who placed his hand on her crotch at dinner, only to become defensive in the more private area of his apartment, and says, "You know, when I was a kid, I honestly used to have fantasies of being a prince in a castle with a winding staircase, dancing in a ballroom with a beautiful little princess. I'm a romantic—at least, I think I am." (The therapist agrees. Women who profess to be romantics invariably turn out to be extremely practical in dealing with life's exigencies; men may deny being romantics and profess being pragmatists despite hopeless realities to the contrary, but rarely if ever will a practical man lay false claim to romanticism, such an act being romantic in itself.)

"The ones who want to marry me I find unappealing; and the ones I want to marry don't want to get serious," he says. "Do I want too much? I want a pretty face, a good figure, a bright mind, a really pleasant personality. I guess that's the acid test—my checklist. If I find a girl who has everything I want, who meets that description, and I still don't marry her, I never wanted to get married to begin with. . . . What are you thinking?" The last question, shot abruptly at the therapist, is an outgrowth of Carlos's three previous attempts at psychotherapy; when a patient is silent, therapists break the impasse by asking that provocative question.

"The shaggy dog," the therapist answers honestly. "Do you know the original shaggy dog joke? No? Well, it's interminably long, but it's basically about a king who offers a fantastic reward to whoever finds his lost shaggy dog. He assures the searchers that they can't mistake the dog because it's the most shaggy dog they could possibly imagine. So, one man undergoes incredible hardships, travelling throughout the land, discarding each dog he finds for a still shaggier one, finally returning with a dog that seems to be nothing more than a giant mop of hair. But the king looks at it in dismay and says, 'Oh, good heavens, he wasn't *that* shaggy!' You see, people can always change the description of what they think they want to find."

Carlos sighs, then brightens. "I love a *challenge*. What do the mountain climbers say? 'Because it's there.'" And Carlos departs for another assult on the mons veneris, to keep a date with a 19-year-old.

Will Carlos marry again? One's first response is likely to be that he is far too selfish; yet, if by that we mean he is concerned with his own pleasure and well-being, is he really so different from everyone else? Do people marry out of some sense of philanthropy and sacrifice, or because they believe marriage will bring them the greatest good and happiness? Very well, we concede, people today do not marry from some sense of moral obligation, saints having, as a matter of fact, an exceptional rate of celibacy; but men like Carlos are very narrow in their definitions of what is pleasant and good—they want sensual pleasure without obligations. If this were the case, Carlos should be a happy man indeed, instead of sitting in a psychiatrist's office complaining of depression. Not that he would argue at these accusations; he himself questions if he is capable of a relationship beyond a brief encounter, momentarily denying the fact that for six years his attachment to one woman, regardless of how ambivalent and stormy, drove him to extremes of anxiety and despair.

As you may have guessed, Carlos's relationship with his mother is not a particularly loving one. He has never met his father, who abandoned the family when Carlos was 2 years old; mother, the breadwinner in an extended family, sent Carlos off to various boarding schools, allowing other children to remain at home, and he has never forgiven her for that. But his emotional deprivation in childhood does not mean we can dismiss his dilemma as an artifact of a neurosis, for the unvarnished truth of the matter is that Carlos's present lifestyle offers more freedom, leeway for extravagance, and variety of sensual pleasure than marriage would. Add to this his identity as an artist, who is far more capable than most of having creative sensibilities aroused in him by encounters with young and exciting women, and we find it yet harder to picture him enmeshed in the prosaic routines of marriage.

"Maybe it's an ego thing," Carlos says, "but I want children of my own. And I'm getting older."

When the writers of the Declaration of Independence sat down two centuries ago, it was one of the few times in history that men who dealt with questions of liberty and rights really had to confront potentially serious consequences for the product of their intellectual deliberation. This was no classroom exercise in logic and ideology; the rights they would maintain to be inalienable to the nature of man would have to be defended at the cost of bloodshed, property, and even life. The trio of rights deemed essential at any cost were life, liberty, and the pursuit of happiness—all worthy goals, but among them one is paramount, to the extent that the other two are readily sacrificed to preserve it. To preserve the existence of life and the quality of life we desire, we often dispense with individual liberty and happiness, as the Continental Army conscripted men and endured the hardships of Valley Forge. Viet Nam reinforced our growing cynicism towards flag-waving, yet never before have we prattled more about the sanctity of individual freedom and the unabashed indulgence in pleasure, particularly when attempting to dissect and restructure contemporary marriage.

But when these all-American rights run at cross-purposes with the somber demands of life, we must abandon the star-spangled fantasy that all three will flourish equally and in harmony. When Carlos, the big city swinger, confronts his mortality and the fate of his unborn children, the carefree meanderings and the bedroom romps weigh light at the other end of the balance and his equilibrium sways precariously. We can no more disparage his longing for purpose and parenthood as conventional and mundane than we can denigrate his materialism and hedonism as immature and superficial; they are all aspects of Carlos, and, whatever he chooses, part of him must die with that choice. There will be self-growth, to be sure, but there must also be destruction to clear the way for change and growth. And some of what is destroyed will be sorely missed, for we cannot abandon part of our selves, no matter how dispensable, without a sense of loss.

People change within a marriage; but then people change

throughout their lives. It would not be valid to watch a snake molt at the zoo and conclude that captivity causes snakes to shed their skins. On the other hand, any change in environment is bound to affect at least the quality of a creature's life, liberty, and happiness. Our interest here is not the relationship between two partners in marriage, but the changing status of each partner as an individual. "For better, for worse" acknowledges that the vows may be constant, but little else remains so.

Matched Pairs and Odd Lots

John and Janet were 12-year-old twins. Janet was studious and compliant, but John was always on the verge of academic failure and initiated as much horseplay among his peers as the limits of their upperclass Catholic upbringings would allow.

After one particular outburst, the seventh-grade teacher, a prim young nun, exclaimed in exasperation, "John, you and Janet may be twins, but you're not at all alike!"

She suppressed a red-faced giggle and waved him into silence when he began to explain, "No, Sister. Janet's a girl and I'm a boy...."

Even Aristotle quoted the old saying, "birds of a feather flock together," but among hens and cockerels of the same species, there is bound to be some variation in their respective plumage. But is the old axiom still essentially true, or, in view of our modern regard for individuality and the erosion of class and ethnic boundaries, do people often marry spouses considerably different from themselves in temperament?

How would you describe your emotional temperament? How would you compare it with your spouse's?

Socrates was one of the wisest men who ever lived, but people may question his choice of wives. Just as Socrates is still remembered for his unemotional logic, Xantippe is immortalized by her fiery temper. Chaucer's Wife of Bath tells the tale of the time Xantippe, in one of her usual rages, emptied the chamberpot on her husband's head, whereupon the stoical old man observed, "With the thunder comes the rain."

Socrates was finally done in by accepting that one last drink, but some modern couples emulate the Socratic marriage, wherein a highly emotional wife may have her temper tempered by a more placid husband, now that indoor plumbing has removed the hazard of chamberpots.

WIFE: "I am more apt to show my emotion and feelings than my husband. However, I manage to keep a lot of my emotions from being very evident to others. Certain things such as love and concern for family, friends and neighbors, the ill and needy, affect me deeply and the emotion shows.

   "My husband keeps his emotions—except anger—well contained within himself. If grudges may be called emotion then he shows that in every way he can to the extent of making everyone aware of how he feels and it puts his friends and family in a very awkward position."

HUSBAND: "I keep my emotions under control. My wife shows every type of emotion even to becoming extremely upset and ill at times."

She's 51 or over, and says even though they never or rarely ever have sex, she still feels they have a loving marriage. He's in the same age range, and works in the technical field. She's a homemaker.

WIFE: "I'm pretty emotional—go from moody to really gay, or sexy and affectionate to feeling like my husband and I are just good buddies. He can get down from job problems or a hassle with someone he works with, or if his golf game goes bad or gets rained out—but he is really affected by my moods. If I'm in a good mood, he soon is cheered out of his bad mood—but if we both feel depressed, it's really rough. I make friends easier than he does, but when he feels like being friendly, he sometimes kind of goes overboard—I mean, is overly-friendly too soon, and makes people (and me) uncomfortable. We argue about that, too."

HUSBAND: "Without her, I'm lots more reserved. I'm very warm
    with her—and she is lots more outgoing, and doesn't need me
    as much as I need her. She is lots more excitable and moody
    than I am—I don't understand why she is—it makes for lots
    of upsets—."

Both are white collar workers between 41 and 50. Both say that
sexual dissatisfaction is their major problem, and both feel tied
down and trapped. This is her second marriage.

In America, we think that a woman's moral number is higher
than a man's, Hector Malone explains to Shaw's revolutionary,
Jack Tanner, and that "the purer nature of a woman lifts a man
right out of himself, and makes him better than he was." Tanner
retorts, "No wonder American women prefer to live in Europe!
It's more comfortable than standing all their lives on an altar to
be worshipped."

Wives are not necessarily more pure than their husbands, but
they are often the more silent partner, even if their taciturn temperament is more a product of inhibition than virtue:

WIFE: "I'm usually rather quiet, particularly in groups, although
    I express both affection and anger more readily than my spouse.
    Spouse is more outgoing, tends to draw attention to himself.
    Sometimes I'm a bit uncomfortable about this."

HUSBAND: "We are both easygoing and communicative gener-
    ally, with some areas more difficult. Both accepting of other's
    eccentricities."

She says they never argue. They lived together for 3 to 6 months
before marrying. He's had some college, is between 41 and 50,
works in management. She's a college graduate between 31
and 40, a professional.

WIFE: "Have strong emotions, but frequently find it difficult to
    express them, particularly towards other adults; somewhat freer
    with children.
        "Spouse is considerably more uninhibited—I envy him his
    greater freedom of expression but also at times find it annoying
    or embarrassing."

HUSBAND: "I am fairly levelheaded and become upset when a person does not try to do the best they can. I have a temper but have learned to control it fairly well.

"My wife in her job is levelheaded, but at home is short-tempered with children and yells at them fairly constantly when they do not do as she wishes."

In our objective question that asked spouses to describe themselves, 19 per cent selected the adjective "emotional," but men chose it far less often than women, 8 per cent versus 29 per cent of wives. Men likewise used the term "reserved" for themselves twice as often as women did. We tend to associate youth with impetuosity, and this was borne out in the self-selection of the term "emotional" by 27 per cent of the married people under 30, the percentage decreasing with age to a low of 12 per cent in those over 50.

In our subsample of 869 matched couples, 31 per cent of them both used the term "considerate" to describe one another, but rarely did the spouses select the same adjective for one another. Fourteen percent agreed on "affectionate," 9 per cent mutually selected "mature" as the prime characteristic, and 8 per cent coincided on "warm." In only 3 per cent of the couples did both call the mate "emotional." This was corroborated by the handwritten responses of wives, who usually saw themselves as high-strung and their husbands as easygoing, or the opposite. Sometimes very emotional wives found that their husbands' tranquility aggravated the situation:

WIFE: "My emotional temperament is to yell when things go wrong. His is to walk away cursing. He laughs at my yelling and that makes me madder. I'm learning to laugh at myself too!"

The worst crisis in this blue collar wife's marriage was the death of her two children and alcohol. Says lack of money and alcohol are her major problems. During arguments she and her husband have struck each other. Still she feels her marriage is fairly stable and loving. Between 41 and 50, with a high school education.

WIFE: "Due to my illness and treatment, my emotions vary greatly. My greatest fear is leaving my husband with the care of a sixteen-year-old by his first marriage. Our son is on drugs and has had several arrests. My husband denies this. He is unable to face any upsetting situations. He was adopted at six months of age after being kept in a hospital from birth. This lack of bonding as an infant has stunted him emotionally."

She feels that her worst crisis concerns their children, and says she is overwhelmed by responsibility. Describes herself as anxious, and her husband as inconsiderate. Definitely would not marry the same person again. A white collar worker between 41 and 50, with some college background.

WIFE: "Highly emotional. Lately would be considered almost unstable. Spouse very low-keyed. Never gets emotional and does not understand my emotions and being high-strung."

Some high-strung wives either found their husband in tune with them emotionally or able to key things to a lower pitch:

WIFE: "I am very emotional and ultra-sensitive. I cry more out of joy than I do out of sorrow! The littlest things make me very happy. I guess I'm somewhat insecure, I need to hear 'I love you' even though I *know* that he truly does. My husband is also quite emotional, although he doesn't show it as freely as I do. He is *extremely* sensitive to my feelings and emotions. He understands me and my emotional outbursts."

She's a white collar worker with some college education, between 18 and 30. They have no children. She describes their sex life as very good and says they have sex once a day. She describes the marriage as always stable and loving.

WIFE: "My emotions change easily and I have a very quick temper. My spouse is pretty easygoing. He's very fair in letting me make some suggestions in our life."

Though she's only between 18 and 30, this homemaker feels she lives only for her children, but thinks her marriage is loving and stable.

WIFE: "Moody at times, often convey wrong impression, not an easy person to get along with. He is easygoing and very understanding most of time, but often expresses doubt of my love for him."

She's 51 or over. A college graduate, working in management. While her marriage is stable, she says she cheated on spouse with more than 3 men, with one affair lasting over a year. Her extramarital affairs have been her worst crises.

WIFE: "I'm an emotional, sensitive person...perhaps too sensitive about myself, but have matured enough to be able to recognize this and to deal with it when these feelings arise.

"I'm very sensitive toward others also and for this I thank God—that I care for, truly feel for and love others. This is a sensitivity I try to cultivate.

"I believe my husband's temperament is similar to mine—or at least that we are both growing in the same direction. Again—Thank God."

The term most often used by our respondents to describe themselves as spouses was "considerate" (47 per cent). In Chapter 2, we saw that this was also the term most often chosen to characterize their spouses (49 per cent). Some wives saw themselves as easygoing or at least considerate enough to keep their emotions under control, but they couldn't say the same for their husbands:

WIFE: "I try harder to be agreeable, and to avoid controversy. I also cannot say things that are hurtful, because I know they cannot be unsaid. My husband lashes out as mean and as he feels like, regardless of my feelings. I am much less volatile and temperamental."

Her worst crisis was her husband's retirement. She is 51 or over. They no longer have sex, and she's sexually unsatisfied. Admits that they both have struck each other during arguments, and says her marriage is generally hostile.

WIFE: "I can control my temper unless it builds up inside of me for so long. My husband is awful. He breaks things, but he has never hit me."

WIFE: "I hold my feelings inside—when I feel neglected, I become mean or withdrawn. Inside, I could explode, what is the use. He is a disciplined man who is always either a martyr or perfect."

Perfect and disciplined men often suffer the fate of martyrs, as in the case of Savonarola, who burned up so many people that they finally returned the compliment.

Some husbands saw their wives as having definite emotional problems, whether or not the man claimed himself to be more stable:

HUSBAND: "I am stable and usually optimistic. My wife is moody and sometimes depressed."

He feels sexually unsatisfied, and says that money is the major problem in their marriage, yet still believes it is generally stable. He's a professional, 31 to 40, with a postgraduate degree.

HUSBAND: "My wife is just like a child due to her illness."

HUSBAND: "We constantly fight, always snapping at one another, but get along great in bed."

Conjugal affection has undoubtedly solved more arguments in history than binding arbitration. Next to "considerate," the term people used most to describe themselves (24 per cent) and their spouses (25 per cent) was "affectionate." High-income earners chose this term more than twice as often as the low-income group, indicating that cold cash does not necessarily inhibit warm hearts. Non-religious people saw themselves as slightly more affectionate than those with firm beliefs, the latter preferring more dispassionate terms, such as "mature" and "considerate." Blacks far less often used terms such as "affectionate" or "warm" to describe themselves, and were more likely to characterize themselves as "passive" or "dominant" than whites; note, however, that some of the discrepancies owe their magnitude to the fact that blacks more often tended to select one answer on the objective questionnaire, while whites exercised their option of checking more than one.

Men cited themselves as "mature" more often than did the women. Those husbands who were mature enough to admit they were short-tempered or otherwise unstable seemed to have shown the maturity to select wives whose personalities complemented their own:

HUSBAND: "Me—short-tempered at times—not assertive enough—really love my wife and kids.

　"She—definitely assertive, loving, good mother and wife.

　"We balance each other off pretty well."

A professional, 41 to 50, with some college education. They have more than 4 children, and the major problem in their marriage is disagreements over the children. He admits to having cheated with more than 3 people, none for over a year. They argue most about her job and career. He describes the marriage as generally loving.

HUSBAND: "Impulsive, forceful, direct, short-tempered, but quick to calm down, persistent. Not always a good listener.

　"My wife is very slow to anger, little inclined to be reserved and not share thoughts—an obvious characteristic is that she does not like to be shown wrong in an argument and won't admit it till later."

He's a professional between 41 and 50, with a postgraduate education. Rates his marriage as stable and loving, but says his major problem is over relatives. Has cheated with another woman briefly.

HUSBAND: "I worry; spouse only worries about me."

HUSBAND: "I am emotional and a bit of a 'flake' at times and a bit unpredictable. My wife is a most stable and even personality. In many ways we are opposites who compliment each other's personality."

To compliment is to express appreciation or praise; to complement is to complete something. With regard to the personality of one's spouse, it would be judicious to do both.

Going Through Changes

"I find that the moment I let a woman make friends with me, she becomes jealous, exacting, suspicious, and a damned nuisance. I find that the moment I let myself make friends with a woman, I become selfish and tyrannical," stated Professor Henry Higgins, confirmed bachelor.

If mere friendship with someone of the opposite sex could cause such deterioration of character in Higgins's mind, one can imagine the total depravity that would be wreaked by marriage. His cynical expectations are no more absurd, however, than the unbridled optimism of many who expect marriage to effect profound ennobling of the human spirit through the exchange of vows and rings. Let a man impregnate a woman outside of wedlock and he is denounced as a scoundrel and she a slut; through the miraculous remedy of marriage, he becomes a man of principle and she a decent woman.

One needs only to contemplate the vows that couples are compelled to take to appreciate how rampant is our naive belief in the magic of this rite to change basic human nature. Liberated women agitated to strike the word "obey" from the promises exacted, yet neither spouse objects to the poetic promise "to love and to cherish, till death us do part." One could realistically, if unreasonably, exact a pledge of lifelong obedience or cohabitation, but love is an emotion, not an act of volition, and we cannot account with certainty for our feelings minutes from now, let alone decades. Kind and docile people are likely to remain so after marriage, whereas bellicose and ill-tempered individuals will pass their days in quarrels. If, as the Devil explains to Dona Ana, the gulf between heaven and hell is merely the difference between the angelic and the diabolic temperament, can we hope to bridge such a gulf by means of a simple ceremony?

Yet, if like Tennyson's Ulysses, we are a part of all that we have met, then we are part of our spouses; and if our partners change, then we are part of those changes, as they are part of ours. What changes do married people perceive in themselves that they attribute to marriage? Are the changes for better or for worse—or both?

How has your marriage changed you as a person?

Only one-third of our respondents said that marriage had changed them for the worse in some way, but more than 9 out of 10 indicated that marriage had changed them for the better in some way. Thus, practically all married people feel they have undergone changes that can be directly attributed to matrimony.

"When I was a child, I spoke as a child, I felt as a child, I thought as a child. Now that I have become a man, I have put away the things of a child," writes St. Paul (Corinthians I, ch. 13, v. 11). It's difficult to think of his ever having been a child, so thoroughly has the dour apostle concealed the remnants of his frivolous boyhood. Maturity, as he reminds us, is not mere aging, but the conscious discarding of old ways of thinking and feeling. Most couples said that marriage had made them more mature through increasing the amount of responsibility they were willing and able to undertake and by making them more considerate of the feelings of others:

WIFE: "Made me more aware of my actions and marriage has given me a deeper outlook toward a future with two people rather than one. I'm not as selfish and more willing to compromise to satisfy my spouse. I'm able to budget money for necessities rather than frivolous things."

HUSBAND: "Marriage has mostly increased my sense of responsibility to spouse (i.e. protection, health, food, clothing). Also marriage has introduced new goals to me as a person, in that I plan more for the future as opposed to the now.

"Marriage has given me a sound financial and emotional base from which to grow. The togetherness that marriage promotes has increased my decision-making to the positive thus benefitting both of us, rather than just one."

She works in the white collar field, and has some college education. He's a blue collar worker, with a similar educational background. Both are between 18 and 30.

WIFE: "Made me grow into a more mature person."

HUSBAND: "It has made me more of a man. I am thirty-seven, we have been married for seven years and I have just lately grown up."

This is his fourth marriage, her first. She's a homemaker, between 18 and 30. He works in the technical field, is in the same age range, and a high school graduate.

WIFE: "I'm more sure of myself as an individual. I also feel confident in his loyalty in all circumstances, so when I take a stand on something, I know he'll stand behind me."

HUSBAND: "Marriage has allowed me to mature and enjoy life more fully by sharing with my partner."

Responsibility is not so much a course of prescribed duties, but rather a more precarious state of readiness to respond to the needs of others as they happen to arise. It is less the vital but predictable routine of the surgeon in the operating room and more the fate of the emergency room doctor who must cope with everything from splinters in the finger to massive hemorrhages. Since responsibility involves perceiving and meeting the needs of other people, it is not a matter to be taken lightly, and Plato long ago said that the trouble with democratic government was that the truly wise man felt inadequate to meet great responsibility while lesser equipped and more self-aggrandizing men sought power over others.

Marriage certainly brings responsibility; some spouses felt it had made them better people, while others just noted that it had changed their lives by entering it.

WIFE: "I'm more responsible, it's enabled me to cope with the many problems that arise in life."

HUSBAND: "It's made me more responsible and considerate."

WIFE: "Put more demands on me."

HUSBAND: "More responsible."

The two ways in which our respondents felt most often that marriage had changed them for the better were the feeling that life had more purpose and meaning (28 per cent) and that they had become better at handling responsibility (27 per cent). People under 30 most often (36 per cent) cited their improvement in handling responsibility, while those over 50 gave this a relatively low priority, possibly because years of marriage had dulled their memories of more turbulent years or maybe because they were part of a generation that learned responsibility before marriage from early employment and large families. The oldest group felt, more than any other age bracket, that they had become more considerate through marriage.

Some couples included partners who felt that marriage either had not changed them at all or had wrought changes for the worse:

WIFE: "I'm a lot more mature in some areas, involving the give and take of cohabitation."

HUSBAND: "First marriage and divorce drained me physically and mentally. After seven years still have little or no self-confidence, self-respect. Emotional problems. Present spouse is great help during stress."

He's between 41 and 50, she between 31 and 40. This is her third marriage, his second. She says they no longer have sex, he says it's "variable" having sex once a week. He has some college education, but makes less than $8,000 a year.

WIFE: "I don't feel it has changed me now. First marriage made me feel quite important but choice of mate was wrong for me and eventually gave me an inferior person.

"I am now remarried and feel very confident and quite equal to everyone. I believe I would feel this way with or without a husband. No, I don't feel my marriage has changed me as a person."

HUSBAND: "Made me a better person.

"Calmer.

"More patient.

"More tolerant."

Both never argue. He married because of pressure from others and to have children, she because of love. This is the second marriage for both of them. They are 51 or over, with high school educations.

WIFE: "I have no life of my own. He is the Boss."

HUSBAND: "Causes me to drink more. All her family fussing all the time."

While approximately one-third of our sample claimed that marriage had changed them for the worse in some way, there was no one complaint that predominated. Feeling tied down and trapped, being overwhelmed by responsibilities, and domination by the spouse were selected with frequency within a single percentage point of one another, none claimed by as many as 10 per cent of the sample. Women did not feel marriage had changed them for the worse any more than men did.

The one complaint that women made more than twice as often as the men was that marriage had made them more nervous and irritable. This lends some credence to those female skeptics who claim that so many women report they are happy with their marriages only because they equate happiness with conformity and fulfilling the role prescribed for them by society. Critics point out that single women are invariably more content and better adjusted than their married counterparts.

Is marriage hazardous to female health? Unmarried, widowed and divorced people have higher death rates at every age than the married, and while the difference is less impressive in the case of women, it is nonetheless significant; as expected, married people have a lower incidence of serious illness. What about *mental* health? Again, there is a lower rate of suicide and psychosis requiring hospitalization among the married, women as well as men.

In good conscience, however, we cannot close the case by concluding that marriage promotes mental health. For one thing, it is obvious that people with severe mental problems do not get married to begin with, or quickly wind up divorced. The same would hold true of physical illness; people with congenital or acquired chronic diseases are not generally desired as marriage partners and they themselves are unlikely to take on the burdens of marriage. Yet, though we assume married women were at least as healthy as their single sisters to begin with, studies have shown that the married ones are more sensitive, moody, indecisive, guilt-ridden, depressed, hypochondriacal, and dissatisfied with their appearance. Married women suffer more from insomnia, vertigo, anxiety, fatigue, headaches and palpitations, despite their relative lack of serious disease.

Perhaps we can draw an analogy here with Rollo May's discovery in his training years that anxiety was not related so much to environments in which youngsters suffered emotional deprivation and misery, but rather to atmospheres in which the frustrations were more subtle, but the victim was confronted with a facade of loving treatment and forbidden to acknowledge the essentially negative forces in operation. Women live in a society that tells them they should be content in their roles as mothers and homemakers, even when these roles subject them to onerous inequities and inhibit their development as persons. Such women may claim their marriages are happy and be at a loss to explain their symptoms of anxiety, depression, and physical discomfort.

The wife below, in giving us a chronology of her marriage, demonstrates how the same marriage, in its various phases, can have both salutary and detrimental effects on the psyche:

WIFE: "I'm not certain that my marriage has changed me or if the changes in my personality are attributable to the natural maturation that comes with age and increased responsibility. After the first five years of marriage, my husband changed companies and we moved out of state, away from our family and friends. It was my first experience away from my very supportive parents. (I was an only child and the oldest grandchild on both sides of the family.) This was good for me because I was really on my own for the first time in my life. When my husband had to travel for business, I could not stay with Mom and Dad; I had to stay alone. My husband never pampered me at all. In fact, I control the distribution of money, pay bills, etc. My husband believes in my capabilities and so do I.

"Having children changed me and our marriage. When my first was born, he never slept, and I felt very trapped and alone. My husband could go out to play tennis, or swim, or play cards, and I had to stay home with the baby. After the first few weeks, I had a 'discussion' with my husband during which I tearfully established the fact that we were "in this together" as it were. He got the message.

"Having kids curtailed my career. I was no longer able to work full time, and part-time jobs are few and far between and not necessarily in my line of work. While I find being a parent important and sometimes frustrating, I do not find it challenging. What's worse, nobody ever pays me for any of the jobs I do at home or tells me I'm doing a great job. Of course, having been an achiever all my life, I feel unappreciated, sometimes unloved, and often 'put-upon.' I often feel uninterested and uninteresting. Hopefully this will soon come to an end. My second and last child is approaching school age. Soon I may be gainfully employed at a job I love, and I'll be able to contribute some interesting dinner table discussion once again."

A professional, 31 to 40, a college graduate. She says that their sex life is variable. They argue most about her job and career. She says the marriage is generally stable and fairly loving.

"Are there no prisons? Are there no workhouses?" sneered Ebeneezer Scrooge one Christmas Eve. Shaw responds, "Home is the girl's prison and the woman's workhouse."

The wife above was able to assume adult responsibilities for the first time only after she had left the home of her overly supportive parents, thanks to a husband who was willing to cede areas of control despite her inexperience. The second major change in her life came with the birth of a child when the traditional male-female role division initially left her with exclusive responsibility for child care; again, her husband was flexible enough to participate in this role, once she made the demand. The third, and least resolved, crisis point is the loss of career, although she has the hope of returning soon to her former occupation, an option that would not have been available in days when women had, on the average, more than two children to raise and no career to begin with. This is a typical marriage with a husband who is probably no worse than average; it emphasizes that marriage invariably involves far more changes for a woman than for a man, since a man does not give up the work he has been doing all his life, and a woman usually does, at least for part of the time, if she has children. Homemaking and motherhood are careers in themselves, and require adaptation to an entirely new lifestyle.

An understanding husband can actually enable a wife to achieve levels of self-confidence and independence she might not have otherwise reached, as these women attest:

WIFE: "Marriage has caused me to realize my own full potential as an individual person. My partner has encouraged me to fulfill my objectives and we both have developed into strong individual people with a strong love for each other."

A professional and college graduate, 31 to 40. She says their sex life is good. They have no major problem in the marriage, which is generally stable.

WIFE: "My marriage has given me a tremendous sense of emotional security because I know there is one person in the world who is completely supportive of me. I am the most important person in his life and he is the most important person in mine.

"Because we have experienced ten years of life together, we have suffered anguish and had great joy. This has given me greater understanding of, and empathy toward my spouse. It has also enabled me to be more understanding of others.

"Being married and having a family has challenged me to cope with all the aspects of life that children and husband and running a home produce."

Her worst crisis was awaiting the arrival of an adopted child. However, she feels her marriage has no major problems, and generally it's a loving one. She's a homemaker with a post-graduate education, between the ages of 31 and 40.

WIFE: "I have a feeling of emotional security and of being loved. He has also given me more confidence in myself. Being the youngest of seven children, I was always treated as the baby, no matter how old I got. He gave me the feeling of maturity that carries over into my job and my family so that I can communicate with them better."

Jack Tanner in recalling his adolescence praises his tailor as the only person who behaved sensibly, since he took Jack's measurements anew each time he saw him, whereas everyone else went on with their old measurements and expected Jack to fit them. Spouses usually have known us only as adults and thus have a very special role in our lives as the only people who love us without subjecting us to their embarrassing recollections of our youthful foibles and failures.

Eighteen per cent of our sample said that marriage had made them more considerate people. Perhaps it is due to the narcissism of the current generation or just the effect of gradual maturity, but this response was selected progressively more often by older people and was higher among those who had remarried.

WIFE: "Instead of thinking about myself all the time and how I come first, I feel that now I think about my husband first and my children. I used to be the type of person that kept their problems inside of them. Now, I feel more open about how I feel and the problems I feel."

While she feels sex is very good, and her marriage stable and loving, she also feels tied down and trapped, and says that marriage has made her more nervous and irritable. Also believes her husband dominates her. A professional, she's between 31 and 40, with some college background.

WIFE: "I don't feel marriage basically changes anyone. However, I do try to control my dominant nature—try to be more considerate. I am reading *The Total Woman,* and am, at last, following some of the advice given in the book. I do feel working (outside home) could make a difference in many of my attitudes. It would enable me to better understand what the man needs when he comes home."

Sixteen per cent of our wives attributed greater self-confidence to their marriages. In addition to the women who credited loving marriages with their becoming more sure of themselves, there were some who had become self-reliant through problematic unions:

WIFE: "Made me realize how much I had to depend on myself. Through this I learned to trust my own judgment and rely on my hunches to make my mark in the world.

"I've become a much better person. After our first child I became a Christian and my whole life has a new meaning. Marriage itself hasn't changed me. It's the man I married that helped bring a change."

She's become disillusioned about love and romance, and says her marriage alternates between periods of remoteness and closeness. Says sex is generally dull, and an extramarital affair was her worst crisis. A professional who is 51 or over, she has a college degree.

WIFE: "Has made me a more secure person. Although I'm now bitchier and bossy, I feel like I like myself better because I don't take people's shit anymore."

She's definitely planning to divorce her husband. Says she no longer has sex with him and married only because she was pregnant. Describes herself as irresponsible, and her major problems involved jobs. Her husband is unemployed. She's a homemaker between 41 and 50 who didn't complete high school.

WIFE: "Made me stronger and angrier."

Not all women who are dissatisfied with their marriages become angry and assertive; some become apathetic and depressed, particularly those who feel trapped in their homes and enslaved by their lack of options. In this world of liberated women, many are still imprisoned. In this world of emancipated wives, many are regarded and regard themselves as the property of men, subject to their wills in everything from daily activities to choice of friends.

The concept of women as property is not only condoned by society, but sanctioned by religion, far before the misogynistic sermons of St. Paul. The Catholic Baltimore Catechism prudently incorporated the Second Commandment with the First so that there could be discrete Ninth and Tenth Commandments: "Thou shalt not covet they neighbor's wife" and "Thou shalt not covet thy neighbor's goods." The Bible does not indulge in such concessions to feminine sensibilities. The Commandment we find in Exodus (ch. 20, v. 17) reads: "You shall not covet your neighbor's house. You shall not covet your neighbor's wife, nor his male or female slave, nor his ox or ass, nor anything else that belongs to him." This has nothing to do with adultery, which is covered by a separate Commandment; it deals with property, pure and simple, and a wife has the same status as a slave, ox, or ass.

Female slavery today is basically economic, not religious.

Women, despite some social advances, still constitute a small minority of the more lucrative professions, hold few top-level jobs in government and business, and earn fewer advanced and academic degrees. Even those few women who are fortunate enough to establish themselves in profitable careers will have to drop out of the work force for a period of time to bear and raise children. Marriage is more than a way of life for women; it is for many a livelihood. Let a woman whose husband has deserted her go to the unemployment office and demand financial compensation or a new position as a domestic or a sex partner, and she will be at best referred to the welfare department as any unemployable misfit, if not arrested for plying an illicit trade. One hears echoes of Eliza Doolittle: "We were above that at the corner of Tottenham Court Road. . . . I sold flowers. I didn't sell myself. Now you've made a lady of me I'm not fit to sell anything else."

Self-concept is vital to the happiness of either sex, but for women the self is often so totally bound up with marriage that its failure dooms them to a dismal present and a non-existent future:

WIFE: "Worn me down to doing most things with his permission. I used to be very headstrong. I'm less emotional but more depressed and quiet. I dream and think of the past a lot and after death."

While this homemaker believes her marriage is generally stable, she says they have separated, and she has cheated briefly with 2 or 3 other men. The major problem is conflicts over relatives and their children. Also differences in personal interest. She's between 41 and 50, with some college education.

WIFE: "I lost interest in life because he doesn't care what happens to me or the kids."

A homemaker, 41 to 50, who didn't complete high school. She has more than 4 children, and got married because of pregnancy. She says that she definitely plans to divorce.

WIFE: "I found out, too late, that I had married too young and did not know what the meaning of love is!"

This white collar worker has had an affair that lasted over a year, and says sex with her husband is dull. Major problem in marriage is sexual dissatisfaction and lack of communication. Describes her husband as inconsiderate. A high school graduate between 31 and 40.

WIFE: "I have had the opportunity to stay at home for years and if I was not into reading, I would have had a very bored life. My husband doesn't care to go places with the children and I, therefore, take them places they would not have an opportunity for. However, I am never approved for various friends and, therefore, stay alone."

She is a homemaker, 31 to 40, with some college education. She feels she lives for her 4 children. They have had a period of separation. Before they married, they lived together for less than 3 months. She says that they now "rarely or never have sex" and says specifically that they have sex 2 or 3 times a month. She describes their marriage as a failure.

WIFE: "I don't feel as free to do what I want. So I don't feel as an independent person, but as a maid or slave. So I don't feel free."

It should not come as a surprise that people in the lowest income bracket felt tied down and trapped or overwhelmed by responsibility nearly twice as often as those making at least $25,000 a year. Just as women may feel enslaved because of their inability to support themselves, husbands, too, may be pressured by incomes inadequate to support the responsibilities they have undertaken or acquired:

HUSBAND: "More mature, greater financial security has become possible, enabling me to take greater risks at work and become more confident in my job."

A professional, 31 to 40, with a postgraduate education. He married to have a companion, but only specifies financial security as being important for a good marriage.

HUSBAND: "Has increased maturity, but decreased self-esteem and limited lifelong dreams and goals."

"Liberty means responsibility. That is why most men dread it," wrote Jack Tanner in *The Revolutionist's Handbook*. The minor who is governed and supported by parents, the citizen of a dictatorship, and the beneficiaries of the state welfare system lack responsibility and liberty to some extent. They may have duties and, indeed, their very survival may be imperiled by their failure to perform them, but carrying out an order that cannot be questioned is not a responsible act in the personal sense of responding to our own will and conscience. In the context of a marriage, however, one is tempted to say that the more responsibility one has, the less freedom there is to pursue individual dreams and goals. In our survey, slightly more of the people with children (9 per cent) than without (7 per cent) said they felt overwhelmed by responsibility and an additional 7 per cent felt they lived for their children, but there was no difference between the percentages of parents and non-parents who complained of feeling tied down and trapped.

If we freely choose to take on responsibility for the welfare of others by marrying or reproducing them, we cannot realistically complain of loss of freedom in the pursuit of other goals; given a choice of highways to take, we cannot protest that this is no free choice because we cannot take both at the same time. Eric Berne, in *Games People Play,* describes an interaction he calls "If It Weren't for You" by which a person chooses a spouse who will restrict him from doing things which frighten him, then makes the spouse feel guilty about the restrictions to gain other advantages. For every man who claims his marriage prevented him from doing the things he wanted with his life, there was at least one husband who maintained that it helped him be something more:

HUSBAND: "Enabled me to be able to help another person enough to give me confidence that I would be strong enough for two. While at the same time could be in need of someone else. This helped to resolve many inner conflicts and reduce much tension so that I could face the world as I really am without worrying about how I am received."

He is a blue collar worker, 18 to 30, with some college education. They lived together for 3 to 6 months before getting married. Their sex life is good, he says, and they have sex more than once a day. He says that he does feel tied down, and that money is their major problem.

HUSBAND: "I feel more confident knowing that my wife is always around to stand behind me and believe in me."

He's a professional, 18 to 30, with some college education. They have no children. Their sex life is very good; he says they have intercourse more than once a day. He describes their marriage as always stable and loving.

HUSBAND: "It has made me a more stable person. It has made me much more considerate of others. I have enjoyed doing for others that I probably would not have done as a single person."

Doing for others is laudable provided you do not automatically do what you would have done unto you. People rarely share the same tastes. Not all men become more saintly as a result of marriage; for example, the man below for whom the Golden Rule was "Who has the gold, rules":

HUSBAND: "Made me greedy."

This is his second marriage. Though he feels more nervous and irritable since he remarried, he admits that he also feels loved and appreciated. However, lack of communication is his major problem. A college graduate, between 41 and 50, he works in management.

HUSBAND: "It has made me a little resentful, and dominant. Often not caring when I should."

HUSBAND: "Friends tell me that I seem to have become bitter. I feel that I understand people better, and act more fairly."

HUSBAND: "It has been a rude awakening because my wife is a runaround."

He says the marriage is a failure, and has considered divorce. But says sex is very good, and has intercourse more than once a day. The extramarital affair of his wife was his worst crisis. A blue collar worker between 18 and 30. A high school graduate.

HUSBAND: "It's made me a more mature person. After nine children, I'd say it gave me more of a sense for responsibility."

We wonder if the conjugal domain of the above father of nine extended to family planning, in which case his acquisition of a sense of responsibility may have been a bit slow. Several other men stressed the importance of children in their marriages; the gentleman below who says marriage made him a better father did not supply information about premarital experience:

HUSBAND: "Better father."

He's unemployed, 18 to 30, and didn't complete high school. He has cheated with one person briefly. He and his wife lived together for 3 to 6 months before marrying. They argue most about the children and money.

HUSBAND: "I feel more responsible and I love my two children. I want to be a better daddy to them than my daddy was to me. My daddy cares more for himself than he did us. There are five of us—three boys and two girls."

While he believes his marriage is stable, he feels overwhelmed by responsibility. Admits that both he and wife have struck each other during arguments. Says their major problem is conflicts over relatives. A blue collar worker who didn't complete high school.

HUSBAND: "It has given me a sense of responsibility. At one time I was wild, hung around beer joints and drank all the time. It settled me down."

"Settled down" conveys the rather disappointing image of a balloon that has lost all its helium lying inertly on the ground, no longer to fly among the clouds and dance with the breezes. Ill-fated high-fliers like the Hindenburg would have settled for such a fate, we presume, and if courtship is a flight of fancy, the nest is its inevitable destination.

Self-image is determined to a large extent on how others see us—or, more accurately, how we perceive others' view of us. Our self-concept as spouses should be influenced by how we think our mates regard us. Just about two-thirds of our sample, wives and husbands alike, thought their spouses loved and appreciated them "fully." Twelve per cent felt "taken for granted," women a bit more so than men, but only 4 per cent of each sex said their spouses wished they had never gotten married. 15 per cent thought they were appreciated as lovers, but considered in want of improvement otherwise, while 6 per cent felt their spouses were dissatisfied with lovemaking aspects of the relationship. Younger people saw themselves more often needing improvement in the non-sexual areas, whereas the progression was the reverse with regard to sex, the older groups feeling their spouses were more discontented than their more youthful counterparts. Spouses in the crucial midlife period (41 to 50) most often felt appreciated but not truly loved. Those with firm religious beliefs were considerably more secure in feeling they had partners' full approval.

The fact that only 1 in 8 of spouses with firm religious beliefs apparently believed their mates to need improvement in non-sexual areas may be a heartening indication that the gospel of Laodiceanism, preached by Samuel Butler near the turn of the century, is finally being heeded. As Aristotle preached the Golden Mean of moderation in all things, Butler contended that too much goodness was dangerous and must be kept under control, citing as his model the Laodiceans, who were nearly as famous for their indifference as the Laconians were for keeping their mouths shut. If Harpo Marx exemplifies the Laconians, the Laodiceans could claim *Mad* magazine's Alfred E. Neuman, who has taught two generations of American youth to say, "What, me worry?"

"One great reason why clergymen's households are generally unhappy," wrote Butler in *The Way of All Flesh,* "is because the clergyman is so much at home and close about the house." This is gross exaggeration, of course, since we would no more expect or desire clergymen to be pious and extraordinarily virtuous outside their churches than we would expect Muhammad Ali to start a barroom brawl or auto racer Bobby Unser to break 100 mph on the Los Angeles Freeway.

There's a joke about three boy scouts who were all able to wreak their daily good deed on the same old lady whom they helped across the street. It took three of them to do it because she didn't *want* to cross the street, showing that a world full of people who spend their time solely in altruism and penance would be as irrational as a world full of burglars and muggers. Today's mugger plea-bargains himself into release in his own recognizance or a suspended sentence, whereas although St. Joan might not be burned were she to return, she would undoubtedly be incarcerated long enough to have electric shocks administered to her brain. In this world where, when the deity deigned to make itself visible, we promptly crucified it, are we any more ready today to respond to the plea of the Maid of Orleans: "O God that madest this beautiful earth, when will it be ready to receive Thy saints? How long, O Lord, how long?"

No one believes in saints anymore, you scoff. Over a decade ago, even the Catholic Church tried, as best it could, to rid itself of them, shunting their crumbling images into dusty anterooms where only the most reactionary of the faithful would seek them out and light their candles, a habit they could no more discard than lighting their cigarettes. Ah, but the saints remain with us as staunchly as the Christophers that beam from our dashboards in defiance of their exile to the realm of mythology; they abound in the marriages of our friends and acquaintances, who lead us to believe they lead lives of camaraderie and daily orgasm right up to the final divorce decree. The lives of these saints are chronicled in the pages of the women's magazines and the self-help books, tales of ideal marriages which can come to any couple who expend the least bit of mutual energy to improve their relationship. We experience moments of sainthood in the therapy offices where we show our good faith by our exorbitant offerings to the Freudian and Sullivanian priests who lead us into revealing and undistracted communication with our spouses that we could no more sustain on an hour-to-hour basis than we could spend an entire day prolonging a 30-minute jog.

Yes, there is always room for change and improvement, but how cramped and hopeless our lives would be if the humans we married and the humans we are should exhaust that vital space for improvement through an intemperate debauch of immoderate goodness.

The Enchanted Forest

In 1917, James Barrie, creator of Peter Pan, wrote a fantasy entitled *Dear Brutus*, in which people who were unhappy with the way their lives worked out were given the chance by a puckish spirit to enter an enchanted forest where they had a second chance to shape their lives as things might have been. The drama's title comes from Cassius' words in Shakespeare's *Julius Caesar*: "The fault, dear Brutus, is not in our stars, but in ourselves, that we are underlings." As the title forewarns us, nothing really changes for the characters, who ultimately wind up making the same choices and following their original destinies.

While children dream of flying to Never Land with Peter Pan, adults are equally drawn to Barrie's enchanted forest of Might-Have-Been. No matter how happily married, who can resist the fantasy of a single alternative?

How would your life be different if you had remained single?

In the movie *How to Murder Your Wife*, Jack Lemmon was hopelessly framed by circumstantial evidence for the murder of his wife, though in actuality she was alive and well. Rather than continue in his attempt to prove his innocence, he put his own confused lawyer on the stand, asked him to envision what his life would be like if he had never married, entranced the lawyer into enacting a symbolic wife-murder, and got himself acquitted on the grounds of justifiable homicide—just in time for a contrite and happy reunion with his wife. Forty-four per cent of our spouses said they would definitely marry today, if single, and an additional 25 per cent said they probably would as well. Only 13 per cent said they would favor remaining single.

More money, more freedom, fewer children, more pursuit of happiness—there's always some possibility to tempt one or the other spouse to wish things had been otherwise:

WIFE: "More freedom definitely."

HUSBAND: "Probably would have gone on to school, and would have pursued a dream until I reached reality and turned to something more sensible!"

Both are high school graduates between 18 and 30, and both work in the white collar field.

WIFE: "More peaceful and I would have a good job and feel better about myself."

HUSBAND: "Cannot imagine life without being part of a family unit."

Both agree that their marriage is in constant turmoil, and they have been separated. She said that alcohol was the cause of most of their arguments. She's between 41 and 50, a high school graduate. He's a blue collar worker, in the same age range, with the same education.

WIFE: "Much more pleasant."

HUSBAND: "Wouldn't have financial problems I have now."

WIFE: "One word—freedom."

HUSBAND: "Would have stayed in Army."

WIFE: "I would not be loved and be as happy as now."

HUSBAND: "I feel sure that I would not have the great sex life that I now have."

At least one couple above agreed that they would rather be married, even if they were not in complete accord about what they would miss most.

The Lord God said that it is not good for man to be alone, and many wives would add that it's not good for women either, stating that they could not bear the loneliness of single life:

WIFE: "I would be working, having a place of my very own, go out a lot (I'd hope) and probably be very empty and lonesome inside. If I were single, one of my goals would be to get married."

Though she's only between 18 and 30, she says her sex life is already dull, and feels overwhelmed by the responsibility of marriage. She also believes she is only living now for her children.

WIFE: "I wouldn't have near the security and probably would feel a loneliness—not having anyone, besides the children to love and care for. Also—no one to plan and share with, which I think is a very important part of life. Also, I think I would have more problems with the children, and have much more strain and work to do."

WIFE: "I'm sure a lot different. However, I need to belong to a family. I need the secure feeling of a marriage. To me, it's what life is all about. Sharing with the people you love.

"I do love and respect my husband and would not want a life without him.

"I do wish we had both not been married before. There are enough problems."

Other wives felt that marriage had either helped them develop as persons or brought them such satisfactions that they would have been unfulfilled without it:

WIFE: "I would be a quiet withdrawn person, lacking confidence in myself, as marriage, as well as maturity, have made me the person I am today."

While this homemaker believes her marriage to be fairly stable, she feels more nervous and irritable these days. Says her major problem is disagreements over their children. However, sex is very good. Between 41 and 50, with some college education.

WIFE: "I would have continued my successful career, but would certainly have missed the fullness of family life and the chance to further my non-professional interests. I'm certain I would never have felt fulfilled."

This homemaker says she feels that she lives only for her children, and is overwhelmed by responsibility. Also says that sex is dull, but still would marry the same person again. Between 18 and 30, a high school graduate.

WIFE: "I'd probably be a miserable old lady."

When children play "Rich Man, Poor Man" with their coat-buttons, the outcome is supposed to indicate the boys' future careers and the girls' future husbands. Without marriage, women can contemplate careers of their own, such as doctor, lawyer . . . and if Jane Fonda ever gets the squaws liberated, even Indian chief:

WIFE: "I would probably be a calculating business executive or professional in the medical field, and be more independent than what I am now."

She has some college education, works in the technical field. She says they argue mostly about money, job and career, and would definitely not marry the same person again. Her sex life is dull, she thinks her husband takes her for granted, and she's cheated on him with 2 or 3 other men, in brief affairs. Says both she and her husband have considered divorce. Between 18 and 30.

WIFE: "I would have probably been really into my career. Like a lot of men, my work would have been my whole life; instead, my children are."

While this wife considers her marriage to be fairly stable, she admits to a lot of problems. Says an extramarital affair was their worst crisis, and cheating (by her husband) is a major problem. Also she feels dominated by her spouse, and taken for granted. Both have considered divorce, but no further action has been taken. Between 31 and 40, a homemaker.

WIFE: "Probably would work myself to death, earning a living. Would have more freedom to do all things I don't have time for—crafts, art, etc., etc."

WIFE: "I'd be a career woman and play the field a lot instead of being tied down."

Not all women dreamed of immersing themselves in work. Some were enchanted by the prospect of travel, freedom, and just plain fun:

WIFE: "I would travel, I would have an opportunity of meeting a man I could truly love and enjoy."

She's a white collar worker who says sex is dull; she's sexually not satisfied, and feels trapped. Has cheated, and believes her marriage alternates between very remote and very close periods. Between 31 and 40, she's a high school graduate.

WIFE: "I feel I would have been better to have waited several years longer to become married, and enjoyed life more. Now it seems I've been married all my life and never know life!"

She married because of pregnancy, and says it's all bad. Sex is unsatisfying, she and her husband have struck each other, she's disillusioned about love, and her husband takes her for granted. A homemaker between 31 and 40.

WIFE: "I would have traveled more, become president and been the first woman on Saturn."

WIFE: "I would be happy."

The women who would not have considered remaining single said they would have been lonely and unfulfilled as spinsters. Men who are glad they did not remain bachelors not only beat the drum for marriage, but the tambourine as well, testifying that marriage had been their salvation from a life of selfishness, alcoholism, and depravity:

HUSBAND: "I'd probably be a goddamned drunk who was screwing every woman in town. My wife has certainly contributed to my character. In fact, I can virtually guarantee that I'd be a picture of the above."

He works in the technical field, and is between 31 and 40. While alcohol was his worst crisis, he feels he still has a loving marriage.

HUSBAND: "I would have drunk myself to death."

HUSBAND: "I think I would have died early from running around."

He's 51 or over, and has some college education. Works in the blue collar field. Says sex is very good, and his marriage is a loving one.

HUSBAND: "A bore—without purpose—little or no cause to achieve."

This professional (51 or over) says his wife is dominating him, and has control over all the decisions in their marriage, and he would definitely not marry the same person again. A college graduate.

HUSBAND: "Yes, more inwardly drawn, more self-centered and egotistical. I feel single people must be selfish in nature and look out for 'number 1' to survive in the competitive world.'"

Assuming the respondent above is not a Ringer, his image of a drawing inward upon a self-center suggests a dying star, collapsing under the pull of its own gravity. This creates first a vacuum, then a void—which is what other husbands said single life would have left them with:

HUSBAND: "I would probably have more material things in order to fill a void in my life."

This blue collar worker says his wife is irresponsible, and sex is just variable. His major problem in the marriage is a lack of communication between them. Between 18 and 30, he has some college education.

HUSBAND: "I would live with the perpetual belief that I was missing up on some great and mysterious fulfillment."

Even the husbands who did not defend marriage as essential to happiness and fulfillment never conjured up the dreams of prestige, adventure, and romance such as we obtained from disgruntled wives. Where they would be without marriage was often a mere place of residence, the status quo, or vaguely better off:

HUSBAND: "When I married my present wife, I was living in a commune and would have stayed there."

He's now between 41 and 50, has some college and works in management. This is his second marriage, yet admits he's cheated in this one with 2 or 3 other women, briefly. While he believes his marriage is generally stable, he says their major problem concerns his jobs.

HUSBAND: "In my case, I believe if I didn't get married things would be basically the same. I think I would still be living with my lover but that it might be easier to separate if we hadn't made the commitment of marriage."

This spouse says that while his marriage is a loving one, he argues with his wife mostly about his attention to members of the opposite sex. Lived with her less than 3 months before marrying. Between 18 and 30, with some college, works in management.

HUSBAND: "Wouldn't be living with a no-good wife."

He's between 31 and 40 now, but married because his wife was pregnant when he was under 18. Has a postgraduate degree. Says his children have driven them further apart, and he's considered divorce. Admits to cheating, and says he never or rarely ever has sex with wife. Marriage is in constant turmoil, and he's overwhelmed by it all.

HUSBAND: "I might not be as unhappy as I am."

This husband says his wife is irresponsible, and the marriage is a failure. Believes sexual dissatisfaction is their major problem, even though he has sex more than once a day. He's disillusioned about romance, and has considered divorce. A blue collar worker between 18 and 30, and a high school graduate.

HUSBAND: "Would have more material things and money. More time for hobbies, travel, etc . . ."

One writer spoke of the concept of self-transcendence as follows: "Its . . . more modern sense is that man is in a constant process of evolving into higher and higher forms of humanness, that his self is constantly going beyond previous selves. Man's human potential is not finite; it is infinite. There are no limits to the process of becoming."

This is fine poetry, but as psychology or science it is dangerous drivel. If the marital therapists have misled us into seeking saints within our marriages, the leaders of the consciousness-raising groups have conned us into a treasure hunt for the superman within ourselves. Preaching doctrines of self-concern and preservation of individuality, they have made their followers the islands which no man should be. On these islands, people dig introspectively into their psyches, convinced that the glittering promised treasures patiently wait to be unearthed.

Room for improvement is one thing, but talk of "constant process of evolving into higher forms" and "infinite potential" and "no limits" is the greatest excess of egotism since Narcissus took the plunge. A few hours with Aristotle or Marcus Aurelius should convince us that to evolve into any higher form of human will probably take as long as it did for a pterodactyl to become a Frank Perdue oven-stuffer. In *Back to Methusaleh,* Shaw felt that Englishmen would finally realize that they were such an advanced evolutionary species that they would die of old age before they outgrew their mental adolescence; having reached this sad conclusion, they would devote their lives to their childish golf games and leave the running of the world to the likes of Chinese men and black women, whose less complex intelligence could mature to an adult level during their years of biological maturity.

What harm is there to believe we have "infinite potential," that we can acquire the emotional equilibrium and psychic wisdom that will enable us to lead maximally productive and stress-free lives, write great books and paint marvelous artworks, earn incomes commensurate with our vast untapped talents, and live happily ever after? The harm is that when these things fail to come to pass, we look around for someone to blame and engage our spouses in a rousing tournament of Berne's "If It Weren't For You." If we had not saddled ourselves with mortgages and pediatric orthodontia, if we had not wasted so much time in super-markets and driver's seats, if we had waited and married some special person who could have seen our true brilliance and prom-ise, how different life would have been!

Let us heed, therefore, the admonition of Shaw's Devil: "Be-ware of the pursuit of the Superhuman: it leads to an indiscriminate contempt for the Human." Let us view our human relationships with clear-eyed appreciation, not starry-eyed idealism—for the fault, as Cassius observes, lies not in the stars.

6

Minor Grievances:

Children in Marriage

She's a born wife and mother, ma'am. That's why my children all ran away from home.

—*George Bernard Shaw*, GETTING MARRIED

Henry and Cora were the type of couple whom you would never expect to see in a psychiatrist's office. Not that their 30-year marriage had run that smoothly—it was just that the problems with which they were now coping were essentially the same ones that had plagued them for the past three decades. Even handling the difficult demands of a small child was the same problem they had always faced, for although Henry was 50 and Cora only a few years younger, 10-year-old Jimmy was around to disrupt whatever tranquil moments between them occasionally occurred.

Stormy seas and the feeling that there was one too many in the lifeboat were nothing new to the marriage; what now rocked the boat was Henry's sudden inexplicable passion for truth when Cora and Jimmy returned from a two-week vacation with relatives and the wife asked the perfunctory question, "Did you miss us?" Instead of giving an automatic, non-controversial response like "Sure," Henry perversely confessed that he had not missed them at all and had really enjoyed the peace that had come into his life. As the shocked Cora proceeded to turn a routine greeting into an interrogation, one revelation led to another, until Henry was actually saying that if she were dead, he would probably find it a positive factor in contributing to his general happiness.

Cora began talking seriously about divorce, and now it was the placid Henry's turn to be ruffled. Death wishes are just harmless fantasies, after all, but a divorce is rather drastic. They had been through some rough times together, and children had always made them rougher. Henry had put himself through college during the post-war years when the influx of returning veterans made housing a nationwide problem. They were both nuptial virgins and Cora became pregnant on their wedding night; they soon had a child sharing their first home, which was actually the attic of a two-family house. Their first child shared their bedroom for nearly 3 years. Just as they managed to find a slightly larger one-bedroom apartment, Cora became pregnant with their second child, and the first one wound up in a small alcove converted into a sleeping room.

By the time Jimmy was born, Henry had progressed from an accountant to a high-paid executive and the family was living in a roomy suburban home. This did not make Jimmy any the more welcome. He was a frankly unwanted child, and Cora, having raised two children into adolescence, had hoped to escape the routine she had come to hate. She was a bright and sensitive, but relatively uneducated woman, and the only way she could have escaped the equally unfulfilling fate of the sales job at which she worked intermittently was through some formal college training. If abortion had been legal at the time of Jimmy's conception, she would have undoubtedly elected this route; but it wasn't, so she found herself doomed to two more decades of motherhood, a career for which she had neither the inclination nor any particular aptitude.

It did not take Jimmy long to perceive that he was unwanted. He also soon understood that his parents, especially his mother, felt considerable guilt about these negative attitudes toward him. His interaction with Cora came to follow a predictable pattern. His day would begin with some sort of a demand on her, such as to buy him a record or to let him wear sneakers instead of shoes to school. Cora would refuse. Jimmy would then begin a series of pleas, whinings, tantrums, questions, and intrusions until Cora would explode in an angry outburst and then give him his way to get rid of him. There was never any question of outcome in Jimmy's mind; mother *always* gave him his way, so it was only a question of how obnoxious he had to be before she capitulated.

Henry fared somewhat better with his son. Cora would occasionally spend a weekend with relatives, and Henry would become the sole parent. At such times, Jimmy would show genuine consideration by letting his father sleep as late as he wanted and by playing alone for an hour or two when his father wanted to catch up on some work he had brought home. Henry, in turn, played ball with Jimmy and took him to sports events. Henry tried to be consistent in his behavior; when Jimmy asked for ice cream after they had been shopping together, Henry remembered he had taken him to an ice cream parlor the last time, so this was a reasonable expectation. On the other hand, when Henry refused to buy him some toy, Jimmy knew this was not an invitation to begin the wearing-down process he used with mother.

Of Jimmy's three types of interactions—with mother, with father, with both—the father-son relationship is smoothest. Henry says, "I'd rather be a husband than a father, though. I tell Jimmy frankly that when Cora's around, she comes first." Jimmy responds by asking, "Wouldn't you be happier if I wasn't around?" Jimmy nevertheless persists in trying to be a part of all of his parents' interactions. "He wants to join all our conversations," Henry explains. "He doesn't understand our half-sentences and wants to know what we've just said, when it doesn't concern him at all." Cora doesn't want the child around, but can't seem to let him go, either. Although they live in a crime-free, upper-income neighborhood, she feels she has to be home whenever Jimmy is out of school. "If I give him a key, he brings friends into the house and they ruin everything," she explains. "He's just so gullible and careless." The one summer they sent Jimmy to camp for two weeks, he badgered them with lengthy long-distance phone calls every night, begging to come home—calls they accepted collect.

Occasionally, Ted, their middle child, spends a week or two and baby-sits with Jimmy. He is a free-spirit, who, having completed a B.A. in philosophy, wanders from city to city, "crashing" with friends, taking odd jobs behind hamburger counters long enough to accumulate a few dollars, then moving on. Henry is furious at him for not going on to law school or doing something more productive with his life. Cora says she is disappointed, too, but she also sees Ted as an emotionally stable friend in whom she confides her deepest feelings. Ted is the opposite of Henry, a work-oriented obsessor who brings reams of paperwork home with him and takes an hour to arrange his clothing for the next morning. Cora sees and envies in Ted the liberty she and her husband have never known.

Since starting therapy, Henry has managed to quit the lucrative job he hated and find a new position. Cora is becoming more active in community affairs and is not sticking as close to home. Jimmy is the unseen patient, whose progress can only be charted by the biased reports of his parents, who are only vaguely open to the idea of having him seen by a child specialist. Psychotherapy is, for most adults, an expensive luxury rather than an important aspect of health care; as with the patient who sees his dentist only when he has a toothache, most patients come to therapy only when in acute distress. In the case of children, however, options are less available. A fever or a bout of diarrhea invariably compels a parent to seek out a physician, but when the most acute distress in a malfunctioning family system is experienced by the child, parents are more likely to view the symptoms as misconduct or a disagreeable personality rather than a condition requiring treatment. Since we *expect* children to be immature, emotional, belligerent, or shy, it is indeed often difficult to draw the line between acceptable childish behavior and emotional disturbance. Moreover, in a disturbed family relationship, the troubled child is often acting precisely the way the parents have unconsciously programed him to do, so there is little motivation for them to change the current state of operations.

Even in the best adjusted of families, however, children pose difficulties; in a one-child family, the original one-to-one relationship has been expanded to three, now including a mother-child and father-child interaction. In a two-child family, there are six possible two-party relationships. And thus the complexity increases geometrically as new children are added. Complexity does not necessarily lead to malfunction, but it certainly increases the variety of potential problems; one good swat with a buggy whip might have been sufficient to get a one-horse shay moving down the road again, but it's not likely to aid a non-starting Toyota or a child who has become a slipped cog in the American dream machine.

Treacherous Triangles

The extramarital affair is generally regarded as the Bermuda Triangle of matrimonial seas, but there is a far more common troublesome three-cornered situation than that of two adults vying for one member of the opposite sex. When we add a child to a pair of loving adults, we disrupt an established equilibrium and set up the most unwieldy of combinations, the threesome. In intimate interactions, this situation produces not a true three-cornered trade of attentions, but a pair and an outsider. Sometimes it is the mother-child bond that excludes the father; less often, the father seems more preoccupied with the child than with his wife. Some couples resent the baby as an intruder. When there are two children in the family, the siblings may align against the parents or parents may each favor one child—not necessarily healthy situations, but ones in which no one is doomed to isolation.

Parenthood is a lifestyle which most people enter with no preparation. Our dating patterns, courtships, cohabitations, and compulsory sex education do much to ready us for the early days of marriage. We all think about falling in love, even when we are not in that enviable state, and of having a loving partner, but we rarely think of parenthood in any but the vaguest of terms. With the predominance of small families, few children experience caring for a much younger sibling or even observing one, their view impaired by their chronological proximity in age to other children in their families. We are probably more romantic about parenthood than about love and marriage, having at least acquired some firsthand experience about love relationships in adolescence.

Whereas our present society gives parents little realistic training, its expectations of them are higher than ever. Since parents are better educated and more psychologically astute than their own mothers and fathers, they are supposed to be progressive and increasingly efficient in their parental role. People have been around to offer expert advice on child-raising since Eve became a grandmother, and child psychologists and other scientific mentors have been constant in their proliferation, if not their viewpoints, since J.B. Watson took the theories of behavioral conditioning out of the lab and into the nursery half a century ago; no matter what a parent does, there is sure to be a book on the shelf to tell him what he is doing is wrong. Television also gives us a picture of what family life could—and, by implication, should—be like; perhaps we have become more sophisticated in evolving from the wholesome simplicity of Ozzie and Harriet Nelson to the grimmer world where Ann Romano's one-parent family takes things "one day at a time," but the denouement is always the efficient resolution of all problems in 22 minutes, a track record that few off-screen families can match.

Since we mostly live in urban or suburban communities rather than isolated rural areas, our children come into contact with and are supervised by more people; it is not enough that they accept the values and meet the standards of their own families, they must be able to interact in a compatible way with peers and authority figures from widely divergent backgrounds. In our youth-oriented consumer culture, children have their own cereals, radios, alarm clocks, and illustrated underwear; they have bras at 10, Princess phones at 12, and automobiles at 16. In addition to providing these luxurious necessities out of the family budget, parents are expected to insure that their children wind up in more prestigious professions and higher income brackets than their forebears.

Yet, while the Seventies parent has more expectations of him than ever, time and energy resources are dwindling. The non-working mother is frowned upon for neglect of self-development in acquiring a meaningful career, as her own mother would have been ostracized for neglecting her physical person by failing to bathe. Husbands are expected to assume the more traditionally female role of nurturing to a greater extent, but the rising divorce rate means that many of these men will be limiting their parenting to bimonthly weekends or whatever visitation rights were negotiated in court.

Raising a child today poses more difficulties than ever before. Whereas the great economist Adam Smith estimated in 1776 that the average American child represented 100 pounds in financial profit to its family in terms of its labor, today's child costs anywhere from $35,000 to over $100,000 to raise, depending on its education, from the time it is born until the time it leaves home. Families compensate by having fewer children, the average number having decreased from approximately four in the Fifties to two in the Seventies (we won't indulge in grotesque images of fractions of children). But more than 95 per cent of women who marry today want to have at least one child, and over 92 per cent have reached their goal before age 35. While pessimists note that 4 out of 10 children born in this decade will spend part of their childhood in a single-parent home, 4 out of 5 are currently living with two parents, even if one is not an original. In a culture where step-parents are no longer regarded with the Grimm suspiciousness of fairy-tale villains, sociologist have rechristened the growing number of such "deviant" families with the more desirable appellation of "variant."

Wider acceptance of our mix-and-match reassortment of families may help children to become accustomed to acquiring siblings by routes other than the stork and the maternity hospital, but some will undoubtedly continue to suffer the bewilderment experienced by the boy who told an older classmate, "My father can lick your father," and was rebuffed with, "Don't be silly. Your father *is* my father."

Planned Parenthood

One cynic observed that people used to have children in order to enjoy them and so that they would be taken care of in their old age. Since no one takes care of aged parents besides the Social Security Administration and you never seem to meet anyone who enjoys his children, people would soon come to their senses and stop having children entirely.

George Bernard Shaw, who had a solution for everything, postulated in *Back to Methusaleh* that man would undergo a reverse evolutionary process and return to egg-laying. The eggs, unattended, would hatch into full-grown adolescents who would amuse themselves for a few years with music, art, and lovemaking, lay their eggs, and metamorphose into bald, ascetic ancients who would spend the next few centuries contemplating deep Shavian thoughts.

Science will not very likely help us develop egg-laying capabilities, but existing techniques of embryo transplantation and the development of artificial wombs will undoubtedly spare women so desiring the burdens of child-bearing. And if, as the Book of Common Prayer tells us, the essential function of marriage is the bearing of children with romance and sexual gratification being mere accidental ones, contraception techniques make it possible for all marriages to fulfill their accidental functions while neglecting the essential.

But why speculate on possibilities? The fact is that while it is possible for everyone to avoid having children, everyone continues to have them anyway. Fifty-one per cent of the people we surveyed had one or more children—we assume they mean children living at home, as opposed to adult children living elsewhere, since this would equate our findings with the 53 per cent of couples shown by the latest census to have children under 18. Two was the number of children most frequently encountered, but there were more couples with three children than with one and 10 per cent of our sample had four or more children. Large families were more frequently encountered among the non-whites, blue collar workers, the unemployed, and those with firm religious beliefs.

When these people who had children were asked why they had wanted them, almost half said it was to acquire an additional source of love. The second most common reason was to fulfill oneself as a man or woman, and women (27 per cent) felt this to be more crucial than men (17 per cent). Having someone to care for was the only other answer selected by more than 6 per cent, and it received an 18 per cent response. Men more often selected a sense of moral obligation or pleasing the spouse—and, of course, perpetuation of the family name.

It has been found that couples who desire children adjust better to marriage than those who do not want to have them, regardless of whether or not children are actually born. More than half of divorces involve childless couples, though it must be remembered that many divorces occur in the early years of marriage during which many couples defer pregnancy. Regardless of sincere desire for children, the birth of the first baby will be experienced as a crisis by most couples, meaning it is perceived as a stressful experience that involves reorganization of the marriage with regard to such variables as roles, values, and ways of meeting needs. Couples who adapt best are those who are best prepared, having acquired through reading or direct experience with children a realistic notion of what caring for an infant means.

With regard to number of children and their spacing, it has been found that good adjustment depends not so much on the number or years of spacing themselves, but how successful the parents were in achieving what they had planned. Most planned first babies are born 18 months after the wedding, with siblings generally born 2 to 2½ years apart, although smaller families tend to have longer intervals between births.

As in the case of the partially deaf old gentleman who began spiffing himself up for an evening of sin when his son announced he was taking him to the poorhouse, many parents have great anticipation, but are disappointed when they arrive there. A nationally syndicated advice columnist caused a furor a few years ago when she reported that a majority of parents responding to a poll said they would not have children if they could live their lives over. The problem with write-in polls is that contented people don't take the time to write letters about how happy they are, while disgruntled people welcome an opportunity to unburden their chests. Do most parents still regard their children as bundles from heaven or as excess baggage on the journey down life's highway?

Baby Makes Three

Psychologist Urie Bronfenbrenner of Cornell University points out with alarm that children today are hardly ever brought up by their parents. They leave early on the school bus, they return at dusk; mother is apt to be out working along with father when they do get home, and father returns to a suburban home after they are already fed and bedded. Every effort is made to throw the child into the company of its peers and segregate it from adults—after-school intramural sports, weekend Little League tournaments, day-care centers, and neighborhood or housing project recreation centers keep the child out of the home, and when he is within the confines of the familial abode, his companion and mentor is the great one-eyed baby-sitter, the television set.

Schools still handle formal education, but morals, interests, and values are increasingly imparted not by parents but by peers—which, in sociological language, simply means 7-year-olds are being raised by other 7-year-olds. This is merely a trend and even the most radical alarmist would not claim that parents have totally abandoned their traditional relationship with their children; yet, the amount of time a parent spends with children will invariably depend on his regard for the child as a beneficial or deleterious influence in the home. To be frank, most children and adults have limited tolerance for one another over extended periods of time, due to the vast differences in the interests of the parties. The pause in the day's occupation that was known as the Children's Hour might have indeed been a pause that refreshed, but when such doings *become* the day's occupation, parenting becomes a less poetic experience.

Most of the parents we surveyed felt that the children had affected the marriage in a positive way, either by actually drawing them closer (36 per cent) or adding a new and positive dimension to the relationship (28 per cent). While 15 per cent said the children had been the source of many quarrels, only 3 per cent felt they had been driven apart by their offspring. About a quarter felt the children had not affected the relationship between spouses.

In our subsample of matched couples, only 17 per cent agreed that the children had brought them closer and a similar percentage said the children had added a new dimension; however, if we include the pairs where one said "closer" and the other spouse said "new dimension," we get 58 per cent of couples agreeing on a positive effect, close to the 64 per cent of individuals who were enthusiastic. The matched couples, incidentally, agreed with one another significantly in their reason for having children only with regard to an additional source of love (31 per cent); their motives otherwise diverged.

More specific effects of the children on the marriage were elicited from the handwritten responses.

How have your children affected your relationship with your spouse and your marriage in general?

Children have been forced into many roles throughout the history of marriage: pets, servants, slaves, property, companions, tyrants, and apprentices. The one role a child can never fill is that of savior to a bad marriage. Six per cent of those surveyed said they had children to insure a stable marriage. Occasionally a child will keep an unhappy spouse in a failing marriage for at least a time, but that no more insures that the marriage will be stable than locking in the guests will insure a successful party.

WIFE: "When baby was first around, she drew us closer. Then months later, my husband finally decided that since I had a baby to pay attention to, he could safely ignore me. He is wrong. I need his love and attention more than ever. I believe having a child was a strain on an already 'lacking' marriage."

HUSBAND: "I love my child, but if a marriage doesn't work, having children isn't going to make it work."

WIFE: "Made me stay in a difficult marriage."

HUSBAND: "Children are the catalyst."

Both are between 41 and 50. She's unemployed now, and feels overwhelmed by the responsibility of it all. He's a blue collar worker and feels unloved and unappreciated. They have 3 children.

WIFE: "I feel he thinks twice now that he has a child with this marriage. He would leave for months at a time but now only leaves for weeks."

HUSBAND: "Love my child. Would never give her up."

People who had remarried most often said that children had not affected their relationship, although they slightly exceeded those in first marriages in citing adverse effects and were much lower in finding children beneficial. Children in remarriages tend to be products of former marriages, and may be too old to consider the new spouse a true parent; however, a child is never too old to cause some conflict:

WIFE: "No kids of my own. Usually enjoy my spouse's adult children (19, 20, 22) but am sometimes annoyed that he will drop everything and go to considerable inconvenience to bail them out of problems."

HUSBAND: "First marriage was out of a sense of duty and children were for the same reason. They were adult when I remarried, but they still visit me. Doesn't really affect the marriage except how I feel about myself when I feel used for helping them out of scrapes."

She's a college graduate, and he has some college education.
She married him for companionship, he married her for her
intelligence. He's between 41 and 50; she's between 31 and 40.
They have 3 children.

Children can be very taxing to parents, and vice versa. We
give cases of such taxation the following representation:

WIFE: "Children have been very taxing on our nerves but we
accept it to be. We were no picnic to our parents either."

HUSBAND: "They have generally forced us apart from each other
and kept us from doing many of the things we would like to
do."

This white collar worker wanted children as an additional source
of love. They have 2. The husband says right now his worst
problem is the lack of money. Both are between 18 and 30.
He's a high school graduate working in the technical field.

WIFE: "They are closer to me in all ways."

HUSBAND: "Ignore me—more than her—because I'm drinking."

Where there is considerable taxation, it is usually because there
is substantial income, and many women readily admit that for all
their drain on our physical and emotional resources, children do
contribute joys and satisfactions:

WIFE: "They take up quite a bit of time. I also feel tired by the
end of the day after running after the baby all day. I sometimes
get snappy with my husband. But most of the time we enjoy
watching our child grow up and learn new things. We often
talk of future children."

WIFE: "Children have created *strains* and *burdens* on us both that
we would not have had. But they have also brought many
moments of joy."

While she says their 2 children have led to many quarrels she
still feels her marriage is very loving. Only real major problem
is the lack of communication between her husband and herself.

This high school graduate is between 18 and 30, and a home-maker.

WIFE: "We feel like a happy, close family. We appreciate our children as individuals and enjoy seeing them develop into responsible adults."

It is indeed, a rare and happy family that appreciates its children as individuals. Few parents can resist the inclination to turn the minds and morals of their offspring into Xerox copies of their own, an act of vanity which is compounded by blasphemy when they pronounce anything the child does that runs counter to parental standards, wishes or comfort as bad, wicked, naughty, or other term indicating that the act is offensive not to the parent but to God. Most parents would do better to hold themselves up as warnings rather than examples, yet they persist in stretching a child beyond its chronological abilities or truncating its unique proclivities (as Handel's parents tried to dissuade him from music) to fit the Procrustean trundle-bed they have constructed.

The recent non-fictional fantasy entitled *In His Image: The Cloning of a Man* raised cries of indignation tinged with a bit of envy from those who felt the rich and powerful should never be permitted to commission exact duplicates of themselves as a means of immortality. The point everyone seems to miss is that a clone is no more than a younger "identical twin" of the cell donor, and anyone who has been personally acquainted with identical twins knows they are generally so completely different as people that we soon have no trouble telling them apart, even without the telltale moles and blemishes we initially seek out to help us. Moreover, such twins rarely have any more genuine affinity for one another than any less similar pair of siblings and generally strive from infancy to be as different as possible, in defiance of attention-seeking mothers who connive to convert them through uniform garb and grooming into a traveling sideshow attraction. Let one twin detect the slightest advantage over its womb-mate in some aptitude or the ability to exert dominance in one circumstance, and it will exploit that potential to the hilt. Thus, unless the cloning process could alter rather than directly reproduce the blueprint of human nature, we can only expect a clone's first acts to be the conscious alteration of its physique and physiognomy, its politics and morals in a direction completely opposite to the preferencès of its model, who could only be reduced to muttering imprecations about serpents' teeth and thankless clones.

Vanity will always promote the triumph of hope over scientific fact, as in the recent case of the man who received a testicle transplant from his brother and expressed his delight in now being able to "father children," despite unheeded explanations that the results would have been no different had his brother been a sperm donor rather than an organ donor. Having discovered what no animal can understand, the profound consequences of a natural act of sexual enjoyment, and also being the only creature aware of its inevitable death, man cannot be faulted for consciously deciding to join with the forces of nature in replenishing the cycle of birth, death, and evolution; he must be content, however, in the physical reproduction of his body, for the mere perpetuation of his own rapidly outdated ideas and unmet goals thwarts the whole purpose of nature's plodding progress. We and our children alike are experiments of nature, and when older experiments start tinkering with the newer ones, the laboratory becomes a chaotic disaster.

In our attempts to preserve the individuality of children, discipline and structure are often totally abandoned. Especially where one parent is determined to make the children's behavior conform to his expectations, the other—usually the mother, who is with the children most of the time—relaxes all restrictions, her *laissez-faire* approach protecting her from a confrontation with the spouse by directly opposing his demands. Quarrels about children were more common, according to our survey, among people with little education and those without firm religious beliefs; perhaps the dogma of the psychology text, as well as that of the Scriptures, lends some consistency to discipline. The remarried seemed to quarrel more over children because of the complex problems that arise in mixing full-, half-, and foster-siblings, an American pattern immortalized by such films as Lucille Ball's *Yours, Mine and Ours* and Doris Day's *With Six You Get Eggroll,* and television's *Brady Bunch,* whose syndicated reruns permit us to observe five years of familial evolution in a single viewing afternoon. High-income families quarrel more; reasons are uncertain, but we might postulate that families where both parents work have higher incomes but less distinct role assignment in parenting; parents with high income are older, have more children and have more complex problems developing with time; it takes money to remarry and raise large combined broods, so only high-income people can afford the luxury of a two-crisis-per-day Brady-model household.

Some wives blamed the husband's tyranny, some their own inadequacy, and some merely blamed the children who seemed to emulate Topsy and "just growed" to be "the wickedest critters on earth."

WIFE: "Both of us love and enjoy our children. But he expects more of them than I. Though I see his views, we clash a lot. We try to prepare our children to be responsible adults, but I suppose I do too much mothering."

She's a high school graduate between 31 and 40. This is her second marriage, and they have 3 children. They lived together over a year before getting married. The worst crisis of their marriage has been actions of children from her previous marriage. She feels overwhelmed by responsibility, and describes the marriage as having alternating periods of closeness and remoteness.

WIFE: "They have added extra pressure to our marriage. They are very *demanding* and *selfish*. They are very thoughtless and can cause conflicts."

While her major problem is lack of communication between her husband and herself, she argues mostly about the 4 kids, and feels overwhelmed by all the responsibility she has. A college graduate, she is between 41 and 50, and works in the professional field.

WIFE: "We argue quite often over children because he is too strict. Also he never gives them credit for anything they do— he says it is expected of them. If they do something against his wishes he calls them names and always keeps berating them."

One can always turn to the experts for advice in discipline— but it would be easier if the experts didn't indulge in so many 180-degree turns themselves. At the turn of the century, mothers were admonished to develop their children's character; maternal instincts were virtually infallible and it was mother's duty to inculcate virtues such as honesty, neatness, obedience and thrift. Seventy years ago, strict discipline was advocated and father's rod often replaced mother's guiding hand; the growth of behavioral psychology in the Twenties substituted terms such as "conditioning" for "discipline," but the inflexible regulation of childhood activities remained the same.

Interest in Freud's theories of psychoanalysis changed America's focus from children's "characters" to their "personalities," and parents began to tread lightly for fear of fixating or regressing young egos in their formative stages. By the years of World War II, baby was dictating its own schedules and permissiveness had replaced the era of direction and discipline.

Our present era will probably be recalled as that of contradiction. On the one hand, we have conservatives such as Dr. Bronfenbrenner who cry that parents have abandoned their children's need for guidance and even authoritarian control, which results, not in self-confidence and individuality, but low self-esteem, poor achievement motivation, uncontrolled aggression, and susceptibility to peer pressure resulting in delinquency. On the other side, we have liberals such as Dr. Virginia Satir who advocate treating the child as a whole person from birth, treating its feelings with respect and dignity, and teaching him to value "realness" above approval—goals we should not quibble with in theory, but the practicality of treating with respect and dignity a three-year-old boy's real desire to relocate the contents of the jam jar on his one-year-old sister's head is a bit unreal in itself.

There are two basic points, often forgotten, which will help us to resolve this directional muddle. The first is to avoid confusion between the child's rights as an individual and its obligations to society. We have become so obsessed with children's rights, that we tend to forget they also have obligations—which easily explains their own frequent disregard of such social restrictions. Although we, as adults, consider ourselves free, we are not free to be rude, slovenly, vandalistic, noisy, or intrusive. Society will not condone it in us, so we cannot condone it in our children.

The second point we must always bear in mind is the child's age. It is fine to talk of treating children as persons and individuals at every age, but it is absurd to expect them to be capable of the same degree of comprehension, intellectual abstraction, and behavior conformity at every age.

The biggest single mistake parents make in relating to small children is in communicating to them as though they were talking to adults. If we draw an analogy from Western movies, we might term this the "Bullet" fallacy. Example: Roy Rogers has been locked in a jail cell by unscrupulous varmints who have taken over the town. Spotting his faithful dog, Bullet, sitting forlornly outside the jailhouse window, Roy calls through the bars, "Bullet, go back to the ranch and get Trigger. Bring him back here and bring a long rope, too. Have Trigger hold one end of the rope, run it around the tree over there, toss the other end to me, and I'll . . ." It makes a dandy movie if you never stop to question the limitations of a dog's comprehension. It's useless, as well, to tell a three-year-old, "Stop crying, I'll take you next week," when the child has not the foggiest notion of how long a week is. Appeals to such virtues as honesty and purity are meaningless to a five-year-old if he is expected to deal with them as abstract universal principles. A six-year-old might be expected to sit quietly through a movie, provided it interested him, but such demands on a three-year-old would violate the natural laws of its nervous system as well as the rights of the surrounding six rows of patrons.

Similarly, a simple command, such as "Stop playing ball in the house," must be enforced in some meaningful way. The child's natural response is "Why not?" Reasons such as "You might break the chandelier" or "You're making me very upset" may be ineffective if the child would get as much delight out of breaking the chandelier or seeing you upset as it does from playing ball. Vague allusions to the universal immorality of indoor ballplaying are equally likely to go unheeded, since no one, including a child (possibly excepting Tom LaSorda's impertinent references to "the big Dodger in the sky"), is likely to believe the deity cares what anybody, from a toddler to Reggie Jackson, does with a ball. The only way a child can be dissuaded from following its own inclinations is, unfortunately, to make it perfectly clear that if it persists, something unpleasant will happen to it. This consequence may range from taking the offensive ball from its possession to converting its tousled head into an object for batting, but the parent must exercise his awesome power, however tempered with love and mercy it may be.

A simple raised voice is usually quite sufficient for a very small child, since loud noises are among the earliest unpleasant stimuli perceived in infancy; a quick swat immediately following a potentially noxious action is an effective form of behavioral conditioning instinctively practiced by bears and apes, as well as human parents. "No television for a week" may be a fine warning for an older child but is useless for the youngster who knows what television is, but has no concept of a week.

Older children present more of a problem. The young child behaves itself, or at least fears misbehaving, in the absence of its parents because its immature mind believes the omniscient parent somehow knows everything it does. The older child is soon able to conclude that it can do things contrary to parental wishes as long as the parents are not around; thus, the natural course of discipline based on parental prohibitions is the development not of virtue but treachery and stealth. There comes a point when the main emphasis in the disciplinary process (and this element is present nearly from the beginning) becomes aiding the child in its natural drive for self-improvement. Growth is, after all, a process of increasing mastery, and the child actively strives to stand, walk, run, talk, socialize, and learn. The passion for self-improvement is even stronger than the passion for mischief, for the devil cannot have all the strong passions as well as the best movies. It is only the child who has learned to perceive himself as incorrigibly bad and unlovable who abandons all attempts to win approval from his parents and society, for no one quests after failure. It is here that some introduce religion to a child, as a convenient embodiment of those concepts of perfection that the unspoiled child instinctively aspires toward as God, though our disillusioned culture avoids that name as the ancient Hebrews, for different motives, kept their deity nameless. In this context, God becomes an extension of the child towards which he moves, not an incorporation of everything in the parent that stands opposed to the child.

The unhappy constellation of a father who is strict because he expects the child to live out his own erratic values and a mother whose "leniency" is a euphemism for inaction and lack of direction does not prevail, fortunately, in most marriages. Even in marriages where there is conflict between the spouses, children may be a uniting bond rather than a divisive wedge between the parents:

WIFE: "Sometimes I think I gave too much attention to our baby and just drifted away from my husband. But if my love for him were stronger I don't think our baby would have been my whole world. If not the baby it might have been something else that caused the damage in our relationship. Our baby does keep a certain bond between my husband and myself. We both love her dearly and where the three of us are concerned we are very close and a real family. But take me away from the role of 'mother' and I can't act like I was before she was born."

She's a homemaker, 18 to 30, and a high school graduate. She admits to having cheated with one person over more than a year. She says their sex life is unsatisfactory (they have sex 2 or 3 times a month), and sexual dissatisfaction is the major problem in the marriage. She rates the marriage as fairly stable. They have 1 child.

WIFE: "We know that we must stick together because neither one of us will give the children up so we have to make it, and it has drawn us so close. I didn't love my husband when I married him, but I couldn't live without him now."

She's a homemaker, 31 to 40, a high school graduate. This is her second marriage, and they have 4 children. She says that she married for economic security. The major problem in the marriage is "smothering love." She says that the marriage is always loving, but that it has alternating periods of closeness and remoteness.

WIFE: "My daughter is the only reason we are still together."

This homemaker didn't complete high school, and is between 18 and 30. She admits to cheating on spouse, and says she feels tied down and overwhelmed by responsibility. Sex is variable between the two of them, and lack of communication is their major problem. They have one child.

WIFE: "If it wasn't for my children I would get a divorce."

Since the natural relationship between father and son or mother and daughter is ultimately one of rebellion, emancipation, and the supersession of the old and declining by the young and capable, it would seem that mother-son and father-daughter love would be more intrinsically beneficial, freed as it is from these inevitable subconscious rivalries. Unfortunately, sexual tensions and social convention drive parents and offspring of the opposite sex apart during the period they need each other most, and fathers either limit their attention to sons or detach themselves from children completely:

WIFE: "The children are not as close to their dad as they should be—I had to be both mom and dad, many times—due to his being away . . . evenings. Although, since our boy turned teen-age, he spends many and most weekday evenings being with him, teaching him many of his skills, and I spend my time with the girls. . . . All three children have high honors in school (16, 17 and 21 year old).

"We could use a higher income—we are just existing on wages like this—we need to live a little. Right!"

This homemaker says that her worst crisis in the marriage was her husband's unemployment, and money is their major problem. They argue mostly over the children, but she rates the marriage as being a stable one. However, she says she feels she lives only for her children at this point. She's between 41 and 50. They have 3 children; 2 other children died.

WIFE: "As a rule the children have caused a great deal of friction between us. He tends to ignore them and I overcompensate by being too lenient."

This homemaker is 41 to 50, with some college education. They have 3 children, and argue most often about them—these disagreements are the major problem in the marriage. Their sex life is very good, and they have intercourse twice a week on the average.

WIFE: "Trouble they've gotten into, and the disrespect they show for their stepfather—this isn't serious because I've learned to let him discipline the children without interference. Probably my leniency causes some problems."

In this age of increasing divorce and remarriage, the presence in a family of parents who are not blood-relatives of the children is common, and if the code of the blood cult had the validity here that necessity demanded in the Scottish highlands where a fifth cousin readily girded his sword for a clansman in distress, we would have some severe problems in family relationships. Actually, our religious heritage is based on a dismissal of the blood-tie as relatively unimportant, as witnessed by the Bible from the injunction in its very first book that "a man leaves his father and mother, and clings to his wife," to the mournful image of Zebedee bobbing behind in the fishing boat with the hired men while his sons, James and John, go off with Christ (Mark, ch. 2, v. 20). Even the Holy Family avoids blood-ties, consisting as it does of a stepfather, a universal Mother, and the Son of Man, a homeless wanderer who says, "The foxes have dens, and the birds of the air have nests; but the Son of Man has nowhere to lay his head" (Matthew, ch. 8, v. 20). There is a conspicuous absence of a holy home, holy mother-in-law, and holy extended family, giving us an inherent warning against the excesses of subservience and affectionate displays we demand in the name of the "natural" love that is supposed to accrue to every hearth and kinsman.

It is a rare husband who does not cite some of the responsibilities and hardships of raising a child, despite a basic love and appreciation of his offspring:

HUSBAND: "Brought us closer together, yet it also makes it hard for us to get up and go somewhere, but for the most part there is more joy and love in our lives."

This blue collar worker has some college education and is 28 to 30. They have one child. He says that they never argue, sex is variable, and the marriage is generally loving.

HUSBAND: "The children are an extension of our love and as such a source of joy to both of us. However, it will be nice when they are grown and wife and I will have more time for each other."

He's between 41 and 50, and a high school graduate working in the technical field. While he admits to cheating briefly, he says his marriage is on a stable footing, but wishes for better communications between them. They are parents of 3 children.

HUSBAND: "If it were not for the children's sickness, we would probably be financially better off, which automatically would make both of us have more outside interests to enjoy. My faith has kept our family close together. I would say our children have had a lot of effect on us."

He's retired, 51 or over. His children have led to many quarrels, and it's what he and his wife argue the most about. He's overwhelmed by responsibility, and feels his marriage alternates between very remote and very close periods. They have 4 kids.

HUSBAND: "Plus the added responsibility, it has added joy and pleasure to my life, to see the birth and growing of my children. It has made our marriage closer and less selfish."

Some saw the expenditure of time and money not as a loss but as an investment, so that their ledgers showed only gains as far as their children were concerned:

HUSBAND: "I believe they have been a most solidifying factor. We have invested a lot of affection in them and through them, in each other. Our lives wouldn't be the same without them."

He is a professional between 31 and 40. They have more than 4 children, and he says their marriage is generally loving.

HUSBAND: "They have been our fun, joy and pride. Another reason to want to be successful."

He's 41 to 50, a high school graduate. They have 2 children, and argue most often about them. These disagreements are their major problem. He says that the marriage is generally loving, but that there are alternating periods of closeness and remoteness.

HUSBAND: "Since my wife spends an inordinate amount of time with the children, I feel ignored. Ironically, I feel warmth toward my children. I conclude that I never had a real relationship with my wife, and would have quit the marriage if the new recruits did not enter into the combat."

Not every infant must be relegated to the infantry in an atmosphere of family combat. But since a mind of its own is regulation issue for each of life's conscripts (there are no volunteers), and since wills are never uniform, conflicts between parent and child or child and child are inevitable. Minors' grievances can become major problems when the communication in the chain of command has a few missing links.

The Matter with Kids

Diana, a 25-year-old mother, is out with her own mother and two-year-old daughter, Lisa, who is riding a tricycle. Grandma is the one watching the child, who suddenly pedals out into the road, where a car narrowly misses her, for which Diana berates her mother.

Lisa is riding a Ferris wheel and Diana is watching from the ground. A woman with an infant is sitting beside Lisa, but she is so preoccupied with feeding the baby that she ignores the older child, who is standing precariously on the seat.

Diana goes into Lisa's bedroom and finds her bed folded up. Lisa is gone and a mysterious stranger explains calmly that she has been taken to Italy. Other strangers are moving out furniture, and ignore Diana's pleas for information about Lisa.

Diana is about to breast-feed an infant. Its face begins to change demonically and she knows it is a child of Satan. She throws it into the air, and it promptly vanishes.

Diana throws Lisa out a window.

These are the dreams of an everyday housewife, as the song goes. Diana is a conscientious, loving, and effective mother, and Lisa is thriving despite the dangers from others and mother that beset her in Diana's nightmares. One can argue that the problems that brought Diana into psychotherapy four years ago make her dreams so disturbing; but one can also contend, in view of her excellent progress, that psychotherapy has enabled her to confront and recall dreams that less introspective mothers would repress. Diana's conscious negative impulses towards her child are no stronger and are better handled than the unperceived hostility of the overprotective mother who projects her animosity onto every stranger, raindrop, and germ in the environment.

Better to be brought up in a home such as that of the nineteenth-century clergyman whose father's practice was to strike automatically the head of any child who wandered within his reach, than one in which a mother totally preoccupied with affection and sentimentality imposes her own demands on her entrapped children in the name of love. The buffeted clergyman always expressed his gratitude to his father for respecting, if not the outside of his head, the unmolested thoughts within it.

Where there is freedom of thought, there will be conflicts of interest, and conflicts are translated into problems. Some are defined by the combatants as the parents' problems, some as the children's—but it's all in the family.

What are the main problems you've faced as a parent, and how have you handled them?

Possession is said to be "eleven points of the law," according to a seventeenth-century play, and where children are concerned, society tends to award parents the extra point and make them the sole law. If wives have often been reduced to mere possessions of husbands, children were, and still are, often the slaves of both. The establishment of the Bureau of Child Welfare and the Society for the Prevention of Cruelty to Children has dispelled the old fantasies that only wicked stepmothers abuse children, but anyone who has routinely dealt with such agencies is aware that only the most vicious extremes of battering, fully documented by X-rays and medical reports, are sufficient to effect official intervention. Getting a child placed in foster care (a hardly ideal alternative) on the grounds of *emotional* neglect is about as easy as getting it admitted to Harvard Medical School. It is still not uncommon to see Puerto Rican women whose educations have been terminated by their families after two or three years of elementary school because they were old enough to serve as nursemaids and house-keepers at home. Compulsory education was not instituted in England in defense against truant children, but against the op-position of lower-class parents who kept children home as a source of free labor, while those with servants would settle for nothing less than full-time boarding schools for their offspring. Physical slavery has been abolished by child labor laws and compulsory education, but emotional bondage persists:

WIFE: "Being too possessive. Wanting to protect them from the world. Telling them to be grown up and then not letting them . . . still trying."

HUSBAND: "The different feelings of what is fair and equitable for the children. I have many times given into the more per-missive nature of my spouse."

This homemaker and mother of 3 is between 41 and 50. She wanted children to have someone to care for. Her husband is in the same age range.

Fathers frequently defer to the wives in matters of child-raising, sometimes by frankly denying any problems, sometimes by trying to establish and accept a role limited by the child's greater dependence on a mother who may even be employed, and sometimes by abdicating all responsibility except financial:

WIFE: "There are so many more responsibilities as a parent. At times it can be overwhelming. Becoming a little less selfish was hard.

   "We as parents face our responsibilities as best we can crossing each bridge as we come to it.

   "Budgeting our income so there's enough for necessities is a challenge, but one that we can work out.

   "We don't always agree on forms of discipline, but we come to an understanding."

HUSBAND: "Our children are quite young yet and we have not faced any great problems as parents yet."

She's a blue collar worker, but is a college graduate. He has a high school education. She's between 18 and 30; he's 31 to 40. He believes that the lack of money is their major problem. They have 2 children.

WIFE: "Leaving my child when I work. Tried to love her more and spend all the free time I have doing what she likes to do."

HUSBAND: "Accepting my child's dependence on her mother. I try to show her how much I love her."

WIFE: "Like most parents, I feel that for each of us communication is the biggest problem in homelife, so I try to include my teen-age son in everything concerning our life together. I share with him the problems and the good times as they come about.

   "We have a very good line of communication between us and there is very little anger or misunderstanding."

HUSBAND: "I have had no problem there because my wife takes care of most major problems with the child—I furnish the finances to take care of him."

The husband wanted their 1 child to please his wife. She now feels their son has driven them further apart. Both are 51 or over. She's a homemaker; he works in management.

Communication with grown children may pose more of a problem for the child than the parent. It is not uncommon to see adult or even adolescent patients who are anguished by their parents' desire to confide intimate details of their lives from chronic sexual dissatisfaction to marital infidelity. Even if frankly rebuffed, the parent will persist with, "But you're the only one I can possibly talk to," making the child feel guilty for the potential danger of a nervous breakdown or suicidal depression. Using the child in this way disrupts further the communication that might develop between parents and may force the child to take sides in the dispute; but its worst effect is to destroy the parent-child relationship, which is intrinsically different from an adult friendship or love relationship. The adult has known the child all its life, whereas the child has known the parent for only a fraction of the adult's life. The child's early perceptions of the parent are of an omnipotent, invulnerable being, and often the insensitivity children show towards their elders is the natural outgrowth of the childish conviction that the adult has the potential for anger, but not for the emotional pain of rejection or inconsideration. The child who leaves a parent, particularly a single parent, when it marries often inflicts a depressing loss upon its lifelong nurturer, but neither the child nor society is apt to let this mar the nuptial celebration. Parents who react to such losses with anything but brave smiles wind up as objects of ridicule or psychiatric patients, for they are violating the natural order of things that is as old as Genesis. Just as therapist and patient must have good communication without the therapist's ever burdening the patient with his own foibles and traumas, so, too, must parents within the context of their special relationship refrain from pressing their offspring into the role of surrogate parents unless they are quite prepared to destroy a child-parent relationship that most children would welcome up to the day that death disrupts it.

One advantage of prison is that prisoners do not have to pretend love for their jailers. Some couples equate parenting with surveillance:

WIFE: "Our children have gone wild or at least it seems to me that they have. The biggest problem I guess is skipping school, they just walk off the school grounds whenever they please. We have talked to teachers and counselors at school and they keep a close watch on them."

HUSBAND: "Rebellious children. I simply clamped down on them—threatened to take the boy's car from him if he didn't straighten out. The girl I just have to watch closely for twenty-four hours a day."

There will always be a breed of parents that worries about what their sons might do and what their daughters will have done to them. Cutting the wheels out from under a boy may inhibit his access to dens of temptation, but girls are believed to carry their temptation around with them, and it is not easy to cut their legs out from under them. Many a young girl victimized by the hysteria of chastity-watching concludes bitterly that "if you've got the name, you might as well play the game." Some, unfortunately, are too young to play, as in the bizarre case of the 10-year-old brought to the mental health clinic by her mother and the male guidance counselor who had "detected the odor of sperm on the child's panties."

Not all parents are dedicated to the preservation of premarital chastity in their daughters. When Nancy Friday appeared recently on a TV talk show to discuss mothers' negative attitudes towards sex as explored in her best-seller, *My Mother, Myself,* another guest was an actress who not only approved her teen-aged daughter's decision to start having intercourse, but also volunteered to sit down with the young man, a virgin, to give him some guidance about how to proceed. The daughter declined, feeling such groundwork was better left to self than mother. Most wives, however, would share the opinions voiced by the lady below, and if we must have an author to warn us that such maternal concern is a mixed blessing, thank God it's Friday:

WIFE: "It is hard for me to look back, my children are nineteen and twenty-two (both girls) and of course the things that I most readily recall are the most recent. . . .

"We tried to bring the girls up to be ladies in the truest sense of the word . . . loving, affectionate, kind, gracious and *chaste,* to be loyal and honest, to love their God, their family, their fellow man . . . to *truly care* about others. NOT to follow the crowd—but their convictions.

"This is how the problems were handled before they arose . . . we tried to bring the children up properly in the first place—trusting that 'when they were older, they would not depart from it.' We trusted them and *prayed* a lot.

"They have made mistakes, of course, but they have grown from them. . . . We've cried together over things that could not be undone and trusted the Lord to somehow let us use our mistakes to benefit others in the same boat . . . to turn it into a blessing as I said . . . to us the tragedy would be if we didn't grow and learn and benefit from our mistakes.

"We as parents and as Christians have always tried to DIS-CIPLINE with love—but *emphatically* to *discipline!*

"However, when mistakes were made we've tried to handle that with love also—never to point the finger and say 'I told you so'—but as I mentioned earlier 'cry together,' ask God's forgiveness and start all over again. We've shared our fun and our sadness.

"*The biggest problem has been the moral climate of the times*. . . . To teach them how to cope with temptations; sexual permissiveness, drugs, alcohol.

"Since they both were and are beautiful and leaders in their peer groups there was the problem of responsibility not only for themselves but as an example to others.

"Another big problem—a trend of the times—*hedonism* . . . to steer them away from 'looking out for Number 1' and to teach them that a headlong dash for happiness is certainly not the way to find it—that it can only be had as a by-product of unselfishness and love for man and God."

She's a professional, a college graduate, and 41 to 50. She says that their sex life is satisfactory. They argue most often about their 2 children.

Virginia Satir has actually advocated celebrating not only the child's first day at school, first menses and first date by means of a party, but also the first sexual intercourse. This sounds rather extreme in an era when most parents would throw jabs and uppercuts rather than a party for a child naive enough to confess such an act. The noted family therapist may risk giving children the idea that life is one big party, especially when she extends the practice to "the first obvious and costly mistake," which may closely follow the first-intercourse party. We can accept the concept (less easily the wording) advocated by the doctor in the book *The Family in Search of a Future:* "that the cover of secrecy be removed from the sexual part of the human being. With this cover off, ignorance can be removed." But when she goes on to urge "that there be as much attention, care, and implementation, openly, creatively and confidently given to the care, maintenance, and use of the genitals as there is, for instance, to the teeth," the impatient parent is tempted to retort, "Why, are they likely to decay and fall out?"

If we are to follow the advice of experts, we cannot deal with general exhortations such as "Charge!" which stir the blood but give us little information as to where we are going and what are the consequences. Only a monster would want its child to be ignorant and guilt-ridden, but do we want our children engaging in intercourse; if so, at what age and with whom; and do we have plans for dealing with mistakes, other than throwing parties to celebrate the milestone? Let us not give our children mixed messages as did the schizophrenic mother who wanted her 14-year-old daughter to remain a virgin, but gave her birth control pills regularly just so "nothing could possibly happen." When the child came home with gonorrhea, the mother launched into such a rage that the child extricated herself the only possible way, by punching her way into an institution via a glass door at the mere cost of a few tendons.

In this age of agnosticism, we cannot say, flippantly, "The Devil made me do it." Even children do not believe in him, as shown by the boy who responded to the question of a peer, "No, the devil is sort of like Santa Claus. You believe in him for a while, but then you find out he's only your father." Many wives were content to blame their husband for poor parenting, indifference, or absence:

WIFE: "My husband did not share enough in the actual family relationship to suit me. I was always the one to take our children on picnics, swimming, etc. I took them to special things going on most of the time. His own interests (listening to sports on radio, TV, etc.) came first. He never took our five-year-old son to a ball game or played catch with him until he was dying of leukemia. He bought a gym set for our son at age two and then when we moved into our new house he wouldn't put it up because he didn't want neighbors' kids in the yard. For many years our daughter asked about it with no results.

It took me a long time to get over my resentment towards him. When our son died at age five I became slightly neurotic over the loss and it affected our daughter to the point where we had to go for counseling for her for three years. The counseling helped me as much as her and I feel now, after six years have gone by, that we have a much better relationship than we would have had. It was not easy for my husband to accept all this and the few times he was asked to come in to participate, he did so reluctantly. My daughter, through her counseling, finds she is able to speak up to her father now and understands him better. Our whole family relationship is more open in many ways since then."

This homemaker is 51 or over now. Though she considers her marriage at this time to be fairly stable, she complains that she feels unloved and unappreciated, and disillusioned about love. Says both have considered divorce, but took no further action on it. They have 1 child.

WIFE: "I was a single parent for several years—my ex-husband did not see the kids much. They really resented this. I felt it very hard to be only parent, but had live-in young couples as baby-sitters, so my sons and daughter had some men around. Also, really got a lot of static from kids about men in my life— this is main reason I didn't consider remarriage until they were all out on their own."

She's been separated from her husband. Married to have companionship and economic security, and support in times of crises. Now in her second marriage with 4 kids, she feels tied down and trapped. Says sexual dissatisfaction and differences in personal interests are their major problems.

WIFE: "Lack of support from husband—silly pseudopsychology that tends to disrupt order. I opposed him and set strict discipline where possible."

This wife has a postgraduate degree, and works as a professional. She believes that their children (more than 4) have drawn them together, yet led to many quarrels. At his point she feels she would not marry the same type of person again. She's between 31 and 40.

WIFE: "When my husband was sent to Korea and South Viet Nam while in the service, I was left with four small children to care for. We took one day at a time, we shared all letters from him. I found the children needed the company of a male. My brother and father would spend their extra time with the children on a one-to-one basis."

She says now alcohol was their worst crisis, and they have struck each other during arguments, which are usually over their children (they have more than 4). A homemaker.

WIFE: "Finding that my husband is a manic-depressive and totally disinterested with life. Refuses medical help. He has an IQ of 190, feels superior to everyone in his misery."

She's definitely divorcing her husband, and has already cheated on him with 2 or 3 other men, with one affair lasting over a year. At this time she feels she lives only for her 3 children. Says her marriage is hostile and in constant turmoil.

WIFE: "My child is only 12 months old and the main problem I have had is dealing with my fatigue when my husband is on the road away from home. He is wonderful *when* he comes home. He understands and gives me time away from the baby to rest."

Among the women who had received help from one or more husbands, the steadiness of a male hand did not necessarily keep the child in check. Sometimes the expectations were unrealistic. When the nervous bride in *Getting Married* asks indignantly if anyone wants her to flatter and be untruthful, one of her guests replies, "Well, since you ask me, I do. Surely it's the very first qualification for tolerable social intercourse." The truth, the whole truth, and nothing but the truth may be demanded in court, though it has probably never been obtained, yet if the child described below followed his mother's wishes in all situations, he would inevitably be ostracized from polite society:

WIFE: "Rebelliousness in oldest child even though he is only eight. Haven't had a real discipline problem with him but he definitely tests parental authority, is opinionated, wants to do what he wants to do, etc. Guess it is a part of growing up. We try to be loving yet firm with him. At times I think we're too strict—other times I think we are too lenient . . . wish we could reach that ideal medium. We haven't caught him in an outfaced lie, yet he hasn't always been *entirely* truthful with us. The whole truth even though it might hurt is one thing I prize. I want the whole truth.

"Our youngest (18 months) from my second marriage hasn't reached the age yet where we've had much problem as far as discipline, etc., is concerned. He will eventually give us problems though. I just hope I can raise both so they have a high moral and ethical code."

In actuality, "the whole truth" is generally demanded not when a parent wants virtue, but information. At other times, when a neighbor asks what was thought of her new decor or grandmother asks how you all liked her rutabaga casserole, flattery is not only preferable to honesty, but mandated in the name of civilized relationships. Children become more adept at flattery than honesty because they soon learn that the former promotes ease and survival, while the latter invariably leads to trouble.

Parents also often expect, consciously or unconsciously, perfect obedience, which is not a virtue at all. Unsocialized aggressive reactions, characterized by overt or covert hostile disobedience, quarrelsomeness, physical and verbal aggressiveness, and destruction of property, and withdrawing reactions, characterized by seclusiveness, detachment, sensitivity, shyness, and self-isolation are both serious psychological disorders of children, but mental health clinics see scores of the disruptive aggressive children and hardly any of the withdrawn ones since school guidance counselors and parents are apt to misdiagnose the latter as perfect children.

WIFE: "1. Children's failure to be 'perfect' children and my 'failure' to be a perfect parent. Accepted fact that none of us are or ever will be perfect but that we can love one another as we are.

"2. Fighting among children—as an only child the sibling rivalry disturbs me a great deal. I try to realize a certain amount is normal and try to enforce rules of fairness and courtesy. It sometimes does not work!"

Children from large families fare better in the outside world because a large family is essentially a community where lines of authority, cooperation, cross-alliances, and independent thinking become necessary for survival, while a family with one or two children too often becomes bogged down in sentimental conventions of affection and domination that prevail when parents become preoccupied with too few offspring, who do not have the offsetting influence of skeptical older siblings. Since children desperately need their parents but have little practical use of siblings, relationships between the children are free of much of the hypocrisy of perpetual familial affection that colors the parent-child relationship. Siblings are good for children in that the rivalry and uneasy truces prepare them for the competitive world ahead; alleged benefits of sources of brotherly love and devoted companionship have been rarely visible since the first parents raised a little Cain.

"O tempora! O mores!" ("What a time! What a civilization!") moaned Cicero several decades before the birth of Christ. In nearly every era people are likely to look around them and conclude that morals have never been lower and youth more decadent. True, more kids are literally going to pot these days, but were things really much tamer a half century ago when people drank bathtub gin, Cole Porter wrote that he got no kick from cocaine, and some of the mini-skirted flappers just might have kissed a boy on the first date? Not the way most mothers tell it:

WIFE: "Right now I am not facing a problem as a parent. Yes, I did rear some children. They are all grown and married. The way I see the children of today, I just couldn't cope with them. With all the pot smoking, drinking, telling the parent where to go; it is a pity. Some of them are agnostic. They stop school for spite, so they think. I have a solution for such problems. Don't tell them off. Appeal to their intelligence, their pride and their hide. Do hope this answers your question."

She's retired now, and is between 41 and 50. While she says there is no major problem in her marriage, she and her husband do argue a lot about their children. A college graduate.

WIFE: "Trying to unite two families—his boys and my boy and girl. His boys are on drugs and have been picked up by the police. My two are ashamed by the boys' behavior. My daughter is married now and my son is leaving in June so things should get better."

This white collar worker of 41 to 50 has some college education. This is her second marriage. They have struck each other, and never or rarely have sex. She feels overwhelmed by responsibility, says her spouse wishes they never got married, and says they have alternating periods of closeness and remoteness. There are 4 children.

WIFE: "Problem of raising a child in this sex-oriented era. Trying to teach *that child* right from wrong and not pay attention to peer pressure."

The family is even more variable than the heterogeneous institution of marriage, because the latter involves two people, whereas a family can comprise ten times that number. Some are organized along political or military lines, as the Baron von Trapp drilled his irregular troop in *The Sound of Music* with as little sentimentality as one can get away with in a wide-screen musical. In the Orient, fathers often capitalized on the practice of ancestor worship by enforcing it in advance of their demise, while some American fathers function more as playmates and year-round Santa Clauses than authority figures. Some husbands of career women are full-time homemakers and nannies, while men in military service may not see their offspring for months at a time.

Since there are so many types of families, there will be many types of situations and problems, some common to most families, some distinctly uncommon:

WIFE: "Learning. Every problem seems to be a major one when I became a parent. I thought of smooth, easy sailing, but being a parent is the hardest job I have ever had. There is no one specific thing I could name, all of them. You handle them as they come—each in their own way—with lots of love, patience, and understanding."

Though this homemaker says she and her husband never argue, their biggest problem is lack of money. A homemaker with a high school education between 41 and 50.

WIFE: "Birth of handicapped child. Handled one day at a time."

This young homemaker (18 to 30) is religious, and says she and her husband never argue, and their marriage is on a stable footing. They have 2 kids.

WIFE: "Explaining to my daughter that I had her *before* marriage. I handled it by being truthful and answering all of her questions."

A homemaker between 18 and 30, she says she has no major problems regarding her marriage now, though she and her husband do argue mostly about their kids. They have more than 4.

WIFE: "Raising the children—wondering if you're making the right decision since the outcome has a direct bearing on life other than your own. Have always tried to keep a promise. We have always been able to say 'sorry' when we are wrong. With a lot of love and understanding I think most children understand."

Dr. Haim G. Ginott would probably tell the mother above that the best way to avoid breaking promises is not to make them. In *Between Parent and Child,* he writes, "Promises should neither be made to, nor demanded of, children. . . . When a parent must make promises to emphasize that he means what he says, then he is as much as admitting that his 'unpromised' word is not trustworthy. . . . Promises about the future good behavior or the cessation of past misbehavior should not be requested or extracted from children. When a child makes a promise that is not his own, he draws a check on a bank in which he has no account. We should not encourage such fraudulent practices."

Promises are untrustworthy in the sense that they imply something that will come to pass with certainty, when life is to filled with uncertain mitigating circumstances. To be honest with our children, we must tell them, as Mary Poppins told her charges, that promises can be like pie-crust, easily made and easily broken. When we have the confidence to confront our children with the truth of life's uncertainty, we often win a deeper trust than we could have gained with myths of invulnerable steadfastness. The answer below citing the difficulty of acquiring such trust came from a truly native American—honest Injun!:

HUSBAND: "Getting the trust of my children. Always being honest with them and setting a good example."

An American Indian, he's 51 or over, and a college graduate. Works in the blue collar field. Admits he's become disillusioned about romance and love, and says his major problem is differing views on women's lib. His marriage alternates between periods of closeness and remoteness. They have more than 4 kids.

The end of the rainbow, a precious gem, a bright and shining star, the spirit of Christmas, sugar 'n 'spice, all go to make up Daddy's little girl, according to the song. When daughter gets as big as her mother, the only ingredient left seems to be the spice she adds to a formerly tranquil home:

HUSBAND: "The fighting between the wife and daughter. I got some counseling for both."

A blue collar worker between 41 and 50, with some college education. He has cheated with one other person briefly. He and his wife lived together for 6 months before marrying. He feels more nervous and irritable since marriage. He says their major problem is conflicts over relatives.

HUSBAND: "Both daughters pregnant before marriage. Soon calmed down and told them that they had to live their own lives and that I loved them."

He's retired now, 51 or over. He calls his own sex life dull, and says he feels sexually unsatisfied. He's the father of 4.

HUSBAND: "Our daughter's marriage to another race and the attendant problems. We were facilitative—non-critical."

Not all fathers govern their children with calm, non-critical authority. Some lose control, some leave control in the hands of the wife, and some need to receive more emotional support than they can give:

HUSBAND: "Coping with children. Their constant demands and lack of consideration for me or my spouse.

"Probably do not handle them too well. Usually fly off the handle at them."

He's a professional between 41 and 50, with a postgraduate degree. He says he never argues with his wife, and has no major problem in his marriage. They have 2 children.

HUSBAND: "The main problems I have faced as a parent are children interfering with sexual activity. (Still needs handling.) Also children not minding and taking time away from other activities. (Usually leave child to wife.)"

A white collar worker, 18 to 30, a college graduate. He has cheated with one person briefly. He says their sex life is satisfactory, and they have sex 3 or 4 times a week. He describes their marriage as fairly loving. They have 1 child.

HUSBAND: "A period of unemployment in 1977 (eight months) through which we survived and which brought us all closer together through family meetings in which we all worked together to pull me through the crisis."

Good parents are concerned with the quality of their children's schools. Many care less about education than about having a place that will relieve them of child-care for six or more hours a day. While we have somehow managed to extricate ourselves from the sadistic rituals that were romanticized as being "taught to the tune of a hickory stick," many urban schools are mere publicly supported detention cells from which the inmates eventually are paroled, unbeaten and unlettered.

Even eager students may find it difficult to learn from poorly motivated teachers, a problem not entirely modern. Young Abe Lincoln was reputed to have been told by a teacher, "You are better fed than schooled," to which Abe replied, "Yes, sir. I feed myself."

The best of parents cannot be with their children at all times, and must try to motivate the child, then match it with a motivated school:

HUSBAND: "Stressing importance of a good education and choosing friends carefully. Pointing out examples from time to time and never giving up."

HUSBAND: "Children having trouble in school—illness forcing them to miss school.
   "Moved because of trouble to more understanding school."

Much has been written about the low esteem in which non-working mothers are held and the unlikelihood of attracting qualified people to run the community day-care centers liberated women are demanding so long as child-care is denigrated and undersubsidized. We tend to overlook the equally low esteem accorded to elementary school teachers, who are generally the lowest paid and least prestigious of pedagogues in the academic hierarchy, although their influence upon the developing child is probably the most crucial of all the instructors it will encounter.

We have not advanced much beyond the turn-of-the-century world in which an impulsive Englishman once blackened the eye of an elementary school teacher for pursuing and striking a child. Haled into court by the teacher, the defendant anxiously asked what would be his punishment. "Six pound fine if he was a gentleman, two pounds if he wasn't," replied the constable. Informed the victim was a schoolmaster, the fine was set at two pounds. To this day, most educators would agree that you can blacken three eyes of a teacher for the cost of one belonging to a professional man.

As much as we should value teachers for giving us a needed daily respite from the trials of parenting, let us admit that some people are better natural parents than others. And by this we do not necessarily mean the mother who keeps children clean, well-fed and cuddled or the father who manages to elicit obedience without undue punishment. The parent who fares best is one who truly enjoys children. The man whose imagination can relish the panoply of a circus or the whimsy of a Disney film may not be a good captain of industry but he can navigate the straits of parenthood better than the parent who impatiently wishes he was at a football game or in a fishing stream instead. The mother who delights in observing the changes in a child's intellectual perception of its world and its constantly developing motor skills will have more patience and less irritability than the housewife who stoically "puts up with the kids." The ability to think and experience as a child does is not a symptom of immaturity; flexibility and empathy are among the hallmarks of the truly mature person, and the true man for all seasons is as much at ease among the buds of early spring as he is in the ripe autumn harvest. The father below sums up the secret of success well:

HUSBAND: "Try to understand why my children think the way they do. Hope I've given them a good example to follow. Have tried to guide them when they need it. Supported them money-wise and emotionally."

To understand why children think the way they do is to be able to think as they do, and no parent could be more fair in his judgment than by first viewing the situation through his child's eyes. To set an example to be followed, rather than pointing down an arduous untraveled road . . . to guide when they needed a guide, but allow them to take steps on their own. To support, not carry.

Would it not be wonderful if all parents could be competent! Reformers keep writing articles advocating licensed parenting, proposing measures ranging from enforced administration of contraceptives to removal of children from parents who cannot pass a licensing exam. Is is not as important to be able to raise a child as it is to drive a car, they argue.

The reasoning is sound, but to effect such changes without turning America into a totalitarian state is impossible. The institution of marriage licenses never stopped people from cohabitation, pregnancy and child-raising out of wedlock, and attempts to regulate childbirth, even if we could construct and support the bureaucracy needed to implement such control, could still be easily defied. It has been proposed that children born to "unlicensed" couples be removed to foster placement until the required examination was passed; in our present system, the state is hard-pressed to find humane accommodations for those miserable few who are battered or abused sufficiently to be removed from their parents, and the prospect of assuming full care for a sizeable percentage of the newborn population is unthinkable.

At the 1978 summer program conference at Indiana University's Institute for Sex Research, a psychological expert described a case in which a Southern mother and father introduced their teen-aged son and daughter to sex education by having intercourse with them, which the siblings later engaged in between themselves; the expert decried the court decision that sent the children to live with relatives in California for five years, because these were basically loving parents and one of the "victims" was a 10-year-old boy who hadn't even been included in the family orgy. Rather than being lynched or at least hissed off the stage, the speaker was warmly applauded by the assembly of mental health professionals, whose concept of good parenting covered a multitude of sins, incest included.

But assuming we could somehow mandate and implement a procedure for parental licensing, let us not be naive about its effectiveness. The world's most incorrigible speeder will dutifully answer a driver's license exam with the correct local speed limit; and the world's most reprehensible child-beater can mouth platitudes about the proper handling of children. Even if the experts cannot agree on answers, we all can describe approximately the saintly ideal methods of raising children, though, being honest men and women, we would never lay claim to being able to practice them at all times.

What was George Bernard Shaw's solution? He, too, advocated licensing, proposing that licenses be issued for the hunting of children. Noting that the foxes and geese of England were better protected than children, he reasoned that the dangers of being shot during a two-month season would be more than balanced by the care and preservation of their welfare during the remaining ten months.

Perhaps the most practical solution at the moment is to throw the burden on our schools, which have already assumed the non-academic responsibilities of child health and nutrition. Compulsory education insures a ripe captive audience for a series of lessons in parenting similar to the sex education lectures that have added reproduction to the three R's. If we can tolerate frogs, hamsters, and rabbits in the classrooms in the interest of biology and natural history, surely we can expose the children to an occasional baby or toddler on loan from a neighborhood family.

Even the sex education curriculum is working the bugs out. One Scarsdale mother was explaining how her 10-year-old had received his very first lesson—homosexuality. "What the hell happened to heterosexuality?" the aghast listener demanded. "Oh," she explained, "the other half of the class got that one."

If we stick with it long enough, maybe someday we will get it all together.

7

Battlegrounds:

Fighting in Marriage

This is not quarreling... it's only English family life.

—*George Bernard Shaw,* GETTING MARRIED

"I'm not allowed to subtract!" Phyllis complains bitterly.

The therapist listens in mock horror. He has heard of men who beat their wives, men who interfere with their wives' choice of friends, men who deprive their spouses of even enough money to buy milk for the children. But to prevent a 25-year-old woman from subtracting is the greatest infringement on personal liberty since the Stamp Act! One could argue that her husband has left her the pleasures of addition and apparently overlooked the higher pleasures of multiplication and she can, if sufficiently secretive, indulge in a bit of division—although long division does involve a certain amount of subtraction. The psychiatrist is about to ask the couple whether the ban extends to long division, when Phyllis resumes her grievance.

"I made a lousy eight-cent error in balancing the checkbook. I subtracted wrong."

"All I said to her was if you're going to do something, take the trouble to do it right," husband Martin says with calm authority. "Besides, it's not just the eight-cent error. There was a check missing that we couldn't account for, and then she finally remembered that she had written one and forgotten to record it."

"Well," Phyllis snaps indignantly, "if he's going to be such a perfectionist, he can do all the checkbook-balancing. I won't touch it anymore."

"You won't let yourself subtract anymore," the therapist nods, finally understanding the nature of the prohibition.

Phyllis and Martin have been married less than two years, and they estimate they have been separated about 18 times. Phyllis always initiates the separation by fleeing to her nearby mother's house, Martin always ends it by cajoling Phyllis back with declarations of love and promises to be more understanding. Phyllis's flight generally puts and end to a quarrel which has been raging for several hours. Psychologically speaking, Phyllis and Martin are as excellently matched for fighting as a cobra and a mongoose. She is a hysteric and he is an obsessive. These terms are not used in a perjorative sense or as a diagnosis of severe mental disorder, but as the acknowledgment of two different personality types that approach the world in vastly different ways. The hysteric is a person who lives by emotion, acting impulsively, expressing feelings openly, and trusting to intuition. The obsessive lives by intellect, guards displays of emotion, and acts slowly, always questioning the wisdom of the decision so laboriously made. The average personality is a blend of the rational and emotional features. While usually one set of defenses merely tends to predominate, a few people are entirely governed by one of the two spheres, unlike Chaucer's Wife of Bath, who said, "For I belong to Venus in my feelings, though I bring the heart of Mars to all my dealings."

Since Martin prides himself on his reason, he feels that logic will prevail in settling any quarrel, provided emotions are kept under control. Since he is more reasonable than his wife, he invariably holds the correct viewpoint, so if he persists in presenting it to Phyllis and can keep her from exploding, sooner or later, she is bound to see things his way. Phyllis may be emotional, but she is no dummy—when Martin has persisted in his unrelenting arguments for more than eight hours, she realizes that she can only capitulate or run; so she flees, forcing Martin to come to her with protestations of love and need, which puts the fight on her turf. Martin is, to his consternation, not perfect; at least according to Phyllis, he does rant, curse, and even come to blows with her. Much of this is unacceptable to Martin's image of himself, so he simply denies that it ever happened. Since Phyllis is such an obvious hysteric and he is so clearly calm and logical, it should be apparent that the more brutal sides of the fights are products of Phyllis's imagination.

Probably there is no therapeutic situation that requires as much self-discipline on the psychiatrist's part as treating the battling couple. From the moment they enter the room, they engage in a spirited debate, recounting not only their most recent dispute, but dredging up great battles of the past like a professor of ancient history. If he is not careful, the psychiatrist will find himself a rapt ringside spectator as the clock ticks away the dollars like a taxi-meter. Well, he can alibi, their interaction gave vent to a lot of emotions, and catharsis is therapeutic—but in cases such as this the "catharsis" is continuous and one does not give a cathartic to a case of typhoid dysentery. The therapist must not intervene just for the protection of the office furnishings; he must, once he has reached a glimmering of what keeps the conflict in a steady state, provide enough friction through his questions, direction, or interpretation to bring the battle to a halt, slow it down, or transfer it to a more appropriate battleground. Like the drunk who was searching for his wallet six blocks from where he lost it because the light on that street was better, many couples are fighting over totally irrelevant issues because the real issues are too painful or threatening to confront. Phyllis and Martin came into the office not quarreling really about subtraction, or eight cents, or even balanced checkbooks; the issue was basically one of trust. Phyllis, it turned out, had committed far more grievous financial offenses than careless bookkeeping; several months ago, after a disagreement with Martin about how much she should spend on household furnishings, she lied to her husband about the actual cost of some drapes, hoping somehow later to replace the excessive expenditure in their joint savings account. To her, money was an expression of love, and when Martin refused to let her buy the things her wealthy parents and more prosperous brothers were accustomed to, she saw him as rejecting her. Martin was understandably incensed by her deception and any disagreement over money was bound to bring up the incident of the curtains.

Is such fighting inevitable in a marriage? Occasionally, one encounters couples who never fight, but this is because their personalities are such that they will give in on any point of contention because they cannot bear displays of aggression or any threat of loss of affection. Many are the type who would never question a waiter's addition or return an unsatisfactory piece of merchandise. Others may be absolute tyrants and harridans at work or in the nursery, venting their frustration on every subordinate, public employee, and defenseless child because they dare not oppose a domineering spouse to whom they defer as they generally did to a similar parent. Occasionally, there is a subtle *folie-a-deux* form of paranoia, where the couple bands closely together against what is perceived as a totally hostile and untrustworthy world.

These atypical couples notwithstanding, there will be disagreements in any marriage, whether or not they qualify as true quarrels or fights. Nearly half of the people we surveyed chose the term "considerate" to describe themselves or their spouses. "Considerate" implies that we consider the wishes of other people and anticipate that they will often differ from our own. Tyrants are not considerate and they are the least quarrelsome people imaginable; they simply do not tolerate quarrels and eliminate those who disagree with them not by putting an end to the disagreement, but to the disagreeable party through incarceration or even more through means of dispatch. We have probably all encountered supervisors who usually consider their subordinates' questions by listening very carefully and then replying, "Yes, but do it my way." And we should not consider such tyrants "considerate" for true consideration means substituting another will for your own. When we encounter someone like our patient, Martin, who feels that by virtue of his superior education, age, and unemotional processes of logic he possesses a superior will to that of his wife, we can hardly ever imagine his substituting an inferior will for his own. And when a wife such as Phyllis has too much self-respect and a desire for liberation to defer her preferences in all matters, plus a personality so different from her husband's that they are bound to have dissimilar tastes in more instances than not, we have a state of constant war.

Even if a degree of disagreement is inevitable in all marriages, it is not necessary to refine the arts of warfare, for it has been observed that when one nation wins most of the battles and its adversary wins most of the treaties, the latter wins the war. What people fight about is not more important than how they go about fighting and peacemaking, so we shall inquire about all these aspects of domestic strife.

Aphrodite in Arms

Homer, author of the first popular war novel, tells us in the *Iliad* that Aphrodite, goddess of love, was so distraught at seeing her Trojan hero, Aeneas, about to be killed by the Greeks that she pitched into the battle herself, sustaining a spear-wound of the hand in the process. Sibling rivalry being what it is, even back then, Athene, goddess of war, told father Zeus that her sister must have scratched her hand on one of the brooches worn by the Greek women she was forever luring into Trojan arms.

The smiling Zeus took Aphrodite aside and gently remonstrated, "Fighting, my child, is not for you. *You* are in charge of wedlock and the tender passions. We will leave the enterprising War-god and Athene to look after military affairs."

Three thousand years after this story was first told, the goddess of wedlock still has not managed to keep out of warfare and as many of her charges are under arms as in each other's arms. Virgin Athene may have been incapable of loving a man, but her more versatile sister was never unable to fight one.

What are the most frequent grounds for battle in the armed camps of Aphrodite? The leading cause of friction was money, far above the second most common grievance, unpleasant personal habits. Fifteen per cent of the people we surveyed said they never argued, but only 7 per cent of the couples in our subgroup of matched pairs agreed that they never argued, so we can conclude that a high percentage of such peaceful households is a matter for argument. One out of six couples in this matched group agreed that money was the most common grounds for dissension.

Of course, there are minor spats and major donnybrooks, and perhaps the best way to approach the field of conflict is to skirt the skirmishes and focus attention on the sort of battle that makes marital history.

Describe the worst fight you and your spouse ever had.

Only about one in 20 of our respondents said that attention to members of the opposite sex was the most frequent cause of arguments. But when the problem of infidelity arises, real or imagined, the ensuing battle tends to be memorable:

WIFE: "Where I caught him and his brother-in-law at two girls' apartment. They were in bed and would not come to the door. I called the Vice Squad and they knocked the door down and took them all to jail. When he got out, he beat me terribly. We had a fight. That was the worst or one of the worst fights we ever had."

HUSBAND: "She caught me one night at a nightclub with a girl, and I think that was the worst one. I had a black eye and she had two."

She's a blue collar worker, 41 to 50, a high school graduate. She has never cheated, and says their sex life is satisfactory. She feels tied down, however, and that she lives for her children, and dominated by her husband. She feels that their marriage is in constant turmoil, and sees cheating, jobs, alcohol, lack of communication, conflicts over relatives and children, difference in interests all as major problems. He's a blue collar worker between 41 and 50, as well. This is his second marriage. He would harm her physically, he says, if he were to find that she was cheating. He feels tied down, and rates the marriage as fairly stable.

WIFE: "Fight because of jealousy. I'm not jealous anymore, because I love him and our sex life is great!"

HUSBAND: "Violent—she caught me talking to another girl, who was a relative, unknown to her."

WIFE: "He was working *all* the time—or it seemed to me. A 'friend' convinced me he was having an affair, and my own insecurity and poor self-image made me believe her. I cried, and even took off in the car for an hour. When I came home, he assured me he was not having an affair. We then made up a schedule of work and time at home that satisfied both of us— and we stuck to it."

HUSBAND: "Wife thought I was unfaithful and walked out on me for fifteen minutes. She came back and we talked about it and made up."

WIFE: "When he fell in love with a young starlet and brought her home to *live with us*. I left and wouldn't come back 'til she was gone."

HUSBAND: "When I brought a young woman to live in our place for a while."

She is a homemaker with some college education, 41 to 50. They have had a brief period of separation. They have a variable sex life, she feels. She feels more nervous and irritable since marriage, dominated by her spouse, and overwhelmed by responsibility. She sees conflicts over relatives and the children, as well as different interests as their main problems. He's a professional with some college, 51 or over. They lived together 3 to 6 months before marriage. Both feel their spouses appreciate them as lovers, but think they need improvement in other ways.

WIFE: "It was during a very unsettling period when my husband was out of work. Because he was free most of the time, I thought he might be playing around with one of our neighbors. However, I was proved wrong, thank God."

HUSBAND: "Nothing more than a lot of hard talking."

Notice how husbands tend to minimize things, whether it was the seriousness of the matter, the duration of the conflict, or the intensity of the battle. Even when the problem is serious enough to drive husband home to mother, he is not as likely to take it seriously in retrospect:

WIFE: "Was when my husband left to go home to his parents because he didn't get laid enough."

HUSBAND: "Normal fight."

Sexual problems were the prime cause of arguments in only 6 per cent of our respondents, although nearly twice as many were found in the 31 to 40 age bracket. Children as the most common source of arguments also rose sharply in this age group, but the sexual complaints dropped to a level lower than in the youngest group at age 40, whereas the percentage complaining about children held at its elevated level. The two factors are probably related, younger children interfering with sexual activity more than older ones who are less demanding of time and attention. Boredom with the spouse when the sex drive is still high and unattached young partners relatively available probably also lead to sexual maladjustment in the thirties, which is either resolved or accepted with time.

Some couples were in unanimous agreement about which fight was their worst, while with others it was a split decision:

WIFE: "We were arguing. My spouse slapped me in the face and I threw an iron skillet at him and almost hit him in the head, so we both shut up before it went any further and we hurt one another."

HUSBAND: "We were arguing and my spouse clammed up and wouldn't argue. So I slapped her in the face and she threw an iron skillet at me and almost hit me. We both shut up."

WIFE: "Lost in Kansas City (at night) we couldn't find the right highway to lead home. I was blamed for not giving better directions and watching signs. Both were shouting at one another senselessly! I was screaming defensively because he was tired and wanted to be home. Also, he didn't want me shouting so loud in a strange place where someone could see we were lost and take advantage of us both. I was also shouting because I didn't want him to look bad with him driving and lost. (Each was trying to protect the other. . . .)"

HUSBAND: "My spouse was worried as to whether we had enough money to pay our income taxes. I felt we should just cross that bridge when we come to it, and if we didn't have enough money we could borrow from relatives. Well, it wasn't enough reasoning for her to stop worrying, so she continued to let it upset her and finally we both came unglued over the fact that if she didn't like the way we handled the money, she should just take care of all the money herself."

The less money people have, the more arguments it causes. Those earning under $10,000 a year cited finances as the main source of arguments over 50 per cent more often than those making more than that amount. Blacks prevailed by a similar margin over whites. The age group that argued least over money consisted of those over 50, who might be assumed to be most financially secure; this was borne out by the low percentage picking this answer among the retired/unemployed, a group in which the oldest age bracket outnumbered all those under 50 by a comfortable margin.

Men may be warriors by tradition, but with a few ancient exceptions like Homer and a few modern ones like Howard Cosell at ringside, they don't do a very good job of describing fights. As the wife below illustrates, embattled husbands are often outspoken—by their wives:

WIFE: "Our fights usually start over nothing. Once, he spilled his cereal on my head, pulled out a handful of hair, and hit me because I said something true to him that he couldn't face. I have no physical ability to get back at him, so I use my tongue, and when I hit the mark, he sometimes gets completely out of control."

It's not likely that Vidal Sassoon spends much of his time picking raisins and bran flakes out of his customers' coiffures, but such daytime cereal dramas between husbands and wives aren't half as funny as when W.C. Fields would crown some mischievous babe with pablum on the screen. But little girls do start to talk earlier than little boys, and most males never do catch up. Thus, many husbands are so badly outmatched by their wives' lashing tongues that they ultimately resort to some sort of physical action. Husbands who participated in our survey hardly ever described fights in more than one sentence, and so we will have to rely on the wives for the gruesome details.

Pre-Liberation mothers used to chant to their babies, "Clap hands, clap hands till Daddy comes home. Daddy has money and Mommy has none." Adam Smith never agonized over this glaring inequity in the distribution of wealth, but many a wife has gone to war—or work—over it:

WIFE: "The worst fight we had was a matter of my independence at the expense of his. I wanted to go back to work. It meant I would have to work weekends for at least part of the weekend. This interfered with his tennis on Sunday morning and it also meant he had to give the children dinner on Saturday evening. I wanted to work to earn enough money to accompany him on a business trip to the Orient. He felt the trip was foolish for me and said, 'You are not going to spend so much of *my* hard-earned money frivolously.' This made me angry because whenever I have worked, I have always contributed to *our* bank account, not one for me alone. Regardless of this, I may not be gainfully employed, but I *do work* as a wife and mother, etc. I, therefore, feel that he is not the only one earning a living—unfortunately, he is the only one getting paid in dollars and cents.

"I decided to earn the money for *my* trip, myself. He argued that if I wasn't going on *his* money, I wasn't going.

"When I started working, he used every excuse he could to try and make me feel guilty. Finally, it caused a big blow-up. I demanded to be *paid* in money for my wifely duties. That did it. He has never used the term 'my money' again. I did stop working eventually, and he did agree to take me to the Orient with him on his next trip."

Money and jobs are inseparable, so it is not surprising that jobs should also be a cause of arguments. About 1 respondent in 12 cited jobs and careers as the biggest cause of friction. In a separate question involving attitudes towards the spouse's job, only half of the wives had no complaint about it. The most common complaint (one in six wives) was not enough pay and close behind it was that it took up too much of the husband's time. Lack of opportunity for advancement was cited by one in twelve wives. Husbands of working wives likewise complained most often of insufficient salary, with proportionately less concerned about hours and promotion.

WIFE: "When my husband wanted to enter a new business venture, he came home and told me his exciting news. I thought the venture was very risky and I told him so. He became very upset and insisted that I wanted to put a damper on all his ideas. After we calmed down, I agreed that the business should be seen, the books examined, and then a decision would be made."

Two per cent of wives felt their husbands' occupations were too dangerous. Not all dangerous occupations involve strenuous physical feats. Musicians, for example, may develop a short-circuit in their electric guitars, become deafened by their amplifiers, suffer brain degeneration from modern music, or confront even more frequent hazards:

WIFE: "He's a part-time musician, has played with many groups—at the time, this group wasn't the best—had him drinking quite a bit—which made living very difficult for children and I . . . opposed and he hit me. . . .

"After thirty years of being a musician, it's not him I don't trust—but there is always one evil woman after any handsome man. Therefore, a wife should accompany him if he plays music more than once at the same place."

A wife cannot always be where her husband works to defend him against evil women. The thing 2 per cent of wives most disliked about their husbands' jobs was his co-workers and this prejudice would probably apply to the lady below whose husband apparently was putting in some overtime with a fellow-employee. However, as some of the other wives explain, you don't have to leave home to find temptation; it can be as close, for either spouse, as a next-door neighbor or the girl upstairs:

WIFE: "Only two years married, I discovered my husband was carrying on with a woman at work, through letters she wrote to our home. I confronted him with the knowledge in horrified recrimination. He made all kinds of promises. We kept our marriage going, but I think I lost all confidence in myself as a woman, and it probably influenced our sexual life together from then on."

She no longer has sex, and says she's very unsatisfied sexually. This is the major problem in her marriage. She's now 51 or over, and has a postgraduate degree.

WIFE: "Over my love for other people."

She's between 41 and 50, and has some college background. Works in the professional field. Admits to cheating with one other man and the affair lasted over a year. She says she rarely has sex with her husband. His job keeps him away from home a lot, and he takes her for granted. Says she lives only for her children.

WIFE: "We were married almost a year. I just found out I was expecting a child. There was a girl living in the apartment above us. She didn't have a husband anymore, also she was an ex-girlfriend of my husband's. My husband was also her little boy's godfather. It seemed to me, since her husband had left, that she was looking for any excuse to see my husband. I thought he was encouraging her with looks and little sayings. At the time, I was pregnant and I wasn't feeling well. Also, his mother always said he should have married her. I just blew up one day when he was making cute remarks to her and I started throwing things and hollering. At one point, I even asked him if he wanted her instead of me. Of course, he said no. This fight went on for three days."

This homemaker is between 41 and 50. She has 4 children, and never completed high school. She says they argue most about money and the children, though their sex life is very good, and the marriage is generally stable and loving.

WIFE "After having found out my husband had been seeing our neighbor and my best friend, we had a terrible fight. Blows were exchanged. I threw a full glass of gin and tonic and hit him in the back of the head."

Getting hit in the head with a gin-and-tonic is one of the least problems caused by alcohol in marriages. About one in 16 of our respondents said that most arguments were over alcohol, and wives mentioned this problem more often than husbands. White collar workers, professionals, and those with college backgrounds had this as the major problem less often than their blue collar or high school-educated counterparts, and people over 40 found it the main source of argument more often than younger people.

Some therapists believe that wives of alcoholics may often be the type of neurotic women who deliberately choose a man they can manipulate and dominate; Alcoholics Anonymous chapters now usually have Al-Anon groups for the spouses of drinkers, and it has been noted that wives will often decompensate emotionally when their husbands become sober. However, many of the more stable wives divorce alcoholic husbands early in the marriage and it is understandable that the stresses of living with an alcoholic will produce ill effects on mental stability in any woman who elects or is coerced by circumstances to remain committed. Alcoholism is not limited to males, and whereas male alcoholics once outnumbered females 5-to-1, the ratio is now less than 2-to-1, whether due to Women's Liberation and the acceptability of women drinking in bars, or merely the emergence of secret drinkers who no longer limit their imbibing to the sherry in the pantry.

Because the most severe male alcoholics are unemployed drifters who never would be considered candidates for marriage, we are likely to find a higher ratio of female to male alcoholics within marriage than in the general population.

WIFE: "We argued one night about the fact that I was drinking too much. He gave me a choice of drink or him. I chose him. He was right of course. I was drinking too much every night. This was just shortly after our marriage. It changed my life around and it all was for the best."

WIFE: "The worst fight was when my husband took a drink at a Christmas party when he promised me he would never drink. It wasn't the drink; it was that he went against something that meant so much to me. My husband didn't understand it and tried to explain that it didn't mean anything while at the same time felt really ashamed for hurting me so much. This made him get very defensive when he would normally just have apologized and ended the matter."

A high school graduate and white collar worker, she says her marriage is loving, and her sex life is very good, having intercourse once a day. She's between 18 and 30.

WIFE: "We have had a lot of them. I guess the morning my daddy died, my husband had stayed out drinking and I found him out in the car asleep (the next morning) and I fussed at him. And he came in the house and threw his pants at me while I was laying in the bed, and his knife in his pocket hit me on the leg and made a knot and made it bleed. Then he went to bed and made me stand with my nose on the wall, until I got the final call that my daddy had died."

In a separate question relating to the major problem (as opposed to source of arguments) in the marriage, 4 percent selected alcohol, with wives claiming this as the major problem twice as often as husbands. It was a more prominent problem in those over 30 and significantly higher among the remarried, who would, of course, be generally older.

The major problem in marriage, as cited in the responses to this question, was again money, but lack of communication trailed it by two-tenths of a percentage point. We did not list lack of communication among the prime causes for argument, since argument is, in itself, communication; however, it apparently caused not only arguments, but more severe consequences at times.

WIFE: "This was no physical fight, and actually very little was said. It was what was said and the way it was said. My husband was reading a magazine when I approached him. I told him that I was greatly concerned about our marriage and wanted to talk with him. He raised the magazine in front of his face and said, 'You so rarely have anything worth listening to or to say.' To which I replied, 'I never again will try to talk things over with you.' (I've seen an attorney and engaged a moving van.)"

She describes her husband as dominant, irresponsible, reserved, possessive and inconsiderate, and is definitely planning to divorce him. Says she feels unloved and unappreciated, and complains that her husband controls all major decisions, except the raising of the children.

Another factor seen as the major problem in marriage was difference in personal interests, which took fourth place with 13 per cent, 9 percentage points behind money and communication problems and only one point behind relatives. The most highly educated spouses found this more likely to be a problem, possibly because wives still tend to be less educated than husbands. In the question about most frequent causes of arguments, the categories of friends, social activities, religion, and politics—all likely to be areas of potential conflict aggravated by differences in interest—added up to 14 per cent, just about the same as those claiming differences in interest as the main marital problem. Sometimes the failure of spouses to agree on doing something that one of them desires can lead to bloodshed:

WIFE: "Wanted to go camping and he didn't. When I went to make up, he ran from me to the the bedroom, shut the door, and I ended up losing the tip of my little finger on my left hand. He bought me a stuffed dog and his insurance paid for my cosmetic surgery."

She's a blue collar worker, 31 to 40, a high school graduate. They never argue, their sex life is good, and she says she'd definitely marry the same person again (she describes him as considerate). Alcohol was the worst crisis in the marriage. She says it's a generally stable marriage, and always loving.

WIFE: "We had company coming. He wasn't pleased as they were my friends. I just got tired of all the hassle and said I didn't care if he stayed home for them (as he had mentioned doing). He stayed away until they were gone, the whole day. It never happened again. During the years, he became more amenable to having company, but he's broken up some of my friendships. No, they are not lower class people."

She's 51 or over, and says they no longer have sex. Admits to cheating briefly with one other man. Says she feels appreciated as a wife, but not as a lover. A homemaker.

WIFE: "My second husband, of four years, and I never argue. The worst fight I had with my first spouse was when he played cards 'til five in the morning and I disapproved because he had a heart attack previous to that and I said it was too much excitement for him. I took an overdose of sleeping pills. He played only until 1 A.M. after that and one day died at the card table. I survived!"

The grim story of death and triumph above recalls Myron Cohen's story of a similar card player whose companions, after standing up to finish the hand out of respect, decided to break the news to the widow in the kindest possible manner. "Your husband just lost over $100," they began. "He should drop dead!" she exclaimed. "He did," they obliged.

We can choose our friends, and sometimes even those of our spouses, but not our relatives. While twice as many respondents named conflicts over relatives as the major marital problem compared with those designating children, the percentages who argued about relatives and children most frequently were identical. This probably means that disagreements over raising and disciplining children are common, but handed with more acceptance than those involving in-laws, seen as a more grievous problem. Children can, however, be the cause of some rousing fights:

WIFE: "We have had no really bad fights. The worse disagreement we had, was over an adult child who had borrowed the car.

Something happened to the car which he blamed the child for. This thing would have happened to the car no matter who was driving it. He blew his stack, said terrible things to the kid (nineteen to twenty years old) and told him to get out. At the time the child was a college student. The child held his temper and went for a long walk, which was the best way to handle it. I asked him to be reasonable, that it wasn't the child's fault, that no matter who was driving the same thing would have happened and he answered that if the kid was so right maybe he should move out and the kid should stay (sarcastically). So I dropped the whole conversation: All this over eight dollars worth of anti-freeze, lost out of the radiator.

"A short time after that, my husband had a heart attack. Now, his whole personality is better. He only works forty hours a week (he used to work sixty to sixty-five) and he doesn't bring his job home with him. (Well, only occasionally.) I put the whole unreasonable fight down to the fact that he was overworked and under a lot of pressure at the time."

She's a homemaker, between 41 and 50, a high school graduate. They argue most about the children, but they have no major problems, she feels. Their sex life she describes as satisfactory.

WIFE: "When he hit our three-year-old son—not a spanking, but three hits across his back—I think I saw red. He has never hit our son again, who is now twelve. I approve of discipline and spanking on the seat of wisdom, but never any form of battering."

This is her second marriage, and she says that her children have led to many quarrels. She married her present husband because of pregnancy, and has already been separated from him. They never or rarely ever have sex, and she feels the marriage is a failure.

WIFE: "He has a son from a previous marriage, and I'm having trouble concerning him. At first, I resented his son and we fought terribly over him."

The least surprising statistic in the survey is that children are a bigger source of arguments for those who have them—yet, 2 per cent of those without children said this is what they argued about most. We assume these responses came from those who married someone with children from a previous marriage, and there was a slightly higher percentage of major arguments about children among the remarried. Professionals and other high-income people argued more over children, either because there was more potential for spoiling the children, or merely because they argued less about money.

Do men quarrel more with women who are dependent or independent? Is the dutiful wife who always has dinner on the table likely to have a quieter house than her liberated sister, or does the prospect of being saddled with a helpless helpmate make a man more irritable and belligerent? Apparently either course can lead to storms:

WIFE: "He came in from work one night and the baby and I were out shopping. I didn't have dinner fixed. He hates to come home without dinner waiting on the table for him. I came home about thirty minutes after he got there. He raised all sorts of hell. I had been out shopping for a present to give him for no reason other than being loving. That crushed me, so I just started raising hell back. We yelled back and forth and my temper rose so I started throwing things. The fight lasted for about three hours."

A white collar worker between 18 and 30, she feels dominated by her husband, and is not sure whether she'd ever marry the same person again. However, she still rates her marriage as "fairly loving."

WIFE: "The worst fight my husband and I have had were the ones where I always apologized and did the making up, even if I wasn't wrong. Only because I was scared of being alone. But once I finally realized that I might be making things worse by doing that, I started to quit being so dependent on my husband and it eased things for both of us. I didn't feel like a burden to him anymore, and I found I could be an independent person in some ways, yet be dependent on him for some needs without weighing him down. All of our fights were the same though, none worse than the others. Now that he knows I'm not going to fight him anymore, we don't fight."

While she admits they've struck each other during arguments, she says her marriage is a loving one. She lived with him 3 to

6 months before marrying, and is between 18 and 30. Didn't complete high school.

WIFE: "We do not have *fights*—just disagreements which are usually discussed and resolved."

"You turn round and make up to me now that I'm not afraid of you, and can do without you," Liza Doolittle snarls at her Pygmalion. "Of course I do, you little fool," retorts Henry Higgins. "Five minutes ago you were like a millstone round my neck. Now you're a tower of strength: a consort battleship."

Independence does not necessarily lead to smooth sailing, but when consort battleships start firing at one another, a discussion between equals tends to lead to peaceful resolutions quicker than slave rebellions.

After reading some of the stirring battle stories above, the entry below, describing the worst fight of a husband's marriage, reads like a routine entry in a ship's log:

HUSBAND: "February 20, 1978—throwing object."

As we said before, most men are not very talkative and if all males were equally succinct in the telling of war stories, *A Farewell to Arms* would have been a telegram instead of a novel. Nevertheless, to give the husbands some say, we will reprint their versions, in their entirety, of the major causes of argument in marriage, which, to recap, are money, personal habits, relatives, children, job and career, sexual problems, alcohol, and attention to members of the opposite sex:

HUSBAND: "We argued over alimony payments. She screamed, hit me, and ran out of the house, when I refused to discuss the situation. I was wrong for not communicating and she was wrong for acting like she did."

His marriage is a loving one, even though they argue mostly over money and their children. He lived with his wife for 6 months to a year prior to marriage. He's a professional with a postgraduate education, and is between 31 and 40.

HUSBAND: "Not a fight, but a vicious quarrel over the house and how little time she spent in keeping it 'presentable.'"

This husband married to have a homelife, and whereas he feels his marriage is fairly stable and loving, he feels sexually unsatisfied. Says it's a major problem. He has a postgraduate degree, works in the professional field, and is between 41 and 50.

HUSBAND: "About her family. They are so bossy—just blacked both her eyes."

A blue collar worker who didn't complete high school, he's between 41 and 50. Admits to cheating with more than 3 women, and says he married his wife because of pregnancy. Feels his marriage is in constant turmoil. Worst crisis was about relative living with them.

HUSBAND: "It was a disagreement over one of the children, we almost came to blows, we ended up giving each other the silent treatment for about three weeks."

He's retired, 51 or over, a high school graduate. They have 4 children, and argue most about them. He feels overwhelmed by responsibility, and says the marriage has alternating periods of closeness and remoteness.

HUSBAND: "Our worst fight was out of her boredom for the lack of time I spent with her in a strange town that we lived in. Due to work, I was unable to be home very often and when home, was tired from the pressure of my job. The fight was yelling and screaming on both sides and a separation for about one week."

He says moving was his worst crisis, but his marriage is on a sound footing. Works in management, and is between 18 and 30, with some college background.

HUSBAND: "Really not a fight, I just told her that I was tired of living this way and that I was going to leave her."

He says both he and his wife have considered divorce, but took no action on it. Admits to cheating with more than 3 women, with one affair lasting over a year. Sex is dull, and he feels tied down. Still rates his marriage as being "fairly stable" though.

HUSBAND: "I stayed out all night drinking and came home about eight in the morning. My wife went wild. I had to stay away from her and let her go off by herself until she got over it."

He's a high school graduate, 31 to 40. This is his fourth marriage, and they have 5 children. They lived together for 6 months to a year before getting married. He has cheated with 1 person, briefly. He says their major problems involve jobs, and that they have alternating periods of closeness and remoteness.

HUSBAND: "Four years ago, I got drunk and we got in an argument. Thought she was going to leave. I drank too much many times, but this one made her angry. I joined AA; haven't drank since."

This is his second marriage, and he says it's a stable one. He works in management, is between 31 and 40. Has a high school education.

HUSBAND: "I came home early one day and found her with another man and the words and her fist flew. I then left till I cooled down."

HUSBAND: "When my girlfriend told wife we were together. Lots of cry, yelling, etc."

"Lots of cry, yelling, etc.," pretty well summarizes marital fighting, especially "etc." Throughout nature, we find many distinct ways of dealing with hostile situations, coming under the general categories of fight and flight. Some creatures attack with paws and claws, some with their mouths, some use venom, and some take refuge behind shells or spines. Some run away, some go underground, some camouflage themselves, and a few make believe they're dead. Humans are just as varied in their styles of dealing with an attacker, as we shall investigate.

Choose Your Weapons

"I know there are discussions in which the poker is the only possible argument," concedes the liberal Bishop Bridgenorth. One of the problems with central heating is not only have we lost the hearth, but the poker as well. This has not eliminated physical violence, however, one-quarter of the people we surveyed admitted that their arguments had at some time resulted in physical attacks. Married people under 30 were considerably more likely to engage in physical assaults and we presume this is a product of our violent times, since the question asked if there had *ever* been a physical attack. Low-income earners, people who did not complete high school, non-whites, and blue collar workers were more likely to give histories of blows being exchanged. People who were remarried were more violent, which might explain why their first marriages failed.

Although there were twice as many instances where the husband's attack on the wife was unrequited, 4 per cent of the respondents said only the women had struck blows. Wives seemed capable of returning tit-for-tat in all age groups, but among the more educated classes the ratio of marriages where only one spouse beat the other evened out, wives actually outnumbering the husbands in making unilateral assaults among the white collar workers, students, and people with some college education short of graduation. In our subsample of matched couples, only 58 per cent agreed that their quarrels never came to blows and only 8 per cent agreed that both had indulged in physical attacks, the rest generally not able to get together on who did what to whom.

Physical violence among married people has become epidemic—or acknowledged—enough for the government to subsidize the construction of shelters for battered wives and their children, to offer a haven for women who lack the economic independence to otherwise escape. There was considerable community opposition when one of these was started in a lower socioeconomic area in Brooklyn on the grounds that the shelter would bring bad women into the neighborhood, that women who got battered probably deserved it, and that the state should not meddle in family affairs.

Given our current passion for equal rights, it should be only a matter of time before shelters are constructed for battered men. Lest we are too prone to blame Women's Liberation for the recent attention to husbands who are beaten, let us not forget the venerable Anglo-American heritage of comic marriages, from the Punch and Judy shows where Punch carried the stick but got most of the lumps, to Maggie and Jiggs who appeared for decades in the comic-strip *Bringing Up Father,* where Jiggs was barraged with crockery and rolling-pins without raising even a voice to Maggie. A turn-of-the-century deck of playing cards reproduced by Tiffany & Company portrays an inebriated king of clubs coming home while the angry queen carries a candle and a blunt wooden instrument. The king of spades has his arm in a sling, his foot in a cast, a patch over his eye, and carries a cane. It is a curious feature of our culture that we can find a battered husband hilarious, but would be outraged at a portrayal of a woman similarly maimed.

Fortunately, even if a sizeable percentage of spouses resort to physical attacks on rare occasions, most fights are characterized by more human, if not humane, styles of fighting.

How do you conduct yourself during a fight? Do you yell, remain silent and cold, walk out, break things, etc.? How does your partner's style of fighting differ from your own?

"Home life as we understand it is no more natural to us than a cage is natural to a cockatoo," Shaw maintained. As we observed before, the natural world deals with hostility by fight or flight and it stands to reason that if there is no exit, there is no flight. People who are forced to live in cramped, overcrowded quarters are far more apt to come to physical blows than those who can escape behind the wheel of a car, to a corner tavern, or a den or bedroom with a door to slam. Put two shrews in the same cage or two piranha fish in the same tank with no means of egress, and soon only one will be left; this applies only to pairs of males—humans seem to be a rather unique species in possessing males who attack females. In any event, flight is usually an option, even if a temporary one, and the flexible fighter knows how to retreat as well as attack.

Sometimes it is the husband who tries to be the prototype of the silent hero. In its section on memorable quotes, *The Official Encyclopedia of Baseball* gives us the following from Charlie Gehringer, baseball's strong, silent man: "———."

WIFE: "I calmly try to make my opinion understood. He usually says 'the decision is made.' So any discussion ends after he clams up."

HUSBAND: "I keep my mouth shut and take it. But someday, someday!"

WIFE: "I'm very calm and never lose my temper."

HUSBAND: "I don't fight. Besides, Homo sapiens have a brain so they can talk out of it. Or if I can't I will kill the other person."

She is a white collar worker, 18 to 30, a college graduate. They lived together for over a year before they got married. They argue most about friends, and she says it's a fairly stable marriage. He is a professional with a postgraduate education, between 18 and 30. He says that the marriage is in constant turmoil, and they argue most about attention to members of the opposite sex.

When someone is very contented, he is sometimes described as "happy as a clam at high tide." The saying has been shortened at times to "happy as a clam," leading people to ponder what a clam has to be happy about, other than staying out of chowders and cocktail sauce. For one thing, however, clams are bisexual, so in quarrels with their mates (they do mate after a fashion, since they take turns laying and fertilizing eggs, rather than handling the whole operation themselves), they could easily see both sides of the argument. And when things got really bad, a clam could simply isolate itself from the environment until its disposition improved. Wives are as apt to be the one who clams up or tearfully retreats like an oyster to a watery cloister, whether or not they are married to husbands who similarly emulate the selfish shellfish.

WIFE: "I sulk, don't want to talk. My husband wants to air it all out—get it out in the open."

HUSBAND: "I want to reconcile and never leave a fight until we have reached decisions. My wife likes to pout and becomes very stubborn. My wife remains silent and cold. Every once in a while either one of us may walk out."

WIFE: "Me—I try to talk it out. Him—states his opinion, has tendency not to listen to my point of view. Criticizes my point of view."

HUSBAND: "I do raise my voice if provoked or else it's the silent treatment and/or cold shoulder. Don't break things (illogical). Spouse becomes emotional—cries silently in bedroom or bathroom but no physical violence or breaking things."

She is a blue collar worker, 18 to 30, with some college. They have no children. They have struck each other. She says she feels unloved and unappreciated, more nervous and irritable since marriage. Although the sex is good, she says, they have alternating periods of closeness and remoteness, and she thinks her spouse wishes they never got married. He is a professional with some college, 18 to 30. He says the marriage is generally stable.

WIFE: "I remain very silent and distant after an argument. My husband does the same thing."

HUSBAND: "I remain very silent and refuse to talk. I give her the cold shoulder and act as if she is not in the house. My wife's style is about the same."

Comedian Sid Caesar used to do a zany professor routine in which he was supposed to be an expert mountain climber. Asked what one should do upon falling off a mountain, he advised screaming at the top of your lungs all the way down so that searchers could easily locate the body. When the dissatisfied interviewer asked if the professor had nothing better to suggest, he replied that you could flap your arms and fly to safety. When the exasperated interviewer objected that people cannot fly, the professor retorted, "What have you got to lose? You might be the first one.... You can always go back to screaming!"

When spouses try their best to be mature and competent, they can take heart, when their stamina fails, in the professor's advice:

"You can always go back to screaming!" And some wives do, after initial attempts at quieter coping, fall back on yelling:

WIFE: "I start out quietly discussing things, then if I am not getting through I yell and swear. He is very quiet at the beginning and usually walks out unless I push him to the point of destroying household objects."

A white collar worker between 18 and 30, she definitely plans to divorce her husband. Says she and her husband rarely ever have sex.

Some women begin by yelling, and then try less noisy methods of resolving the conflict or relieving the frustration. Others begin by yelling—and keep right on going.

WIFE: "I am an impulsive fighter—I like to yell for a minute and relieve my frustration and then discuss the situation calmly. My husband refuses to confront me when I'm mad—he ignores the issue, but remains warm and friendly until I calm down. Then we discuss it. I will occasionally (instead of yelling) do housework at a furious speed to work off my anger until I calm down. My husband never gets angry at all."

This homemaker says she is the dominant one in her marriage and her husband is passive. However they don't argue, and rates her marriage as stable and loving. Between 18 and 30, with some college education.

WIFE: "I scream—which accomplishes nothing—because my husband is calm and just doesn't answer. This infuriates me so that I really scream. Finally, I resort to tears and my husband responds sympathetically at once."

She's a professional, 41 to 50, a college graduate. They argue most about relatives. She feels overwhelmed by responsibility. The marriage, she feels, is generally stable.

WIFE: "Yelling—both of us. But he walks out in the middle— terribly frustrating."

WIFE: "I yell. He hits me, or a wall or door."

She is retired, 51 or over, with some college education. This is her second marriage. She and her husband argue most about the children, money, and social activities. She feels dominated by him, tied down, and disillusioned about romance and love. She thinks it's a fairly stable marriage, but has alternating periods of remoteness and closeness.

WIFE: "I yell to get my feelings out of my system. That way I don't stay mad. Partner yells, but I feel comments made are 'hitting below the belt' and said in anger. When I'm angry I try not to say things that won't be forgotten when the fight is over."

Not all spouses guard their remarks during a quarrel as the lady above does. Martin and Phyllis obviously say wounding things to one another in the heat of battle that fester later, since they recount them in therapy sessions. Martin tells Phyllis she's self-centered and has "a weak character." Phyllis goes for the groin and says things such as "You've never satisfied me sexually" and "Your body disgusts me." These charges, if valid, would not be changed by a state of truce and will leave bitter feelings in the minds of the accused long after the brawl is over.

Some wives confessed that they kept their tongues honed to a sharp edge during quarrels, whether they threw things up or just threw things:

WIFE: "I either pout or become sarcastic, neither of which are very constructive. My husband is more direct."

She's between 41 and 50, with a postgraduate degree. Says she argues mostly about sexual problems, and an extramarital affair was her worst crisis. Works as a professional.

WIFE: "I become very hurt. Feel I don't deserve all these accusations. Throw up to him how hard I work and that I am ill too but can't lay back and expect to be cared for or at least share some of the responsibilities. He screams and is verbally abusive and ridicules everything. Threatens me physically but has never hit me."

She has been separated from her husband and has considered divorce. This is her second marriage. Admits to cheating with another man for over a year, and while she has many negatives feelings about their marriage, believes it is still a loving one.

WIFE: "I am very vocal and good at making cruel remarks—if very mad I throw things. Husband more likely quiet—if angry enough, walks out."

The French have a proverb: "A deaf husband and a blind wife are always a happy couple." A man can achieve some measure of happiness and still retain his hearing for the play-by-play sports broadcasts by marrying a woman who is silent, or at least soft-spoken, during arguments:

WIFE: "During a fight, I try to remain calm, then become silent and cold for a long period afterwards. My husband states his mind and then abruptly walks away before we have finished the 'discussion.' I am the one who in the end always says 'I'm sorry!'"

She's a college graduate, now a homemaker, between 31 and 40. While her arguments are mostly over her children, she feels her marriage is stable.

WIFE: "We don't argue a lot. Sometimes we know of a matter some people would fight openly about but we don't say a lot and it dies down. For serious matters we talk freely and it's usually a long conversation. He avoids arguing more than I do."

Where the daily fare seems to be a choice between hot tongue and cold shoulder, many husbands elect the latter even if the chill creeps in under the bedcovers:

HUSBAND: "My partner and I both have the poor fighting habit of 'clamming up.' We don't talk. Occasionally yelling may come into the picture but that's the extent. Usually we remain silent and cold. Both of us do the same things. My wife may get mad and I won't know it until I try to get friendly with her and have sex on my mind—then I get the cold shoulder."

While money and jobs are this husband's major problem, he feels his marriage is on solid ground. A professional, with a postgraduate degree, he's between 31 and 40.

HUSBAND: "It used to be talk but as the lying and cheating increased it went to silent and cold. I stayed to finish raising the family. The partner is a little noisier."

In baseball, when a pitcher finds a troublesome man at home, he often can be eliminated by means of an intentional walk. Some husbands give themselves a walk to eliminate the risk of hitting:

HUSBAND: "Remain silent and cold until I reach boiling point at which time I walk out. I return only after I have come back to my senses without the aid of drugs or alcohol. My spouse yells, and occasionally breaks things. After she calms down she is very perceptive of the problem and attempts to iron it out."

He says they argue mostly about his attention to members of the opposite sex. Describes himself as dominant, his wife as possessive. Lack of communication between them is his major problem. A college graduate, he works in management.

HUSBAND: "I walk out of house and go to the nearest bar."

He's a high school graduate, between 18 and 30, who says he cheated with 2 or 3 other women, briefly. Says he feels tied down and trapped, and his major problem is lack of communication.

HUSBAND: "I yell a lot and have walked out. I find that I give in quite often, more than my wife. She is quite emotional in a fight and usually cries."

> "Sayin' nothin'," says the goldsmith, "is a woman's rarest skill."
> "Birds should sing," remarked the Doctor, "but a woman should be still."
> —Wallace Irwin, THE CHAMBER OF TRANQUILITY

It is not a woman's natural proclivity to be silent, but husbands occasionally drive them to unnatural acts. Some husbands get so excited during a quarrel that they don't really listen to much except the sound of silence.

HUSBAND: "I yell—don't listen to what she tries to say. I don't stop to think about why the fight started before flying off the handle. I never hit or would ever hurt her in any way, but tend to throw things around, that I have in my hands at the minute."

While his marriage is a loving one, his major problem involves his jobs. He's between 18 and 30, and a high school graduate. Says he's "retired."

HUSBAND: "We both are excitable. We start out rationally, but I like my decisions to be respected. She should consider I've had a heart attack and can't run around doing things, except to play golf. I get very angry with her and I know I'm unreasonable. We both holler a little but lately she doesn't say much."

He's retired now, 51 or over, and admits to cheating on his wife with one other woman, and the affair lasted over a year. He argues mostly about career and social activities. Says he's overwhelmed by responsibility, and is more nervous and irritable than ever before.

HUSBAND: "I usually try to remain calm and attempt to see my wife's point of view, however she will not tell me what is wrong most of the time. This results in a cross-examination by me to determine the problem and I usually end up aggravated and then just leave her alone. My wife does not fight, if she's angry she usually keeps to herself, and when I leave her alone she talks to herself."

He's a professional, 18 to 30, with some college. They argue most about money. An extramarital affair was the worst crisis in the marriage (he's never cheated). He feels their sex life is unsatisfactory, and he feels unloved and unappreciated. He thinks lack of communication is their major problem, and rates the marriage as being in constant turmoil.

HUSBAND: "I am, perhaps, more vociferous than my wife but not to the point of yelling and never walk out or throw or break things. My wife is the 'quit talking type' for a while and then we, 'talk out' our problem."

HUSBAND: "It depends on the subject and intensity. Overall when I respond one way my wife usually responds the opposite and the reverse is true. Therefore, our disagreements are short lived. We have one rule: Bedtime is makeup time! and it works!!"

"And so to bed," as Samuel Pepys wrote in his widely circulated diary. Pepys was himself widely circulated among the ladies of London and frequented more beds than the one his wife shared. Still, he was an affectionate husband and Shaw wrote, "Imagine being married to a liar, a borrower, a mischief maker, a teaser or tormentor of children and animals, or even simply to a bore!... What woman would not rather marry ten Pepyses?" Ultimately we each make our own beds and lie in them, generally not alone, deciding whether they are to be hotbeds of contention or demilitarized zones. Would that every night could bring us the valediction of Romeo: "Sleep dwell upon thine eyes, peace in thy breast!"

War and Peace

"Born enemies don't fight.... Just as nature, when she foresees a struggle between two kinds of insects, equips them with weaknesses and weapons which correspond... all our weapons and habits correspond with each other and balance against each other like the beams of a gable."

The speaker, Ulysses, is talking of Trojans and Greeks, not men and women, but the words often apply as well to married couples. The play is Jean Giradoux's *La Guerre de Troie N'Aura Pas Lieu*, translated into English under the title *Tiger at the Gates*, missing the irony of the original title, which is literally "The Trojan War Will Not Happen." Married couples stay together because of their similar values and love for one another. The problems arise, not because they are so directly opposed to one another, but because of the subtle differences in their goals and temperaments, sometimes no more than the differences that are inevitable between two sexes with dissimilar life orientations since birth, whether we consider this inate or conditioned. Men and women are not natural enemies, but their complementary natures may bring antagonism as well as cooperation. To say that a newlywed couple can exist in perfect harmony without a trace of dissention is to say, *"La guerre de Troie n'aura pas lieu."* In nearly one out of three marriages today, the conflict is great enough to annihilate the marriage, but in the majority, the unions survive with the battling parties as acknowledged allies—not a true war, but a series of skirmishes and truces. We have dealt with the war, now let us consider the peacemaking, which inevitably follows the inevitable battles.

How do you usually make peace after a quarrel?

Sex is the most fun you can have without laughing. A by-the-book career army sergeant once confided that he and his wife, tempted by glowing accounts of the aphrodisiac qualities of marijuana, mooched some from their teenagers, but were too convulsed with giggling to accomplish much in bed. Laughter and sex may be incompatible, but both are even less compatible with anger and either may be used in peacemaking:

WIFE: "I make him laugh—can't laugh and stay mad."

HUSBAND: "By talking it out and apologizing. Sex is not considered because spouse is not willing to forgive and forget."

She is a homemaker, 41 to 50, with some college education. It's her second marriage. Her husband has struck her. Both say they argue most about the children. This and lack of communication she sees as their main problems. She says the marriage has alternating periods of closeness and remoteness. He is a professional, with some college, 41 to 50. This is his second marriage, also. He, too, says they have periods of closeness and remoteness.

WIFE: "Well, if things get too hot, he tries to force me to kiss him, which really makes me madder, if things are still up in the air. Once we get everything said, we usually hug and kiss and snuggle. Sometimes, after that, we make love—but not always."

HUSBAND: "Hug, kiss, stroke—usually ends up with sex."

The English used to say that the sun never set on the British empire (to which the Irish would retort that the Lord wouldn't trust them in the dark). Some couples believe the sun should never set on a quarrel, though this policy has probably led to the loss of more sleep than caffeine and Carson combined; one suspects that as many apologies are motivated by somnolence as contrition.

WIFE: "Usually I say I am sorry, or agree to do it his way, we kiss and make up."

HUSBAND: "We have had a prior-to-marriage rule—never let the sun go down on a disagreement. The few times we've reached bed—both sleep under the same cover—we always kiss and hug before falling asleep."

She is a homemaker, 51 or over, a high school graduate. Both feel they argue most about personal appearance. She feels dominated by her husband, but describes the marriage as always stable. He's a professional, with a postgraduate education, 51 or over. He says it's a marriage which is always loving.

WIFE: "One or the other usually apologizes and all is forgiven. My husband usually makes the first move."

HUSBAND: "Quarrels are seldom. I apologize (even if I consider myself correct) and kiss. As I view it, there is no other solution."

When asked by Dona Ana in hell if he has not repented, Don Juan replies, "Do you suppose heaven is like earth, where people persuade themselves that what is done can be undone by repentance; that what is spoken can be unspoken by withdrawing it; that what is true can be annihilated by a general agreement to give it the lie?" Perhaps not in heaven, but on earth apologies are *de rigueur* for restoration of domestic harmony, according to some wives:

WIFE: "Apologize, kiss and make up, make love. Quarrels are very few around our house."

Her marriage is loving. Lived with her husband for less than 3 months before marrying. She has some college, and works in the technical field.

WIFE: "Apologize if wrong. Accept gracefully if someone else apologizes and don't hold a grudge."

Apologies sometimes take the less perfunctory form of gifts or special treatment:

WIFE: "Once he has made me feel rotten he gives me gifts."

WIFE: "I pout for a bit, then I try to do something special for him, fix, cook, miss my favorite TV show and let him watch what he wants or run his bath for him, something to say, 'Hey, I'm sorry.'"

This homemaker is between 31 and 40. She says that the lack of money is a major problem in her marriage, and they have been separated. Also she admits that they've struck each other during arguments.

WIFE: "I treat my husband like a mother would a child. Motherly love does it every time. If I give in and let him have his way, everything is fine."

When a boy bangs his head or scrapes his knee, he runs to his mother or the nearest female surrogate to find comfort in her arms, and when he has grown and he wounds his sensibilities on one of life's many hard surfaces or rough edges, he will often seek that same maternal comfort from some loving woman. Most wives would prefer to engage in a more mature form of resolving differences rather than coddling their spouses. Some may refuse to argue in the first place, some recommend a cooling-off period, and others enter into immediate negotiations:

WIFE: "There is no common sense in my husband's head, therefore, no point to quarrel—I learned years ago. Now mostly silence."

WIFE: "We usually cool off and then discuss why we overreacted. Sometimes we yell our opinions until we understand why we are so angry."

This professional is between 18 and 30, a college graduate. She says they argue most about personal habits. She feels more nervous and irritable since marriage. Money is their major problem, she feels, but the marriage is always loving.

WIFE: "Let time pass. Try to talk out differences, to understand each other's point of view. To reach a solution so anger doesn't continue."

She has a postgraduate degree, and is a homemaker. "Emotional illness" was her worst crisis, but says her marriage is always stable. Between 31 and 40.

WIFE: "We usually talk for a while and try to make sure all negative feelings are resolved. It helps when we reaffirm our love for each other and stress the positive points in our relationship. We try to leave quarrels in the past."

Undoing was one of the basic defense mechanisms described by Anna Freud in her classic work *The Ego and Mechanisms of Defense*, published in 1936. It is simply the act of doing something to undo, at least symbolically, a previous act. Restoring stolen money would be a very effective act of undoing; apologies are considerably less effective. Saying "I'm sorry" after stepping on someone's foot does nothing to alleviate the pain; on the other hand, our rules of social conduct not only compel us to perform this ritual, but they likewise demand that the trodden one smile through his tears and say, "Quite all right." If we omitted the apology, the offended one would be more incensed by the social insult than the physical injury and would feel free to berate us and possibly inflict some physical injury in retaliation. Other examples of undoing are throwing spilled salt over your shoulder, knocking wood after proclaiming good fortune, and saying "bread and butter" when an object separates you and a companion—all of which make about as much sense as apologizing; that is, if the apology is not more than a prescribed ritual of a few words, as husbands may engage in. If the party initiating the reconciliation has gained some insight into the basic problem and feels he may be able to circumvent future ill feelings, the apology may be less a senseless attempt at undoing and more a positive act of prevention. When one has just recovered from an illness one would rather have a vaccine to prevent recurrence than a treatment for the past illness.

HUSBAND: "There seems to always be a surge of remorse and a mutual coming together, triggered, perhaps, by a few key words."

This is his second marriage. He lived together with his wife for over a year prior to marriage. Says sex is dull, and he feels sexually unsatisfied. He's between 31 and 40, and has a postgraduate degree.

HUSBAND: "Kiss, apologize, admit my errors or shortcomings, if indicated."

HUSBAND: "By saying 'I'm sorry' and 'I love you deeply.'"

Lack of communication between them is his major problem, but he still feels his marriage is a stable one. He's between 31 and 40, has a postgraduate degree, and works in management.

HUSBAND: "Usually she asks for a truce in some—in later years I have frequently initiated the truce."

What can you say after you say you're sorry? You can add a joke, a kiss, a gift, or, best of all, a bit of enlightenment:

HUSBAND: "May sit around and pout for a while to see what spouse's next action may be to give her a chance to make amends first. After a while I try to change subject to a humorous mood, light talk, calm down and re-enter the quarrel calmly. Usually just talk it out."

A college graduate, he has become disillusioned about love and romance. His worst problem is lack of communication between himself and his wife. He works in management.

HUSBAND: "Make love, kiss and make up."

A blue collar worker between 31 and 40, who sees his marriage as a loving one.

HUSBAND: "I make up by getting my wife something pretty for herself."

A blue collar worker, he says his marriage is on solid ground, and is always loving.

HUSBAND: "Mutual communication, to enlighten one another of the other's feelings—if the reverse situation occurred."

"Blessed be the peacemakers, for they shall be called children of God" (Mathew, ch. 5, v. 9).

The Turning Point

Crisis! The word connotes a great emergency, when everything seems to be in confusion and nothing is sure. How curious that this word is derived from the Greek word, *krinein*, which is also the root of the word "certain." The meaning of the Greek word is "to separate," and a crisis does, in fact, compel us to sort out our lives. The old, unthinking patterns simply will not work for us anymore and the magnitude of the events forces us to make definitive decisions, to choose certain paths to take, whether they prove to be right or wrong.

The term "crisis" has a venerable medical history, meaning a sudden change in an acute disease, generally in the positive sense, such as a fever dropping; the antithesis of this positive change was "lysis," a destructive process.

We are familiar with the term in the political sense, as with the Cuban missile crisis during the Kennedy administration. While there may be factors of considerable danger, the actual implication of the term is that some definite course of action had to be adopted, that the current status could not continue unimpeded.

Since our psychologically-oriented society now regards the term particularly as it applies to individuals' lives, we interpret crisis as an unusual instability caused by excessive stress and the endangering of the continuity of the person or his family. Continuity is not necessarily a desirable thing, especially if the path one has been traveling leads to further unhappiness and self-negation. The crisis is a turning point, with emphasis on the "point" rather than "turning." It is not the motion of deviation from an original course, but that moment when all motion ceases, when the victim is immobilized by opposing forces that block forward progress but are not yet felt sufficiently to produce a change in direction. In the mental health field, we speak of crisis intervention, meaning not only helping a patient who is under such stress, but reaching him at that moment, without the bureaucratic rigmarole of endless screening procedures and waiting lists, for unlike a problem, which might go chronically unsolved like a Gordian knot, a crisis poses such urgency that those it affects must make moves of their own or be swept in some unwelcome direction by the unbearable pressures.

Some crises in marriage are caused by voluntary actions, such as extramarital affairs; others, such as illness, may be beyond any sort of control. Some are unequivocally traumatic, such as accidents or death, while others, like the birth of a child or marriage, may be happy occasions that, nevertheless, force drastic changes in accustomed routine. Times of life, such as puberty and menopause, are crises because the body is undergoing changes, while certain life events may vary in time, but are generally encountered at some point, such as the death of parents or the departure of children from the home.

Where there is life, there is change; and where there is change, there is crisis. Few marriages escape major crises, though not all would agree, even within the same marriage, on what was the worst of the crises thus far encountered and shared.

What is the worst crisis that you have had to face—and how was it resolved?

Bishop Bridgenorth chides his celibate chaplain with an admonition to fall in love: "Think of what it would do for you. For her sake you would come to care unselfishly and diligently for money instead of being selfishly and lazily indifferent to it." It is difficult not to care about money when one is married, and in the objective portion of the questionnaire, the crisis most often selected as the worst was debts, chosen by more than a quarter of those who responded to the question. Those under 40 were more preoccupied with debts than their elders, and husbands more so than wives. 41 per cent of black respondents chose this response, twice the white contingent. One third of people making less than $10,000 per year said that debts posed the biggest crisis.

WIFE: "Losing a house almost by changing jobs and everything else we owned."

HUSBAND: "Debt problems compounded by an adverse real estate transaction after changing jobs and relocating.
    "1) Took another job which did not require relocation
    "2) Got a raise of $1,000.00 per year
    "3) Refinanced my home to improve my debt ratio."

Illness was the second worst crisis. While it was a negligible factor for the youngest group, it tripled in the 31 to 50 brackets, and continued to rise to a high of 22 per cent in those over 51. Was Don Juan being overly cynical when he exclaimed, "ages of faith, of romance, and of science are all driven at last to have but one prayer: 'Make me a healthy animal'"? Pain, debilitation, and the prospect of death, as doctors well know, make wealth irrelevant, sweep away careers that took a lifetime to build with one sharp pang, and shake the philosophies by which we have charted our courses for decades. Poverty, guilt, sorrow, and frustration grip the loved ones of the ill person, forcing drastic alterations in lifestyles and relationships. Mental illness can be even more devastating, for the outcome is usually far less certain than in physical diseases, and families must deal not merely with a weakened body but a drastically changed person.

WIFE: "Husband's cancer—isn't yet resolved, though will probably not be life-threatening. Makes one realize that one is not immortal."

WIFE: "Husband's emotional instability causing excessive pressure on wife. Has lasted for years—with some periods worse than others. Resolved somewhat with wife returning to school—taking courses to gain more insight into husband and self.

"Have learned to cope with husband's depressions, am more tolerant of husband, and have helped him develop methods of coping with his depression. Also, since wife is now independent emotionally, is able to take some of the pressure off of husband which she placed on him when first married. (I leaned on him too much and expected him to make all decisions. Has now changed to where we share decisions.) Am working so husband may return to school and find out what he wants to do with his life regarding career."

HUSBAND: "Money."

She's a professional, 18 to 30, a college graduate. They have 2 children, and their family income is between $25,000 and $49,999. Her husband has struck her, and they argue most about sexual problems. She feels that conflicts over relatives is the main problem in the marriage. He is a blue collar worker with some college education, 31 to 40. He says they argue most about money, and he feels he lives for his children.

WIFE: "Mental growth of myself only."

HUSBAND: "Spouse's mental problems. Years of therapy."

WIFE: "The worst crisis in my life was a bad relationship (not sexual) before I even met my husband. It was resolved when I finally realized it was a lost cause."

HUSBAND: "The worst crisis I have had to face has been my occupation. My dissatisfaction with my job was giving me an ulcer. With the support and understanding of my wife we were able to attack the situation and change my occupation."

Not all illnesses are beyond our control or non-related to our life situations. Ulcers are among the most frequently encountered stress-related illnesses, but high blood pressure, colitis, asthma, and skin conditions likewise may be brought on and aggravated by conflicts on the job or at home. A variety of non-specific symptoms, such as headache, back pains, nausea, tremors, dizziness, and weakness, may be emotional in origin, though the symptoms have physical roots in the resulting muscle tension, gastrointestinal spasms, or chemical imbalances caused by rapid breathing. The body may precipitate a crisis and force a change when the spirit would otherwise struggle in a frustrating and nerve-wracking situation.

Weaknesses of the flesh leads to marital crisis in more ways than through illness. One out of ten who specified a crisis said that extramarital affairs wrought the worst havoc. People in their thirties were most vulnerable to this problem, with those in the forties a close second.

WIFE: "I strongly believed in marriage vows, had my husband very high on a pedestal, and one night he came home and confessed he had taken a very young girl, whom he worked with daily, to her apartment and had sexual relations. The young girl confronted me several times. It lasted a year before I was told and around six months after I was told. Our children were involved as this young girl told them of the sordid affair (in detail). Our family literally fell apart. It broke our sixteen-year-old girl's heart, and did much more to the seventeen-year-old son. We have older daughters; older than the girl he fell for. Our family was always very close. We are not the same at all. I tend to give in too much to the children, feeling they have been given unjust treatment that wasn't expected from their father. I have become the buffer, giving my paycheck mostly to their needs. We don't pull together in raising them.

"I can't forget, even when making love, I feel he would rather be with her. I think of it often, several times a week, although I am sure he isn't seeing her still. *I can't forget,* I can forgive."

HUSBAND: "Extramarital affairs by myself were brought out into the open by my telling wife of same. After much heartbreak and counseling, everything is now under control."

She is between 41 and 50, a high school graduate, with more than 4 children. She says they've consulted a lawyer about a divorce. She says that the marriage is both in constant turmoil and fairly stable. She sees the major problems as money, disagreements about children, and lack of communication. He is a professional with some college education, 41 to 50. He feels fully loved and appreciated, and thinks the marriage is generally stable.

WIFE: "Joining the church.

"Solved with love, patience, understanding arrived at through constant prayer. I am very thankful to my Heavenly Father for the help He gave me during this time. We now both are members of the same belief and are growing in the gospel together and because of this our marriage is so much better; so strong and loving."

HUSBAND: "An extramarital sex affair where wife was found guilty of noon-time fucks.

"We went into mate-swapping, and group sex for a short time (seven months), and then straightened our act out. It's now straight, without problem.

"We now have found a new way of life through Christ in the Church of Jesus Christ of the Latter Day Saints (Mormon)."

WIFE: "Extramarital affair. Talked out and resolved problem."

HUSBAND: "Problem with wife's ex-husband wanting her back. Discussed and had a stronger marriage."

She's a professional, 31 to 40, with some college. They lived together for 6 months to a year, and this is her third marriage. She feels tied down and overwhelmed by responsibility, but believes their marriage is fairly stable and loving, with alternating periods of closeness and remoteness. He is a professional, with some college, as well, 31 to 40. This is his second marriage, he's never cheated, and he thinks the marriage is generally stable.

Seven per cent of our respondents said they had experienced no crisis. Nine per cent said their crisis had been something other than one of the ten listed choices. This couple's crisis, for example, dealt not with an extramarital affair, but premarital ones:

WIFE: "Telling my husband of the affairs I had had before marriage, after we were married.
    "We resolved this through talking and a lot of time."

HUSBAND: "My wife going out on me before we were married and not telling me. Looking to God!"

A man's job is a major part of his identity, and it is not surprising that among the 9 per cent who found unemployment their worst crisis, 11 percent of the men made this choice against only 7 per cent of the women. This crisis was hardest experienced among the low-income and blue collar groups.

WIFE: "My husband lost his job. He got another one, but the three weeks in between were hell."

HUSBAND: "I can't think of any, except losing my job, and I knew I'd get another one, but it was over Christmas and very traumatic."

There is a nostalgic myth rampant in our current culture that the larger households of the past included doting grandparents, maiden aunts and Dutch uncles under the same roof, creating a communal atmosphere of extended sources of love, child care, and emotional support. While it is true that families were larger in the sense that more siblings led ultimately to more aunts and uncles, and these family members were less likely to live what is now a 4-hour jet ride away, households throughout America's history have consisted essentially of parents and children. Any naturally developing frictions between two loving spouses and their children are only aggravated by the addition of outsiders, no matter what good intentions and common genetic composition they bear. One in 12 respondents said their greatest crisis was a live-in-relative, and this complaint was most common in the 41–50 age group, when spouses' parents would most likely be over 65 and infirm. Sometimes, the couple had moved in with a relative rather than the reverse, but the tension was just as bad on alien territory:

WIFE: "We moved to Florida and thought we could do better money-wise. We lived with his aunt. She had to watch our son; he was only ten months old.

"I worked daylight to dark and so did my husband. We never saw each other or the baby. We weren't making any money, and his aunt was driving me crazy. So we moved back home."

HUSBAND: "We moved to Florida for a better living. It didn't work out so we moved back home."

She's a homemaker, a high school graduate between 18 and 30. They have 2 children, and their family income is between $8–9,999. He's a blue collar worker, 18 to 30, with some college education. He says conflicts over relatives is their main problem. He agrees with his wife that they have a generally loving marriage.

There was a case of a man who wanted to keep his extramarital relationship a secret and found a perfect plan to cover his wanderings. Before returning home from his paramour's nest, he would stop at a bar and have a drink or two, and then tell his wife he had been in the bar all night. His wife never did find out about the girl friend, but the plan went awry when she divorced him for being an alcoholic. Seven percent of our sample said that alcohol was the biggest crisis, and the problem plagued remarriages twice as often as first unions.

WIFE: "Remoteness of husband.

"Drug and alcohol problems of husband.

"Dishonesty at times, non-trust of husband.

"Help of marriage counselor, AA—not totally resolved."

HUSBAND: "Loss of business—became better.
"Sickness—became better."

WIFE: "My husband had his own business for a couple of years, and was away from home from early morning until late at night, sometimes seven days a week. We had a three-month-old baby. It was difficult for me to be virtually husbandless, and a single parent. It was partially resolved when his hours decreased and he had an occasional day off, and completely resolved when he changed businesses."

HUSBAND: "I was becoming an alcoholic a few years ago. My wife was so concerned that she sought professional advice. The fact that she was so concerned made me realize that things had to change. There has been no problem since."

She is a homemaker, a college graduate, 18 to 30. She says their marriage is generally loving, but lack of communication is their major problem. He is a professional, college graduate, 31 to 40. He thinks their marriage is generally loving and always stable.

Every year about one-fifth of Americans move to a new home. While this has dropped about 2 per cent to 18 per cent in 1977, career pressures still often induce families into a somewhat nomadic existence. Moving is often a major crisis since it involves not only a change in house, but new schools for the children, possible separation from relatives, adjustment to a new neighborhood or even region, and the necessity of making new friends. Six per cent of our respondents said that moving caused their biggest crisis, and this was a particular bane of the highly-educated, the professional and white collar workers, and the upper income group.

WIFE: "My worst crisis in marriage was leaving my home state and moving to California. I missed my family and the familiarity of Philadelphia, where I felt very secure. I was very unhappy and insecure. As a result I began to dislike myself and set about proving that I was a capable and intelligent human being. I still do not like California, but am too busy to think about it."

HUSBAND: "(I assume this question relates to the worst crisis in my marriage.) My wife is an only child. She lived with her parents until we were married. We moved away from her parents (and mine) the day after we were married. The many adjustments that were necessary for me, and especially for my wife after we got married, were formidable. The abrupt separation from her parents coupled with the new responsibilities of married life, caused my wife a great deal of anxiety. As a result of the above, my wife developed many fears (flying, driving on freeways, death, etc.). In some cases it has been a problem dealing with the above."

She's a professional with a postgraduate education, 31 to 40. Her husband has struck her. She feels tied down, appreciated as a spouse but not as a lover. She feels his job takes up too much time. He is a professional with a postgraduate education, also 31 to 40. He feels their major problems involve jobs.

Children are occasional sources of crisis, and given the time span over which they can cause problems, it is surprising that no more than 6 percent saw their birth or actions as the major impetus. Not only young children and teenagers were mentioned, but the actions of adult offspring were also cited. Pregnancies often triggered a crisis when it was felt the marriage could not stand the burden of another child. Homemakers, possibly having more children than employed wives, were more beset by crises centering on children.

WIFE: "Unwanted pregnancy. I already had a toddler and our marriage was shaky at that period. I already felt over-extended in emotional, mental, and physical areas. I wanted an abortion. My husband didn't want the baby either, but he was scared of the 'cosmic' consequences of abortion. We never really agreed about it. My husband just let it be my decision. We had a big problem with him laying a moralistic trip on me. We started seeing a psychologist. We've reached a sort of understanding. For one, we're *very careful* about birth control now. Two, he has also agreed if such a situation occurs again, to work it out without laying such a big guilt trip on me."

HUSBAND: "When my wife became pregnant; I was morally against an abortion, even though I knew that having another child would put a tremendous strain on us. She wanted (or felt she needed) an abortion. I left the decision with her. It was resolved by a tremendous effort to understand each other and live with our differences. We are much more careful with birth control."

WIFE: "The worst crisis was when one of our children was diagnosed as having emotional problems at the age of three. We worked together (my husband and I) and sought professional help. After eleven years of therapy, our son seems to be fairly normal mentally now."

HUSBAND: "It's difficult to say we had *one* worst crisis. We really have had *two*.

"(1) Lost my job in 1958 when we were in Florida and had no money. It was very difficult, but I got a second job and it worked us out of a difficult situation.

"(2) Our third son is emotionally disturbed. We discovered it by his second birthday, and placed him in therapy. He is now sixteen, and while out of therapy (psychiatric), is doing reasonably well."

WIFE: "The worst crisis we had to face was with our oldest daughter at thirteen, running away, rebelling. It caused a great strain on our marriage. We got professional help. She is fourteen now and calming down, so the strain she put on our relationship is not as bad."

HUSBAND: "When our thirteen-year-old ran away. She wanted more privileges and wanted to be out in cars with older boys nineteen to twenty-one. We went to family counseling. She wanted to be able to stay out late seven days a week and wanted to go and come as she pleased without answering to anyone. After counseling for a year, things are being worked out as far as bending a little both ways."

She is a homemaker between 31 and 40, who didn't complete high school. They argue most about the children, which is the major problem in the marriage. She feels overwhelmed by responsibility, but thinks they have a generally loving marriage. He is a blue collar worker, 31 to 40, who also didn't complete high school. He says they married because of pregnancy. He also feels it's a generally loving marriage.

WIFE: "The divorce of one of our sons. We faced it together and prayed for healing of their marriage."

HUSBAND: "The marital problems of our children. We were and are sustained by a strong religious faith."

She's a homemaker, 51 or over, with some college education. She feels they have no major problems, and says they never argue. She describes the marriage as always stable. He's a professional, with a postgraduate education, 51 or over.

WIFE: "An autistic son. It has never been resolved."

HUSBAND: "Problems with actions of grown children had to be resolved between spouse and myself, or marriage could have floundered. Love for each other over-rode, finally, the problems."

We can get fairly accurate statistics on divorce, but we cannot begin to estimate the number of separations that occur, especially brief ones where the abandoned spouse had no way of knowing when and if the departed mate was coming back. This had happened to at least one in 20 of our respondents, who were upset enough by the incident to consider it the worst crisis the marriage had faced. People under 30 reported separation more frequently, and couples without children cited it twice as often as parents.

WIFE: "Fell in love with husband's best friend. Moved out of friend's house and renewed commitment to husband."

HUSBAND: "Infidelity on her part. I felt somehow incomplete in meeting her needs. Left her the option of fulfilling her true nature. Once she let me know *I* was all she needed, we proceeded from that point to rebuild our marriage."

She is a homemaker between 18 and 30, with some college. She thinks money is their major problem, and finds their marriage generally stable and loving. He is a professional, with a postgraduate education, 18 to 30. He and his wife lived together for 6 months to a year before getting married. He feels sexually unsatisfied, and says the marriage is fairly stable, with alternating periods of closeness and remoteness.

Not all separations are abandonments. Military service, often compulsory, has been responsible throughout our country's history for disruption of marriages, leaving wives to care for children alone or move in with relatives.

WIFE: "I believe the hardest time in my life was my husband being away in the Marines during World War II and having to care for our two-year-old son alone. Most of that time I had to live with my in-laws; the other half with my grandmother. With God's help I came through it alright."

Not all reunions prove to be happy ones. The shadow of impending military service and separation often precipitates marriages among young people whose commitment is not strong enough or maturity advanced enough to sustain the hasty union. People invariably change with time, but when these changes occur without the presence of the spouse, subsequent adjustment is difficult, if not impossible.

WIFE: "My first husband, after we both returned from overseas (Navy), decided I wasn't the type of woman he wanted. Eventually, he began beating me and abusing me. I felt degraded and lonely. After being left without food, heat, transportation for a few days, I finally got the courage to leave, even though it made me feel bad and hurt my pride, to ask for outside help. I went back home, got a job, and sought a divorce."

This is her second marriage. She lived with her present spouse for 6 months to a year before marrying him. Her major problems involve the lack of money, and conflicts over relatives. She's between 18 and 30, and a blue collar worker.

To some women, a husband's affair with another woman is abuse enough, even without beatings and with professions of love. People with an income over $10,000 said that extramarital escapades were the worst crisis twice as often as the low-income group. Financial security is no substitute for emotional security, which is hard for a wife to regain even if she stays in the marriage.

WIFE: "His love for another woman. He made the decision to stay with me, but I'm sorry he did. I've never felt the same security or mutual love, though he says he really loves me. There have been other and worse crises, but our love always saw us through everything."

She's 51 or over now, and says they've been separated. She has cheated on her husband with one other man for over a year. Says her worst problem is that her husband is inconsiderate, and they don't communicate. She feels unloved, thinks her husband dominates her, and is more nervous these days.

WIFE: "Finding out after eight years of marriage that my husband has cheated on me from the first year.
"Resolved: Divorce."

There was no difference between the percentage of spouses in first marriages and those in remarriages with regard to having children as their major crisis source. Perhaps this is because in our sample the percentages of people who were married for the first, second, and third time were identical whether or not they had children. Remarriages may cause unique frictions with non-blood relatives. How come, this woman might ask, none of our fairy stories talk about wicked stepchildren?

WIFE: "Very difficult stepchild. Tried everything under the sun. Finally, went to lawyer to find my legal rights. (Child was over 18, at home, destroying normal family life, and had no direction or goals.) Lawyer made peace, and said 'Get that kid out.' Out she went. Marriage since is beautiful, though all family members are deeply affected by the trouble she caused."

This homemaker who is between 41 and 50 says her marriage is now a loving one.

Wives are at least as apt to experience a crisis when the children are gone for the first time as they are with the children around. The condition is common enough to be termed "the empty nest syndrome" by psychiatrists who treat middle-aged women experiencing depression, boredom, and a sense of uselessness when their life's career of motherhood suddenly ends before the age of 50. The resolution of this crisis often depends on whether or not the spouses can recapture the closeness they had to sacrifice to some extent for the children:

WIFE: "My dissatisfaction with my marriage after raising our family and returning to work, and the children leaving the nest at the same time. A change of location in my husband's work put us in a strange part of the country, away from our children and relatives, and made us much more dependent on each other for companionship and social activity. We are much more companionable now."

She's 51 or over, and is a white collar worker. At this point she feels sexually dissatisfied, and is more nervous and irritable than ever.

And then there are the medical tragedies that dwarf the other crises, because all parties concerned feel powerless in their presence and their wake. One in ten Americans will spend some time in a mental institution. More than 8 husbands and 4 wives out of every thousand will die between the ages of 45 and 55. There are those particularly cruel diseases that single out their victims among children, such as acute leukemia, or young adults, such as Hodgkin's disease, where the average life span after diagnosis is five years. The certainty of early death and the uncertainty of the time involved imposes a terrible burden of courage on victims and spouses, who must live each day as normally as possible without dwelling on the catastrophic future. And, even for wives whose spouses live a "normal" life span, the prospect of years of living as elderly widows increases as women continue to outlive men for progressively longer periods, despite a lengthening of life span for both sexes.

WIFE: "My illness (Hodgkin's disease)."

While her marriage is stable, she feels more nervous and irritable these days. She's between 18 and 30, works in the technical field. Has some college education.

WIFE: "My husband has had two nervous breakdowns that required hospitalizations of six weeks each, since our marriage twenty-six years ago. Each time he has seemingly recovered after undergoing psychotherapy."

She says her husband dominates her, and sex between them is dull. In addition, they've struck each other during arguments. Her major problem involves conflicts over relatives. Between 41 and 50, with a post-graduate degree, and works in the professional field.

WIFE: "Trying not to compare with deceased, first husband."

She never or rarely ever has sex, and says her worst crisis was illness. A homemaker, 51 or over, who didn't complete high school.

WIFE: "Death, lost a son; it was hard to believe and learn to live again without his presence."

Husbands face the same crises as wives, such as extramarital affairs and troublesome children, the only unique one possibly being confrontation with a wife who has been caught up in the Women's Liberation Movement:

HUSBAND: "Wife suddenly feeling the need to become independent. We were both too immature to handle it properly. Came to point of divorce, before willingness to communicate."

He has been separated from his wife, and cheated on her with one other woman for over a year. Says he dislikes wife's co-workers, and describes her as irresponsible. Admits they have a communication problem. He works in the technical field, is between 31 and 40, and has some college.

HUSBAND: "Stepson caused a continual hassle, he married, moved away, and problem solved."

This husband feels his marriage alternates between periods of remoteness and closeness, and admits to a brief affair. He's 51 or over, with some college, and works in management.

HUSBAND: "I had extramarital affair.
"I broke it off."

He's retired now, 51 or over. Cheated with 2 or 3 other women, briefly. Says his sex life with his wife is unsatisfying, he has sex with her once a month, and feels dominated by her. Believes he's tied down and trapped.

HUSBAND: "Finding out she's a cold fish—went elsewhere."

Middle-aged men are particularly vulnerable to financial stresses, because just at the point in their lives when the children are ready to enter college, with its heavy expenses, their own parents become frequently infirm, financially dependent, or otherwise problematic:

HUSBAND: "My mother, who needed home, living with us, finally, because we were unable to give her proper care for advancing age, and, more especially, a terrific imbalance problem, then because of weakness, being unable to get up off floor, had to be persuaded to enter rest home for her own protection (we feared she would get hurt in fall, etc.). Enlisted aid of her doctor, then a little talking with her and explaining situation, especially the price—$124 for three eight-hour shifts at home; or $600 a month in rest home."

He's 51 or over, and a college graduate. Says his marriage is a loving one, and he has no major problems, other than his mother living with them.

HUSBAND: "My father's drinking. Resolved when he quit and family business was saved. Periodically he hits the bottle which irritates me and subsequently upsets my wife."

Husbands may tend to suffer in silence more, but they, as their wives, must face illness and death of the very loved ones whose support often made mortal existence bearable.

HUSBAND: "Wife's illness. It was resolved with understanding and patience."

While he says his marriage is always loving, he admits that he has struck his wife during arguments. Works in management, is between 31 and 40, and has some college education.

HUSBAND: "Son has cancer—not resolved—still trying to save his life."

HUSBAND: "Loss of an unborn child. Confidence and support from spouse and faith."

He has a postgraduate degree, works as a professional, and is between 31 and 40. Says his marriage is generally loving.

HUSBAND: "Several deaths in the family over a very short period of time. It was never resolved, but made me a very different person."

> "A tale begun in other days,
> When summer suns were glowing—"

Marriages almost always start in an atmosphere of happiness and youthful optimism. Time brings tribulation, sorrow, and death, and marriage cannot protect us from confronting these darker days—only from confronting them alone. And, in Lewis Carroll's words, "though the shadow of a sigh may tremble through the story," the story is more than Macbeth's tale told by an idiot, for love can abate its sound and fury and give it significance.

Crisis will come, but if we expect it and can face it with confidence, we shall negotiate each turning point with equanimity, including that final crisis point from which there is never a turning back. Our children and other loved ones can carry on the tale which we once shared, no less complete for one man's failure to tell it through.

We can say little more than Lewis Carroll, who abandoned his masterful nonsense for a sobering moment to address Alice:

"Come, harken then, ere voice of dread,
  With bitter tidings laden,
Shall summon to unwelcome bed
  A melancholy maiden!
We are but older children, dear,
Who fret to find our bedtime near."

8

Out of Bounds:

Infidelity

> Look at my old woman! She's never known any man but me; and she can't properly know me, because she don't know other men to compare me with. . . . But Mrs. George she came to know a lot about men of all sorts and ages; for the older she got the younger she liked 'em; and it certainly made her interesting, and gave her a lot of sense. I have often taken her advice on things when my own poor old woman wouldn't have been a bit of use to me.
>
> ——*George Bernard Shaw*, GETTING MARRIED

Rick's first extramarital affair followed 20 years of fidelity; he and his wife were both in their mid-forties with two grown children. Helen was the type of wife who, if her husband got up in the middle of the night for a drink of water, would make the bed. Well, maybe not *that* compulsive, but she literally never let the family use the living room for fear they would mess it up. She was as fastidious about her body as her house, and would demand that her husband withdraw before ejaculating because she did not want his semen inside her. While women across the country were debating whether or not to accept semen in their mouths, Helen was holding her ground back at the vagina.

Rick had premarital experience with many prostitutes in his Army days and had even lived overseas with one. Helen had a brief, ill-fated marriage in her late teens, and had gone to bed with Rick before they were married; sex was better then, he contended. The thing that drove Rick to another woman, however, was not sexual frustration, but Helen's night job as a waitress. When she insisted on adding an extra night to her schedule, Rick stopped spending his evenings with the television set.

Myra, the other woman, was Rick's age, a divorcee with two young children. Rick described Myra as a slob, a bad cook, a bad mother, and a whore. The last attribute was what drew him to her, for although she continued an erratic affair with a younger man, she responded most enthusiastically to Rick in bed. He had been impotent with her at first, but she quickly brought out the best in him. "She made a man of me!" Rick said proudly. Rick moved out on Helen and in with—not Myra, but his mother. "Shacking up" was contrary to his upbringing, and marriage to Myra was something he was less than ready for.

Rick returned to his wife—"my best and only friend"—who welcomed him with open arms, sheer negligees and a voracious sexual appetite. Rick was impotent. "It's not like *her* anymore," he complained to the psychiatrist. "She makes me nervous." Even when his potency returned, he would say of Helen, "The sex was good, but the feeling wasn't." Helen was prettier, cleaner, and a better cook than Myra, but Rick could accept Myra's sexual openness and not Helen's.

He tried to solve the problem by turning to a new woman, Pat, younger and prettier than either. Pat had been divorced two years ago, but had allegedly remained celibate, biding her time and raising her children until a "decent guy" like Rick came along. Rick, with a chance to cheat on both his unsatisfactory women, took Pat to a motel. A sportswriter once said of a plodding baserunner who was thrown out by several yards attempting to steal second base, "His head was full of larceny, but his feet were honest." And so it was with Rick, for while his head was full of infidelity, his lower parts remained true.

Helen came to one therapy session in a desperate attempt to save the marriage. She chastized herself for her past sexual coldness and said she had now really changed, with which Rick concurred. When the talk got around to the initial crisis, her working an additional night, Helen revealed that they truly needed the money because of accumulated bills, including their daughter's wedding costs. Rick admitted he had always left the finances entirely up to Helen, along with the cooking, cleaning, and mothering.

Helen ranted about Myra: "I don't understand it. He puts her down, he calls her a dirty whore, but he can't get her out of his mind. He keeps moving back in with me, but he wants her, too. He wants to have us both!"

"Or," the therapist said, "both of you in the same woman."

Rick stayed in therapy only six months. It relieved his anxiety, stopped him from the heavy drinking he had begun, and kept him functioning at work. He finally took the step of moving out to an apartment of his own, despite Helen's entreaties to stay whenever he wanted, on his terms, with bedroom privileges.

Helen had apparently tried her best, but Rick simply could not accept the mother of his children as a sexually aggressive and uninhibited woman, and it is likely that Helen had subconsciously come to understand this early in their relationship. Her great fault was not her sexual indifference, but her abandonment of her maternal duties by spending more nights at her job. Pat, too, was unacceptable as a sex partner by virtue of her virtue. And Myra, the "bad mother" (who, realistically, did a rather commendable job of supporting her children), was too much the whore.

Rick's dilemma of not being able to meet all his emotional needs through the same woman led him into a classical madonna-prostitute split, and split his marriage in the process. But for every spouse such as Rick whose extramarital affair has profound effects on his marriage and his emotional stability, there are several, of both sexes, who secretly and briefly manage to incorporate some outside sexual activity into their lives without detection, or, at worst, without dissolution of their marriages. In our subsample of matched couples, in only two-thirds of the cases had both partners been thoroughly faithful; that is, in one of three of these marriages, where the couples were not only still married, but were compatible enough to be out answering questionnaires together, the husband and/or wife had been involved in extramarital activity. Thus, we can already see that infidelity is common not only to the sizeable percentage of marriages that end in divorce, but also among the average couples we encounter, as did our researchers, strolling together in shopping malls and business districts.

In this chapter, we will limit our investigation and discussion to infidelity, commonly known as "cheating." We realize that extramarital sexual activity might be carried on, mutually or by one partner, with the spouse's knowledge and consent, and that increasing numbers of couples are experimenting with lifestyles that defy traditional standards of marital monogamy with respect to sexual partners. We shall explore and comment on these trends in the final chapter of this book; here, we will deal with "cheating," as discussed by our respondents, presumably in the context of having occurred in violation of the marital commitment made by the spouses.

Cheating, or doing by stealth what we would never dare with the open knowledge of all concerned parties, is an art acquired very early in life. The two-year-old has no conscience except its mother's prohibitions; when she is not physically around, her presence is often internalized, as in the case of the toddler who slaps its own hand and says "no" repeatedly as it takes cookies out of the cookie jar. As the child acquires a stronger sense of reality, it realizes that mother has no way of knowing what she is not around to see or hear. Since the child is not yet capable of formulating its own abstract morality nor accustomed to thinking in the subjunctive mood of the possible consequences *if* mother finds out, its sense of right and wrong hinges on the actual knowledge of authoritarian witnesses to its acts. If apprehended or suspected of wrongdoing and confronted, the child falls back on the most primitive of defensive mechanisms, denial—"I didn't do it." Denial in such cases is different from a deliberate lie, for the child half-believes that reality is what the child sincerely wants it to be, especially since the only reward for truth will be loss of love and angry punishment. Thus, we learn to lie to ourselves and to loved ones and to live in two or more coincident realities, that where things happen known only to ourselves and that which we share with significant others. The cheater lives in two different worlds, but with detection his life is shaken by the pervasive chaos one would expect when worlds collide.

The State of Affairs

"I could not answer for my feelings for a week in advance, much less to the end of my life; . . . to cut me off from all natural and unconstrained intercourse with half my fellow-creatures would narrow and warp me if I submitted to it, and, if not, would bring me under the curse of clandestinity," Don Juan says of women's demands for fidelity. Secrecy may be a curse, but revelation of an affair scarcely results in a shower of blessings. Under the veil of confidentiality, respondents to our questionnaire were able to describe the causes and consequences of their infidelities, even those hitherto clandestine.

One-fourth of all respondents had "cheated" on their spouses at some point, and this included 30 per cent of husbands and 17 per cent of wives. The figure for women agrees closely with Hunt's 1972 survey, in which he estimated 12 to 24 per cent of wives had been unfaithful, more so among the youngest. Hunt also rebalanced Kinsey's estimate of 26 per cent to correct for the excess of divorced women in that sample, and found the revised estimate to be 20 per cent. Our figure for men indicates a higher degree of fidelity than in Hunt's 41 per cent who cheated, but his figure included divorced men, as well as those still married, whereas all of our men are currently married, 79 per cent for the first time.

In our previous survey for the book *Beyond the Male Myth*, where we asked men if they had ever cheated on their wives *or steady girl friends*, 43 per cent of our currently married sample had *not been* always faithful, whereas currently divorced men had cheated in 61 per cent of cases. We have a more representative percentage of older men in this survey, 22 per cent in their forties and 32 per cent over 50 against only 39 per cent who were 40 or over in our previous study.

Of the husbands who *had cheated*, only one in six had ever been involved with an outside partner for over a year. The wives were less evanescent in their infidelities, nearly one in three with a history of outside involvements reporting a liason that had lasted at least a year. Five per cent of husbands had cheated with at least four other women, but less than 2 per cent of the wives had that many affairs. Forty per cent of cheating husbands and 73 per cent of unfaithful wives had limited their extramarital activity to one outside partner, indicating a dearth of satyrs and nymphomaniacs even among adventuresome spouses.

Numbers have their limitations. Can we make valid comparisons between the traveling husband who has scores of one-night stands and the housewife who conducts noontime trysts with one lover over decades? Can we compare the "swinger," who claims he is happily married but has a need for variety with the wife whose husband is cold and abusive or the husband whose wife denies him intercourse? To get a more valid impression of infidelity in American marriage, we have to go beyond the numbers and understand how affairs happen and what motivates them.

Have you ever had an affair or affairs? How did it happen, and how do you feel about it? Did your spouse find out? What did your spouse do about it? If you've been faithful, what has been your biggest source of or reason for temptation?

Two per cent of our respondents said they had been involved, but with the partner's knowledge and consent. This was reported, however, by double the percentage of husbands as of wives, which is known as a double standard. This phenomenon was highest in the 31–40 age group, and negligible in couples over 50, whose fidelity rate was a mere 6 per cent above the least faithful group, again spouses in their thirties.

WIFE: "I think that if a couple believes in having extramarital affairs it should be equal as long as it isn't detrimental to the relationship."

HUSBAND: "Yes—my spouse also has had an affair—who cares?"

This couple's family income is over $50,000 a year. He has a postgraduate degree, and she's a white collar worker. They

have no children. She cheated briefly with one other man. He
has also cheated. He's also into group sex and mate-swapping.
He married for regular sex.

WIFE: "We do not believe in fidelity. Sex is poor with each
other."

HUSBAND: "When I caught my spouse cheating in my home we
reached a mutual agreement."

The greatest temptation to cheat among our combined respondents would be constant fighting at home. For the 98 per cent of
couples who do not believe in outside sexual activity, nothing
stimulates constant fighting as much as a discovered affair. Revenge is a strong motive for affairs, and many a betrayed spouse
would inform their mates, in the words of Eliza Doolittle, that
they would be grateful for "a chance of getting back a bit of what
you chucked at me":

WIFE: "Yes. After he cheated on me I went crazy and did a lot
of terrible things to get even. I told him I'd make him pay and
pay."

HUSBAND: "My wife likes group sex so I've gone along but
don't like it."

She's a college graduate, between 18 and 30, and works in the
professional field. Is also into group sex and mate-swapping.
Says she feels unloved and unappreciated. He's a white collar
worker between 31 and 40. Says he cheated, but with his wife's
knowledge and consent. He is disillusioned about romance, and
says his wife has even struck him during arguments.

WIFE: "Yes. Spur of the moment. Sexual attraction. I feel guilty.
Yes he did find out. Separation."

HUSBAND: "Yes, I have. It was due to revenge, and want of
sympathy. It was a waste of time. Yes, my wife did find out,
but we talked ourselves back together again."

She's between 18 and 30, and he's in the same age range. She
says her husband takes her for granted, and they don't com-

municate. He's had an affair with 1 woman for a brief period of time. Says their sex life is variable, and feels tied down and trapped. However believes a divorce would leave him depressed.

WIFE: "Yes, after that girl he cheated with. I lost my sense of loyalty to him. Yes, he knew about it. Begged me to give the other man up and promised to forget the girl."

HUSBAND: "I have had affairs. I was very active sexually. My wife knew and would try to understand my needs."

Only 39 per cent of spouses saw themselves as beyond temptation. Several paintings of *The Temptation of St. Anthony* remind us that not even the saints are above temptation, but 28 per cent of husbands considered themselves so, as did a formidable 49 per cent of wives. A compatible marriage circumvents the two most prevalent temptations, fighting and poor sex, but even contented couples might be tempted by someone who understood them better than their spouses (10 per cent), and exceptionally attractive partner (9 per cent), or being away from home (7 per cent):

WIFE: "Spouse unavailable."

HUSBAND: "No. Temptation—a drink and an admiring woman— love to be loved and/or respected."

She's between 31 and 40, and a homemaker and college graduate. She has never cheated, and stated that moral beliefs keep her faithful. They have 2 children. He has a postgraduate education and earns between $25–$49,000 a year. He's never cheated because of loyalty to his wife. Feels their sex life is good, says his wife appreciates him, but doesn't really love him.

The only source of temptation that was greater for wives than husbands was a "person who understands me better." And while only half as many wives would be tempted by exceptional attractiveness, women were not immune to the type of affair that husbands classically alibi as "just a physical thing."

WIFE: "Yes, I've had an affair with a man I was very sexually attracted to. Spouse found out. We broke up briefly."

HUSBAND: "No affairs."

WIFE: "Yes. I met someone I had more in common with during first marriage. Spouse knew . . . did nothing."

HUSBAND: "I have never had an affair, reason being I'm a one woman man. I would never think of it unless we were in the process of divorce."

Poor sex at home is the prime temptation for husbands, one in five saying they would consider looking for outside substitutes; however, an unsatisfying sex life ranked a poor third for wives, although an occasional female respondent cited it as the cause of her affair. Non-physical incompatabilities, such as constant fighting and lack of understanding, ranked in first and second place among wives.

WIFE: "1. Yes.
  "2. I wasn't getting sex at home and I found it somewhere else.
  "3. No, my husband did not find out."

This white collar worker has a postgraduate education, and is ending her marriage for she's consulted a lawyer about a divorce. She says since her marriage, she's been more nervous and irritable, and cheated with 1 other man for over a year. Her major problem though is really about disagreements over their only child.

WIFE: "Yes, I have had an affair. It began innocently. I'm not sorry, but I do feel guilty at times and wished my sex life was more compatible with my spouse. He suspected the affair, but I denied it."

She's a white collar worker with 4 children, between 41 and 50. While she feels her marriage is fairly stable, she says her sex life is generally dull, and has cheated with 1 other man, briefly. Also reveals that during arguments, she and her husband have struck each other.

WIFE: "Yes, have had affairs. Spouse found out. Spouse beat the hell out of me. It probably happened because I was always being accused of it."

WIFE: "Yes, I had an affair. I met someone compatible. I feel good about it. My husband did not find out. I did it because my husband is an egotistical jackass."

Apuleius notwithstanding, it is difficult to find love with a jackass. Yet the spell of a midsummer night's dream about romantic love may tempt even a wife whose husband is not such a burdensome beast. Only half as many wives as husbands would be tempted by an exceptionally attractive new partner but males don't have a monopoly on ego and a wife whose morale is in need of a boost might at least raise the question of an affair:

WIFE: "Probably the only time in my marriage that there was any minute of temptation was when we were married about six years and I had three children rather closely together and a member of the opposite sex paid close attention to me. It made me feel desirable as a woman and built up my ego. However, there was really never any one real temptation and as my marriage grew older and our love matured, these same attentions only made me laugh to myself."

She has more than 4 children now, and while she believes her husband appreciates and loves her, he takes her for granted. She's between 41 and 50, and says they argue mostly over the children.

WIFE: "Yes. It just happened. I had mixed feeling, but had a real love for him. Yes, my husband did find out. He was understanding, supportive, and has never held it against me."

Her biggest temptation to cheat again would be a man who understood her better, for she's become disillusioned about love. This homemaker is between 18 and 30, and has 2 children.

WIFE: "Yes, I was very attracted. My husband never found out. I still am afraid that he may find out. Circumstances have changed and I would not like to lose present spouse."

She's a homemaker, 18 to 30, with some college education. She admits that she's cheated with 1 person for over a year, yet she says that she feels only the husband should be permitted outside sexual activity. She says that their sex life is good, and the marriage is generally loving.

WIFE: "No. The only reason I've ever thought about it is when my husband has been so immersed in his own personal problems that he has completely disregarded my needs. Sometimes he isn't my image of a 'manly' man. I've occasionally thought about having a relationship with this 'perfect image' type of man."

Sometimes the dream of a more perfect man lies not in the future but in the past. Some women stirred up troubled marital waters by casting a nostalgic glance at the one who got away:

WIFE: "Yes, I had two brief extramarital affairs. The first one one year after being married (I've been married two years). It was with an old lover. I hadn't seen him for two years prior and our relationship ended because of family conflicts. I just had to find out for myself if he did mean anything. After seeing him that one time I never wanted to see him again. My spouse knew of the visit but did not know of my having sex with this man. He found out."

She says they've had a period of separation, but feels her marriage now is fairly loving. However, she thinks her husband is irresponsible, and says he dominates her. She's between 18 and 30, with some college education.

WIFE: "Yes. An old friend came by when my husband was gone. I was pleased. My husband does not know."

This young homemaker (18 to 30) says her sex life is dull, and they only have sex about once a month. She admits she has struck her husband during fights, and that their worst crisis is fighting.

WIFE: "Not really. Continued to see old boyfriend after marriage when husband was away."

Some women have learned from experience that the grass is not greener on the other side of the marital enclosure. Others see their husbands so frequently engaged in lying down in outside pastures that they suspect some may be greener than others after all.

WIFE: "I had enough affairs before I was married (this is the second time) to last me a lifetime. The grass is definitely *not* greener on the other side and anyone who thinks so is only kidding himself."

She's only between 18 and 30. Says her last marriage failed because of sexual dissatisfaction, but believes this present marriage is a loving one. Describes herself as emotional, and her husband as impetuous. Married for the first time between 18 and 20.

WIFE: "Yes, because husband had many affairs."

Spread enough cash around and the territory is bound to look a little greener, but only one respondent in a hundred said money or gifts would tempt them to be unfaithful, and women were no more occupied with gold-digging than men. A few saccharine words seem to have more appeal to today's woman than the rich treats of the old-time sugar daddy.

WIFE: "I had a baby when I was sixteen. My baby is sixteen years old now. He lives with us. My husband doesn't want him. Temptation—money."

This homemaker says her husband is irresponsible, and takes her for granted. Her major problem is lack of money, and though she never cheated, she has thought about divorce. Feels it would give her the freedom to fulfill herself.

Most wives are homebodies, by choice or circumstance, so it is not surprising that more than three times as many husbands said that being away from home would constitute a main temptation. However, Satan finds some mischief *still* for idle hands to do, and boredom was as apt to drive wives as husbands into infidelity, especially when one spouse or another is on the road.

WIFE: "Yes, it was on a vacation. I didn't seem to mind, but it created guilt in other party. No, my husband didn't find out."

WIFE: "Yes. It has happened several times when I was away from my spouse and had been drinking. I feel guilty about it as far as emotions are concerned but logically I feel no guilt. My spouse has been in jail for two years. My spouse is very aware of my affairs. The only thing he has done about it is to use it against me as his form of security.

"To whomever is reading this:

"You must understand that questions regarding sex between spouses are answered, in fact, to our activities before he was convicted and sent to prison."

She's a blue collar worker, between 18 and 30. Both she and her husband have considered divorce. She's cheated with more than 3 men, but none for over a year. Says her sex life with her husband (before he went to prison) was very good, but felt dominated by him. Describes him as possessive.

WIFE: "Yes, I was alone and intoxicated. No, he never found out and he never will."

Judging from the above responses and those below from husbands, it seems that in the game of love Cupid does the shooting but Bacchus, god of wine, gets credited with many an assist:

HUSBAND: "Yes. I was in a car out of town. Got slightly drunk and was talked into going home with a woman. Spouse doesn't know. I feel a little bit guilty."

A blue collar worker between 41 and 50, he describes himself as emotional, and has thought about divorce. He cheated with 1 other woman, briefly. He says that sex with his wife is good, and he believes that their marriage is generally stable, but feels that his wife takes him for granted.

HUSBAND: "Yes, I met her in a bar after a business meeting and went home with her. Yes, wife found out and went to an attorney . . . wanted a divorce right away."

He's a blue collar worker, and a college graduate. He cheated with 1 other woman, briefly. Both he and his wife have considered divorce, but took no further action on it. His biggest temptation is when there is constant fighting at home. He's between 31 and 40, and describes himself as emotional, while he calls his wife "possessive."

HUSBAND: "Yes, I had a couple of affairs. We met at a bar and (one) at a gas station. It was OK. They say a spice of life is good for the soul. No, she never found out about it."

If the plural of "mouse" is "mice," would not the plural of "spouse" be "spice"? Some wives do not apparently agree, and consider husbands who followed this philosophy something akin to lice:

HUSBAND: "Yes. It just happened. She found out and got angry and hurt."

He's 51 or over, retired or unemployed. This is his second marriage. Says he no longer has sex with his wife, and feels tied down and trapped.

HUSBAND: "Yes, one affair. I worked closely with this person. I am sorry it happened. Yes, my spouse found out and got in touch with other person. That ended it."

He's a blue collar worker, a high school graduate, 41 to 50. He has cheated with this person for over a year, and says he'd be tempted to cheat by poor sex at home. He says that an extramarital affair was the worst crisis of their marriage. He feels they have a fairly loving marriage, and says their sex life is good.

HUSBAND: "Yes. Spur of the moment thing with married girl much younger than I. She told her husband. He called my wife."

It's frustrating when a narrator interrupts his tale just when the exciting part is about to happen. Perhaps there's too much violence in books these days as it is; besides, wives don't always take much action against faithless husbands anyway, if we are to believe the following:

HUSBAND: "Yes, have had numerous affairs. Yes, spouse found
    out but does not really care as it relieves her of sexual duties.
    The biggest reason for temptation has been lousy sex life at
    home."

He considers his marriage a failure, and says he cheated with
more than 3 women, with one affair lasting over a year. Says
sex with wife is dull. Also he had children only to please
his wife. He's between 31 and 40, and has a postgraduate
education.

HUSBAND: "Yes, I have had and have many affairs. My spouse
    found out and much was said. Not much was done about it.
    It happens that I love to make love to other women, and I feel
    very good about loving my women. As for temptation . . . it is
    mainly sex and whatever else the relations bring."

He's unemployed now, and has some college education.
Cheated with 2 or 3 other women, with one relationship lasting
over a year. Says he's sexually unsatisfied in his marriage, and
though he's only between 31 and 40, he no longer has sex with
his wife. He's been separated from her, and says a divorce
would give him the freedom to fulfill himself.

HUSBAND: "Yes. Did it just by coincidence. Wife found out and
    did nothing about it."

HUSBAND: "Yes, with my wife's consent. I find that I need
    extramarital sex."

One husband in ten said he would be tempted by the prospect
of finding either true love, or at least better understanding, so not
all cheaters want a quick, impersonal relationship, though stronger
motives vary:

HUSBAND: "Having one now! It is the most positive experience
    in my emotional development in a long time. We had strong
    feelings for each other for 2 years before the affair actually
    started. The event has been gradual over 2½ years and very
    positive for us both. Presently our spouses don't know."

He's a professional and has a postgraduate education. Between
31 and 40. He says he would be tempted to cheat with someone

who understood him better than his wife. He feels affairs should be tolerated, but fidelity is preferable. This is the only person he's cheated with. He feels their sex life is generally dull, and they have intercourse 2 or 3 times a month. They have struck each other. He feels the marriage is fairly stable, but it has alternating periods of closeness and remoteness, and he feels lack of communication, difference in personal interests, and conflicts over relatives are major problems.

HUSBAND: "Someone showed great interest in me and great approval. I should not have allowed it to happen. My wife suspected but was not sure."

He thinks his wife wishes that they'd never married, and has cheated with 1 other woman, briefly. Says he and his wife argue mostly over personal habits, and he has considered divorce. He's between 41 and 50, and a college graduate. Works in the technical field.

HUSBAND: "Her cheating."

Despite complaints of the feminists that employers exert sexual pressures on subordinates through the implied threat of withheld raises and promotions, only one married woman in a thousand and three husbands per thousand said that a chance for job advancement would tempt them to cheat. Not all office affairs are strictly business, but proximity and secrecy seem to be the inherent temptations. Deep motives are not always necessary. Ten per cent of husbands and 4 per cent of wives would most readily respond to an affair that promised to be brief and casual.

HUSBAND: "I have had affairs. I've had them with people from place of work (office). Spouse does not know. Am currently engaged in an affair. Boredom has been main reason for temptation."

He's definitely planning to divorce his wife, says she's impetuous and their major problem is differences in personal interest. He has cheated with 2 or 3 other women, in brief affairs. A professional, between 18 and 30.

HUSBAND: "Yes. I was looking for extra sex. No my wife did not find out about it. It was just in fun that I did it."

For the 70 per cent of husbands who had remained faithful to their wives, some did so out of strong moral convictions, some out of a sense of responsible adult behavior, and some rather reluctantly:

HUSBAND: "My strong belief in life and faithfulness and being (or at least trying to be) a self-actualized person. I also want to create a safe, peaceful life for the new generation and society."

He's a postgraduate student, and says he would never be tempted to cheat because of loyalty to his wife. His marriage is a loving one, and he says sex is good.

HUSBAND: "Nope! No affairs. If I wanted to have affairs I wouldn't have gotten married. Sure, I see women every day with whom I'd like to go to bed, but my own maturity prevents me from pursuing such action."

He's a professional, has a postgraduate education, is between 31 and 40. He'd be tempted to cheat if he were away from home, but says he's faithful because of love for his wife. He feels they have a very good sex life, and they have intercourse 3 or 4 times a week. He feels fully loved and appreciated, and describes their marriage as generally stable.

HUSBAND: "I have never had an affair. Sometimes I feel tied down. Arguments lead to daydreaming about leaving it all behind."

Sigmund Freud made a discovery about 50 years ago that people today would assume was always commonly known; through the intimate revelations of his psychoanalytic patients, Freud learned that adults have daydreams. Before Walt Disney and *Playboy*, adults no more talked about daydreams and fantasies than they talked about masturbation. Freud said children were proud of their daydreams because they reflected the wish to be adults, whereas adults were ashamed of their fantasies because they were childish in nature. Some men scoff at the fantasy of extramarital sex as immature and others regard cheaters as bold heroes who accomplish what meeker men only dare to dream about. Virtue consists, not in abstaining from vice, but in not desiring it, so the virtue of a faithful man must be measured not by his experiences but his wishes and motives. Is the prevalence of virtue a reflection of the triumph of love or the default of cowardice?

Faith and Reason

In his short story, "Go Back to Your Precious Wife and Son," Kurt Vonnegut, Jr., describes a conversation between two men, one of whom reveals that he married at age 18 and has now spent 20 years with the same woman.

"Don't you ever feel like you got gypped out of your bachelor days, your playboy days, your days as a great lover?" the acquaintance asks.

"Well," comes the reply, "in New Hampshire those days generally come between the ages of fourteen and seventeen."

Of course, the more urbane and sophisticated we get, the longer we prolong our adolescence. Our technological evolution seems to establish an intellectual counterpart of our most laborious physical evolution, wherein the simple creatures, such as the mayfly, live a matter of days, while large mammals like us and the elephants take over a decade to reach adolescence. Whereas any self-respecting aborigine would be waging mortal combat or bearing children at the age of 13, our most highly educated young adults can reach pinnacles of acclaim only by toting synthetic pigskin bladders across a grassy plain or outmaneuvering other females for a beauty crown via a mock display of puritanical sensuality. Progress for the vast majority of adults means fiberglass golf clubs, electronic Pong games, and "Laverne and Shirley" beamed across an entire continent. When our culture prolongs every other aspect of our adolescence right through our lives into our Sunset City retirement villages, how are we to put a selective end to the carefree, indiscriminate liaisons of our premarital days?

Whereas 23 per cent of our respondents admitted to having cheated at some point during their marriage, only 6 per cent said that they were currently unfaithful. This included 8 per cent of husbands and half that number of wives. What keeps them faithful when the singles and divorced all about them are waging a sexual revolution and all our media promote an exciting world of sexual variety and innovation?

What prevents you or inhibits you from extra-marital affairs?

A minister was greeting his congregation after a service and he stopped one male parishioner upon whom the sermon seemed to have had profound effects. "I noticed," the minister said, "that at one point you seemed deeply concerned, but as I spoke a great weight seemed to be lifted from your shoulders. Could you share your thoughts with me?"

"Well, Reverend," the man confessed, "you were talking about the Ten Commandments, and when you said, 'Thou shalt not steal,' I realized my umbrella was missing. But then you went on and when you said, 'Thou shalt not commit adultery,' I remembered where I'd left it."

While the National Council of Churches probably does not draw a Sunday audience as large as that of the National Football League, moral beliefs were the second most common reason for fidelity, according to 23 per cent of our sample:

WIFE: "I love my husband and my God."

HUSBAND: "We are Jehovah's Witnesses and our lives are centered around the Bible's teachings . . . love of God and love of neighbor."

She says loyalty to spouse keeps her faithful, and says her marriage is a loving one. Her worst crisis was over her husband's ex-wife. This is his second marriage, and he says he would never be tempted to cheat. He describes his wife as considerate, but feels their major problem involves jobs. He's between 31 and 40, and works in management.

WIFE: "My love for him and because of religious feelings."

HUSBAND: "Before the church nothing inhibited me. Now the fear of the wrath of God only prevents me. No proper living Christian will ever indulge in extramarital activities."

Fear of the wrath of God prevents extramarital affairs for many, but a few are more inhibited by fear of the wrath of the spouse, an answer selected by a timid 2 per cent:

WIFE: "Fear of spouse and I don't want a divorce anytime soon."

HUSBAND: "I love my spouse."

Nearly three million people have read Eustace Chesser's pre-Kinsey sex guide, entitled *Love Without Fear*. Fear seems to be quite dispensable, since love alone was by far the number one reason for fidelity, chosen by just about two-thirds of our respondents.

WIFE: "My husband and I have had an incredibly beautiful twenty-seven years of marriage. He knows me better than I know myself and makes life very easy for me. I, in turn, feel I do the same. I would not attempt to do *anything* that would jeopardize our relationship—nor would I want to."

HUSBAND: "Consideration of my wife; doesn't allow for double standard. I feel she wouldn't, so why should I?"

This homemaker and mother of 2 says her marriage is a loving one, that her sex life is good, and they never argue. He feels that his marriage has given his life more purpose and meaning and because of his marriage he has become a better lover. She's between 41 and 50, and he's 51 or over, and is a professional, making between $25–49,000 a year.

WIFE: "Before this marriage I had many affairs because there was no love at home. This man loves me enough to keep me satisfied."

HUSBAND: "All the love I want is at home."

This is her third marriage. She has no children. She says this marriage is a loving one, and has never cheated on her present spouse. He's considerate, but her only major problem with him has been alcohol. He's a white collar worker between 31 and 40, and this is his second marriage. He says he has a feeling of emotional security and of being loved, and though he describes his wife as possessive, he believes she loves and appreciates him fully.

Wives were even more motivated by love than husbands, with a 70 per cent mark to the men's respectable 61 per cent. Couples in the youngest age group and those married for the first time placed a higher stress on love, though there was more current infidelity in the respondents under 40.

WIFE: "I have a wonderful husband. We are very much in love. I don't think I could find another man like him."

She's a homemaker who didn't complete high school, 51 or over. She is faithful out of loyalty to her spouse, and says she'd never be tempted. She feels that their sex life is good and that her spouse loves and appreciates her fully. She does say that she's become disillusioned about romance and love, however. She says their marriage is generally stable.

One in five husbands cited moral beliefs as the prime deterrent to cheating, and the wives exceeded this with one in four keeping faithful through faith in religious or other ethical precepts:

WIFE: "I really have no desire for a lover. I also have a strong moral and religious objections. But basically, I have a low sex-drive and have no real need for sex outside my marriage."

She's a high school graduate and a homemaker, 18 to 30. She would be tempted by constant fighting at home. Their sex life is variable; they have intercourse twice a week. She finds she's more nervous and irritable since getting married, but she rates her marriage as generally stable and loving.

WIFE: "Religious beliefs. There is one person if I had the opportunity I couldn't refuse, but probably won't have the opportunity."

We wonder if Joanne Woodward would be the prime obstacle for the lady above. Whether the person who could make our respondent a godfatherly offer she couldn't refuse is a remote fantasy or a nearby temptation, she shares the feelings of many wives who experience a measure of discontent with their husbands, but whose sense of loyalty keeps them faithful. Loyalty ran a close third, just behind moral beliefs, and husbands and wives were equal in the percentage choosing this rationale.

WIFE: "I would feel guilty because I strongly believe my husband has never had an extramarital affair since our marriage. Although our sex is not the greatest (from my point of view) I don't think I'd enjoy it any more with another man. I would probably feel very guilty."

A professional woman with a postgraduate education, 41 to 50. She says she'd never be tempted out of loyalty to her spouse. She feels their sex life is generally dull (once a week). She feels dominated by her husband, but loved and appreciated fully, and thinks their marriage is generally stable.

WIFE: "My husband is in the Navy and often gone for long periods of time (eight to twelve months), so there is ample opportunity for an affair. However, I want my marriage to remain as solid and satisfying as it is. Consequently, I would have to make sure (1) my own head was 'together' and I could trust myself to seek sexual gratification *only* (impossible to guarantee!) and (2) the partner felt the same also. I would also demand respect during and after the affair, and that again is difficult to guarantee."

All other reasons for being faithful received only a smattering of support, none chosen by more than 3 per cent of the respondents. Lack of opportunity was among these, some wives demanding far more than the usual lover is willing to give and some feeling nobody would want them.

WIFE: "The fact that I want a person who is interested in me as a person and not someone just to have sex with. So far I have not met anyone that I feel a strong love for and vice versa."

She has more than 4 children, and is between 31 and 40. She married for economic security, and says her marriage now alternates between periods of closeness and remoteness. Lack of communication and sexual dissatisfaction is her major problem.

WIFE: "I am heavy."

Other factors weighing less heavily in the balance but nevertheless influencing fidelity on a small scale were fear of spouse (nearly twice as common in women), fear of losing children, shyness, and fear of social censure:

WIFE: "Fear is the first thing that comes to mind. I really have no interest in it. I am happy where I am or else I wouldn't be here."

She's a homemaker, a college graduate, 18 to 30. She's been involved with her partner's knowledge and consent.

WIFE: "Commitment to family togetherness. Sexual commitment is a part of total family commitment. Strong belief in the importance of communication between spouses—extramarital affairs would interfere in this honest sharing."

She would only be tempted if there was constant fighting at home, but she considers her marriage to be a loving one, and a very good sex life. She has a postgraduate education, works in the professional field, and has 2 children.

WIFE: "I have been out of circulation for so many years."

She is a homemaker, 51 or over, a high school graduate. She says that she'd never be tempted because of love for her spouse. Their sex life she finds satisfactory, but she feels tied down and trapped, and difference in personal interest is their major problem.

WIFE: "Satisfaction in my own marriage and knowing it is wrong. I am far-sighted enough to realize affairs are temporary and destructive, whereas my marriage is permanent and healthy. I would not want to impair its chances of success.

"Friends would be extremely disappointed in me."

While fear of an affair's hurting a career was the main motive for fidelity in only one man in a hundred, this consideration was practically exclusive for males. Fear of losing children was just as high in males as females, and lack of opportunity was, somewhat surprisingly, more frequently chosen by husbands than wives, despite their greater range for temptation.

HUSBAND: "(1) My profession, both internally (theologically) and externally (standing in community), but (2) more importantly, I don't care to become involved because I value highly the family we have set up."

While he believes his marriage is loving, he says that sex with his wife is dull, and feels sexually unsatisfied. His biggest temptation would be an exceptionally attractive woman. He's between 31 and 40, and works in the technical field. Has a college education.

HUSBAND: "Fear of venereal disease and possible loss of present family, especially my son."

He says both he and his wife have considered divorce, but took no action on it. A college graduate, he believes their only child has driven them further apart, and he had him to please his wife. Poor sex at home would be his biggest temptation to cheat. Says his sex life is not satisfying, and his wife takes him for granted. He's between 31 and 40, and works in the technical field.

HUSBAND: "Fear of wife discovering and possibility of termination of marriage or of destroying marriage relationship. Possibly the effect of divorce on the children and ruining their relationship with me is even a greater concern."

Fear of his spouse usually keeps him faithful, but he has cheated already with more than 3 women, none lasting over a year. Says he and his wife have struck each other during arguments, and feels dominated by her. His major problem is money. He works in management, is between 31 and 40, with a postgraduate education.

HUSBAND: "Shy with women, no money to waste on flings, general lack of opportunity."

The road to hell is paved with good intentions and not all motives—such as not wishing to hurt one's wife—are sturdy enough to keep a man on the straight and narrow path. Men with no intentions at all, either of having affairs or staying faithful, may find that unpaved roads also lead to the damnedest indiscretions.

HUSBAND: "Although I do cheat on my wife occasionally, I always have the fear that if she ever found out she would be hurt deeply. This I wish to avoid over all costs."

He's had affairs with 2 or 3 other women, and being away from home is his biggest temptation. He says he feels overwhelmed by responsibility. Works in the technical field, is between 18 and 30, and some college background.

HUSBAND: "An extramarital affair can be planned or just happen. I do not go out looking for one. Mine just happened. Right time and place, etc. I would not look for one."

The most convincing answers of all came from husbands who said the reason they did not have extramarital affairs was simply because they didn't want them. Love, moral beliefs, and loyalty to their wives certainly played a role on an intellectual level, but fidelity was not really a matter of will; rather it was a natural course of their desire for an exclusive sexual relationship and lack of desire for outside liaisons:

HUSBAND: "I had been married once before and engaged in extramarital affairs and found it unrewarding and a result of a poor marriage and sex life. Now I am remarried to someone whom I truly love and with whom I enjoy a good sex life and I haven't had any desire to have an affair with anyone."

This is his second marriage, and he has not cheated on his present spouse. Says he feels loved and appreciated fully. The only temptation would be if he was away from home or sex at home was poor. He's between 31 and 40, a professional, with a postgraduate education.

HUSBAND: "I do not feel the need for extramarital affairs. My wife fulfills my needs. Although my attraction toward females continues, I always find that on further contemplation none of the legs on parade or associates' acquaintances which may originally catch my Playboy machismo (the social power of this shitty imagemaker is incredible) ever holds up to my wife's personality, charm and loving embrace."

This white collar worker with a postgraduate education says his marriage is a loving one, and his sex life is good, but believes while his wife thinks he's a good lover, she feels that he needs improvements in other ways. Describes himself as methodical, emotional, and anxious.

HUSBAND: "A belief that intercourse remains a 'special' act between a couple, and an affair would destroy that reserved specialness. We have engaged in sex with another couple, touching one another, but have stopped short of actual intercourse with one another."

He's a professional, with a college education, 31 to 40. He says he'd be tempted to cheat by the chance of a brief, casual affair. He and his spouse engage in group sex and use mechanical aids in their lovemaking. He feels their sex life is generally dull, nevertheless. They got married because of pregnancy. He says they have no major problems.

HUSBAND: "Totality of contentedness in my present marriage— ego satisfaction in an emotional, physical and spiritual manner that precludes that need."

When people have achieved a true intimacy, they do not desire outside relationships because their own love and concern for one another is so pervasive that they simply have no room in their lives for more than one such relationship at a time. People who contend that married couples, liberated from strong social and religious taboos, would pursue sexual partners as indiscriminately as barnyard animals, fail to understand that monogamy, not promiscuity, is a product of freedom. Just as the wild birds can be perfectly contented with one mate, unlike the penned-in fowl of the barnyard, adults who select spouses freely will be quite pleased with them, whereas those who have been pressured into unions by social and familial demands are less likely to be content. The final freedom must be a release from the neurotic inhibitions that direct us towards "safe" choices, such as the surrogate father or asexual madonna, whom ambivalence or our own belated maturity will eventually cause us to reject, at least partially. The truly valid love relationship does not involve a constant struggle against temptation; where needs are met, there are no unslaked appetites seeking appeasement. And where vice is undesired, rather than merely unrealized, we have a condition known as virtue.

Revelations and Retribution

"O curse of marriage! That we can call these delicate creatures ours, and not their appetites. I had rather be a toad, and live upon the vapour of a dungeon, than keep a corner in the thing I love for others' uses." The name of Shakespeare's Othello is as synonymous with jealousy as that of Judas with betrayal or Jezebel with temptation. And we can learn much about this common emotion from the murderous Moor, even just from the speech above, where we see that jealousy is an attitude towards something we own, a piece of property, rather than love. When Othello speaks of keeping a corner in the thing he loves for other's uses, we may think of Desdemona's strategic strawberry handkerchief, if we have ever watched a mother scrutinize her own handkerchief for a clean corner to offer a runny-nosed child. It has been said that our society does not love people and use things, but rather loves things and uses people. Women commonly react to the possibility of a husband's extramarital affair by saying squeamishly that they could no more tolerate that than sharing their toothbrush. We do not demand doctors, lawyers, or teachers that are exclusively ours, but spouses are considered strictly private property.

This claim is enforced by society. Othello affirms that we *can* call our wives "ours," though their affections are irrelevant, just as we may own a dog or horse though the creature detests us. Society supports our jealousy in cases of marriage or betrothal, though other circumstances dictate that society oppose this feeling, namely when there has been no such establishment of claim. In cases where the one desired has made no formal commitment, rivalry between suitors is not only accepted but encouraged; jealousy among rivals certainly occurs, but once a formal engagement or other indication of commitment has been declared, the rules of good sportsmanship are supposed to prevail, and any disgruntled rival who would attempt an act of revenge—a frequent theme in the old melodramas—would be sternly punished by the law. Conversely, a betrayed husband who killed the interloper would undoubtedly receive considerable clemency under society's acknowledged "unwritten law" for here the other man was not a rival, but an encroacher or trespasser.

Jealousy is not related so much to the violation of exclusive sexual relations with the spouse, but with the usurpation of property without consent of the owner. There are tribes in this world where, under the rules of hospitality, a host offers his wife to the guest and would be offended if the guest declines. In underworld cultures, men may prostitute their wives and would become angry only if the client reneged on payment. Some European wives would not raise their blood pressures a millimeter over their husbands' patronizing a common street-prostitute, but would fly into a rage if a woman of their own social class began flirting with the male. We are now seeing a striking example of this attitude in our own culture, where couples engage in mate-swapping and other forms of group activity. Sexual intercourse is encouraged without jealousy but the spouses may do so only if the other spouse knows with whom and when this is done; let a mate start seeing another partner, even one who is a member of the sanctioned group, without the spouse's knowledge and consent and there will be a scene to rival any which would have occurred in the house of a 19th century Sicilian.

Jealousy may occur in all sorts of property situations and the marital situation is unique because here the object has some choice in its acquisition. Objects are rarely valued for themselves. In the case of need, value depends more on the intensity of the void that must be filled than on the object; a canteen of water would be worth more than vintage brandy to a parched castaway and a camel is invaluable to an Arabian merchant but a nuisance and hazard to a suburban homeowner. Some objects, such as diamonds, mink stoles, and limousines have no utilitarian value and their worth lies in impressing others with the wealth and social status of the owner, provoking envy (which differs from jealousy in that the envier does not feel he has a claim to the desired object). Other objects have value in reflecting the merit of the owner, such as trophies, plaques, executive washroom keys, and committee chairmanships. Again, none of these objects have any exercise of will in the matter of their ownership; but even in interpersonal relationships, people reach points where the love object is wantonly destroyed, as in Othello's murder of Desdemona. This makes no sense according to the concept of love, but is comprehensible in terms of property; angry spouses who say "I'll never give you a divorce!" know they no longer have any love, but react as they would to a caged canary who was attempting to find a way out.

When NBC television sponsored a nationwide survey on the topics of love, sex, and marriage, they presented people with 31 multiple-choice questions, and then compared the answers of the general population with the opinion of experts. In only two questions did the American populace disagree. One was a marked discrepancy in response to "People are often less satisfied with their marriages if they have children. True or false?" 84 per cent said "false," which correlates well with the 82 per cent of our sample who did not feel their children had a negative effect on the marriage. The "experts" apparently had either a different conception of "often" or were basing their answer on studies of childless couples, because they contended the answer was "true." The other question where the majority ruled against the experts was "Jealousy is natural if you really love your mate," to which more than half replied "true." Obviously, if the majority of people feel this way, they have probably personally experienced feelings of jealousy, so the experts can only argue semantically about the word "natural." Jealousy, if we define it as driving away rivals to preserve the exclusivity of a sexual relationship, certainly occurs in nature among birds, deer, elephant seals and just about every type of creature that has managed to put more than one cell together and, therefore, requires a mate. Thus, the "experts" might have better said that jealousy was not worthy of such an advanced creature as man, who should rise above his natural urges, rather than denying the naturalness of the reaction. (It is the unfortunate tendency of our social scientists to try to have the argument both ways. If they believe in free love, they extol sex as a "natural" thing and encourage us to follow our urges. If they disapprove of aggression, they define war as animalistic [although only five species of ants and two of termites are known to wage war, out of all the denizens of the animal kingdom] and condemn such behavior as atavistic.)

Perhaps what we should say is that two people who love one another will handle their jealous feelings in a different way from those more concerned with property than people. We cannot predict with certainty how we would react in a specific crisis, but we nevertheless engage in fire drills and disaster plans. We asked our respondents how they would handle the discovery of their spouses' extramarital affairs.

What would you do if you discovered your spouse was having an extramarital affair?

At least in the unemotional planning stage of dealing with such a crisis, nearly half of our spouses said they would discuss the situation *calmly* with their mates. Peaceful negotiations constituted "plan A" for 43 per cent of our respondents.

WIFE: "I would have a discussion with him and find out how he felt and if he still loved me or whatever."

HUSBAND: "I would just discuss it with her and find out the reasons for having an affair. If the fault was mine I would seek to correct the faults. If the fault were hers I would ask her to think more about commitment to each other."

The second most commonly selected answer was to demand that the spouse give up the outside lover. Even though they might engage in calm discussion, this demand was non-negotiable for 18 per cent:

WIFE: "Be shocked and extremely hurt. Ask what I was doing wrong to cause him to seek another. Try to discuss it calmly. If the situation continued we would have to be divorced."

HUSBAND: "I would be hurt and would confront her with the accusations. I would try and discover why she would want to hurt me and if she really wanted to be free I'd seek a divorce. There could be a possibility of taking her back or forgiving her, but any further extramarital action would definitely end our relationship and marriage."

One-sixth of the spouses we surveyed said they would seek a divorce immediately. Husbands were considerably more likely to consider infidelity irrevocable grounds for divorce, 19 per cent choosing such precipitous action compared with 14 per cent of wives:

WIFE: "First I would look at myself and ask why. What had I done to cause my spouse to look elsewhere? Then I would sit down with my spouse and try to talk with him, to get some kind of reason. Ask why he had an extramarital affair. Then, if not satisfied, would take myself right out the door and leave."

HUSBAND: "Divorce."

WIFE: "Definitely ask him about it. Ask whether it was a one-night stand. Ask if there was something we could do together to remedy the situation."

HUSBAND: "Throw her out."

In our subsample of matched couples, only in 27 per cent of the pairs did we find both partners wanting to discuss the situation calmly in lieu of other solutions. There were twice as many situations where the wife would have opted for calm discussion and the husband for immediate divorce as the reverse. While both sexes chose calm discussion by a wide margin as their favorite option, wives led husbands in this choice, 46 per cent to 40 per cent.

WIFE: "That is hard to answer. I would be very hurt I'm sure. I don't think I would leave him as that would be childish. I probably would sit down and have a good heart to heart talk to see in which direction our marriage was going to go in the future. The question of 'why' did he stray must be answered *honestly* by him. There is always room for improvement on both sides, but if he strayed, I would suppose that I need a good look at myself and my habits to see why he lost interest."

Both she and her husband have considered divorce. She says her sex life is generally dull, and feels tied down and trapped. Says her husband is reserved. Between 41 and 50, a white collar worker with 2 children.

WIFE: "First I would be very upset but I would want to know why he felt he needed the affair and what his future plans were (to continue the affair or work out the problem that led him to it) also; I really wouldn't want to know who the person was as I would probably then feel I would have to compete with her."

The more education people had, the more faith they put in calm discourse. High school drop-outs trailed college-educated people by nearly 10 percentage points in selecting this response. Professionals picked this answer 49 per cent of the time, 9 percentage points above white collar workers and 17 above blue collar employees. Blue collar workers and high school drop-outs were far more likely to seek immediate divorce or harm the partner physically. Blacks were the only subgroup that did not pick discussion as their probable reaction; instead, in one-third of their responses, they would demand that the spouse give up the lover.

Wives would be slightly less tolerant of a continuing affair, one-fifth demanding a prompt halt, compared with one-sixth of the husbands.

WIFE: "Probably try to leave. If he'd let me leave then I would know he was serious about the affair. If he wouldn't let me leave then I would demand the affair come to an end."

She's a homemaker, with a postgraduate education. Says she would never be tempted to cheat, for she feels her marriage is a loving one.

People who were married more than once were far more likely to seek immediate divorce, choosing this over a demand that the affair be ended; perhaps many of them ended the initial marriage in precisely this manner. Those with firm religious beliefs were more opposed to infidelity than divorce, since they selected immediate divorce more often than their non-religious counterparts. Surprisingly, the presence of children in the marriage had no effect whatsoever on the percentage choosing divorce.

WIFE: "I would appreciate it. He has had an affair but it was only a one night stand and I actually pray that he'll find somebody else so I can get out of this 'Made in Hell Marriage'."

She says her marriage is a failure, and is definitely planning to divorce her spouse. She married him out of "pity" and their major problem is lack of money. She's cheated, and says both have struck each other. Between 18 and 30, a white collar worker. No children.

Fifteen per cent of our respondents said they would seek professional counseling, but wives were twice as likely to go alone if the spouse refused to cooperate.

WIFE: "Would be *extremely* upset. Would sit down and discuss the problem completely as to what caused it . . . the possibility of it recurring and his feelings about it. I really couldn't tolerate it, but if it was a one-time fling I would seek counseling. I need to know that it is only one."

While she feels her marriage is loving and sex is good, she feels more nervous and irritable since her marriage. A homemaker, 31 to 40, she has a postgraduate education and has 2 children.

WIFE: "I would not be surprised. I'd discuss it with him and encourage him to seek outside counseling to discover why. It would be an easy way out of the situation. Definitely not preferable, but an easy way out."

Responses chosen by wives in less than 5 per cent of the cases included having affairs of their own, withholding sex, and inflicting physical harm on the spouse:

WIFE: "Have one myself if I couldn't ignore it."

This mother of 2 says she's emotional, and has considered divorce. She cheated on her husband briefly with 1 other man, and says her husband wishes that they'd never gotten married.

WIFE: "I'd leave his ass high and dry."

A white collar worker between 18 and 30, with 1 child, she says her marriage is in constant turmoil, and has thought about divorce. Argues mostly about personal habits, and feels trapped.

WIFE: "Probably crown him for not saving it all for me. I can handle it."

One spouse in twenty, husbands and wives, would "ignore it." In the case of many wives, this apparent inertia seems to be rooted in feelings that they have been inadequate or lacking in their marital roles:

WIFE: "My pride would be hurt I am sure. But there isn't much I could do about it. I would deserve it. I know I am not a very good wife and he deserves better. In our case it would either make or break our marriage. If my heart was hurt then it would prove to be a shot in the arm to make our marriage work. If I felt no pain it might force the end of a marriage that has been in limbo for some time as far as I am concerned."

This homemaker says her spouse is considerate, but she's dominant, and their biggest problem is sexual dissatisfaction. She's thought about divorce, says it would give her the freedom to fulfill herself. Has cheated on her husband with another man for over a year. She has 1 child, is between 18 and 30, and a homemaker.

WIFE: "Be very hurt because his moral standards are very high.
    "I really don't know what I would do. I could tell you one thing and do the opposite.
    "If he had to turn to another woman, I would ask myself, 'What's wrong with me?'
    "Then take it from there."

This is her second marriage, and she believes this one is stable, and that her husband loves and appreciates her fully. A blue collar worker with 3 children, she is between 31 and 40.

WIFE: "I would feel it was mostly my fault. If I had been a good wife and lover he wouldn't need someone else."

Do husbands differ much from wives in their reactions to infidelity? Four times as many men said they would inflict physical harm on their partners, but this still constituted fewer than one man in twenty-five:

HUSBAND: "Kill the fucking bastard and beat the shit out of her."

He's 51 or over and in management. Makes between $25–$49,000 a year and has 4 children. He himself has cheated with more than 3 women, with one lasting over a year, and believes that only husbands should be allowed outside sexual activity. Says his marriage is a failure, and sex life is dull.

HUSBAND: "Probably, go completely out of my mind! Who knows what I would do? Probably something I would be sorry for later but would get great satisfaction at the time if I was to do something drastic."

Men did not differ much from their wives in turning to professionals for guidance, 14 per cent of husbands electing this option against 17 per cent of wives. And there were just as many husbands as wives willing to ignore or otherwise fail to interfere in the matter.

HUSBAND: "Seriously analyze how I may have contributed to her desire to have an extramarital affair.
"With my spouse, *I would seek professional aid.*"

He is a professional with a college education, 41 to 50. He says he'd never be tempted to cheat because of love for his wife. Their sex life he rates as satisfactory, and they have sex 2 or 3 times a month. He describes the marriage as always loving.

HUSBAND: "Join her."

Traditionally, women have been far more accepting of infidelity than men, a double standard with a nonetheless firm biological rationale. Cuckoldry for a husband could mean his working years to support a child that was not his own. Likewise, a wife pregnant with another man's child would deprive him for about a year of siring his own offspring. For a wife, infidelity by the husband held no such hazards. The only risk to her own progeny was the possibility of his desertion to another woman. She could more easily live with the knowledge of shared affections than cope with supporting a family by herself.

Husbands today, according to our survey, are less likely than wives to demand that an affair be terminated and are no more eager than women to confront the interloper. While it is true that husbands slightly more often demand an immediate divorce, the total of percentages wanting either immediate cessation of the affair or of the marriage differs by less than 2 percentage points between the sexes. The modern husband may show considerable patience before demanding that his wife give up a lover:

HUSBAND: "I would wait to see if she would tell me first. If she didn't I would confront her and try to openly discuss it with her. I would tell her if it was over I could forgive her, but it would take me a long time to forget. It would be through love and her faithfulness that would eventually erase the affair from my mind."

He's a professional between 18 and 30 with a postgraduate education. He definitely plans to divorce, though he says his sex life with his wife is good, and he's never cheated. He says that he'd be tempted to cheat if he found someone who understood him better than his wife.

HUSBAND: "My wife has had an affair which I discovered, and lived with for over a year. After a year of torture I rendered an ultimatum to her to end the affair or I would end our marriage."

Even among husbands who would seek an immediate divorce, not all are motivated by moral indignation. Some would apparently welcome a good excuse to get out of a dissatisfying marriage, invoking the immortal words of Henny Youngman: "Take my wife . . . please!"

HUSBAND: "If she had one I would be pleased. Then I could leave with no hard feelings or moral obligation but I really do not think if she was able she would."

A college graduate between 31 and 40, with no children, he says that he and his wife have separated at one time. He believes that husbands alone should be permitted outside sexual activity, and has cheated with 2 or 3 other women. Says his wife is sickly.

HUSBAND: "Confront her which I did and divorce her which I did."

He's in management, earning between $10–$15,000 a year. While he never cheated on his wife, he has become disillusioned about romance and love.

HUSBAND: "I think a divorce would be inevitable. We have discussed this question and my spouse knows my feelings on this. There would be no point in continuing the relationship under such conditions; if problems have gone to that extreme where discussion comes *after* action, then the marriage is beyond saving."

More than half of today's husbands would discuss the situation with their wives, with or without the aid of a therapist, before taking more drastic steps. They are not beyond strong feelings of anger and depression and are not blind to the possibility of having to plan a new life, but they have enough faith in communication and common sense to try to hold the marriage together:

HUSBAND: "First—swear a lot. Then—*cry a lot all to myself.*
  "I would try to have a calm discussion with my wife to find out why . . . whether it is for real or an outlet for something else. If the latter, there is a *chance* of salvaging the marriage, with common sense, reasoning and communication. Otherwise, make plans for a new life."

Perhaps modern couples are winning the battle against the green-eyed monster. Othello was not Shakespeare's only character who spoke of jealousy. It was Portia who noted how jealousy, along with other unpleasant passions, could be routed by love:

> "How all the other passions fleet to air,
> As doubtful thoughts, and rash-embrac'd despair
> And shuddering fear, and green-ey'd jealousy.
> O love! be moderate; allay thy ecstasy;
> In measure rain thy joy . . ."

Portia, of course, made another speech involving rain that is far better remembered, something about the quality of mercy which she delivered in a court of law. With a little more concern with mercy and less with justice, couples can weather even the more turbulent of storms.

9

Split Decisions:

Divorce

What sort of servants? what sort of friends? what sort of Prime
Ministers should we have if we took them for better for worse
for all their lives? We should simply encourage them in every
sort of wickedness.

—*George Bernard Shaw,* GETTING MARRIED

Phyllis and Martin, the battling couple previously discussed, had
their final fight seven weeks after Phyllis had left him for the
eighteenth time in as many months of marriage. This time the
separation had lasted more than the customary three days because
Phyllis's parents were not several blocks away, but vacationing on
the Jersey shore, where Phyllis joined them. Martin decided, after
several fruitless telephone calls, that he was not going to kneel
in the sand and beg his wife to return; instead, he took off for a
vacation of his own in Puerto Rico.

During Martin's absence, his father was called by his father-
in-law who complained of Martin's callous treatment of Phyllis,
left without financial support while Martin sat on a beach. Father

341

responded that if Phyllis could sit on a beach in New Jersey, Martin could sit on a beach in Puerto Rico.

Two days after his return from Puerto Rico, Martin, being in his own neighborhood on business, decided to have lunch at home. There he was surprised to see his father-in-law and his wife's cousin, Viola, standing on his front steps, the door ajar and the hallway piled with cartons. Some of the furniture had already been moved out, and Phyllis was at the moment with the moving van making a delivery to her father's house.

"Sir, this is outrageous," Martin respectfully informed his father-in-law.

The older man, a diminutive but dapper banker, shrugged. "I'm sorry, it's Phyllis's decision," he replied. "Besides, we can no longer trust you. You might change the locks on the house."

"If I had wanted to do that, I would have done it two weeks ago," Martin protested. "I want you to leave right now."

"I am sorry," the elder said impassively. "This is Phyllis's decision."

"Maybe someday you'll have the guts to stand up to your wife and daughter," Martin said, less respectfully. "I can't permit you to do this. If necessary, I will use physical force."

At this point, father-in-law called Phyllis, who soon was back on the scene with three moving-men. Phyllis was immediately upon her spouse, kicking, clawing, and screaming, "How dare you talk to my father that way!" Martin tried to call his lawyer, but Phyllis kept interfering via the extension phone.

Now Martin confronted the moving-men and said this was a domestic dispute and they had no right to take anything. The chief of the crew said he had a contract, and he was living up to it. So, Martin got back on the phone to summon reinforcements in the person of his sister, Julia. Then he called the police emergency number and asked for help. The movers continued to take things out of the house.

Martin realized he didn't even know what was being taken, so he began to unpack the cartons Phyllis had packed. Finding one carton unyielding, he went to the kitchen for a knife, whereupon cousin Viola shrieked, "My God! He's coming at me with a knife!"

Martin, who always prided himself on his logic and control, abandoned the knife, and turned his attention back to the busy movers. The bedroom set was gone, but, after all, that had belonged to Phyllis before they were married. But the living-room set was definitely his, and there was no way they were going to take that! If he could only delay the movers until the police arrived, he could at least preserve that much. So, each time a mover would lunge for an armchair, Martin would say, "No, not that. Take *that,"* pointing to a carton or other article he was willing to sacrifice. Sister Julia arrived, and deployed herself across the sofa. Phyllis, needless to say, was meeting his pleas for reconciliation with a harangue reviewing every lowpoint of their internecine association.

Like a storm-tossed captain jettisoning everything possible overboard, Martin was running out of things to sacrifice to the movers. Again, he called the police, not realizing that city police never come until hours after you have reported a crime, unless you say it's in progress, and they never come at all if the problem lies between husband and wife. (Really sophisticated urbanites say a policeman is being attacked, the only sure way to draw six squad cars and two dozen armed patrolmen in under ten minutes; obviously, the reason for summoning them had better be good.) Finally, Martin made his last desperate stand. In his denuded living-room, he drew himself up to his full 66 inches and told the three behemoths that the living-room set was going over his body. They also had Julia's body to contend with, still obstinately supine on the sofa. For one heart-stopping moment two of the giants flexed their muscles at opposite ends of the sofa. The foreman cocked his head to listen for police sirens. Martin guarded the door like Horatio at the bridge. Cousin Viola and father-in-law tried to be inconspicuous in a room devoid of cover. Then, Phyllis raised her arm like a merciful angel. "Okay," she told the movers, "leave it."

Phyllis and Viola hopped in a car and followed the laden van. Julia righted herself and headed for the nearest bus. And on the front steps stood Martin and his father-in-law in the silent wake of the hours of noisy chaos that had suddenly ended. Martin, ever respectful, extended his hand to the gray-haired man beside him, saying, "Sir, whatever has happened between Phyllis and me, I hope it won't affect our friendship."

The above is Martin's version of the start of a divorce. In Phyllis's version, Martin comes across as far more disorganized, weeping, groveling, and charging that he has been emasculated. Both agree that the episode was a blend of high tragedy and a

Keystone Cops farce. But such is the American way of divorce, and it is difficult to conceive anything else so capable of reducing not only a couple, but their proud families to such extremes of anger, hysteria, and near-violence.

The American system of divorce is traditionally an adversary system, whereby one spouse must charge another with some wrongdoing that meets the state's requirements for dissolution of the marriage. The spouse who filed suit had to prove the wrong-doing, and, when under New York State law, the only admissible grounds was adultery, the wife would usually produce photographs in court of her husband in bed with another woman. Collusion was not technically allowed and any couple caught in the reprehensible act of helping one another to get evidence would have been punished in the worst possible manner, by being sent back to live together under pain of marriage. Needless to say, no reasonable judge ever bothered his head with figuring out how on earth a photographer happened to know where the husband was illicitly engaged and how the photographer gained access to the trysting place at the most intimate moment. Couples sensitive and wealthy enough to refuse to be party to such tasteless and embarrassing shenanigans would fly the wife to the one state in the Union sensible enough to see not only the plentiful revenues it could obtain from legalized gambling, but also from easy divorce; the state did institute a residency requirement which was just long enough to lend its laws some credibility and its hotels some tourist income.

Today, most of our states have relaxed their previously stringent requirements for legal grounds, but one spouse must still charge the other with such atrocities as physical abuse, inhuman treatment, or mental cruelty. No-fault divorce can only be obtained at the cost of a lengthy separation and the type of "progressive" law, practiced in Sweden for over 60 years, whereby a divorce can be granted at the simple request of either spouse, is yet to be enacted in the Land of the Free. Divorce is then essentially a punishment by which one partner, having been proven guilty of a grievous wrong, is banished from the marriage. In such a system, one spouse becomes plaintiff and the other defendant, though, through countersuit, they can simultaneously play both roles. Couples who may have been merely incompatible are transformed by the divorce laws into bitter enemies. The merest hint of divorce is enough to send the spouses scrambling in all directions in a frantic race to empty out all joint savings accounts and safe-deposit boxes, just as Phyllis engaged the moving van on the advice of a lawyer who was not around to be embroiled in the ensuing chaos. "Woe to you lawyers also! because you load men with oppressive burdens and you yourselves with one of your fingers do not touch the burdens (Luke, ch. 11, v. 46)," said a Man who managed to found a widely followed religion on only two laws.

The Semi-Permanent Relationship

A woman telephoned a Los Angeles radio station at the invitation of one of those talk shows which encourages listeners to phone in questions to guest experts. "Doctor," she said, "I don't know what's wrong with the men I've been meeting. I'm 29, attractive, divorced, and have no children. I fly my own charter plane and meet a lot of interesting men. We have a few dates, the sex is good, but then they lose interest. *I* want a semi-permanent relationship..."

The source of her problem was as obvious as a dagger in the back of a patient complaining of muscle spasms. Men, she was gently advised, would accept a casual relationship or even a permanent one, but nobody is going to invest in a "semi-permanent" one. The concept itself is highly dubious, seemingly akin to "semi-pregnant" or "semi-dead."

With deference to our lady pilot who can't seem to get things off the ground, however, we must admit that American marriage appears to be in the process of becoming a semi-permanent institution. We assume that nearly all the people who marry take their poetic though often unrealistic death-parting vow seriously; yet, since nearly one in three couples will dissolve that union through divorce, the commitment to permanence is something less than absolute. As in the case of the man who defended his act of expectorating on a subway platform in defiance of a "No Spitting" sign because it did not read "Positively," we pursue our natural inclinations in opposition to the spirit of the laws we pass and the religion we profess.

The annual ratio of divorces to marriages has changed from 1-to-4 in 1958 to 1-to-2 in 1978. In 1958, the divorce rate was 210 per 100,000 population, which had not risen appreciably over the previous two decades; it rose to 370 in 1971 and then to 500 in 1978. Our present rate dwarfs the 1908 Japanese figure of 215 per 100,000 population, then a world record, which scandalized an England that had a mere 2 divorces per 100,000. One can look at our divorce situation in a more optimistic light by saying that, if there are four people in the average family, the rate of marital failure in any given year is a mere 2 per cent; however, each succeeding year brings a similar chance for a family to disrupt into a statistic, and only 2 out of 3 first marriages survive as long as 30 years.

What has stopped our freedom-loving nation from letting marriages dissolve, as in Sweden or the Netherlands, simply because at least one of the partners no longer desires it? For many people, of course, what passes for marriage in those countries would be regarded as "free love" here, and many a puritan's descendant limits his patriotic love of freedom at freedom of love. To some, letting people do whatever they want is the same as simple immorality.

But as deeply rooted as the contention of some that sexual liberty is intrinsically immoral lies the more pervasive influence of our Christian heritage which regards marriage as an irrevocable sacrament. Obviously, for vast numbers of people joined in civil ceremonies, matrimony has not the slightest connection with religion. Devout Catholics officially believe that such irreligious couples are not truly married in the sight of God and are doing no more than living in sin; in practice, however, they fraternize as warmly with such people—and, for that matter, people living together without any sort of ceremony—as they would with members of their own congregation. In a Long Island church recently, the priest announced from the pulpit a forthcoming social event "for single and divorced Catholics," and in some areas, the Church has been so cooperative in granting annulments to divorced faithful in order to make their spiritual status compatible with their civil that the archdiocese of Brooklyn, for example, has become an ecclesiastical Reno. Yet, otherwise liberal Christians will solemnly intone "What therefore God has joined together, let no man put asunder," illogically equating the bureau of licenses, the local justice of the peace, or old Father Flannigan with God. The staunchest advocates of lifelong marriage are celibate clerics who seem to believe that the unhappily married deserve their fate much as the rich are often imbued with the notion that the poor got that way through their own fault.

But our most convincing argument for divorce comes not from

denying the sacerdotal nature of matrimony; rather, in admitting it, we see the importance of weeding out those who would profane it. Christ's admonition, "Whoever puts away his wife, *except for immorality,* and marries another, commits adultery (Matthew, ch. 19, v. 9)," indicates that there are, indeed, grounds for divorce. (Mark, who was not one of the original twelve apostles, omits in his gospel the qualifying phrase, giving the injunction an absolute nature quite different from that in Matthew.) One could quibble about what constitutes immorality, but St. Paul in his epistle to the Corinthians is quite severe in his castigation of those who participate unworthily in sacraments, saying that he who eats and drinks unworthily eats and drinks his own damnation. It is difficult for a religious person to perceive anything more immoral than the profaning of a sacrament based on mutual love by one or both spouses who harbor a contrary attitude of hostility, and denigration. It is one thing to defend the rights of a newborn baby as a child of God, but quite another to condone its acts of murder and theft twenty years later as the outcome of God's creation. The insistence that a spouse continue in a lifelong union characterized by deceit, brutality and callousness on the grounds that God has created and willed such a state is the sort of blasphemy we should expect from a cult of Satanists rather than a synod of devout deists.

Under Consideration

Whereas marriages arranged by parents or governments have been readily accepted in many cultures, we would be aghast at any attempt to force Americans to marry someone they did not desire. Where one party is extremely eager to marry, even to the point of incessant harrassment, hysterical weeping, or suicidal threats, we might have our courts intervene to suppress the ardent pursuer, but we would never dream of compelling the reluctant party to enter a marriage on the basis of unilateral desire. Our attitude is inconsistently the reverse once a couple is married. Even in states which grant divorces on such grounds as incompatibility or irreconcilable differences, these charges are contestable and a matter for trial if either spouse presses the matter. Our legal system retains the assumption that a marriage can somehow remain viable even if one spouse is totally opposed to it.

Would most modern spouses agree that a marriage should be ended if it proves unsatisfactory to either partner? Apparently not, for in our survey fewer than one in five respondents held this viewpoint, and neither sex was more in favor of it than the others. Slightly over a third believe that marriage is a lifelong commitment *never* to be broken; women might be expected to have a greater interest in insuring permanency for marriage, but actually the men prevailed in this attitude by 3 percentage points. The most commonly indicated feeling (44 per cent) was that marriage is a strong commitment, to be broken only under exceptional circumstances, and this was the only choice where women held an edge over men. A mere 2 per cent of husbands and 1 per cent of wives said that marriage should be entered with the expectation that it may be temporary.

In our subgroup of matched couples, only in 15 per cent of the cases did both partners feel that marriage should never be terminated, neither spouse prevailing in holding a more rigid view when there was disagreement.

The most surprising finding on this question was that 32 per cent of those remarried, nearly the same as those first-married, said that marriage was a commitment never to be broken, despite past experience to the contrary. Older spouses were far more conservative, 49 per cent of those over age 50 advocating an irrevocable commitment, compared with 25 per cent in their thirties. The youngest group was slightly more dedicated than the next oldest bracket, 28 per cent holding the most conservative view. The essentially religious basis for lifelong commitment was borne out by the large margin separating those with firm religious beliefs (45 per cent) from those not firm (19 per cent) in selecting this view. Those who never attended college, low-income earners, blacks, blue collar workers, homemakers, and the retired/unemployed, most tended to believe marriage was always for life. The liberal opinion that marriage should be ended at the discretion of either party was most prevalent among those without firm religious beliefs, high-income earners, professionals and white collar workers, the remarried, spouses under 30, and our small sample of Hispanic-Americans. In no subgroup, however, did the number advocating virtual divorce on demand run as high as one-third.

Nearly a third of our respondents admitted to having considered divorcing their present spouses, with no appreciable difference between the husbands and wives. Seven per cent had taken such serious steps as separating, consulting a lawyer, or having definite plans to divorce. One spouse in eight had thought about it but not discussed it, and a similar percentage had discussed it but not taken further steps. Three percent of our respondents under age 30 said they definitely planned to divorce. The younger the spouses were, the more likely they were to have considered divorce. Parents of children were only 3 percentage points below the childless spouses in frequency of having considered divorce.

A dignified matron was once asked if she had ever considered divorcing her husband. Indignantly, she replied, "Never! Murder on many occasions, but divorce—never!" We asked all our respondents to consider divorce, not only the experiences of those who had been through it, but also the positive and negative factors in current marriages that might ultimately determine the marriage's stability.

If you have been divorced, why did that marriage fail? If not, what dangers and strengths do you see in your marriage's stability?

It is a rare couple that on careful scrutiny cannot find some flaw in their marriage among its many facets. Those who felt their union would undoubtedly endure would generally cite a strong initial commitment, understanding, and self-criticism rather than blame of the partner.

WIFE: "Strengths—my husband's support always and his objectivity in times of arguments or misunderstandings."

"Dangers—my husband finally becoming fed up with some of my reactions and childish behavior during arguments."

HUSBAND: "The fact that we both consider the marriage contract to constitute an extremely strong commitment is a strength. Our child is also a strength."

A homemaker and mother of 1 child, she's between 31 and 40. While she says her husband thinks she's a good lover, he thinks she needs improvements in other ways. Says her marriage is a loving one. He's in the same age range, and has a postgraduate degree. He says he feels tied down and trapped, and his worst crisis is his general disillusionment with everything.

Among the couples where at least one spouse admitted to having considered divorce, some gave evidence of general compatibility, but most indicated that the marriage's weaknesses were prevailing over the strengths:

WIFE: "The danger that we have right now is financial instability. Our strength is general understanding."

HUSBAND: "Dangers—possible moments of weakness on either side that escalate to real problems. Strength—true belief in each other's ideas and intentions."

This homemaker and mother of 3 has some college education. She says their worst crisis is their debt, and her husband's job leaves no room for advancement. He's a blue collar worker making between $15–$25,000 a year, and admits that the lack of money is his major problem. Also he feels overwhelmed by responsibility. She's between 18 and 30, and he's between 31 and 40.

WIFE: "Dangers—dissatisfaction with spouse's job. Strengths—lots of 'guts.'"

HUSBAND: "Dangers—possible boredom or taking for granted; developing expectedness and consequent resistance to change or new ideas; dependency; lack of substantial outside interests. Strengths—dependency; lack of surprise thru stability; children's future happiness is common goal along with present happiness of all."

She says her husband's job is (family income is between $25,000–$49,000 a year) their major problem. He's between 31 and 40, and has a postgraduate degree, and works in the professional field. Describes his wife as anxious and says while she appreciates him, she doesn't really love him.

WIFE: "The strength is the security and peace of mind. The danger for me is sometimes such stability is a bore and I feel I would like to have some fun."

HUSBAND: "The only danger I see in stability of my marriage is passiveness or complacency with respect to the relationship as well as boredom.

"Many times, due to the pressure of other things (invariably my business) her needs and our relationship are considered last. Every time we take or make the time to talk things out and spend time with each other our relationship becomes revitalized."

WIFE: "Use of alcohol which led to unemployment. Lower self-esteem for the whole family especially the youngest child."

HUSBAND: "Danger—children growing up and leaving. Strength—trials and tribulations associated with twenty-five-plus years of marriage have a binding effect."

Both are between 41 and 50. She's a mother of 3, feels that her husband wishes that they'd never gotten married. Says they argue mostly over money. They had a period of separation. He's a blue collar worker who makes less than $10,000 a year. Describes his marriage as being in constant turmoil, and says his worst crisis was over alcohol.

HUSBAND: "Dangers—I'm in love with someone else and want a divorce."

Money and the spouse's occupation were often cited as vulnerable points. Insufficient funds often results in loss of interest:

WIFE: "Financial and maturity."

HUSBAND: "Money would improve it."

Both are between 41 and 50. She's a homemaker and mother of 1, he works in the blue collar field, earning between $10–$15,000 a year. She says their major problem involves her husband's job which leaves no opportunity for advancement and feels overwhelmed by responsibility. He says his wife is dominating, and marriage has made him more nervous and irritable than ever. Says their worst crisis is their debts.

WIFE: "Strength—communication; Danger—job instability."

HUSBAND: "Money, immaturity."

She says they've assaulted each other during arguments, and he says they argue mostly over money. He makes between

$15–$25,000 a year. She feels his job doesn't pay enough. Both though consider their marriage as being fairly stable. He's between 41 and 50, and works in management. She's between 31 and 40, and is a homemaker.

WIFE: "Dangers—naval separation; different social circles; financial problems; Strengths—Closeness; enjoy each other's company; common goal."

HUSBAND: "Dangers—guilt from the past; loss of trust; financial; Strengths—dear friendship; love deepening with each crisis; great desire to build our family."

Some who focused on the failure of their past marriages indicated on the objective portion of the questionnaire that they were experiencing difficulty in their later marriage, such as the couple below:

WIFE: "My ex-husband walked out on me for another woman—probably because of the responsibility of a baby and I was not holding up my end."

HUSBAND: "Ex-wife ran around, picked at weak points in my personality, i.e., laughed at me when she made me angry, was 'cheap' looking and acting. She set me up for divorce."

This is her third marriage, and his second. She's the mother of 4 children, and says her present marriage alernates between periods of closeness and remoteness. Also she has the feeling that she's unloved and unappreciated, and says they rarely have sex. He's between 41 and 50, she's younger, between 31 and 40. He works in the technical field. While he describes his wife as passive, he feels tied down and trapped. Yet he feels his marriage is stable and loving.

The macho male, celebrated in men's fiction and castigated in women's non-fiction, is hard-headed, hard-fisted and hard to keep at home. The remarried women below found such first husbands hard to take—so they left the marriage:

WIFE: "My marriage failed because my spouse was self-centered, hard-headed, un-thoughtful (and a couple of other things—but I don't use that kind of language—in front of strangers, any-

way). I have a new man with whom I am faithful and loyal
and hope to marry eventually. Communication, understanding
and thoughtfulness are very important in a relationship."

WIFE: "Battered wife."

This wife is a college graduate between 31 and 40. This is her
second marriage and she has 2 children. Her major problem is
money—the family income is between $15–25,000 a year.

WIFE: "Immaturity. Present marriage based on agreement of personalities. We like each other and can be quite compatible
though have terrific disagreement based on personal interests.
Husband's obsessive sports interests and lack of interest in
other fields endangers stability of marriage."

This is her second marriage, and she feels that her present
husband takes her for granted, and feels tied down. Her worst
crisis is her husband's obsessive interest in sports, and she has
considered divorcing him. A homemaker between 41 and 50,
with 1 child.

WIFE: "Husband left home for another woman. We were not in
touch with each other's feelings."

To a husband, an extramarital affair may be the mere outcome
of a perfectly simple impulse of his manhood towards some third
party's womanhood, but the wives of such men may suffer severe
trauma to their own self-esteem and doubts about the stability of
the love relationship. Women whose husbands travel in the course
of business are especially prone to stress, particularly in our culture
where the traveling salesman is more renowned for seduction than
sales.

WIFE: "Dangers in marriage would be unfaithfulness. It causes
self-doubt about one's self and distrust in mate. Unfaithfulness
can be a result of a momentary weak moment, not necessarily
lack of love for one's mate, but is still dangerous to a marriage.
"Strengths in one's marriage I feel is in knowing that each
is always in reach of the other. Standing by each other in daily
trials and happiness."

She's a blue collar worker, between 31 and 40, with 3 children.

WIFE: "I have not been divorced, I have been married thirty years. The dangers were mainly difference of opinion in raising three children. The dangers were my husband traveled and was away for a week or two at a time.

"Strengths in our marriage is our ability to talk things out. Also in never to forget 'love' and show it as well as say it."

This college graduate who is between 41 and 50, says she has a loving marriage and a mature husband, and sex between them is very good. She works in the professional field.

WIFE: "His extramarital affairs, gambling, drinking, away from home on average of six days a week twenty-four hours a day— for me to care for two small children."

With regard to gambling, John Tanner made the curious observation that whereas the only person who consistently profits from a gambling table is the fellow who runs it, passion for gambling is rampant but a passion for keeping roulette tables is unknown. Husbands with a passion for gin may be addicted to rummy, martinis, or both, since Lady Luck and John Barleycorn keep pretty steady company in the late hours.

WIFE: "My marriage is not a success because of my husband's drinking and gambling. I am a Christian person and this problem is very bad. I came from a very good father and mother, too, and all I remember from my childhood is love and happiness because my father was a religious person and my mother."

This wife describes her husband as irresponsible, and says they no longer have sex. She's 51 or over, and is a homemaker. She has thought about divorce, but her biggest obstacle would be their only child. They argue mostly about her husband's personal habits.

WIFE: "Too much alcohol and inconsiderate. No help with children's disciplining."

Embroiled spouses have been known to keep a marriage together for the sake of the children; it's probably a rare marriage that breaks up because of them, but conflicts over child-rearing certainly take their toll:

WIFE: "Dangers—too much pressure from work to be done (from jobs, housekeeping and child-rearing); Stability—similar ethical, moral and social committments. Share similar goals and ideals in life.

"Looking forward to sharing experiences together when children are gone—helps marriage through difficult times with young children."

She has a postgraduate degree, and is the mother of 2 children. Though she says her marriage is a loving one, and sex is good, she admits that raising children leads to many quarrels, and dealing with temperament is her major problem. She's between 18 and 30.

WIFE: "My husband is dependable, reliable and only danger to our marriage is that he is a perfectionist and expects myself and children to be the same."

She's a homemaker, 41 to 50, with a high school education. She finds their sex life satisfactory. Their major problems involve jobs and disagreements about the children. She thinks it's a generally loving marriage.

WIFE. "We can't agree about relatives; we can't agree whether he should stay at his present job. We never agree about how to discipline the kids."

Wives who felt they communicated well with their husbands indicated that they suffered little risk of ever having to communicate through a lawyer.

WIFE: "Our marriage has always been open. I never feel that I can't discuss my every thought. We have always worked out all disagreements. At the beginning my husband was reluctant to take responsibility, but after a few years of tolerance, patience and arguments he has improved greatly. Most essential to our marriage has been a sense of humor."

She says her husband is a mature man, and her marriage is on a loving footing. If she ever considered divorce (which she hasn't) money would be her biggest obstacle. She's between 18 and 30, with some college education.

WIFE: "The strength of our marriage stability is the mutual consideration we have for each other and also having the attitude of thinking of all of us as one. We also provide time for myself and spouse to be alone as a couple and not just always parents.

"The dangers would be differences in personality and what we each feel is important to obtain materially. I love to spend money and he is very practical."

This homemaker says that her major problem is lack of money, and she feels she is impetuous. Money problems would be her biggest obstacle if she ever considered divorce. Between 31 and 40, with 4 children.

WIFE: "There was a time when our marriage seemed to be going wrong. I think we just stopped communicating with each other. Since my husband never truly showed his emotions I thought he didn't care and I couldn't express my needs. I in turn became very depressed—not just because of our marriage—and went into therapy. It helped because it made me understand myself and understand what I was doing wrong."

WIFE: "Not being able to communicate. We hardly ever carry on a conversation."

Husbands agreed that difficulties in communication and reaching agreement were a danger, but love and care reduced much of the static.

HUSBAND: "Danger—Non-communication.

"Questionable health—(Heart patient).

"Strength—Have a responsible, caring wife whose calm offsets my higher emotional temperament."

This husband says he feels tied down and trapped. He's 51 or over, retired or unemployed, and has a postgraduate degree. He says his wife appreciates him as a husband, but not as a lover. Both have considered divorce, but money problems would be his biggest obstacle.

HUSBAND: "The dangers are my wife's big mouth, and her sometimes unreasonableness. Love and affection for one another, our sincere interest in one another's being."

Si jeunesse savait, si vieillesse pouvait, lament the French: "If youth only had the knowledge, if age had the power!" Unfortunately, the most difficult years of marriage in terms of economic hardship and other uncertainties tend to be the early ones when spouses are still lacking in maturity. How quickly maturity can be attained will often determine the fate of the marriage:

HUSBAND: "Infatuation—bloom of young love, etc.—has been gradually replaced with a deep sense of commitment and love tested and tempered by the pain and joys—ups and downs—of everyday living. During the first few years of our marriage we went through more problems as a team than most couples see in a lifetime—we faced them at a time when we could grow and be strengthened by the experiences."

He says they argue mostly over money, but he's never considered divorce. The father of 4 children, he works in management and is between 31 and 40.

HUSBAND: "Previous wife was immature. Not satisfied to put up with the hardships and inconveniences of military life during World War II."

While 43 per cent of our respondents who were not firm in religious beliefs had considered divorce, only 24 per cent of the devout had done so. Only half as many of the devout had undergone a period of separation, consulted a lawyer, or made definite plans to divorce.

HUSBAND: "I see no dangers in our marriage. Our strengths stem from our mutual love for and dedication to God made individually before we met and renewed during our engagement and at our wedding. Working together to imbue in our six children this same love of and dedication to God serves to increase the bond of love between us."

He sees no major problem in his marriage, and says his wife is a loving spouse. Describes himself as possessive and impetuous. Works in the technical field and is between 31 and 40.

HUSBAND: "The dangers are the poor respect for marriage and children upbringing. The dangers are the breakdown in our society of the family unit and low respect for life in general. The dangers are the poor esteem woman at home has in our society being a homemaker. The stability is in the growth of our children, our religious beliefs and our maturity in growing in love."

Husbands with previous divorces often blamed past failures on sexual difficulties of one sort or another:

HUSBAND: "My wife did not fulfill me sexually. Besides the fact that I was young, she was a virgin and older than myself and wasn't everything I expected."

HUSBAND: "Poor choice in first spouse. Money problems. Unfaithful spouse, very shallow relationship."

He's a professional, 18 to 30, with college education. He admits to having cheated with 2 or 3 women, briefly, although he feels that affairs inevitably lead to separation and divorce. He describes their sex life as very good. Although they have struck each other, he thinks their marriage is generally loving.

HUSBAND: "Married because of possible pregnancy—stayed for children—had no use for each other—finally decided staying together was harder on children than separating."

He has 3 children now, and has never cheated, or considered divorce. Says he's emotional and possessive, and his wife takes him for granted. Between 41 and 50, and works in the professional field.

HUSBAND: "My first wife denied me sex."

Thus, where divorced wives tend to complain of poor communication, inconsideration and irresponsibility on the part of their ex-husbands, men seem more driven to divorce by errors of commission and ommission in the sexual sphere, and the possibility or actuality of such threatens any a marriage still in existence.

HUSBAND: "Trust has broken stability. Wife has cheated on more than one occasion with different men. Separated, filed, forgave and came back, now seriously considering refiling."

He's between 18 and 30, and is a white collar worker and father of 2 children. He's cheated on his wife but only after their separation. Says their major problem is his wife's cheating, and though he has consulted a lawyer about a divorce, feels money problems are his biggest obstacle.

HUSBAND: "The only danger I have is that she may fall for someone else. Other than that we are very feeling for each other."

This blue collar worker says that while his wife thinks he's a good lover, she feels that he needs improvements in other ways. Says his marriage is always stable. He's between 41 and 50.

HUSBAND: "The first wife wasn't happy with sex either."

"Plus ça change, plus c'est la même chose," the French also say, when they are not lamenting about the problems of aging— "The more things change, the more they remain the same." Changing partners does not always insure a smoother dance, particularly when you have not mastered the basic steps.

No Exit

No room feels like a prison if the door is left open. We have seen responses from disgruntled spouses saying they wished their mates would have an extramarital affair so that they could get rid of them. When the door is always open, there is no need for people to bolt through for fear it will never open again.

But not all the obstacles to divorce are legal ones, and despite the one-third of our respondents who had considered divorce at some point, few people really have a favorable view of it. Only 17 per cent of those we surveyed said that the major effect of divorce on their life would be a positive one, either in terms of freedom for self-fulfillment or to find true love. Husbands were slightly more positive in their expectations for divorce, but still less than one in five saw it as advantageous. We might have expected people who longed for the freedom to fulfill themselves to come from the ranks of disillusioned older people or those burdened with children, but the reverse was true: this attitude was held by 20 per cent of the youngest spouses in contrast to 9 per cent of the oldest, and by 17 per cent of the childless versus 12 per cent of parents. Perhaps a mature and fruitful marriage imparts a sense of fulfillment in itself.

The average spouse does not think about divorce in terms of the exhilaration and light-heartedness we associate with liberty and freedom from responsibility. The answer selected by more than a third of our respondents was that divorce would leave them depressed. Close to a fifth said divorce would leave them alone in the world, and another third split their answers among such dismal alternatives as suffering lowered self-esteem, becoming alienated from their children, and being forced to lower their standard of living.

We have seen that while more than 30 per cent of our respondents have considered divorce, less than 2 per cent have definite plans to go through with it. Obviously, whatever factors were present to cause them to consider divorce have been strongly opposed by deterrent forces. Having learned something of what motivates people to think of divorce, what are the obstacles that hinder spouses from leaving problem marriages?

What obstacles would prevent or inhibit you from getting a divorce if your marriage was bad?

Starting with the smallest obstacles, the molehills among the mountains, we find that one in 20 of our respondents selected disapproval of others as the primary obstacle. Some people find in their in-laws more satisfactory parents than their original ones, and are reluctant to lose them. Some spouses feared the disapproval of their grown children. Still others felt that the divorced were stigmatized by society and would suffer socially and professionally.

WIFE: "Money and a deep love for his relatives. Marriage is a lifelong commitment never to be broken. Married for love."

HUSBAND: "Mostly parental disapproval on both my side and spouse's side. Also the feeling of hurting my spouse emotionally would inhibit me, furthermore, failing to succeed at marriage inhibits obtaining a divorce."

About one in nine feared the losses of the spouse's services. This includes not only cooking and housekeeping for men and auto maintenance and home repairs for women, but sometimes, as in the case of the husband below, financial support during higher education that will affect earning power for the rest of one's life:

WIFE: "Children, security, a deep hidden love we have but through lack of communication, it isn't expressed like it should be."

HUSBAND: "Being a student would force me to quit and seek employment. This would stop me because I would never get a good enough job."

Custody of the children was the main concern of one in eight. They were also concerned about psychological trauma to the children as a result of the period preceding divorce and the divorce itself:

WIFE: "The psychological effects on the children would be the major issue. The economy is so inflated that both spouses are required to work to make ends meet. It's best to resolve your current problems because the pasture isn't any greener on the other side."

HUSBAND: "Consideration for the children's welfare."

Moral or religious considerations would deter 21 per cent from thinking seriously about divorce. The wife who answered below is in her second marriage; she may have found religion late, or might have found the one divine ground for divorce in her first attempt:

WIFE: "I do not believe that the marriage vows should be taken lightly. Also the Bible teaches us that there is only one ground or reason for divorce.

"My marriage vows are very sacred to me and I would do everything I could with the Lord's help to keep my marriage and to make it a good one."

HUSBAND: "Losing my possessions, such as house, vacation property and cottage—my position in society and my job."

Money problems reached second place among the obstacles to divorce, with selection by 22 per cent. These include loss of support by non-employed wives, splitting of income between two households, division of property, enforced sale of property possibly at a loss, and the necessity of finding extra jobs. Some people tend to treat their children as objects of property, and the couple below has managed to integrate them smoothly with their other acquired possessions:

WIFE: "Children, grandchildren; we have collected coins, antiques, stamps, etc., throughout our twenty-five years, have several apartment houses, have a beautiful home of our own."

While she has consulted a lawyer about a divorce, her biggest obstacle to getting one is loneliness. However she has had an affair to "feel like a woman again," and is disillusioned about romance and love.

The peak in this range of obstacles, however, was the fear of loneliness, with a response of 30 per cent. People without children were particularly vulnerable to the fear, one-third of them choosing this answer. The youngest group was least concerned about loneliness (though it did barely edge out money problems as their main obstacle); there was no appreciable difference, however, among the age brackets over 30.

WIFE: "I suppose financial problems would be the main concern; along with the fear of being alone, but if the marriage was truly bad there would be no obstacle too great."

HUSBAND: "If my marriage was bad the thing that would inhibit me from getting a divorce would be our children, but I would have to discuss the situation fully with my spouse because sometimes prolonging a bad marriage could have as many ill effects on the children as the divorce itself."

Women have more difficulty adjusting to divorce in many ways. Those who are unemployed or without established careers have a heavier emotional investment in marriage than their hus-

bands, whose jobs occupy much of their time and continue un-
changed by the marital disruption. Women whose husbands initiated the divorce action and who have had little time to adjust to
the idea will have more depression than those who have either
sought the divorce or lived through a long preliminary period of
weighing the split. Women may harbor the conviction that divorce
is morally wrong, or be in the company of relatives or peers who
are critical.

Divorced men seem to be regarded as returnees to bachelor-
hood, whereas the divorcee holds an unenviable status, receiving
neither the solace reserved for widows nor the deference received
by the unmarried. While people today tend to give lip-service to
the no-fault concept of divorce, the divorcee is, in actuality, regarded with approximately the esteem accorded a colonial adul-
tress, ostracized by married women and boldly propositioned by
single and married males. Often struggling with the unshared
burdens of child-care, sometimes compounded by a new breadwinner status, she is hardly in the mood for evening socialization.
At a point where her depression over her broken marriage has
reduced her libido to a prepubertal low, males are assuming she
is walking around in a sustained state of stage-two sexual arousal
from her male-deprivation and is panting for any willing male to
trigger her long-awaited orgasm.

Few, if any, appreciate the mental status of the divorcee, whose
grief is often greater than a widow's, and this lack of understanding
estranges her from whatever friends, relatives, or dates enter her
altered sphere. No wonder, then, that 34 per cent of women, in
contrast to 26 per cent of men, selected fear of loneliness as the
biggest deterrent to divorce.

WIFE: "Knowing my husband is a good man and loves me and
getting back into the singles scene and never finding what I
want.

"I feel my husband is what I want and I just have to work
out minor things. Sometimes feel trapped, like I want to date
others but I know the others would turn out to be nothing—
just a fling."

She's a college student. While she has no children, she feels
tied down and trapped, but believes her marriage is a stable
one. Says she and her husband have considered divorce.

WIFE: "I have no idea what it would be like to have a bad marriage. After twenty-five years I'd be afraid of the loneliness. My only concern is being widowed by death."

A white collar worker with some college education, 41 to 50. She has cheated with 1 person briefly. She describes their sex life as very good, says they have no major problems, never argue, and have an always stable marriage.

WIFE: "Financial responsibilities—being able to support children and myself adequately. Lack of confidence in ability to locate a job that not only provided financial stability but would give me a sense of satisfaction and accomplishment.

"Loneliness—and losing friends because you are no longer half of a pair or they think you could become a threat to their marriage."

Since women are often totally dependent on their husbands economically, it was understandable that one-quarter of wives would be most concerned about money problems, as opposed to one-fifth of husbands. Spouses with children prevailed over those without in money concerns by approximately the same margin.

WIFE: "Lack of money to continue a reasonable lifestyle for the children. Husband could not afford alimony and I could not earn a living at his present salary for at least a few years."

This mother of 2 says her husband takes her for granted. Describes herself as emotional, and has considered divorce. She's between 18 and 30.

WIFE: "Money would be a big problem. There is no way I could do more than barely exist with my age and lack of training. I have college but it was an A & S and won't get me a job of worth."

Because they were so strongly concerned with possible loneliness and financial problems, women were slightly lower than men in their selection of moral or religious considerations as the main obstacle to divorce. Some indicated in their handwritten responses to our essay question that ethical considerations extended to the welfare of the children. Divorce has the potential to inflict emotional conflict on the children at various stages over a period of years during the separation proceedings. First, there is the anxiety aroused in the preliminary stage when the children initially learn of the divorce plans and are witness to quarrels and hostile behavior between the parents. There is the actual separation with loss of the steady presence of one of the parents. Children are often used in the adversary system, being asked to side with either parent, even to the point of testifying in court. Even if they manage to avoid an active role in the parental battles, exposure to one bitter parent and separation from the other generally leads to estrangement from the less frequently seen parent, usually the father. Finally, children often have feelings of embarrassment and inferiority in explaining or presenting a one-parent family to their peers and may even resort to ill-constructed falsehoods in an attempt to hide the divorce from friends.

But an unhappy household makes a bad nursery, and children who have been living in a house where there has been active quarreling and frequent talk of divorce over a long period are far less traumatized than children exposed to a sudden divorce in a home where parental discord had been previously hidden. Even in situations where trauma has been minimal, however, there are the inevitable problems of custody agreements, visiting rights, and adequate child support, and the economic agreements will probably continue to require the services of lawyers and judges long after divorce itself becomes the incontestable right of any married person so desiring it.

WIFE: "Biblical reasons—divorce is wrong, moral reasons—anyone can run from a problem, but it takes character to work it out. Others suffer from it. Close relationships with both sides of family would make it too painful. Also children are always hurt. Faith that God is able to help me work out all problems and is powerful enough to help even in extreme difficulty."

WIFE: "I thought my marriage was pretty bad. Basically I learned through psychotherapy that the bad feelings were what would prevent me from a divorce. Bad feelings like guilt—going against my religious teachings and causing my husband, children, family pain; loss of self-esteem; doubts, perhaps could have made it work, etc. Feeling selfish. Also, God helps those who help themselves and He does have a plan for me, no matter how I may choose to live. I could write a lot more, but then it would be a book."

This homemaker and mother of 2 has considered divorce. While at this time she feels her marriage is fairly loving, she says she is overwhelmed by responsibility. Describes her sex life as "variable." While her strength now is increased maturity, her major problem is lack of communication. She's between 18 and 30.

WIFE: "My vow that I made at our wedding to God 'Until death do us part.'"

She's 51 or over, a homemaker with a high school education. She feels their marriage is generally loving.

WIFE: "I have cancer and a limited life expectancy, my husband is unable to accept this and hides from reality so I must be the strong one to help him survive.
"God sustains me in times of trouble. He will not suffer my foot to be moved."

We each formulate our own system of ethics, which must include attitudes towards divorce and marriage even if merely the rejection of either or both. Some value systems are based on the Bible, some on writings of psychologists, and some on the foundations of the *Playboy* philosophy. The lady below appears to have found her morality in the pages of *Car and Driver* magazine:

WIFE: "All things in a marriage must work if it is to succeed just like a car—if every working part is tuned in good running order, if all parties work together, it will last. Each person has their own idea of which part, if broken, will substantiate a new car or a trade-in. But most of us feel that if one of these things happen we can just trade-in until we get one that lasts on its own. Personally, I wouldn't want a divorce unless there was a crash where the whole thing was totaled and then only if both parties were so injured that they were completely without salvage."

The obstacle that was by the widest margin a greater concern for husbands than for wives was the custody of children. While men seem to be more readily accepted back into society's single groups on their premarital footing, their worst pangs are felt on coming home to an empty apartment when they are used to the company of their children and the comforts of a domestic style of living. Women may feel they are living in a ruins, but men are dwelling in a void. Even 2 per cent of spouses who had no children cited custody concerns as the biggest obstacle to divorce, apparently anticipating the children they wanted to have. Custody problems affected the 31 to 40 age bracket most, that group most likely to have young children in the home.

HUSBAND: "I wouldn't want to have to decide on custody of my son and chance of seeing him once a week and chance of losing everything I have."

He's a blue collar worker, 18 to 30, a high school graduate. Their sex life is good, he feels. Money is their biggest problem. The marriage is generally stable.

HUSBAND: "Children, splitting everything we own, parent's reaction."

While this husband feels a divorce would give him the freedom to fulfill himself, he has never considered it. His strength in the marriage is his increased maturity. Between 41 and 50, and a professional.

HUSBAND: "The children are paramount in my trying to make the marriage work. As I was not raised by my parents, it is a strong desire in myself to see to it that my children do have theirs."

He's a college graduate, between 18 and 30. Works in the professional field. Says his wife is dominant, and their marriage alternates between very close and very remote periods. Lack of communication between them is their major problem according to him. However he believes his children have added a new and positive dimension to their relationship.

HUSBAND: "If my marriage wasn't working out I would confront my wife and talk it over, the only reason we might stay together would be if we had children, but I would try and find an answer first."

In the question concerning what would be the effect of divorce on their lives, 11 per cent of men, compared with only 2 per cent of women, felt that they would be alienated from their children. Women, despite the probability of retaining custody of the children, outpointed men by a narrow margin in the belief that divorce would leave them "alone in the world." Men were not as concerned with loneliness, but fear of it was nevertheless for them as well as their wives the biggest obstacle to divorce.

HUSBAND: "Probably loneliness, and fear of financial insecurity. Having been divorced once previously, I have a better understanding of what it means to lose everything I had spent years to achieve, as well as what it means to be truly alone."

This is his second marriage, and says this present one has better communication and better sexual compatibility. Fear of loneliness if he ever considered divorce (which he hasn't) would be his biggest obstacle. He works in the technical field.

Since husbands generally have control over family income, money problems as an obstacle ranked third for men, whereas they had been the second biggest concern for women. About one husband in eleven felt the major effect of divorce on his life would be a financial one. While the popular maxim that two can live as cheaply as one was always in doubt, no one ever contended that two households could be run as cheaply as one.

HUSBAND: "Wife's income and other financial assets."

He's into mate-swapping, and group sex, and has consulted a lawyer about divorce. Says money problems is his biggest obstacle to getting one. Earns between $25–$49,000 a year, and is a professional with a postgraduate degree, between 31 and 40.

HUSBAND: "I wouldn't have enough money left to support myself."

Husbands are more sensitive to the disapproval of others, despite our tendency to think of men as less conventional and more independent than women. There were more husbands than wives in our survey who said that such disapproval would be the main obstacle to divorce. The divorced man has usually been living in an ark-like circle of friends to which people are admitted in pairs. He is the member of the separating pair most likely to put geographical distance between self and former nest, and, given a choice between the two spouses, friends are likely to omit the male. Women's friendships are generally based on nearness of neighbors, men's on business contacts; marriage involves mutuality of friends, but generally women have had more time for daytime socializing, even if it is a 5-minute chat on the telephone or supermarket line. The children, who usually remain with the wife, provide some continuity of social relationships for their mother through school activities and neighborhood families. Married friends may even offer matchmaking services to the divorced wife, whereas men are presumed to be able to do their own hunting and may even be discouraged from continuing long-standing friendships with married women, much as one accepts a housecat around a canary but would be petrified if a hungry alley-cat entered the home.

Fifty years ago, only one divorced person in three ever remarried. At that time, society regarded them as a basically immoral or neurotic lot, and, indeed, such an attitude probably kept many conservative people in unhappy marriages because they could not adapt to the expected role, leaving the field clear for those who actually were on the wilder side of behavioral standards and emotional stability. Yet, in these days when the liberal "swinger" is glamorized by our media and even emulated by committed spouses, majority rule by the married still makes outsiders of the divorced and social pressure continues to shut many a door against them.

HUSBAND: "Social pressure to stay together would probably play a big part."

A professional with a postgraduate education, between 31 and 40. He feels that the biggest obstacle to divorce would be custody of the kids, and a divorce would leave him depressed, he says. He feels their sex life is very good, and says their marriage has no major problems.

While the women who held firm religious beliefs (67 per cent) outnumbered such men (57 per cent) in our survey, husbands outnumbered wives in claiming moral or religious considerations to be the greatest obstacle to divorce.

HUSBAND: "I have been divorced. My religious teachings caused pangs of guilt for awhile. There were no children so I do not really know if there would have been any obstacle in that area."

He's retired, 51 or over, with a high school education. This is his second marriage. He says fear of loneliness would be the biggest obstacle to divorce, but that a divorce would enable him to find true love. He has cheated with 2 or 3 women, at least one for over a year. However, he still feels loved and appreciated fully by his wife.

HUSBAND: "First, personal standards and ideas. I do not believe in divorce. I married for it to be a forever contract. Life is full of trials and part of marriage is working to make it work, I feel it's a one-hundred per cent–one-hundred per cent arrangement.

"Second, my religious background doesn't look favorably on divorce."

We should respect the rights of any individual to believe that marriage is an irrevocable lifetime contract and to refuse to consider divorce as a personal alternative, whether these views are based on religious dogma or an individual value system; however, we cannot compel such a person's spouse to adopt a similar code when the marriage is deemed highly unsatisfactory. Whether the shackles are imposed in the name of religious or civil law, there is no worse form of slavery than restriction of the pursuit of a happiness based on our own goals and convictions, provided the rights of others are safeguarded. Our present divorce system is a half-hearted hodgepodge that works only because it cumbersomely evades its ancient underlying premise that divorce is a punishment for a grievously errant spouse whose guilt must be proven by a virtuous mate. Let both parties be found innocent or equally guilty and they are sent back to their unhappy home to plot their next assault on the system. Divorce not only requires the airing of dirty linen, it often necessitates the soiling of clean linen. Our vacillating, ambivalent attempts at divorce reform, undoubtedly abetted by a legal profession that prospers by contesting and reinterpreting

the ambiguous, undecipherable laws it composes, have only succeeded in granting freer admission to the costly and agonizing
feuds whose vilifications, mental reservations, and collusions be-
smirch our cluttered court calendars.

Since we must admit that anyone with sufficient funds can
obtain a divorce today, the only realistic solution is groundless
divorce on the request of either partner. Court intervention should
be limited to the more important tasks such as fixing alimony,
child support, and custody arrangements where the couple cannot
reach satisfactory agreement themselves.

Women are probably victimized by faultless divorce more often
than men, although a court decision to divide property in lieu of
alimony may force a husband to sell a house or a business at a
loss. Women have been able to use the threat of opposing divorce
to wrangle higher alimony payments or property settlements out
of husbands, and no-fault divorce robs them of this weapon. We
cannot effect reform of the divorce system unless we also correct
the more difficult problem of the economic oppression of women.
Until we accord the labor of motherhood and homemaking the
dignity it deserves, their dependency reduces the domestic aspects
of marriage to servitude and the sexual relations to prostitution.
Society already shoulders the burden of the deserted mother
through the degrading welfare system; it only remains to reform
our attitude and put the labor of the housewife on the same level
as that of any other tradesman who becomes unemployed. This
would not absolve husbands of their responsibility for child support, including the cost of the labor of child-rearing, and desertion
should be dealt with as harshly as under our present system. Under
no circumstances, however, should women be compelled to remain
in a faithless marriage under economic compulsion or degraded
as social parasites should they leave such a union.

Finally, let us not encumber the areas we have constructively
denuded of archaic punitive structures by implementing a maze
of court-affiliated compulsory conciliation and counseling centers
to question the decision already reached by two presumably competent adults. We have provision for community mental health
centers, quantitatively insufficient and qualitatively underfunded
as they may be, to provide free or low-cost counseling for those
who desire it and it would be far more advantageous to augment
existing facilities offering a broad range of treatment rather than
to construct a bureaucratic network of psychological experts to

prey on the same unwilling clients exploited for decades by legal experts. The establishment of offices and centers for divorce counseling makes about as much sense as constructing medical facilities to specialize in equally restricted areas, such as throat infections or hernia repairs.

Obviously, every change we make in our existing system of divorce must either be accompanied by corresponding changes in other areas of society or, over a long period of time, must induce these changes through sheer necessity. We often plan our social system not according to the needs and realities of human nature, but according to the way we think human nature should be; ultimately, human nature prevails and the result of this triumph over hollow laws leads to the hypocrisy and inequity that passes for jurisprudence.

We can no longer continue to blame God for marriage and expect Him to be responsible for lifetime maintenance of unions He is reputed to have established. As Bishop Bridgenorth warns us, unless the laws of marriage are first made human, it can never become divine.

10

Given a Rematch:

Remarriages

> A thousand indissoluble marriages mean a thousand marriages
> and no more. A thousand divorces may mean two thousand
> marriages; for the couples may marry again. Divorce only re-
> assorts the couples: a very desirable thing when they are ill-
> assorted.
>
> —*George Bernard Shaw*, GETTING MARRIED, Preface

Things are not going well between Martha and Sam, and Martha
is the designated problem. She makes it clear that the fault is hers
and that she is, indeed, the one who should be in the psychiatrist's
office, with Sam's role limited to paying the bills. Her problem
is her temper, which leads her to make "unreasonable demands"
on Sam, sometimes emphasized by slapping him or throwing
drinks in his face. This is the second marriage for both. Martha
is only 23, but she was originally married at 19 after a two-year
courtship; the union lasted less than a year. Of her former husband,
Martha says that he was introverted and uncommunicative, though
since their divorce, he seems much more open. They speak on

the telephone once a week, but though Martha doesn't feel she worked very hard at that marriage, she is content to bury it in the past.

Sam's first marriage is another matter. Sam is ten years older than Martha and was involved in his first marriage for considerably more years than Martha was in hers. Almost all of their quarrels relate either to Sam's first wife or his 6-year-old son by that marriage. Not that Martha has any real cause to be jealous of Sam; she is with him constantly, because they work together. Sam is an executive in a company manufacturing ladies' garments and Martha works along with him. They had met when both were employed in another company; Sam moved on, and when he learned that Martha had once had an affair with a co-worker he disliked, Sam prevailed on her to leave and move to his new company.

Sam took his bride-to-be under his tutorial wing and she has progressed rapidly in skills and salary despite her lack of much formal education. She now makes $12,000 a year and coupled with Sam's $30,000 salary, they are able to live comfortably; however, Martha deeply resents the $600 he gives his ex-wife each month for child support, along with extra money for such luxuries as summer camp and music lessons for his son. If his telephone chats with his ex-wife exceed ten minutes, Martha's rage begins to build and by the time he is off the phone, Sam is bound to get soaked by Martha's dry martini. Sam, on the other hand, does not generally need such cooling-off procedures, since he is a placid sort who tends to accept circumstances stoically, especially anything his lawyer advises him to accept when the ex-wife makes additional financial demands.

Sam not only gives in to his ex-wife and his lawyer; when it comes to his 6-year-old son, Mike, Sam makes Santa Claus look like Scrooge. Mike comes to stay every other weekend, and when he does, he expects the next 48 hours' activity to revolve around his preferences. If Martha and Sam want to go to a party, Mike will usually veto staying with a relative for a few hours, and that kills the evening. Mike also disparages trips to museums, zoos, and movies, preferring to "hang out" in their apartment all day. He bodily intervenes in any displays of affection between father and stepmother. All of this infuriates Martha, but only drives Sam to greater efforts to placate his son. When Mike's unsecured bicycle was stolen from the street, Sam promptly bought him a new one. Sam recently promised Mike that if he should come to visit and the apartment did not happen to be stocked with any particular "treat" Mike wanted, such as cupcakes, popcorn, candy bars, sugared cereals, or soda, Sam would buy him a toy as a penalty for being a poor provider.

Given Martha's background, it is understandable how the sight of such parental indulgence makes her both envious and incredulous. She was one of seven children and neither parent had the time nor the inclination to show much affection. Martha's mother died when Martha was barely an adolescent; she had started taking oral contraceptives after her seventh child and quickly died of a blood clot. Martha's father did not remarry until her late teens. Though a half-brother was born of this new marriage, the stepmother moved out to a separate apartment; not that the marriage was over, the stepmother just could not stand the tensions in the main household. It was not surprising then that Martha had sought escape and love through an early marriage. And when that marriage failed, she tried again.

The problem with the second marriage is that Martha keeps imagining how good it could have been if Sam had not been married previously. She counts the extra money they could have if Sam wasn't paying child support. Sam traveled extensively with his first wife, and now wants to be settled, while Martha dreams of the exotic lands she has never seen. She resents little Mike's bimonthly intrusions on their weekends and his dictatorial control of their house. Sam even told her before marriage that he did not intend to have any more children. At 23, Martha certainly doesn't want children yet, but feels she might change her mind someday. Somehow it was not a big consideration then for a girl who had never had expensive new clothes before and had been introduced to the exclusive Fifth Avenue shops by Sam; children in her early life had meant nothing except competition for inadequate supplies of affection and money.

Now, ironically, with a prosperous and loving husband of her own, Martha is still in competition for love and money with an ex-wife and a 6-year-old. And she broods over the life that might have been, had this been the first marriage for Sam, until her rage boils over in a geyser of gin and vermouth.

Like Jacob Marley's ghost, people entering a remarriage drag along the chains forged in an earlier life, and some, like the chains awaiting Scrooge, are very heavy indeed. There are the debts of child support, alimony, legal fees, and past expenditures. There are often children, not an unmixed bane, but often competitive and resentful of the new spouse and still bruised from the trauma of recent divorce. Finally, the newlyweds are themselves still smarting from the wounds of the embattled marriage that was dissolved and cannot always unburden themselves of old grievances and suspicions, which they proceed to attach to the new partner.

One never starts a remarriage with a truly clean slate. We may clear areas for the new relationship, but the corners of our lives remain cluttered with unerasable marks of past experience, the children we continue to care for and the ex-spouses tied to us through the children. And there are the smudges of past difficulties, the still visible traces of past conflicts on which we superimpose new essays and confuse the marks of the past with the bold new strokes of the present.

Yet, nature abhors a vacuum, and so does the human heart. Bishop Bridgenorth says, "I would not dare go about with an empty heart: why, the first girl I met would fly into it by mere atmospheric pressure." Having wiped the slate as clean as possible, people soon tire of looking at a blank space and begin writing a new chapter to their lives.

Changing Partners

"Two lines! . . . each with a lobster as a partner . . . advance twice, set to partners . . . change lobsters, and retire in same order, then . . . you throw the lobsters . . . as far out to sea as you can . . . swim after them . . . turn a somersault in the sea . . . change lobsters again! . . . Back to land again, and—that's all the first figure. . . ."

Like all great works of fantasy, Lewis Carroll's *Alice in Wonderland* lends itself readily to any type of symbolic interpretation, and Alice has been interpreted by critics as everything from a psychoanalytic autobiography to a satire of the religious controversies of Victorian England. We are sure that Carroll, an old bachelor, did not have marriage in mind when the Gryphon and the Mock Turtle described the lobster quadrille, with the incessant pursuit, discarding, and changing of partners and the dancers frequently all at sea, but the bizarre dance does bear certain resemblances to the serial polygamy that characterizes America's contemporary matrimonial patterns.

Four out of five divorced people remarry today, in contrast to one out of three in the 1920's; and for divorced people in their twenties, the remarriage rate is even higher.

In one out of every four marriages, one of the newlyweds has been married previously, and more than half of these returnees are younger than 35. About 60 per cent of divorces occur in families with children and women with children are as likely to remarry as those without; in fact, possibly due to an atavistic or practical need for supporting a large brood, women with several children remarry more quickly than those with one or two. A history of divorce is no barrier to remarriage, for at every age level, the probability of marriage is higher for divorced people than the single. Some divorces are motivated by falling in love with an extramarital partner, which partially accounts for the fact that one-quarter of divorced people remarry within five months and half within a year.

In our own survey, one-fifth of our respondents had been married previously. Seventeen per cent were in their second marriages; nearly 2 per cent in a third union; and one in every hundred had been married four or more times, women having been so maximally married more than twice as often as men. The trend towards remarriage is increasing, for 34 per cent of spouses in their thirties were already reinvolved, but only 28 per cent of those in their forties were beyond their first marriage. In the group over age 50, the rate was back to 34 per cent, but widowhood rather than divorce probably accounted for a good portion of remarriages. Although our respondents who were firm in religious beliefs had indicated negative attitudes towards divorce, 18 per cent were nevertheless married more than once, with the non-devout leading by a scant margin at 22 per cent; those without firm religious beliefs were, however, four times more likely to be involved in a third or later marriage.

Those in our sample who had remarried tended to be older. 85 per cent were over 30 years old, compared to 72 per cent of those first married, and 37 per cent were over 50, versus only 28 per cent of the one-timers. Fifteen per cent of the remarried had been younger than 18 at the time of their first marriage, whereas this was true of only 9 per cent still in their first marriages. Having been burned once, the remarried were more likely to test the heat before jumping in again—41 per cent had lived with their present spouse prior to marriage, half for at least six months; only 19 per cent of those not previously married had a period of trial cohabitation, proportionately more for less than three months.

When we asked the remarried in our survey why they believed their current marriage would be successful, the answer most often given (29 per cent) was increased maturity, with better communication running a very close second.

Not surprisingly, three out of five had picked spouses quite different from their previous mates, but one-sixth had chosen new spouses very similar in most ways. An additional 8 per cent had picked spouses similar in appearance to their former mates but different in personality, while 4 per cent had opted for a new set of looks, but similar temperament.

You don't have to actually remarry to think about what improvements you would seek in a new spouse. We asked all our respondents, remarried or not, to consider what changes, if any, they would make in designing a replacement model for their present mates.

If you remarried—or were to remarry—what did or would you look for in your new spouse, and how would this compare to your former spouse?

They tell the story of a new bride married to a widower who constantly talked about his previous wife. His reminiscing was posing a serious threat to the marriage, until the wife hit on a simple solution: whenever he started talking about his last wife, she began talking about her next husband.

Couples who were dissatisfied with their present marriages may not have developed new relationships yet, but they certainly had the blueprints:

WIFE: "Someone who would try more to work out problems, not run away from them. Someone who would listen. Someone more open-minded. Spouse doesn't do this."

HUSBAND: "I'd look for an intelligent, bright person who is attractive, neat and can be creative in sex.

"A one hundred per cent improvement would be shown from my former spouse, in that there would be more variations in our relationship, intellectually or sexually."

She says her husband is inconsiderate, he wishes that they'd never have gotten married, and admits they've physically assaulted one another during arguments. The husband describes himself as "anxious," and says his wife is possessive. He works in management; she's a blue collar worker. They have no children.

WIFE: "Someone who would have a little more tenderness, love and caring about me especially under job pressures, home and church. Someone who would listen instead of lecture. Someone who would be aware of feelings and get involved in rap sessions with family, sharing in feelings of others to help each other to feel better about themselves. This 'I know it' attitude turns me off. Solutions are not black and white; they are steps in helping someone."

HUSBAND: "No.

"I would look for one who would listen instead of argue at a drop of a pin."

This college graduate who is between 41 and 50, says her husband has struck her, he's dominating, takes her for granted, and she is overwhelmed by all the responsibility. He in turn says his wife is the dominant one, and takes him for granted. They argue continually about his attention to members of the opposite sex. Works in management, in the same age range as wife.

WIFE: "Someone faithful forever."

HUSBAND: "Loyalty and fidelity, intelligence and pleasantness."

She's been involved in group sex and mate-swapping. Says her marriage is in constant turmoil. Cheated with 2 or 3 other men. A college educated professional with no children, she's between 18 and 30. He's a white collar worker between 31 and 40. While he cheated, he says it was with his wife's consent and knowledge. He describes himself as passive and emotional, and says his wife dominates him.

Some wives wished they had a man who understood their ideas and goals better, but as far as their husbands were concerned, their only wish was for a wife who would be more agreeable:

WIFE: "A person who would share his dreams and thoughts with me and let me share mine with him, without making me feel as though it was not necessary to talk about such things.

HUSBAND: "To get along with people easier."

WIFE: "I need someone who respects my wishes. Job-wise and freedom."

Even happily married couples can come up with a few desirable modifications, in most cases. If nobody ever wanted to change things occasionally, everyone would be driving Volkswagens.

WIFE: "Many things would be similar since I happen to be married to a wonderful sweet, understanding guy. The only thing I wish he would like to buy clothes and dress differently. I also would prefer more of a hustler in business.
   "The longer I am married, the more I appreciate what I've got!"

HUSBAND: "I would want someone exactly like my present wife, only with fewer sexual hang-ups."

WIFE: "Financial and social status. It was not a consideration in choosing my husband—who does fine—but would like rich old man with one foot in the grave if anything should happen to present honey."

HUSBAND: "A sexually mature person, stable, honest, loving."

She's a college graduate who works in the technical field. This is her second marriage, and she feels this one is loving and she has a good sex life. This is also his second marriage. He feels that while his wife thinks he's a good lover, she feels that he needs improvement in other ways. She's older, and has more education, being between 41 and 50, and a college graduate.

He's a blue collar worker (works in construction) between 31 and 40, with a high school education.

WIFE: "The same as my spouse is. Don't need to worry about remarrying unless first husband dies."

HUSBAND: "I don't plan to remarry unless my wife dies. If that sad event should occur, I would look for a person who was very much like her in religious conviction (Protestant) and who had the constitution to be a minister's wife. I would again choose a woman who has a high regard for the church, the Bible, who is a non-drinker, non-smoker and a good worker in home and church and has a high regard for the sanctity of marriage."

She's a homemaker who is religious, and the mother of 2 children. She describes herself as mature and considerate. He's between 41 and 50, with a postgraduate degree. He describes himself as reserved, but warm, and says his wife is the dominating one. Their major crisis is over who's boss in the family.

When we asked people what was their most important reason for marrying, 50 per cent of those in first marriages said "for love," but only 38 per cent of the remarried gave that reason. The remarried were slightly more interested in having a companion and a homelife than were the spouses in first unions. Even for those in first marriages, a little experience seems to increase their desire for communication and respect, as well as love, as these wives indicate:

WIFE: "I would want a very understanding man. I would also want him to be romantic. My husband is not very romantic. He should be considerate and devoted to me. I would want him to be easy to talk to. Sometimes I can talk to my husband and sometimes he makes me feel stupid."

She's thought about divorce, because she's overwhelmed by responsibility. Her worst crisis was their debts, and she says her marriage alternates between periods of remoteness and closeness. This homemaker, between 31 and 40, has no children.

WIFE: "Have a little bit more respect for me and my feelings. I would look for someone that would treat me as the person I am and not otherwise."

Almost three times as many of our remarried spouses said that their most important reason for marrying was for economic security. Again, a little practical experience often leads wives to value a good provider and the goods he provided:

WIFE: "If I were to remarry I'd look for a man who knew how to show love, was mature, but knew how to have fun, was good with kids and had lots of money. He would have to resemble my present husband in all those ways. But the money would become an important factor, where it didn't have anything to do with why I married my husband."

WIFE: "A good provider for me and my children, a loving person and someone I could feel comfortable with sexually. Actually if this were to happen I would want someone that I could feel as good with love-wise but could say loved me not 50-50 but more than I loved him, as I feel the second time around it's easier that way, but I also feel my life would never be the same as my husband now is my best friend, my lover and the father of our children and nothing can really compare to that."

While this homemaker says she has a very good sex life, she admits to cheating, but with her husband's knowledge and consent. Also she has thought about divorce. Describes herself as emotional and dominant.

WIFE: "Someone rich because now we never have an extra nickel. Someone much more affectionate and sexy because I crave this and don't get it from my husband."

Sex for the remarried tends to be better than for the others. Fifty-five per cent of the remarried whom we sampled rated their sex lives as very good, while only 35 per cent of those in first marriages gave theirs the highest rating. Twenty-one per cent of the remarried had intercourse at least five times a week, while only 15 per cent of those married once were as active.

In describing their spouses, the remarried less often called them "considerate" and more often chose the adjectives "mature" and "dominant." Some wives indicated they wanted a man who was confident and mature:

WIFE: "Has: high morals, sincerity, honesty in dealing with others (business and personal), affectionate, sense of responsibility, conscientious worker, sense of humor.

"Doesn't have: self-confidence without being egocentric, has very little self-confidence in his ability to deal with problems, handle responsibility at home, he is a responsible person, but worries a lot."

This homemaker is a high school graduate, and is between 31 and 40. She would remarry someone very similar to her present spouse in most ways. She describes her husband as warm and believes it's a generally stable marriage. The major problem in the marriage is alcohol.

WIFE: "I looked for someone with both feet firmly on the ground. Someone with goals and a dream all his own. But not the Peter-Pan type, chasing rainbows, I wanted a man that knew how to enjoy life—even the humdrum aspects of life. A man mature enough to *give* and *receive* love."

Although the wife above tried to avoid a man like Peter Pan, in the responses from remarried wives below, we see an underlying Peter Pan principle: Some remarriages peter out, and some pan out.

WIFE: "This is hard to answer in some ways because I'm re-married, it will be three years this June 21. I have three boys and he had four girls. (1) Someone who believes in God. (2) Love kids. (3) Someone who loves you because you're just you. (4) Someone who cares for others."

She works in the blue collar field. Her second husband she says has increased maturity, and is quite different from her first one. He also has a stronger sense of commitment. She's between 31 and 40.

WIFE: "Religious, non-alcoholic."

This blue collar worker and mother of 3 is religious herself. This is her second marriage. While she feels her present husband is quite different in most ways from her first husband, she admits both have considered divorce. Both have struck each other during fights, and lack of communication is her biggest problem. Between 31 and 40.

WIFE: "I looked for a stronger man emotionally, one who seemed to know what he wanted in life and was determined to get ahead. Former spouse couldn't keep a job or accept responsibilities and this one is completely the opposite."

In our question about the major problem in marriages, the remarried reported that alcohol was the greatest source of trouble more often than those married for the first time. Other problems a little more common to the remarried were disagreements about the children and cheating. Money was the chief problem for those married once, but it took second place to lack of communication for the remarried. Nevertheless, some husbands, in the event of remarriage, would look for women with large figures—in bankbooks:

HUSBAND: "I'd look for a rich woman, my present wife is not wealthy at all."

This white collar worker between 41 and 50 makes between $10–$15,000 a year, and has 3 children. His major problem is money, and says his wife takes him for granted. He's overwhelmed by all the responsibility, and has thought about getting a divorce.

HUSBAND: "Lots of money."

In listing the components most essential for a good marriage, the remarried did not differ much from the first-timers; both groups picked good communication and similar ideas or interests as most vital, with the remarried giving these factors an even higher percentage rating. One element rated lower by the remarried was individual freedom, and some of the husbands would want a new spouse to be more dependent than their current liberated wives:

HUSBAND: "Perhaps someone who is not so self-centered, more willing to do for others than herself. Perhaps even a little more needing of my support—emotional, physically, but not necessarily financially."

This college graduate describes himself as dominant, yet he says his wife is inconsiderate, and she doesn't love him. Lack of communication is their biggest problem, and he's thought about a divorce. He has no children and is between 18 and 30.

HUSBAND: "I would look for similar characteristics of my present wife as follows:

(1) Intelligence
(2) Similar views and ways of thinking
(3) Competent capable person
(4) Equally sexually attractive.

"I would prefer a person slightly more dependent and less aggressive than my current spouse."

Contrariwise, there were husbands who felt their wives should show more ambition, self-confidence, or sense of responsibility:

HUSBAND: "I would look for a person who thinks positively about herself and our relationship, more outgoing and willing to have friends, capable of handling and enjoying social engagements (but not to excess), capable of making love, not just being a passive receiver, healthy, outdoor sports prone, a good reliable friend."

He's a professional, 31 to 40, with a postgraduate education. He admits to having cheated with one person briefly. He says their sex life is generally dull, and he would remarry someone quite different in most ways. They argue most about social activities. He says he thinks his wife wishes they never got married. Believes it's a fairly stable marriage but has alternating periods of remoteness and closeness.

HUSBAND: "I would probably look for someone with more ambition and common sense. Also she would have to be a good housekeeper. A girl who would rather excel at what she's good at and less interested in being something else."

He says his wife is reserved, and he describes himself as considerate. He's overwhelmed by all the responsibility, and if he remarried again, he would marry a woman quite different. Also he says their sex life is dull, and feels his wife's job takes up too much time. Between 31 and 40, and works in the technical field.

HUSBAND: "Someone who is a lot more mature, and with more responsibilities. My spouse is just the opposite."

In citing important factors for a good marriage, the remarried evaluated mutual sexual satisfaction more highly than did those in first marriages. If some husbands were to remarry, they would definitely seek better performance in this area from their new model wives; and some would not be merely concerned with performance, they would opt for a more streamlined chassis:

HUSBAND: "Would look for one who really loved me and wanted sex for that reason."

He's a professional who says that both he and his wife have considered divorce, for he feels it would give him the freedom to find true love. He's cheated on his wife with other women for over a year. Says his wife is passive. He's 51 or over.

HUSBAND: "I would look for person with similar personality, willing to put home ahead of everything else and thinner."

He's a professional, a college graduate, 41 to 50. Feels their sex life is variable, and overwhelmed by responsibility. He describes their marriage as generally stable.

HUSBAND: "Same as wife except better physical appearance (body not face)."

When asked what influenced them most in their choice of present spouse, the remarried put greater emphasis on ability to communicate and intelligence. Although slightly lower in percentage, the remarried agreed with the first-married in selecting most often personality as the prime influence in mate selection, as in the case below:

HUSBAND: "This may sound strange, but the very thing that attracted me to my present wife, is that of a radiance that shows through telling you there is a strong positive personality behind it. I knew her 2 hours before I knew she was the one I wanted to marry."

This white collar worker has some college education, and is between 41 and 50. Their family income is less than $8,000 per year before taxes, this is his second marriage, and they have more than 4 children. He feels overwhelmed by responsibility and more nervous and irritable since marriage. He says their major problem is jobs, but they argue most about the children.

HUSBAND: "This being my third, I have no intention of separating. However, if she were to die, I would like to meet someone as near to my present wife as possible."

Are remarriages more likely to be successful than first attempts? Ruling out very early marriages which have a high disaster rate, people who marry for the first time between the ages of 25 and 35 have a 66 per cent chance of staying married for life, according to national census figures, while those who enter second marriages in that age range have only a 62 per cent chance. Seventy-five per cent of all first marriages last 20 years or more, while only half of all second marriages do; however, remember that many second marriages occur among the widowed late in life and are interrupted by death, rather than divorce. The figures for lifetime second marriages among those who remarry relatively young are more indicative of the narrowing gap between those married only once and those previously divorced who find a stable and satisfactory relationship.

As for our sample, the differences are not striking, but we can report that the remarried less often felt taken for granted by their mates, less often felt marriage had changed them in any way for the worse, and more often said they would definitely marry the same person again today. And *that* would seem to be the type of "remarriage" most likely to succeed!

Revised Editions

St. John Hotchkiss, Shaw's self-proclaimed snob, says, "Marriage is good enough for the lower classes: they have facilities for desertion that are denied to us." Yet, a wealthy Hungarian actress explained her repeated remarriages with the confession, "If you're not married, it's too embarrassing to carry on an affair in front of the servants." As our survey shows, remarriage comes to the rich (24 per cent of those earning at least $25,000 a year) and poor (17 per cent of those earning under $10,000) nearly alike. If one marriage has not worked out well, there is always hope and Prufrock's consolation of "time yet for a hundred indecisions, and for a hundred visions and revisions. . . ." A remarriage may be no more successful than an initial one, but it is never a carbon copy of the original, and having closed the book on one ill-fated union, a returnee to the wedded ranks is apt to put considerable planning into the revised second edition of matrimonial venture. Even people thoroughly engrossed in first marriages may have visions of what a second union might be like, whether it would adhere closely to the original script or be an entirely different story.

If you have remarried—or were to remarry—what steps would you take to insure its success, and what mistakes, based on past experience, would you avoid making?

The reason most often given by the remarried spouses who answered our questionnaire for the failure of their last marriage was immaturity, listed by 29 per cent. Even those in first marriages often felt they were immature at the time of the wedding:

WIFE: "As much as I love my husband, I never would marry a drinking man. It breaks hearts too many times. Now we are older his drinking is lesser and lesser. We seem to do more together where, before, his drinking buddies were more important.

   "I realized now and even at 22 (my age when I got married) I was very much immature and very easily hurt and wanted very much to be loved my way.

   "To insure a successful marriage—do more talking over values, what you expect of marriage, each other, children, religious beliefs, jobs, money source, contributions, etc. Would avoid premarriage relationship. In his eyes it's okay. It's taken me a long time to rid myself of guilt. Sometimes it still sneaks up on me."

HUSBAND: "Give more time, never drink."

She says they argue mostly about his drinking and the children (they have 2). The worst crisis they faced was the death of 2 other children. While she believes the marriage is fairly loving now, she still feels overwhelmed by responsibility. She's between 41 and 50, and a homemaker. He's a blue collar worker, 51 or over. He feels his wife is considerate, and he would definitely marry her again.

More than one-fifth of the remarried blamed the failure of their previous marriage on a poor choice of spouse. Happily married couples would insure the success of a remarriage by picking a mate similar in ideals and character to their present one:

WIFE: "I would not remarry unless I was very young and had children, my new husband would have to have the same religious convictions. I would pick a man as similar to my husband now as I could find."

HUSBAND: "I would avoid remarriage. Look for someone who was much like my spouse and interested in my lifestyle—I would be more careful about relatives."

Both are between 18 and 30. They have no children. She says their major problem is conflicts over relatives, but her husband is considerate and their marriage is stable. He's a college graduate who works in management. He feels his wife is also a considerate person, and that she loves and appreciates him fully.

WIFE: "Married for love, same religious preference, no smoker, no drinker and no divorce."

HUSBAND: "I would not choose a person without deep religious conviction. I would look for a woman with even temperament who gets along well with everyone, even people who tend to be irritating."

Eight per cent of the remarried blamed the failure of their past marriage on in-law problems. A more frequent cause of marital disruption was money problems, cited by 12 per cent of the remarried. The remarried less often picked money as the major problem in their current marriages, and many a couple in their first marriage would feel more secure in a new marriage with more securities, such as stocks, bonds, notes, certificates, and debentures.

WIFE: "I most probably would not remarry. If I did, we would approach marriage the same way as I do now. A good marriage takes cooperation between spouses, love, consideration, and a heck of a lot of hard work. The only thing that would make a new marriage easier would be a more ample income. This would be one less hardship."

HUSBAND: "Would be more patient, loving and understanding spouse and not take my spouse for granted. Tell my spouse that I really love her."

This college graduate and mother of 2 says her husband is emotional, and their major problem involves jobs. She probably would marry the same person again today. He's a blue collar worker between 31 and 40 and believes their major problem is money. While he describes himself as reserved, he admits to striking his wife during arguments. She's a blue collar worker between 18 and 30.

Dissimilar interests were blamed for marital breakup by 12 per cent of remarried spouses, and making sure the spouses were in agreement on the way major issues should be handled was advocated by people with enduring marriages; familiarity is important, though without commitment the strain on the couple can be as bad as in the case of commitment without familiarity:

WIFE: "Thoroughly talk out principles by which other planned to live and expect we would agree, certainly on major things like commitment, how to deal with anger, hurt, significant persons to our marriage, if children were contemplated, principles of child rearing and part children would be in family life. Reaction of each to criticism should be discussed."

HUSBAND: "Would not try intercourse first night unless we had been copulating prior."

WIFE: "I don't like to think I'd ever remarry. My love for my husband is very true and very deep."

HUSBAND: "The only change I would make would be that we would not live together before marriage. This placed an undue amount of tension on the relationship because of no binding commitment between the two of us."

While there were as many childless spouses in remarriages as in first marriages, the remarried parents generally had more children. Twenty-nine per cent of remarried parents had three or more children, compared with 22 per cent in first marriages; and twice as many remarried spouses had more than four children. More of the remarried said their children had driven them further apart or led to many quarrels, though 38 per cent of the remarried—twice as many as parents in first marriages—said children had not changed their relationship at all. This ability of many remarrieds to detach children from the relationship may reflect a number of late remarriages where the children are already grown, or the advantage of becoming acquainted with and accepting stepchildren prior to remarriage. Still, 4 per cent of our respondents blamed the failure of a previous marriage on disagreement over children, and some wives stressed that this aspect of marriage cannot be taken for granted:

WIFE: "Would make sure open communication exists and that we know what we are getting into as far as children go. The need to discuss children from previous marriages very important. Person I choose would not be moody."

Sexual dissatisfaction was claimed as the cause of marital failure by 14 per cent of the remarried, more than three times the number who blamed conflicts over children. Sometimes both these problems are present, and interrelated, as in the case of the unhappily married lady below:

WIFE: "I was widowed at 39—brand-new baby, too. I was alone for eight and a half years, when I let this present husband talk me into marriage. He put on a front as far as loving and caring for my nine-year-old girl. Even though I dated him ten months it is not enough to find out true feelings. Also where sex is concerned I should have known things don't change that much after marriage. The tension of him not liking my nineteen- and twenty-one-year-old boys changed both our feelings as the months went by. It was one, two and over and the heck with her feelings—woman is not supposed to enjoy sex (by his short way of expressing himself). I would avoid marriage period again—I have had it."

As we noted previously, more of our respondents used the term "considerate" to describe their spouses than any other adjective, and it was selected twice as often as any other offered choice. Not all spouses are considerate, however, and 14 per cent of the remarried blamed past failure on an "inconsiderate partner." Several wives advised finding a considerate man in case of remarriage:

WIFE: "I would look for a person considerate of my feelings and one who could accept my opinions and criticism without hostility."

This homemaker has a postgraduate degree, one child, and is between 18 and 30. She says they argue mostly about religion (she is religious), and her biggest problem is relatives who are living with them. Still she feels her marriage is stable, and would marry a similar type of man, even though she describes him as dominating.

WIFE: "If I would marry again I would be very sure to marry a man with more responsibilities and a real Christian person.
"It is very important to believe in God, pray, be happy and have patience. I read the Bible every day and this helps me in my problems."

She's 51 or over, and no longer has sex. Describes her husband as irresponsible, and lack of communication is her biggest problem. If she ever divorced, she would marry a man quite different in most ways. This homemaker has one child.

WIFE: "I would make my man more assertive from the first day of our marriage."

She says they rarely have sex, and married because of her pregnancy. If she would ever remarry, she would want a man quite different—and says that the immaturity of her husband and their sexual problems could cause their marriage to fail. Feels her spouse is irresponsible and emotional. She's a homemaker with 2 children, between 41 and 50.

WIFE: "I would have a more open relationship. I would want both of us to have a limited amount of freedom. I would like to be treated as a person who is loved and appreciated and not a slave! If it were possible—I would want complete trust and no such thing as jealousy."

Since the wife above who desires a "more open relationship" speaks also of a "limited amount of freedom," she may not condone extramarital affairs. Nine per cent of the remarried—three times as many as people in first marriages—did express the view that both spouses should be free to have outside affairs, with each other's knowledge. Yet, the remarried outnumbered the first-timers, 45 to 37 per cent, in believing that extramarital affairs "almost inevitably lead to separation and divorce." Remarried people in our survey gave a slightly higher incidence of cheating on current spouses and 22 per cent said that previous marriages failed because of an extramarital affair, a cause tied for second place with poor choice of spouse and exceeded only by immaturity.

Whereas only 14 per cent of those in first marriages said they would react to their mates' cheating by seeking divorce immediately, 23 per cent of the remarried, perhaps disillusioned by past experience, would head straight for a lawyer. The remarried were generally more accepting of divorce, just about one-quarter stating that a marriage should be ended whenever it proves unsatisfactory to either partner. Only 7 per cent of the remarried said a divorce would lower their self-esteem considerably, compared with 18 per cent of those in their first marriage. And 19 per cent of the remarried said the greatest obstacle to getting a divorce would be the loss of spouse's services, more than twice the number of once-married who chose this prosaic response.

One area of responsibility in which the remarried exhibited a more egalitarian attitude was in the control of money, where finances were less often placed primarily under the domain of one spouse than in first marriages. A rich husband, or one with better financial sense, was often the dream of wives whose marriage had achieved better emotional than financial balance:

WIFE: "I would find someone with a lot of money, since most of our differences are about money. I would be secure enough to never display jealousy. Early in our marriage I was a very jealous wife, it was annoying and almost led to a separation."

The family income here is less than $8,000 a year, and they have 3 children. She is now pregnant with the 4th. She says her husband is dominant and describes herself as emotional, yet feels their marriage is generally stable. Between 18 and 30, she's a homemaker.

WIFE: "(1) Letting friends' emotional problems interfere.
   (2) Spending money less frequently on splurges.
   (3) A more outgoing person who likes to travel."

She works in the technical field, and has no children. Her major problem is money, and she feels her husband is passive. While they argue mostly about job and careers she would still marry the same type of man again.

WIFE: "If I were to remarry I would make sure I had plenty of money and would make sure I could be independent of myself with no one to rule over me."

Remarried spouses said that alcohol was the major problem in their marriage twice as often as those in first marriages, 7 per cent of the remarried giving this response. We may assume that alcohol caused the breakup of many first marriages, freeing alcoholics to marry again. Some wives related how alcohol had threatened their current marriages:

WIFE: "I am a recovering alcoholic, and would try to remain that way. I would prefer to keep alcohol away from a second marriage, as I believe that is the only cause of this failure."

This blue collar worker between 41 and 50, with more than 4 children is definitely planning to divorce her husband. She says her marriage is a failure, and she made a poor choice. Her husband is unemployed, and money and alcohol are her major problems.

WIFE: "I would know more about a person's feelings towards marriage; social life; raising children; drinking habits. I thought when you married the other person changed considerably; such as stopped drinking completely; this was never discussed, nor did I realize it was to be a problem in marriage but I would still marry the same person."

Knowing a partner well before marriage may help circumvent poor choice of a partner or the immaturity of a spouse not yet ready for marriage, such situations having been blamed for half the marital failures of those in our sample who had remarried.

Since personal growth is a lifelong process, however, it is unlikely that any bride or groom will be fully "matured," and it is important that a spouse does not arrest his or her development by becoming overly dependent on the partner. No matter how similar two people are in their tastes and goals, they are individuals and must support one another in the maintenance of a degree of independence and autonomy:

WIFE: "Make sure I knew the person well before we married so that we think alike and enjoy the same things. Especially need to know their marriage goal is the same as mine. That he be mature and does things that need to be done.

"I wouldn't marry him just because he wants it. I would be sure in my mind that I'm doing it because I want it too and we believe we are doing what's best for both of us."

This homemaker is the mother of more than 4 children. Describes her husband as passive and irresponsible, and feels that a divorce would enable her to find true love. She wants a husband with a stronger sense of commitment. She's between 31 and 40.

WIFE: "I would be more accepting of need for independence of all members of my family.

"I would be more accepting of my own need for independence and develop more individual interests—I waited too long before setting personal goals. I wasted some valuable time."

While she says her marriage is stable, her husband is mature, and sex between them is very good, she admits to cheating with 3 other men, with one affair lasting over a year. A college graduate, between 41 and 50, who works in the white collar field.

WIFE: "There have been no mistakes in our marriage. There have been fights, some failures, but always we end up closer. The biggest success secret is honesty and openness. A sense of humor and understanding that two people can live together but never think alike helps. I feel each spouse's responsibility is to help the other person be the best person he is able to be."

While she argues mostly about personal habits, she feels her husband is warm and affectionate, and they generally have a loving marriage. She works in management, and has one child.

WIFE: "I will never remarry again, even if my husband were to die as I have such a wonderful marriage now—I would not want to risk a marriage that could be bad, and I would have such wonderful memories of this marriage."

Whether married for the first time or remarried, respondents most often felt the key to their marriages' success lay in increased maturity. Both groups chose better communication second, with the remarried emphasizing it more. The remarried made "more love" their third choice, while those in first marriages cited commitment next.

Among married men, whether in their first or subsequent marriages, more than one-fourth felt that maturity would lead to marital success, and they would look for this characteristic in a spouse if they were to remarry:

HUSBAND: "Choose a mature person with interests similar to mine. Choose someone who is sexually uninhibited."

He's 51 or over with a post graduate education. Family income is over $50,000 a year. He says sexual dissatisfaction could cause his marriage to fail. Feels his wife appreciates him but doesn't really love him.

In our question about the most important elements in a good marriage, women selected communication by a wide margin over men; however, husbands trailed wives by only 3 percentage points in choosing better communication as a means of increasing a marriage's success:

HUSBAND: "(1) What I am doing this time is to spend more time with my wife.
"(2) Have a family night once a week.
"(3) Wife and I get together with our children to find out their needs and wants.

"(4) Have a hobby of guitar playing for enjoyment to release my tensions and relax.

"(5) She and I get together to talk over money needs and incomes and reach a decision together without the children being there."

This white collar worker between 41 and 50 is into his second marriage, and believes this one will be successful because of his increased maturity, and now he feels he has a more responsible partner.

A stronger sense of commitment, more cooperation, and more love rated close behind maturity and communication, no more than 3 percentage points separating husbands from wives in choosing these factors as prime contributions towards marital success:

HUSBAND: "I would try to understand my wife better and I would try to give just as much as I receive, if not more. I would listen closer to her feelings and try to understand them and try to better myself in any way that might improve our relationship."

This is his third marriage, and if he ever married again he would choose a woman quite different. Considers his present wife to be a considerate person, and says his marriage is generally loving. A blue collar worker between 31 and 40.

HUSBAND: "I got married partly to have sex regularly, safely. But our love really grew to be a beautiful thing. I think young men tend to put too much emphasis on sex!!"

About one husband in nine felt that development of similar interests was most essential in making a marriage work; however, some apparently were more interested in a wife who would not so much share, but rather keep out of their way:

HUSBAND: "Find girl with more interests the same as mine and to talk about families more."

He feels he is the dominant one, and describes his wife as considerate but reserved. He would marry a woman who is similar in appearance, but one with a different type of personality. He works in management and is between 41 and 50, and the father of 2 children.

HUSBAND: "Would try to see that interests were more similar, would try to understand needs of partner better and determine if I could provide for these needs. Would try to avoid taking partner for granted."

He's a college graduate, between 41 and 50, and works in management. This is his second marriage. Describes himself as reserved and methodical, and while he feels his wife appreciates him as a spouse, she doesn't appreciate him as a lover. He has the feeling of being tied down, and says his sex life is unsatisfying. He would marry a woman quite different if he was ever free again. Says both have considered divorce.

HUSBAND: "I used to drink but no more so I wouldn't go through that again. Make sure we had same interests. Discuss and think things through more thoroughly instead of jumping right into things (financial things more than anything else)."

He's a blue collar worker, 31 to 40. They have had a period of separation. He has cheated with one person briefly. He says he'd remarry someone quite different in most ways. He married to have a companion. Their major problems are sexual dissatisfaction and money.

HUSBAND: "The only thing to do would be to insure that I enjoyed being myself without being harassed."

This blue collar worker says his marriage is in constant turmoil, and they have many major problems. He married only because of pregnancy, and at this time he would marry someone who is quite different from his wife. Though he's only between 31 and 40, he says they never or rarely ever have sex.

HUSBAND: "Doubtful if I would remarry, but would find partner more adaptable to my present 'image'."

He is a college graduate, a professional, 41 to 50. He lived with his present wife for 6 months to a year before getting married, and this is his second marriage. He feels tied down and sexually unsatisfied.

HUSBAND: "I would marry a less opinionated person. I would be less opinionated."

He says his marriage is in constant turmoil, and his wife dominates him. He has cheated on her, and if he would ever marry again, he would marry a woman with a different type of personality, but one who was similar in appearance to his wife now. A college graduate between 31 and 40, he works in the professional field.

HUSBAND: "Marrying a dumb woman. (Wouldn't do again.)"

In James Boswell's *Life of Dr. Johnson*, Samuel Johnson is quoted as saying of a widower, "Were he not to marry again, it might be concluded that his first wife had given him a disgust in marriage; but by taking a second wife he pays the highest compliment to the first, by showing that she made him so happy as a married man, that he wishes to be so a second time."

Of course, we know that today most remarriages are not sequels to death of a treasured spouse but to divorce of an incompatible one. Accordingly, perhaps we would do better to quote from that same work, "A gentleman who had been very unhappy in marriage, married immediately after his wife died; Johnson said it was the triumph of hope over experience."

Johnson's wit rings somewhat hollow, because hope can rarely triumph over experience. We see far more instances of what Charles Dickens called "the hope of happy inexperience." For people who have terminated marriages to remarry consistently as they do—and more often than not then stay married for life—we must conclude that even a failed marriage offers enough positive experience to motivate another attempt.

Shaw's Bishop Bridgenorth points out that common humanity tends to make one man much the same as another, so that a woman who remarries will find at the end of a month it wasn't worth changing. "Then it's a mistake to get married," protests the discontented wife.

"It is, my dear," concedes the bishop, "but it's a much bigger mistake not to get married."

The joke says that a bachelor is a man who hasn't made the same mistake once. The remarried apparently make more mistakes, but they may be considerably smaller ones.

11

As Far as Thought Can Reach:

Lifestyles and the Future of Marriage

MRS. BRIDGENORTH: The world must go on, mustn't it, Collins?
COLLINS: Oh, the world will go on ma'am: don't you be afraid of that. It ain't so easy to stop it as the earnest kind of people think.

—George Bernard Shaw, GETTING MARRIED

"I would like Charlie to complain less and do more.

"I would like to see Charlie sleep less.

"I would like to need Charlie for more than a paycheck.

"I would like a husband to make me feel like a woman to love, hold, kiss and not just unload it.

"I am working three days, Charlie five days. If Charlie took care of his responsibilities with the house and children as he would like me to there would be no problem.

"I would like a human being for a husband, not an animal who has to yell and hurt to get his way.

"I would like a man who can keep his word and make up his mind.

"I would like a loving, understanding, listening father for my child."

What sort of woman would present a therapist with the above list of complaints about her marriage? Ginny is a 32-year-old waitress married to a cabdriver five years older. She was raised by conventional Irish Catholic parents, has a high school education, and was a virgin when she married. She has three children in elementary school. Thus far, Ginny probably fits pretty well the image one would get from reading her list of problems. What one probably could not surmise from her bill of marital grievances or even from first meeting her is that Ginny has been involved in mate-swapping and group sex, and has twice had sexual relations with another woman while her husband watched. Previously unable to reach orgasm except through cunnilingus or with a vibrator, she had her first coital climax after seven years with the aid of drugs, and has been using them since as a sexual adjunct. She has whipped her husband at his request as a prelude to sexual activity. Recently a male co-worker has been propositioning her, and she is about to begin an extramarital affair. And her mid-morning coffee break with a female neighbor downstairs is developing into something hotter than the coffee.

"I would try to be a better mother and housewife . . . a quieter person . . . a less hateful person.

"I would try to trust in someone other than myself.

"I will try to be fair and understanding in my opinions and judgments.

"I will try to have faith in this marriage."

Charlie once had dreams of being a commercial artist, but dropped out of school, and now feels like a failure. "Everything is coming apart," he complains. He is depressed, indecisive, and finds it difficult to approach his wife sexually. He has had several brief homosexual experiences since his teens, and often frequents prostitutes. His purchase of pornographic magazines and frank discussions with his wife initiated her into the unconventional world of "swinging," which the previously staid woman accepted with remarkable ease, and she has now begun to foray into bisexual adventures of her own without her conjugal guide. Charlie actually has more guilt about such things than Ginny, and paying a prostitute to whip him subsequently unnerved him enough to come to the mental health clinic.

This is no simple case, amenable to a weekly hour of joint discussion in a therapist's office. With the referral of two of the couple's three children from the schools because of academic failure and behavior problems, there are now four patients in treatment, and counting individual sessions for the marital problems, joint marital sessions, family therapy sessions, individual therapy for the children, psychiatric evaluations, and psychological testing, at least ten clinicians have been involved in the therapy. One peculiar aspect of this case is the handling of a lifestyle which a generation ago would have been termed sexually chaotic if not frankly schizophrenic; a dozen years ago, we might have seen such cases, but the partners would have been "hippies" or "flower children," easily identifiable by their garb and overt behavior as living on the margins of society; now, we see a middle-class couple from traditional family backgrounds, professing conventional values, immersing themselves nevertheless in an atmosphere of drugs, bisexuality, and extramarital liaisons.

When Ginny says that she views her search for outside lovers, her habitual use of drugs, and her diversity of sexual outlets as marks of liberation, should we, as therapists, respect that? Do we intervene in some way when the ambivalent quest for self-development begins to affect the children, who are highly aware of the increasing marital tensions? And what do you do when confronted, as we were, by Ginny's blithe admission that she was taking money from the cash register on the job because "it's what everyone does"? Do we mutely agree that Ginny is merely looking out for number one in accordance with society's latest manifesto, or do we struggle against the maelstrom, dragging her back to older, firmer territory where spouses had responsibility to spouses, parents to children, and individuals to society?

The answers are not that simple, and when you convene the staff of a mental health clinic around a conference table, one is less likely to emerge with a clear course of action and more to collect six different sets of directions. With the expansion of new frontiers in the American lifestyle, we lose the confidence of having established boundaries, and unless we mark some sorts of limits as we go, we shall, like Hansel and Gretel, trying to retrace a trail of crumbs, find ourselves completely disoriented. One can always keep heading in the same direction, of course; and as the Cheshire Cat explained to Alice you're sure to get *somewhere* if you only walk long enough, provided that, like Alice, you don't much care where you get to. Having had the foresight to ask Ginny to list the direction in which she wanted her marriage to go, her therapist should be able to see that her destinations of responsible parenthood and marital partnership, sexual intimacy in a context of love, and ability to trust lay nearly 180 degrees off her present course of impersonal sexual activity, freedom from familial ties, and clandestine temptations.

There are many therapists who, in their eagerness to follow psychoanalytic ideals of non-directiveness, become little more than spectators, much like a movie audience that knows it cannot possibly change the outcome of the celluloid perils being played out before its eyes and is aware that there is no actual danger to the actors, regardless of the insanity of their risks. The therapist must guide, and not in the pastoral sense of Bishop Bridgenorth, who proclaims, "I'm not a teacher: only a fellow-traveller of whom you asked the way. I pointed ahead—ahead of myself as well as of you." It is presumptuous to assume that everyone should have the same set of goals, and the therapist would do better to heed Don Juan's parting words, "I can find my own way to heaven, Ana; not yours." It is not essential that the guide go in the same direction as the searcher, but it is necessary to ascertain where the traveller wishes to go, and, if it happens to be in the direction from which he started, to turn him around rather than let him press on into a tangled wood of wild and wondrous encounters that lead farther from home.

All progress means war with society and just because new trends of behavior go against past social norms, they are not necessarily detrimental. If married people and those who eschew marriage are developing new lifestyles, at least some of these persons must have aims and expectations which they feel traditional marriage cannot fulfill. The expectations that motivate these lifestyles must be considered as carefully as the innovations themselves, or we shall never be able to understand whether the experiments failed or whether they simply were designed to fill a set of goals that turned out to be unrelated to a more distant goal that lay in another direction.

Without a clear idea of the purpose of things, we will fall into the errors of the reader who complained that the stories in the dictionary were too short or the child who criticized the washing machine for repeatedly broadcasting the same television show. Before we can judge whether marriage today is fulfilling its functions, we must determine what people expect from it.

The Parties of Both Parts

"Now that our Governments refuse to make these contracts reasonable, those whom we in our blindness drove out of the Church will be driven out of the registry office; and we shall have the history of Ancient Rome repeated. We shall be joined by our solicitors for seven, fourteen, or twenty-one years—or perhaps months. Deeds of partnership will replace the old vows," predicts Bishop Bridgenorth, his words first uttered in 1908. As the progressive clergyman indicates, the substitution of private contracts for civil and religious marital commitments is scarcely a new idea. In pre-Christian Rome, the poor needed the protection of marital law, but the property laws that affected the wealthy were deemed so intolerable, especially to women of property, that the rich simply avoided them by forming unions outside the temple and drawing up contracts as they would in any business merger.

Many young couples marrying today are rejecting the traditional marriage vows and composing their own. Some go so far as to draw up actual written contracts, not only for actual marriages, but also for living-together arrangements outside of marriage. In a book entitled *Personal Marriage Contract,* Dr. John F. Whitaker presents a "Declaration of Commitment," to be negotiated for a definite period of years or an indefinite term, containing 96 paragraphs, such as:

"I will consistently remember those qualities and traits that are beautiful about you and consistently communicate my love by recognizing your inner beauty and your outer physical beauty through words and actions. . . .

"I will keep my mind healthy, attractive and loveable. . . .

"While I accept our momentary human response of frustration with disappointment, I will not act rejected, will not sulk or continue to be hurt or angry; nor will I attempt to control your expression of your individuality in any way," etc.

The poetry of such documents is quite lovely, but the sentiments would be more suitable for Valentine's Day cards than for legal documents. The exorbitant promises of saintly behavior at all times make the traditional vow of "to love and to cherish, till death us do part" as easy to keep by comparison as making a monthly minimal payment on your Master Charge card. The notion that limiting the period of commitment will somehow enable the partners to demonstrate superhuman degrees of consideration, personal conduct, unwavering honesty, self-control, maturity, and constant admiration for a period of months and years is akin to saying that a man cannot be expected to walk the same road for a lifetime, but can fly through the heavens if he doesn't have to do it for very long. Such ideal contracts are also filled with apparent contradictions such as "I cannot make you happy or unhappy, but I can make myself happy" versus "I will give OUR time the highest priority." It is never really made clear how these superspouses are to reconcile their total freedom to pursue individual self-actualization unhindered by the needs of others with affirmations of loyalty, love, and consideration which appear to know no bounds other than the period of the contract, at which time the partners have the option to "part in a friendly manner and will go on with our lives separately."

If one wanted to draw up a truly realistic contract, one would have to draw on the experiences of people who had been actually living in a marriage for a while, expecting their advice not to consist of making promises that only someone who had never lived in a real marriage could possibly dream of keeping, but of asking for just enough changes and commitments to keep a union viable. And this is what we asked of the couples we surveyed:

If you and your spouse were to renew your marriage vows and wanted to draw up a contract stating what you expected from one another, what provisions would you include in that contract?

The term "gentleman's agreement" is used to describe a pact based on the honor of the parties involved, without recourse to written documents. The gentlemen in our survey often were opposed to the idea of contracts, while the wives, who desired that their husbands pay more attention to them and less to other interests, wanted to spell things out:

WIFE: "I expect my husband's love and attention. I don't want to come in second to his work. I feel I should come first. I like to be showered with attention. Expensive gifts are nice but I crave for my husband's attention."

HUSBAND: "I don't believe such 'contracts' will hold any validity in future actions."

WIFE: "The only thing I would ask is that my husband doesn't drink. This is the only real problem we've had. At this time he hasn't had any drink of any sort in seven months."

HUSBAND: "I wouldn't want a contract. It would not work under contract."

She says their major problem involves her husband's drinking. However she feels now that their marriage is generally stable, and her sex life is very good. This is her second marriage, and she's between 31 and 40. They have no children. He's a blue collar worker between 41–50, and this is his third marriage. He claims that their major problem is conflicts over relatives, and describes himself as "considerate."

WIFE: "Sex more often, I can't get enough of his loving. He's just so perfect and *great* in bed."

HUSBAND: "To always love me and be honest with me as she has been. That's why I love her so much."

Both are between 18 and 30. They have no children. In addition, both are white collar workers, and the family income is over $50,000 a year. Though she says her marriage is generally stable, she feels her husband takes her for granted, and dominates her, yet she has sex more than once a day. Also she engages in bondage. He describes himself as "possessive" and says their fights involve his attention to other women.

Contracts are very important where money is involved, and since money is involved in marriage, some spouses wanted the contract to be partially an I.O.U. covering financial responsibilities:

WIFE: "Better communications, financial security as much as possible for wife's future. Total honesty in all things."

HUSBAND: "Money, group therapy."

This is her second marriage, and admits that both of them have considered divorce. Lack of communication is their major problem. She's between 31 and 40, and the mother of two children. He's between 41 and 50 and works in management. He describes his wife as "emotional and impetuous," and feels tied down and trapped.

WIFE: "Nothing new."

HUSBAND: "That she didn't spend so much money and nag so much."

Since the ark landed, couples have been under a divine command to multiply, but some feel division is equally important, and would like their contract to specify how work is to be split between husband and wife. Some favor the radical ideal of equal division of all chores without regard to gender, while others prefer the traditional fulfillment of roles designated as male and female:

WIFE: "I would include being a man in terms of doing what should be done around the house and manly responsibilities."

HUSBAND: "That she stay home more and do wifely duties."

Both are between 41 and 50. He works in the blue collar field, and she's the mother of 4 children. She says their marriage is in constant turmoil, her husband is emotional, and they argue mostly about social activities. She married because of pregnancy, and now feels dominated by her spouse. He says they've struck each other during arguments, which are mainly over their lack of money.

WIFE: "We would divide up the household duties."

HUSBAND: "I really don't know."

This wife is a professional with a postgraduate education between 31 and 40. She feels that money is their biggest problem, even though the family income is between $25–$49,999 a year, and they have no children. He works in the technical field, and says his marriage has given him a feeling of emotional security and of being loved.

WIFE: "That I would be able to get away with the same things he does, I believe in a fifty-fifty marriage; he believes in a ninety-ten marriage."

HUSBAND: "None."

This is her second marriage, and she's already had a period of separation. She admits that she had children to please her husband. She feels their major problem involves communication. In addition her husband travels too much on the job. He's between 18 and 30, and works in management. This is also his second marriage. He feels their major problem involves disagreements over their three children, and says his wife dominates him.

WIFE: "Take out the garbage."

HUSBAND: "Only that she let me do my social activities without getting upset."

"The great secret, Eliza, is not having bad manners or good manners or any particular sort of manners, but having the same manner for all human souls," explained Henry Higgins, who delighted in treating duchesses as if they were flower girls. "The question is not whether I treat you rudely, but whether you ever heard me treat anyone else better."

Eliza, however, could tolerate rude treatment, but refused to be passed over, and compared her professor with a motor bus: "all bounce and go, and no consideration for anyone." It was not surprising that Higgins remained a bachelor, for most wives would want the assurance of being treated with respect and consideration, that assurance preferably in writing:

WIFE: "That I would be entitled to be my own person and not have to quiet my own personality for fear I would not meet with my husband's approval."

This homemaker is between 31 and 40. She has some college education, and this is her second marriage. They lived together for less than 3 months before marrying, and they have had a period of separation. They argue most about the children, and married because of pregnancy. She feels that she lives for her kids, and says their major problem is difference in personal interest.

WIFE: "Don't be so opinionated—listen to the other side. Be a little more considerate."

She's a homemaker between 31 and 40, with some college education. They argue most about the kids. She describes herself as considerate, and says the marriage is always stable. The main problem in the marriage is conflicts over the relatives.

WIFE: "(1) Joint help in keeping a home (2) Mutual respect and consideration (3) Effort in keeping lines of communication open (4) Agreement on personal freedom (5) Joint activities we both enjoy (6) No one has more control over the money, or other property."

This white collar wife says money is their major problem, and they argue mostly over personal habits. She believes strong affection is important for a good marriage. A high school graduate with no children.

WIFE: "Moral support."

Some wives would include consideration for children as well as themselves as one of the contractual clauses, whereas others might draft provisions to insure that the heirs of the union did not control everything from birth:

WIFE: "(1) Doesn't drink a lot (2) Works hard and supports me well (3) Accepts me for me (4) Like sex (5) Loves children (6) Gives good back massages (7) Goes to church."

She's religious, a mother of 3 and works in the technical field. Describes herself and her spouse as "emotional," and married because of pressure from others. Now she says she's overwhelmed by responsibility, but feels her marriage is a loving one, and her sex life very good.

WIFE: "A larger period of time alone together or with other friends—without the children. Sometimes it's hard to remember that we got married to each other and loved each other before we had children."

Seventy years ago, Shaw complained of liberated couples who were opposed to conventional marriage: "When they finally give

up the idea of reforming our marriage institutions by private en-
terprise and personal righteousness, and consent to be led to the
Registry or even to the altar, they insist on first arriving at an
explicit understanding that both parties are to be perfectly free to
sip every flower and change every hour, as their fancy may dictate
in spite of the legal bond. I do not observe that their unions prove
less monogamic than other people's: rather the contrary, in
fact. . . ."

While some modern marriage contracts contain such provoc-
atively worded statements as "Since I understand that we cannot
be everything to each other, I will respect and value the importance
of your having separate play and work activities with separate
friends" or "I reserve the right to have private areas of my life
that I will not share with you," few wives would want written
sanction of extramarital sexual activity, and many would want it
specifically prohibited:

WIFE: "That he be faithful to me."

She's 51 or over, and has 3 children. Her worst crisis was her
husband's extramarital affair, and says marriage has made her
more nervous and irritable than ever before. Money and a lack
of communications is her major problem and her husband takes
her for granted.

WIFE: "That he be faithful, doesn't lie, go to work, wouldn't
    steal."

"No man is a match for a woman, except with a poker and a
pair of hobnailed boots. Not always even then," proclaims Jack
Tanner. Some women are not interested in evening the odds; what
is rare in the sports world should be routine in the marital world,
and they would contract for a no-hitter:

WIFE: "Never to threaten one another or to ever hit one another.
    Always stand by one another if one needs a little support at
    any given time."

She married because of sexual attraction, and now says she
cheated on her spouse—but with his knowledge and consent.
She feels her husband is dominating and possessive, and he has
struck her during arguments. Both have considered divorce. A
homemaker.

Jack Tanner knew he was too much of a gentleman to take a poker to his future wife, and was, therefore, doomed to be her slave. He also accepted the fact that "we all lie; we all bully as much as we dare; we all bid for admiration without the least intention of earning it; we all get as much rent as we can out of our powers of fascination." Human nature being what it is, how, then, are we to enter into any sort of contract with such untrustworthy scoundrels? Indeed, some wives were loathe to enter contracts for this reason, or because they felt their husbands would suit the contracts to their own patterns of domination, or simply because they did not need them:

WIFE: "Probably would not remarry—marriage does not seem to satisfy me in any way but financial. People change too much after they marry. I believe they put on too much of a front before marriage during courtship. My spouse is completely different from the person I thought I married."

This blue collar worker says both she and her husband have considered divorce. She hasn't cheated—but only because of lack of opportunity. She married primarily for financial or social status, and she says her husband wishes that they'd never married. Her biggest problem involves communicating.

WIFE: "He would know what to put in the contract, would probably include time allowed for job at home, duties I am expected to perform-schedule, children's freedom."

She's a homemaker with a postgraduate education, and mother of two children. The children have led to many quarrels, and she feels her husband appreciates her as a wife, but not as a lover. At this point she is not sure whether she'd marry the same person again. Between 41 and 50.

WIFE: "None that we have not yet stated. *Obey* was deleted from our vows as it is demeaning to both."

A professional, college graduate, between 18 and 30. She feels fully loved and appreciated by her spouse, and feels they have no major problems. She describes the marriage as always stable.

WIFE: "I would like to keep things as they are now. A contract sounds so businesslike, a marriage is not a corporation which has no feelings, only there to make money. Marriage should not be like that."

In Mary Martin's version of *Peter Pan,* anyone who wanted to live in Never, Never Land would have to take the solemn pledge, "I Won't Grow Up!" Some husbands would require their wives to take the opposite pledge, expecting "Daddy's little girl" to leave the little girl and Daddy far behind:

HUSBAND: "That my wife be a better homemaker, try to be more physically involved in sports and recreation, generally grow up and take better care of herself and learn more about sex. (I should teach her?)"

This blue collar worker says his wife is irresponsible and admits he is inconsiderate. Says his wife has control over their sexual activity, and sex is "variable." He's thought about divorce, and feels trapped. Between 18 and 30, with some college education.

HUSBAND: "Move out of the neighborhood and away from family interference."

If comedian Rodney Dangerfield ever started getting any respect from his wife, he would be out of a job. Husbands in other types of occupations, however, would like their wives to show a little more appreciation and consideration:

HUSBAND: "I don't think any written provisions would ever change anything; but I would want her to agree to understand the responsibilities I have to carry as the only income-maker, and appreciate what I have to do at times. Basically, I guess I have spoiled my wife."

He makes between $25–$49,999 a year, and has a postgraduate degree. Admits that both he and his wife have considered divorce, and has cheated on her with 2 or 3 other women. Says he's sexually unsatisfied, and that's his major problem.

HUSBAND: "(1) Don't try to be dominant in social situation (2) Stop trying to demonstrate 'you know it all' (3) Continue your outgoing friendly approach and consideration to others (4) Raising children requires great input—she isn't always right."

He's a professional, a college graduate, 51 or over. They argue most about alcohol, which he sees as their major problem. He has cheated with one person for over a year. He describes the marriage as having alternating close and remote periods.

HUSBAND: "Consideration, fairness, no personal demands."

The one advantage of personal marriage contracts is that they allow for some highly personal demands. The disadvantage is the nature of some of these demands, some of which are very unconventional and some unconscionable:

HUSBAND: "That my wife would stay on a diet and not get too overweight. That causes more conflicts than any other in our marriage."

This white collar worker says a divorce would give him the freedom to fulfill himself. His major problem is difference in personal interest, and while he feels his wife is warm and considerate, she's also emotional and possessive. He married his wife for her good looks, now they argue over her personal habits.

HUSBAND: "I think that the only thing I would include is that she relax more and not try and fill every moment with things she feels she must get done."

His major problem is sexual dissatisfaction, and says sex is dull. However he feels that his marriage is stable and loving, but he believes he's appreciated only as a husband, and not as a lover. 51 or over, he works in management, and has some college education.

HUSBAND: "She must have wealthy parents."

He's a college graduate 51 or over who makes between $25–$49,999 a year, and has two children. When he feels his marriage is stable, and his wife considerate, he feels tied down and trapped. They argue mostly over social activities.

HUSBAND: "To be able to bring my male lover home."

This professional is 31 to 40, and has a college education. He says he has consulted a lawyer about a divorce. He admits to having cheated with more than 3 others, at least one for over a year. He feels only the husband should be permitted outside sexual activity. They argue most about sexual problems. He describes himself as irresponsible, and feels their major problem is difference in personal interest. Still, he feels the marriage is always loving.

HUSBAND: "80 per cent to 20 per cent, my favor."

"Taking out a contract" has hostile implications in some sectors of society, and there were husbands who felt marriage could do without improvements on our traditional vows:

HUSBAND: "Would leave it as is—vague and nonspecific. Making specific obligations reduces the marriage in spontaneity, consideration of spouse, and so forth."

Perhaps our traditional vows are indeed "vague and nonspecific," but formal contracts are notorious for fine print and loopholes, and, as our world of striking public employees and holdout baseball stars shows us, these days a man's bond is no better than his word.

Dr. Virginia Satir nevertheless writes: "With the expectation of the age of marriage being around twenty and life expectancy being around seventy, close to fifty years of a person's life can be expected to be lived under the aegis of a marriage contract. If the contract does not permit an alive, dynamic experience, with growth possible for both, the result is outrage, submission, destructiveness, withdrawal, premature death, or destructive termination. Maybe this type of marriage contract is impossible."

Impossible to keep, perhaps, but easy to draw up. Dr. John Whitaker's 96-paragraph contract even contains the following prohibition: "I will never threaten to or actually abandon you, 'drop out' or 'go crazy.'"

How in the world can any sane person vow never to become insane? We wonder if Virginia Satir is aware that modern contracts are going to such drastic extremes. But, alas—yes, Virginia, there is a sanity clause.

Forsaking All Others

The minimum of national celibacy (ascertained by dividing the number of males in the community by the number of females, and taking the quotient as the number of wives or husbands permitted to each person) is secured . . . (where the quotient is 1) by the institution of monogamy. The modern sentimental term for the national minimum of celibacy is Purity.

—*George Bernard Shaw,* THE REVOLUTIONIST'S HANDBOOK

Anthropologists Clellan Ford and Frank Beach reviewed scientific studies of 185 societies and concluded that less than one-sixth of these had formal restrictions of their married members to a single mate, and only about one in 20 disapproved wholly of both pre-marital and extramarital relationships. We often conclude that the monogamous structure of Western society is the condition natural to the human species, and draw parallels between our own kind and other species, such as birds, where partners remain true exclusively to one another through one or more breeding seasons or even an entire lifespan. Of course, our closest biological relatives, the chimpanzees and gorillas, have no such standards of fidelity, though monogamy is not strictly for the birds—a few mammals, such as gibbons, marmosets, foxes, and beavers apparently choose lifetime mates when they can.

It is difficult to claim any sort of biological basis for man's method of mating, since we see ample evidence of both types of human behavior, spouses who have never known another mate throughout their life, and spouses who indulge in sexual relations with a variety of partners, even with consent of their avowed mate. The potential for finding outside partners sexually attractive is certainly present, and even encouraged by our society, which exhorts us to be sexy and desirable to the world at large, even though acting out that attraction is taboo for the married. Female liberationists may cite biology for the cause of sexual freedom, pointing out that the human female is rather unique in being sexually receptive and capable of orgasm at all times, while nearly all other mammals have periods of estrus or "heat" and are not remotely interested in sex at other times. Male chauvinists defend the double standard on Darwinian grounds, pointing out that it is nature's way for the male to be as promiscuous as possible while the female is highly selective. A female can produce only one to a dozen ova per breeding cycle, depending on species, and can bear only one litter or single offspring per cycle, regardless of how many males she mates with; therefore, it is important that the male who fertilizes her be as strong and adept at survival as possible to insure high quality offspring, and her safest course is to mate only with the most superior partner. The male, on the other hand, can sire as many offspring as the number of fertile females he can engage, so his best course, from a natural point of view, is to pursue as many females as possible. A single ejaculate from a human male contains half a billion sperm cells, enough to fertilize every female in the United States several times over. King Solomon is reputed to have had 700 wives and 300 concubines, a number exceeded nearly ten-fold by more recent Oriental potentates; we do not know how many children Solomon fathered, but even one child by each woman would have given him a thousand offspring. According to the *Guinness Book of World Records*, the most children born to one woman is 69, by a Russian whose 27 pregnancies included 16 pairs of twins, seven sets of triplets, and four sets of quadruplets.

There is a contrasting natural mechanism, also related to the rearing of offspring, and that is pair-bonding, where the partners maintain an exclusive commitment to one another and drive away intruders. We are closer to the birds in our proclivities than to our anthropoid relatives because we share the need for close cooperation between two partners in the rearing of children, one parent remaining at the nest while the other goes out to forage for food. In primitive societies where there is a strong sense of community within the tribe, children may be cared for as a group without strict parental responsibility for particular offspring; in such a society, there is no pressure for one man and one woman to remain together to meet parental obligations. Similarly, in certain American subcultures where there are large extended families and children are readily passed among aunts and grandmothers to be raised whenever the natural mother, often unmarried and impoverished, cannot provide, we see patterns of sexual promiscuity or shifting of mates.

In mainstream America, we see two conflicting trends. One

is the technical development of contraception to the point where the dangers of a wife's conceiving a child by an outside lover or a husband's incurring financial burdens by siring a child by a mistress are remote. However, most married couples do have children and the rising costs of caring for and educating children through a growing adolescence, without prospect of help in child care from relatives or community, have forced the couple more than ever into the mode of the two-against-the-world nest-builders rather than the protective packs of our simian cousins.

And so, at least in early marriage, much of the basis for monogamy lies in the prospects and actualities of child-raising, for our new standards of premarital sexual experience have laid to rest most of the obfuscating notions that there was something inherently evil in sexual relations or the change of partners. The other strong basis is economic; we regard the Eastern world with awe for its widespread acceptance of polygamy, forgetting that polygamy is actually practiced only by the few men wealthy enough to afford the expense of more than one wife and the corresponding increase in children. Women in such cultures will gladly accept a one-half or one-quarter share in a husband who is an excellent provider rather than to live out their lives in poverty with a socially inferior man who cannot adequately support their children. The strongest opposition to polygamy comes not from women, as we have witnessed by our own experience with the Mormons of Utah, but from the men, for the practice of taking multiple spouses discriminates against the mediocre, who cannot compete with the more powerful and affluent and are doomed to celibacy and sterility. Economic concerns are not strictly related to child-raising; for example, what of the wife who remains with her husband for 20 years, enduring hardships, perhaps working to support him while he pursues higher education, only to have him leave her for a younger woman when he becomes a great success? Even if we concede him his right to change to a partner more pleasing to him, does not his first wife deserve some recompense for her contributions to their partnership over the years?

We can generally rule out a future change in our American lifestyle to one of Oriental polygamy since such arrangements would only serve the interests of the very wealthy and would not be championed by the mass of the population. Some communes, out of a present total of no more than a few thousand, encourage sexual mingling among members of the group and raise the children collectively, but there are no formal group marriages and children are aware of their natural parents. True group marriages are very rare (and, of course, not legal), but according to one study which located about 40 of them, group marriages usually dissolved in less than a year.

We certainly accept the notion that people may change partners through divorce, though we have seen that 80 per cent of our sample still considers this a drastic step and does not recommend that a marriage be ended merely because one partner is not happy with it. But are we any closer to the notion that a man or woman is entitled to more than one sexual partner at a time, even though married? We have already seen (Chapter Eight) that one-fourth of couples currently married have been involved in extramarital affairs, including 30 per cent of husbands. This figure is low because it concerns those couples who, in general, are not about to divorce, and it is fair to assume that many divorces are occasioned by extramarital affairs. Certainly, among the 50 per cent of divorced people who remarry within a year of divorce and the 25 per cent who wed again within five months, many, if not most, have had a relationship with the new spouse that pre-existed the divorce. So, surveying currently married couples for extramarital infidelity is like checking automobile tires on the road for blowout potential; one will find some dangerously worn tires, but since an actual blow-out will remove the vehicle from the road, we have no way of assessing all the casualties if we count only cars still rolling.

Only 2 per cent of spouses had been involved in extramarital activity with their partner's consent, so, in actual practice, few couples seem to accept the idea of sexual variety. How many modern spouses are open, in theory, to the concept of extramarital sex?

Do you believe in extramarital sexual activity for yourself and/or your spouse? What allowances and limits would you recommend? How would you deal with infidelity?

Only 6 per cent of those we surveyed said that both partners should have outside affairs, and 4 per cent felt these should be made known to the partner.

WIFE: "Yes I do. Just as long as I didn't get pregnant it would be all right. No limit."

HUSBAND: "If my wife felt she needed someone else's attention I would probably allow it. I'd be a little apprehensive at first but if I was having an affair I'd like to know that it would be tolerated."

This homemaker has never cheated nor considered separating. Love for her spouse keeps her faithful, and at this point she would not be tempted. However she does admit that she and her husband have struck each other during arguments. He's a blue collar worker between 18 and 30 who believes that while faithfulness in a marriage is preferable, extramarital affairs should be tolerated.

WIFE: "Yes, all allowances and no limits."

HUSBAND: "Presently engaged in swap club."

She's into mate-swapping, group sex and homosexual activities. She describes her husband as irresponsible, and herself as passive, and has cheated with more than 3 men. She married because of pressure from others, and now says her husband takes her for granted, and they've had a period of separation. She's a homemaker, no children, between 41 and 50. He doesn't care about his wife's cheating, and admits he married her because she was pregnant at the time. He's also into group sex and mate-swapping, and reveals that his biggest temptation to cheat is money or gifts. A professional with a postgraduate education between 41 and 50.

Two per cent felt that both partners should have outside affairs, but should not reveal them to one another.

WIFE: "Yes. Only without my knowledge and only 'one-night stands.' Infidelity—first learn why, if first-time offender, dismiss issue. If more often, dismiss spouse."

HUSBAND: "A 'zipless fuck' would be okay. Talk it out to determine if it occurred because of a deep-seated discontent with my behavior or sexual performance."

She has never cheated, and feels it is a serious threat to a marriage to do so. If her husband did, she would demand that he give up his lover. The temptation for her to cheat though would be an exceptionally attractive new partner. This is her second marriage, and she says sex is good, and they never argue. Between 18 and 30. He's between 31 and 40, and works in management, and has a postgraduate degree. This is his second marriage. He believes that while faithfulness is preferable, extramarital affairs should be tolerated, though he's never cheated himself. Temptation to do so would be if he met a woman who understood him better.

An additional 3 per cent said that the husband only should be permitted outside sexual activity—5 per cent of husbands and less than 1 per cent of wives advocating the double standard.

WIFE: "NO—would ignore as much as possible."

HUSBAND: "For me only and would not condone infidelity."

Six per cent said that faithfulness is preferable, but extramarital affairs should be tolerated.

WIFE: "Under extraordinary circumstances it can happen. You should calmly talk out your problem with spouse."

HUSBAND: "No, but if it happened discuss it, reason it out and accept it."

WIFE: "I believe that extramarital affairs happen. I think care should be taken to not hurt your spouse. That would be dishonest."

HUSBAND: "I believe in it, if sex within the family is a failure—
no allowances or limits and I would deal with infidelity in a
mature and direct way."

This left 85 per cent who were definitely opposed to extramarital sexual activity. 46 per cent chose the answer "Faithfulness
is important, and extramarital affairs should be regarded as serious
threats to the marriage."

WIFE: "No, none—probably poorly, quarrelling most likely
though I'd prefer to be calm and collected and discuss it."

HUSBAND: "No, indicates either individual problems or something lacking in relationship. If both parties find something in
their relationship worth saving they may seek counseling and/or
work out another suitable arrangement between them."

This professional with a post graduate degree says she doesn't
believe in infidelity, and has never engaged in it, but what
would tempt her is a man who understood her better. At this
point she feels their marriage is stable, and her husband considerate. He works in management, and is between 31 and 40,
and also has a postgraduate degree. His temptation for cheating
would be an exceptionally attractive woman, but so far he has
never done so. Infidelity to him means a serious threat to a
marriage.

The remaining 39 per cent felt that "extramarital affairs almost
inevitably lead to separation and divorce."

WIFE: "In most major cases I do not believe in extramarital affairs.
I feel in some cases where the partner is ill, mental or similar,
and not able to be a loving partner, someone could find a
partner. It still may not be right but not as wrong as a person
having affairs after affairs."

HUSBAND: "No No No! No allowances. I don't know what I'd
do but would consider divorce."

Though her temptation to cheat would be an exceptionally attractive new partner, this wife says love for her husband and
moral beliefs keep her faithful. She's the mother of 4 children,
and is between 31 and 40. He's a white collar worker between

41–50 who is religious, and says he would never be tempted because of moral beliefs. Describes himself as "mature."

Wives were less liberal than husbands in advocating extramarital relationships, only 3 per cent being in favor of such liaisons with the spouse's knowledge, compared with 5 per cent of husbands. Two per cent, identical with the number of husbands, would condone such relationships if kept secret.

WIFE: "Yes, I believe in extramarital sex if it were kept discreet and you weren't being fulfilled at home. Of course, this is not the answer for everyone but it suits me. If my husband was unfaithful I would suppose I wasn't doing my job as a wife."

This wife cheated with 2 or 3 other men, briefly, and though she feels her husband takes her for granted, she says she has a fairly stable marriage. Her feeling is that both partners should be allowed outside affairs, but they should not reveal them to one another. Between 18 and 30, with some college, and works in the technical field.

WIFE: "Yes—the activity should be kept to oneself and be of the non-binding type—a pleasureable occurrence rather than a love affair. Infidelity—sexual wandering—should be handled as the situation requires."

This wife says that if she found her husband cheating, she would ignore it for while she believes fidelity in a marriage is preferred, extramarital affairs should be tolerated by both partners. She has not cheated herself only because of lack of opportunity. Her marriage alternates between periods of remoteness and closeness. The mother of 3, she's a professional with a postgraduate education.

WIFE: "For me I would be eager for an affair if I could find someone I really cared about and he made me feel important."

Six per cent of wives—1 per cent less than the number of husbands holding this view—felt that faithfulness was preferable, but that extramarital affairs should be tolerated.

WIFE: "I do not really believe in outside sexual activity but I have because of lack of love and need at home. I have knowledge of infidelity on my husband's part and I accepted it as a part of his inability to be mature enough to be satisfied at home."

She has already consulted a lawyer about a divorce, and has cheated on her husband with another man for over a year. If her husband cheated, she would simply ignore it, for she has little sex with him. While she believes he appreciates her, she feels he doesn't love her. She's between 41 and 50, works in management, and is the mother of 2 children.

WIFE: "Not really. I would have to accept it if it was done openly."

She cheated—but with her husband's knowledge and consent, and feels that both partners should be free to have outside affairs with each other's knowledge. Her sex life is good and her husband appreciates her fully, yet if she knew he cheated, she would seek professional counseling—if he agreed to do so. Between 31 and 40 and a college graduate.

WIFE: "I don't believe in extramarital activity. To me there are no limits but allowances would be total boredom with marriage only if spouse just does not solve problem. Infidelity is very hard—but I believe in therapy with spouse, talking calmly and complete understanding and not putting anyone down."

Ninety-one per cent of wives were opposed to extramarital sexual activity compared with 78 per cent of husbands. Some felt, however, that they could deal with infidelity in a patient, understanding way:

WIFE: "I believe in absolutely no extramarital sexual activity for myself . . . I also believe it would be wrong for my husband—but that, of course, is up to him to decide. . . .

"The Christian walk allows only complete fidelity but of course Christians are human . . . and I'm sure many Christians make mistakes. . . . It is not for me to judge. When you're living under the grace of God, rather than rules and regulations, what you do is between you and the Lord. I would deal with infidelity as I try to deal with all of life's problems, with love and understanding and praise to the Lord—because He can turn anything into a blessing!"

She's religious, and is between 41 and 50. A college graduate and mother of two, she says her marriage is loving and her husband appreciates her fully and they only have "friendly" arguments. Her feeling is that fidelity is what marriage is all about.

WIFE: "No, however, if one spouse is unable or unwilling to perform sexually, infidelity on the part of the partner would be more easily tolerated. Certain allowances should be made, but only if one partner is unwilling or unable to perform. Open communication is the only way to deal with infidelity. I would try to find out what my spouse was seeking in an extramarital affair and if necessary, attempt to acquire the characteristics my unfaithful spouse was seeking."

Other wives indicated that they would be very upset if they learned their husband was having an affair—or at least they gave no indication of tolerating it well:

WIFE: "When my husband gave his vows he gave up other women. That's what marriage is all about. I would deal with infidelity in an outrage."

She's a white collar worker with some college education, between 18 and 30. They have no children. She admits she would be tempted to cheat for many reasons, but says that she is faithful out of love and loyalty to her husband. She thinks their sex life is very good, and says they have intercourse once a day; nevertheless, they argue most about attention to members of the opposite sex. Their major problem, she feels, is alcohol. She rates the marriage as generally stable.

WIFE: "No! Seems impossible at the moment to set allowances and limits since I don't believe in the extramarital sexual activity.

"Dealing with infidelity—I'd seek out professional help as my anger and hurt would be more than I could cope with by myself.

"While a friend with a sympathetic ear is nice—it would be better to have a professional work with me—he/she would have no 'vested interests' or involvement."

This homemaker is between 31 and 40, and has a postgraduate education. She says that she would never be tempted to cheat because of moral beliefs. They argue most about money, job and career, and attention to members of the opposite sex. She feels unloved and unappreciated, but rates the marriage as generally stable.

WIFE: "I do not believe in extramarital sexual activity for either husband or wife. I believe that it comes about as a result of a lack of something in the marriage, not necessarily sexual dissatisfaction. I also believe that getting involved with an extramarital relationship further weakens the fiber of the marriage. It's always easier to give up than to fight to preserve something you consider worthwhile. Good marriages take work—Cinderella and Prince Charming only live in storybooks.

"If I discovered an infidelity on my husband's part, I would be angry, shocked, hurt and disoriented. After that I would confront him and try to find out the reasons why. Quite honestly, I do not know if I could forgive and forget even though intellectually I might be able to understand it. Down deep I'm still an emotional romantic. I certainly would try to work it out and even seek professional help, if necessary."

This college graduate with 2 children says her marriage is on a stable footing, and believes that infidelity is a serious threat to a marriage. However she does describe her sex life as "variable," and admits that her husband has struck her during arguments. If she found that her husband had cheated, she would confront him calmly. She's between 31 and 40.

WIFE: "None. I don't know. It's awful. I'm faced with that *now*. Seeking marriage counseling now (both of us). Hope there will be no more."

She's a homemaker, a high school graduate, 31 to 40. This is her second marriage, and they lived together for less than 3 months before getting married. She says that she'd never be tempted because of moral beliefs. She finds their sex life good, and says they have intercourse once a day, though she has orgasm 10 to 39 per cent of the time. She thinks their major problem is lack of communication, and feels disillusioned about romance and love.

WIFE: "No, I do not. The Bible clearly states it is sin—sexual relations are only for married people—Fornication is a sin. It is contrary to Bible teachings and one of the Commandments given by Moses from God: 'Thou shalt not commit adultery.'"

Forty-two per cent of wives were adverse enough to extra-marital affairs that they believed such activity almost inevitably led to separation and divorce—7 per cent more than husbands holding the same extreme view:

WIFE: "I do not believe in extramarital sexual activity in any way. If my husband decided to have an affair I would separate from him. Why go out for a hamburger when you have steak at home! There would be no way I could accept that."

This homemaker has a postgraduate education. Would never be tempted to cheat, and thinks her sex life is very good. They never argue and have no major problems, she says. She rates the marriage as always loving.

WIFE: "(1) Not really too good an idea! (2) If one cannot tolerate partner, one should place sleeping bag elsewhere—either lonely place or near nice companion. (3) If serious infidelity and one needs change of scene for various reasons—leave partner with best wishes! Go visit mother!"

As noted in Chapter Ten, those who had remarried were three times more open to extramarital affairs with the spouse's knowledge than were those in first marriages. Couples without children were considerably more liberal in this regard than parents. There was, however, no difference depending on age, and younger spouses were no more in favor of open relationships than their elders. The more educated were slightly more liberal, but only a single percentage point separated the college graduates from those who had not completed high school.

Even the husbands who saw the possibility of extramarital affairs with each other's knowledge generally expressed reservations:

HUSBAND: "Yes, if it is an unusual circumstance, and both parties see the benefit from such an undertaking to their own marriage. But extramarital activities must be agreed by both parties with definite objectives other than physical pleasure. Communication must always be open between spouses. Otherwise extramarital activities become infidelity."

This white collar college graduate says both husband and wife should be free to have outside affairs with each other's knowledge and consent, but he hasn't done it so far. He's between 31 and 40.

HUSBAND: "If it's okay for both partners, why not? In my own situation no—I don't think I could handle it; nor do I think my wife could. The physical pleasure gained is not worth the psychological pain most likely incurred. Infidelity—I think my wife would leave me—I'm not sure."

He says cheating leads to divorce—and he hasn't done any. If he found his wife commiting infidelity, he would seek professional help. Says his marriage changed him for the better, even though he married because of pressure from others. His only major problem is lack of money. A professional between 31 and 40, with a postgraduate education.

HUSBAND: "I don't think anyone should cheat. But if you both agree you should try it—then do it."

More than three times as many black respondents as white felt that both partners should have outside affairs, but not reveal them to one another. One husband in 20 felt that extramarital intercourse should be an exclusive male prerogative, and we would assume many would keep that opinion and its consequences to themselves:

HUSBAND: "Yes, if I was out of town. I wouldn't tell my wife."

This blue collar worker says a divorce would enable him to find his true love, and has cheated with 2 or 3 other women, briefly. Boredom tempts him, and he admits that he feels that husbands only should be allowed outside sexual activity. Says he is possessive.

HUSBAND: "Occasional affair with no ties."

He's a professional, 18 to 30, with some college education. He admits to having cheated with 2 or 3 others, briefly. He says he's tempted by an exceptionally attractive new partner. They married because of pregnancy, and he finds their sex life variable. He describes his wife as possessive, and himself as impetuous. He believes they have a fairly stable marriage.

HUSBAND: "I'm not against it if it doesn't lead to complications. A little change is a spice for the marriage."

The viewpoint that fidelity was preferable but extramarital affairs should be tolerated was more prevalent among the highly educated, 8 per cent of those with college educations and 11 per cent with postgraduate education expressing this feeling against 5 per cent of high school graduates.

HUSBAND: "While I do not believe in extramarital sex I believe that mistakes in judgment may occur and either one of us having an extramarital affair would not break up our marriage. I would deal with infidelity by discussing the reason or reasons for it with my spouse, then seek to rectify the problems."

This graduate student has never cheated, and says his sex life with his wife is very good. While they argue mostly over personal habits, he says his marriage is a loving one, and married his wife because of her ability to communicate.

HUSBAND: "No, none, try to approach it carefully and maturely. The family is the important factor and sin, like pain, is forgotten in time."

Educational levels did not so much influence attitudes towards extramarital affairs, but rather the way spouses dealt with the situation. For example, 83 per cent of high school drop-outs and 82 per cent of college graduates did not believe extramarital affairs should be tolerated; however, 43 per cent of high school drop-outs believed that such problems inevitably led to separation and divorce, while only 28 per cent of college graduates shared this conviction.

HUSBAND: "No, I believe it is morally wrong. Aside from morals, I think it would severely damage your relationship. Rather than being a cause of marital problems, I think it is a symptom of problems that already exist. I do not know how I would deal with it."

He works in management and has 4 children. This is his second marriage, and he's between 31 and 40, and a college graduate. He now has a feeling of emotional security and of being loved in this marriage, and admits it has changed him for the better. His sex life is very good, and says they have no major problems—so he's never cheated.

HUSBAND: "No! No allowance whatsoever. God's law states: 'Thou shalt not commit adultery.' Divorce only when there has been unfaithfulness (sex with someone else). Then one has no right to marry again! However, there need be no separation—as reconciliation can be made if both parties are willing to admit before God and each other their sin! And confess their sin to God."

He's religious, 51 or over, and works in the technical field. He says he and his wife never argue, and that marriage has made him more emotionally stable, and he knows his wife loves and appreciates him fully. In addition he believes they have no major problems.

HUSBAND: "I am strongly against extramarital sex for either myself or my spouse. I would most likely demand to meet the lover and because of jealous streak in me probably get into a physical fight, I would probably leave my spouse."

He's a student, 18 to 20. He says he'd never be tempted to cheat, and that their sex life is very good. They do argue about personal appearance and attention to members of the opposite sex, however. He says they have no major problems, and have a loving marriage.

HUSBAND: "I don't feel that a friendly feel out in the open, not objected to by the other party, is of any consequence. A behind the back feel, or advance, or one that is made against the wishes of the other party is out of the question. I don't feel intercourse is allowable, either out in the open or 'behind closed doors,' for myself or my wife. I feel I'd be able to 'talk out' any incident of true infidelity but I'd take a long time to build up my trust in her again."

From the data presented here and in Chapter Eight, it should be apparent that extramarital sexual involvement, although widely practiced, is not close to being accepted as part of the American system of marriage. Affairs, as we have seen, tend to be brief, and only one husband or wife in 20 has carried on an extramarital affair for a year or more (wives being twice as prone to long affairs and half as prone to infidelity). Only 5 per cent of husbands and 2 per cent of wives have been, according to our survey, unfaithful with four or more others, indicating that infidelity is more a sporadic phenomenon than a way of life for most spouses.

Our respondents show considerable insight into the fact that affairs often "just happen" and indicate they would be inclined to forgive the spouse provided the outside liaison did not continue. Indeed, the more women become better educated, involved in business, and the equals of men, the more will there be routine communication between members of the opposite sexes and the possibility of temptation. There is no conceivable way to avoid this sort of non-sexual interaction, nor should we strive to. As Shaw puts it, "The impersonal relation of sex may be judicially reserved for one person; but any such reservation of friendship, affection, admiration, sympathy and so forth is only possible to a wretchedly narrow and jealous nature; and neither history nor contemporary society shows us a single amiable and respectable character capable of it." Hopefully, deeper interpersonal relationships between the sexes in the course of carrying on personal business and that of the world will not lead the concerned parties to either underestimate the biological forces that remain constantly in play or overestimate the urgency of the most impersonal of drives.

Finally, the impersonality and evanescence of most affairs should reassure us that a further liberalization of divorce laws will not encourage people to change partners every few months nor abandon monogamous relationships in favor of an endless series of brief unions. No man or woman has ever become infatuated with the entire opposite sex, and, in fact, the quality of infatuation is such that it makes us oblivious to the attraction of all others. No shopkeeper with any business sense or sense of any sort would try to convince a teen-aged girl that a John Travolta poster was just as good as a Shaun Cassidy poster if he happened to run out of her favorite idol's image. Our basic desire to limit ourselves to one exclusive partner has kept the institution of monogamous marriage going when nearly every other warm-blooded, furry creature has followed a different and more varied call.

An ill-informed schoolboy once wrote: "Having two wives is called bigamy. Having one wife is monotony." One man's sameness is ten men's stability and while people occasionally venture outside the marital system which insures that stability, nobody seems very motivated to alter the system.

Coming Apart

> He had bought a large map representing the sea,
>   Without the least vestige of land:
> And the crew were much pleased when they found it to be
>   A map they could all understand.
>
> "What's the good of Mercator's North Poles and Equators,
>   Tropics, Zones, and Meridian Lines?"
> So the Bellman would cry: and the crew would reply,
>   "They are merely conventional signs!"
>   —Lewis Carroll, THE HUNTING OF THE SNARK

Carroll's captain, who navigates with a map that is a total blank, was born a century too soon. He would be quite at home among today's marriage experts who advocate the disregarding of the conventional guidelines that have governed marriage for centuries, but who have not provided us with any visible alternate routes. The captain without a chart "had only one notion for crossing the ocean, and that was to tingle his bell"—and with the divorce rate being what it is, newlyweds might just as well toast their union with Golden Wedding on-the-rocks and not send to ask for whom the bell tolls.

The safest place from which to get directions for avoiding the reefs is from a ship still afloat, and we sought some advice from couples whose love-boat had not yet floundered:

Why do you think the divorce rate is so high today? What would you advise newly married couples to do to prevent ultimate divorce?

One frequently stressed point is that young couples too often go their separate ways. In their quest for independence and self-fulfillment, they find things to occupy them apart from their spouses, and fail to develop common interests. They are individualistic at best, selfish at worst, and do not think of themselves as part of a unit except in times of crisis, at which point they have had little experience with acting in concert with the spouse.

WIFE: "People are selfish and self-centered and not committed to the institution of marriage. If a husband and wife are both actively involved in trying to make their marriage work, it most likely will."

HUSBAND: "There is not enough commitment to each other and to the family. It is very important that there is a strong feeling of family. Every member is important and should be involved as much as possible. Religion is also important in holding a family together."

This homemaker is a college graduate, and mother of two, and while she feels they have a loving marriage, she says they don't communicate, and her marriage sometimes alternates between very close and very remote periods. He's between 31 and 40, a college graduate working in management, and feels his wife loves and appreciates him fully, and that his marriage is always stable.

WIFE: "Couples grow apart. They have different interests and want different things out of life. What is important when you're young and first married seem to change as you get older. I feel doing things with family is very important."

HUSBAND: "Couples fail to realize the extent of the commitment involved in marriage. Be sure to develop mutual interests, otherwise a couple grows apart as each develop their own interests."

WIFE: "Because couples do not communicate with each other. They go their different ways with outside activities and don't spend enough time together.

"My advice to a newly married couple would be go into marriage with a positive attitude and always work on your marriage to improve it."

HUSBAND: "From what I see and judge our relationship as it was and is now would be outside interests such as his golf day, her bowling day. These things are good but both spouses should join and do something together to keep communication open and honest."

Both are between 31 and 40. She's a homemaker, he's a blue collar worker who didn't graduate from high school. She was under 18 when she married, and now feels overwhelmed by responsibility. They have 3 children. Disagreements over their children is a major problem according to her. He believes their major problem is conflicts over relatives, and though he describes himself as passive, he feels his marriage is a loving one.

WIFE: "Because people don't seem to try to keep their marriage together. You have to work at staying together from the beginning, not waiting until problems have become too big to overcome. Don't be so selfish, think more of other person than yourself. Try to put Christ back into the home."

HUSBAND: "(1) The act of divorce is more socially acceptable. (2) The financial ability of women to be self-sustaining (3) The extreme demands of partners for immediate and total satisfaction in the relationship—the prospect of future gratification is simply not acceptable—I have no advice for newly married couples."

She's religious and a homemaker, and mother of 2. Though lack of communication is her major problem, she says their marriage is generally stable. Describes herself as emotional and possessive, and now feels she is living only for her children. He's a college graduate between 31 and 40, and this is his second marriage. He describes his wife as "considerate" and "reserved," yet feels he's loved and fully appreciated, and marriage has definitely changed him for the better.

Since divorces, through law reform, are easier to get, more people will get them. The growing job opportunities for women, coupled with their smaller families and better educations, have offered alternatives to wives whom financial dependency would have previously kept trapped in bad marriages. In the face of such changes, an increase in divorce rate is inevitable and, in many ways, desirable; however, some of our couples felt that newlyweds should better their understanding of marriage through conscientious communication and not rely on the unrealistic portrayals of the mass media.

WIFE: "It's too easy to get married and simple to get divorced. Advise newly married couples to discuss all feelings and troubles with spouse. Always have open communication between the two."

HUSBAND: "Lack of communication before and after marriage. Learn to talk about problems and frustrations and release tensions verbally."

WIFE: "It is too easy to get a divorce. Talk to one another and don't leave a problem inside of you."

HUSBAND: "Couples underestimating the need for similar backgrounds and culture. And the 'well if it doesn't work out, we can get a divorce easy enough' attitude of many people who get married."

WIFE: "Many dwell on sex too much and don't want to assume responsibility of ups and downs. Money has lot to do. One has to be able to manage and not go over one's budget."

HUSBAND: "Divorce rate is high due to a number of reasons. The great drive for freedom of expression has become greater than obeying and following basic moral standards. Women have become financially independent so the need for working harder to save a marriage is not necessary. Television shows and movies portray unrealistic conditions."

Both are 51 or over, she's a white collar worker and mother of 4. Money is her major problem, but her sex life is good and she has not been tempted to cheat. She had children to insure a stable marriage and believes she has one. He says his wife is considerate and loves and appreciates him fully, but that their major problem is differences in personal interest.

WIFE: "Couples marry too young. They are not ready to settle down. Newlyweds should give each other all the privacy each spouse needs. Communication about emotional needs are important."

HUSBAND: "Divorce rate is high because it is easier to get one now and the stigma of a divorce has changed. No advice for newly married couples. There is no answer for a cure to divorce."

Some wives not only felt modern spouses were too self-centered, but they put the blame squarely on women for rejecting the Biblical teaching that wives were supposed to be obedient to the husband and regard him as head of the household. Others felt the blame should be shared between the sexes for putting the self ahead of the spouse, or the couple ahead of their children.

WIFE: "I think the divorce rate is so high today because there is too much 'I' in the relationship. 'I need to be satisfied.' 'I need to be pleased.' The Bible says first, 'Husbands love your wives' then wives, 'respect and obey your husbands.' If a husband shows genuine love to his wife, a wife will want to respect and obey her husband. It can be a wonderful circle of love and respect. My advice—Love, marriage, sex, family, home was all God's idea. He brought it all into existence. He is the authority of it all. Put it all into His care and He will give you the strength to live it day by day. He is the blessed controller of all things."

Her marriage has given her a feeling of emotional security and of being loved, and it's a stable marriage. Her only problem is difference in personal interest. She's 51 or over, and works in the professional field, with some college background.

WIFE: "Give one hundred per cent of themselves to the other. Women are too sure of themselves. They use their sex against their husband. They should never go to sleep angry. Women are generally the major cause in divorce in my opinion. They no longer treat their man like the head of their house. I need my husband and I let him know it. When a woman needs her husband she should tell him to make love to her. It's as good for his morale as it would be for hers."

She's a homemaker, 31 to 40, a high school graduate. This is her second marriage. She says the major problem in the marriage is smothering love, and describes the marriage as being both always loving, and having alternating close and remote periods.

WIFE: "The divorce rate is so high today due to several reasons, some of them being: the unimportance of strong religious and moral convictions, placing the welfare of the children below the desires of the adults, financial pressures, frequent job transfers, alcohol problems, unfaithfulness, etc."

WIFE: "The divorce rate is so high because people are selfish. Everything in our society teaches us to take care of No. 1 first. Most couples go into marriage today to see what they can get out of it not what they can give to it. To prevent divorce, they must trust Christ and let Him be the center of their relationship. They must work at making that marriage work. Love will grow. I thought I loved my husband 18 years ago, but now I know I do and it came through working together."

Ann Whitefield, who weds Shaw's social reformer, Jack Tanner, has no fear of disillusioning her reluctant fiance, saying, "I can't: he has no illusions about me. I shall surprise Jack the other way. Getting over an unfavorable impression is ever so much easier than living up to an ideal." Many wives felt that young people enter marriage with false expectations, anticipating that the course of action between them will be a lot smoother than in actuality. Having no concept of potential bad times, they are not committed to enduring them and working them through, and so they bail out at the first sign of trouble.

WIFE: "The divorce rate is so high because young people expect too much. Nothing is ever perfect, if they have a problem it is too easy to quit. I don't think they want or would take advice. I would advise that they communicate, try to work their differences out even to calling in outside help. Attending a Marriage Encounter weekend before they have trouble might help avoid problems."

She's married for second time, and although she claims her marriage is generally stable, she admits they have a communication problem. Her feeling is that strong affection and good communications are important for a good marriage. Describes herself as "mature," and says her marriage has given her more confidence in herself.

WIFE: "I think the divorce rate is high because people do not have a realistic expectation of what it is like to share another's life. I would strongly recommend learning to communicate with each other, be considerate of each other as an individual, avoid exploitation of partners."

She's the mother of more than 4 children, yet has a postgraduate degree, and is now 51 or over. Her only major problem in her marriage is conflicts over their children from a previous marriage. She feels that good communication is important for a good marriage, and what influenced her the most in her choice of present spouse was his ability to communicate.

WIFE: "I don't believe that people really commit themselves for life. They just want to be married as long as it feels good. When things go bad they head for the divorce courts instead of trying to work things out. Newly married couples should decide that marriage is a lifetime relationship and take their marriage vows more seriously. Also, a lot leave God out of their marriage completely."

This homemaker and mother of one admits her biggest problem is sexual dissatisfaction, and says her husband appreciates her as a wife, but not as a lover. They argue mostly over their lack of money, but she would definitely marry the same type of person again, even though she rarely ever has sex, and is only between 31 and 40.

WIFE: "I believe that unrealistic expectations play a major role in the increasing divorce rate. Also the changing reactions to divorce; its social acceptability. And the breakdown of the family structure throughout the U.S. has been an influence in bringing about divorce. Since a woman has a better chance for job opportunities and a man faces less financial burdens of alimony the monetary path to divorce is easier."

Not all wives welcomed the growing economic independence of women, and some, like the lady above, felt it was influential in the rising divorce rate. Others felt that the more competitive attitude of the working wife was being carried over into the home, playing havoc with traditional marital roles and upsetting the family's equilibrium. And, despite the increasing presence of two careers within the same household, the woman, due to deferred education and employment during the early stages of marriage, often lags behind the man in her professional and personal development, decreasing the equality they felt in their courtship days.

WIFE: "Because women are more self-supporting now and more educated. In past times marriage was about all they could do. Also many are selfish and think of themselves rather than their mates.

"Be a born again Christian and choose a Christian mate. If you do this you will feel all trials and troubles are God's plan to strengthen you and prepare you to help others. Just think what shallow useless people we would be if everything went just right for us all the time."

This college graduate and mother of 3 is between 41 and 50. She feels that marriage is a lifelong commitment never to be broken, and even though she argues mostly about social activities, she says her husband is considerate and thinks she's a good lover.

WIFE: "I think women are too aggressive. I think men have become too feminine. They do not look or act like a man in other ways. They depend on wife to help make the living but aren't willing to help her provide a clean orderly place to live. Both male and female have left their God-given roles and have tried to be too much the same. The only way to prevent divorce is to seek God's way and act accordingly."

This white collar worker and mother of 2 is between 41 and 50. A college graduate, she feels concern for each other's needs and good communication is important for a good marriage, and sees no major problems in her own. However she admits she only has sex once a month, and has cheated on her husband briefly, with one other man.

WIFE: "I think two people come together in their level of maturity at some point in time. This is great. But we do not remain static for the rest of our lives—we continue to grow and at different rates. I see no reason to make the rest of your life miserable just because your level of maturity was the same at one point. Be considerate of the other person. However, even this will not make for a good marriage when you no longer love each other."

Mammon, the personification of money, was one of Satan's original band of fallen angels, according to Milton's *Paradise Lost,* and Carlyle compared him to fire: "the usefulest of all servants, if the frightfulest of all masters!" Mammon continues to put wives in devilish binds, for while outside employment may weaken domesticity and family life, economic hardship perhaps takes a worse toll.

WIFE: "Divorce rate is high today because of inflation, families have to work out more, thus their home life is interrupted.
    "Stay home more, enjoy meals together and not go into debt too heavily."

Marriage has made her better at handling responsibility, but she says she feels tied down and trapped, even though she married for economic security. She believes that similar ideas and interests are important for a good marriage, along with financial security. She's a homemaker and mother of 3 between 41 and 50 with some college education.

WIFE: "I think money has the most to do with it. When we were first married my husband was not working. With all the bills and the getting used to one another was about all we could take. It probably would have broken us up. Now it's a lot easier. I think if you really love your partner you should put him in front and if you want your marriage you have to really fight for it (give a little and take a lot)."

A homemaker and high school graduate, she admits she has thought about divorce. Describes herself as emotional, and her husband as dominant. While she feels that concern for each other's need is important for a good marriage, she says her husband takes her for granted, and isn't concerned with her own needs. She's between 18 and 30.

WIFE: "The world has changed so much people take everything for granted. The money situation has caused many people to divorce—I also think abuse to the wife has caused it too. My first husband beat me every time I just looked at him wrong. Try to solve their problems and talk them out."

People are fond of saying they would not do something "for love or money," but one thing they seem to do for both those reasons is divorce. Some wives blamed various aspects of love and sex, as well as money problems, for our rising divorce rate, whether the fault was inadequate sexual gratification after marriage, too much of it prior to marriage, or possessiveness that stifled all gratification:

WIFE: "The laws should be changed and the colleges should not be so free to have all the children living together—this free love will kill our country."

She's retired, 51 or over, and a college graduate. Her major problem is disagreements over their two children, but feels her marriage is stable, even though her husband takes her for granted. She describes him as possessive, and feels she only lives now for her children.

WIFE: "Sex satisfaction. Get into group scene."

She's unemployed now, and this is her second marriage. A college graduate with no children, she's between 31 and 40. She admits that she's into group sex and has cheated with her husband's knowledge and consent. Married for companionship, and says sex with spouse is good, but her major problem is sexual dissatisfaction. She describes herself as irresponsible and possessive, and says her husband is also irresponsible and inconsiderate.

WIFE: "People don't want to face problems because it's easier to run. If, before going into marriage, things were talked out and they learned to communicate many problems would be solved. Spouses get too possessive, they stifle individual freedom without really knowing it."

One devout husband fortified his opinions with statistics of his own, though since nearly three out of five remarried people in our survey professed firm religious beliefs we doubt the veracity of his figures if not his sentiments:

HUSBAND: "Both married people should devote or give their lives to Jesus Christ and as Christian people God will give the glue to hold the two people together. Among Christian couples only one out of every 1,015 couples divorce and the divorce rate among non-Christian people is fifty-fifty. I have been very fortunate to have a loving Christian wife that loves me and Christ too. This has been the main reason for my marriage working so well. God was the one who performed the first marriage and he knows how it's supposed to work. The Bible tells us what we should do—now if we don't even look, then we may have to pay the price of a bad marriage."

A few husbands blamed preoccupation with sex, both extra-marital and marital, for the rising divorce rate:

HUSBAND: "Ask themselves, 'Why do I wish to get married?' Most promoted reasons for American marriage are invalid. So many marriages fail because the individuals married for wrong reasons. Social acceptance and sex are not the most important reasons."

His major problem is money, even though the family income is over $50,000 a year. His marriage though has given his life more purpose and meaning, and he feels it is a stable one. He's 51 or over, has no children, and is a professional with a post-graduate degree.

HUSBAND: "Infidelity. Stay away from temptation, spend as much time as you can with your family (as long as you feel comfortable doing this), express your love often."

There are many jokes about marriage and prostitution, such as the one about the nervous bridegroom who absent-mindedly left $20 on the bureau before leaving for work and was even more distressed to find that his bride had left $10 change. Sometimes, sex and money seem inseparable, especially as marital problems go:

HUSBAND: "Divorce rates are probably so high because of financial difficulties and/or cheating on the spouse. Learn to understand that in early marriage there are difficulties and you have to bear with the problems until they are worked out. Make sure before you marry that the mate is the right one."

This college student says he has no major problems, and feels loved and appreciated. Unemployment has been his worst crisis, and admits his wife has struck him during arguments. He thinks that extramarital affairs are serious threats to one's marriage, and would never be tempted to cheat.

HUSBAND: "I think that because of the times it is necessary for two incomes in order to survive or at least to live comfortably. This makes one more independent and thus a wife does not depend on her husband. I think working together for set goals and also letting Christ be the head of your house."

His family income is over $50,000 a year, and says sex at home is dull, and that's his major problem. Feels his wife appreciates him as a spouse, but not as a lover. What would tempt him to cheat is being away from home, but he hasn't done so as yet. He's 51 or over.

HUSBAND: "The divorce rate is so high in my age level because there is no communication, wages are low. Credit cards are the worst things to have because when the statement comes in every month everybody concerned has a fit."

Who wants to be committed to an institution? When the institution is marriage, commitment is precisely what is needed, according to several husbands:

HUSBAND: "Unwillingness to make firm commitments. Divorce no longer carries a stigma so people are no longer 'afraid' of divorce. Divorces are generally easier to obtain.

"Think before speaking. Realize that marriage is a partnership. Accept the partner's 'faults'—don't try to change them. A natural adaptation process will occur resulting in a harmonious relationship. Forget role playing. Share the responsibilities of maintaining the home and love life. Share life and love—successful marriage will result."

He married because of sexual attraction, and says that marriage
has given him more confidence in himself. A college graduate
between 31 and 40, his only major problem is differences in
personal interest. Describes himself as "methodical," and says
sex is very good.

HUSBAND: "Too early marriage; not showing enough commitment, lack of deep love, attitude of have your cake and eat it
too, unfaithfulness, also a lot of people should get divorced,
they have just grown apart, marriage doesn't have to be forever
nor divorce end in hate."

The problem most often cited, by husbands as well as wives,
was the prevalence of self-centeredness and independent activity
in a relationship that should be predicated upon compromise and
empathetic concern for the partner:

HUSBAND: "Most young couples have no idea of what marriage
means in terms of giving up their personal wants in order to
effect a good working marriage.
"Discussion of every item on an equal footing, equal rights
in all matters, close communication at all times, tell each other
how you feel."

He's the father of more than 4 children, and while his marriage
is a loving one, he says sexual dissatisfaction is a major problem. He's 51 or over, and works in management. He now feels
he lives only for his children, and has become disillusioned
about love and romance.

HUSBAND: "Young people are raised in a permissive age which
is not teaching them responsibility or morality. And the old
morality which kept people together has been abandoned for
a cheap do-as-you-please attitude. When the youth come to
grips with their sense of personal accountability to God and
man maybe a new foundation can be laid on which a permanent
home structure can be built."

He claims that affairs lead to divorce, and his Christian faith
has kept him faithful. Marriage has definitely changed him for
the better, and he says they have no major problem. His wife
loves and appreciates him fully. Married for companionship,
and his worst crisis was finding out that they couldn't have
children.

HUSBAND: "People are wrapped up in separate careers and are too afraid of losing their independence to devote themselves fully to each other, which is really necessary for a happy and successful marriage."

His wife is affectionate, his marriage is loving, and it has given his life more purpose and meaning. He says they never argue, and there are no major problems, and he is loved and appreciated. He's 51 or over and retired.

HUSBAND: "Too many selfish people—think only of themselves. Be sure you are ready to settle down to a home life and a change of pace. Be sure you are getting married for yourself and not because of peer or parent pressure. Don't rush into it. Always be open with each other. Realize that you are going to expose yourself emotionally and physically to your spouse."

HUSBAND: "I think people are becoming more self-centered and less likely to compromise. Perhaps our society is more strenuous causing the emotional release at home which causes problems. I firmly believe regular exercise such as running will help solve problems and enable them to be more understanding. It works for me."

Looking out for number one is not the safest course to follow in marriage. In so doing, the lookout loses sight not only of the partner but also of the aims with which they entered the new territory of marital relationship. We have suddenly become a society obsessed with the physical act of solitary running, running races with no destination and no victories. Even with a partner jogging in gasping silence alongside, there is none of the good-natured rivalry or the dedicated teamwork of the golf course, tennis court, bowling alley, or even the card table. Perhaps it's time to return to pastimes requiring at least two people—including marriage.

Trial Runs

When Colonel Pickering "naturally" concludes that Eliza Doolittle's parents were married, her father explains, "No, that ain't the natural way, Colonel: it's only the middle-class way."

But as the post-Victorian English middle class morality ultimately forced Alfred P. Doolittle into marriage, the sexual revolution of the American Seventies is pressuring young people into living arrangements once held to be the province of the poor and scorned with such designations as "living in sin" and "living common-law."

According to our survey, 24 per cent of married people lived together prior to marriage. Among the youngest people surveyed, those between the ages of 18 and 30, 42 per cent had lived together prior to marriage, a lifestyle attempted by only 8 per cent of those now over the age of 50.

While only 19 per cent of those married for the first time had held a trial run, 41 per cent of those involved in a remarriage had experimented before making the union legal.

In three out of eight premarital living arrangements, the couple had waited over a year before marrying. One-fifth had lived together from 6 months to a year, one-sixth from 3 to 6 months, and a quarter had waited less than three months.

Couples currently without children were more likely to have lived together before marriage, 34 per cent having done so, versus only 14 per cent of parents. While pregnancies may have accelerated some marriages, the gap is more likely due to a more liberated lifestyle among those who defer childbearing or renounce it in favor of career goals. Those without firm religious beliefs held a similar edge in premarital cohabitation over their devout counterparts, 39 versus 14 per cent.

In a reversal of Alfred P. Doolittle's society, it is now the high-income earners and the most highly educated who live together before marriage more often than those earning under $25,000 or who did not attend college. Twenty-eight per cent of college graduates lived with spouses before marriage, compared with 19 per cent of high school graduates. The highest income bracket prevailed in premarital living experience over the middle-income group, 28 to 22 per cent.

With nearly half of our youngest spouses living together prior to marriage, it is difficult to term such arrangements unconventional. While a practical test of living with one's intended spouse on a day-to-day basis seems the ideal way of guaranteeing marital compatibility, the prevalence of such experiments apparently has done nothing to lower the divorce rate.

What other daring, unconventional improvements has our society made as alternatives to marriage? The communes are scarcely new—the Oneida Community flourished in New York State for three decades, from 1848 to 1879, though it numbered only 300 people and was disbanded by its founder when age sapped his powers and no one foresaw a suitable replacement. Truly agrarian communes are impractical in our industrial society, but even if the country had the land resources to support large numbers of such communists, they would fail to attract even the support of our most liberal elements, since in practice they foster a return to a gender-based division of labor, where the men handle the building, farming, and money management, and women the cooking, housekeeping, and child-rearing.

Group marriages are hardly new, the most successful in history having been the affectionate triangle that existed among Lord Nelson and Sir William and Lady Hamilton a century ago. The problem here is a simple mathematical one, for if it is difficult to obtain harmony between two people, this difficulty increases with alarming exponentiality as new partners are added.

Ironically, as progressive heterosexuals are declaiming marriage as an archaic and non-viable institution, homosexuals are agitating to be permitted to take the same religious vows and be bound by the same legal documents that are being so violently contested.

Single-parent marriages are nothing new, but with new techniques of external fertilization and uterine implantation, we may soon witness the advent of "fatherless" children. No sooner had the newspapers proclaimed the birth of an English child who was the product of an ovum fertilized outside the womb and surgically reimplanted, then a spokeswoman for a militant lesbian group announced her intention to campaign for such lesbian pregnancies, using donor sperm from male homosexuals. Her motives were purely political, she explained, since it was felt the only way homosexuals could obtain rights under the law was through breeding and indoctrination of children who would grow up in sufficient numbers to pressure politicians to pass the desired legislation. She dismissed a reporter's facetious question about whether, with the declining birth rate among heterosexual women, we might not reach a point where any pregnant woman would be assumed to be a lesbian.

Such extreme proposals seem too unreasonable to be taken seriously at this moment, but we would do well to heed Jack

Tanner's warning: "The reasonable man adapts himself to the world; the unreasonable one persists in trying to adapt the world to himself. Therefore all progress depends on the unreasonable man."

Getting It Together

> Marriage is a microcosm, a world within which we seek to correct the shortcomings of the macrocosm around us. St. Paul said it is better to marry than to burn; today, feeling the glacial chill of the world we live in, we find it better to marry than to freeze.
>
> *—Morton Hunt*

Where did modern marriage go wrong? Everyone seems to want it, yet no one knows how to keep it going, and those who do often are dissatisfied with the way it is running.

To answer all the questions that have been raised, you would have to write a book—which is what we have just done; somehow the questions, despite the answers of nearly 4,000 married people, still remain unanswered. What we clearly see emerging, though, is a set of assumptions about modern marriage that run contradictory to our traditional expectations. If expectations have changed and marriage has not, our problem may be that we, like Lewis Carroll's White Knight, "madly squeeze a right-hand foot into a left-hand shoe" and are feeling the pinch.

Rampant assumption number one is that marriage is a private personal contract between two individuals. Far from it, it is a three-cornered pact, involving a man, a woman, and the State. Anyone seriously doubting this has only to note what happens when some starry-eyed reformer advocates some way of decreasing individual responsibility for the couple; he blithely, and correctly, expects the State to fill the void. Free women of domestic chores so that they may pursue careers, and the State shall provide day nurseries. Allow fathers easy access to divorce, and the State shall find methods of determining and enforcing child care payments, or, better yet, take over all child care completely. Prevent immature people from marrying by having the State set up more stringent requirements for marriage licenses.

No sooner is a proposal made that seems to ensure more personal freedom for the married, then a counter-proposal must be made so that the State can fill that void. Margaret Mead proposed many years ago a double system of marriages, a limited, easily dissolved form for those without children, and a more traditional long-term one for parents—all regulated by the State, of course; modern couples simplified this proposal and bypassed the State by simply living together until they were sure they wanted to incur the legal obligations of marriage. Yet, as actor Lee Marvin now knows, even those who think they have evaded the long reach of the State by foregoing marriage may be told by the courts that an unwed partner, on petition, shall be granted rights and damage payments in all respects equal to someone who played by the State's rules from the start. Alarmists who were advocating mandatory contraception to curb the population explosion should not rest complacently with our achievement of Zero Population Growth; the government of Argentina within recent memory banned the sale of contraceptives not for religious reasons, but simply because the population was too low. The State is a partner to every marriage and we must never presume that increased individual freedom will be accompanied by corresponding anarchy.

Basic new assumption number two is that marriage is somehow a vehicle for personal growth and happiness. On the contrary, marriage has been a bulwark for survival against the vicissitudes of life—allowing for sexual fulfillment without the competition and insincerity that characterizes the world of the singles, providing security for the children who are our defense against our mortality, and insuring some sort of aid and companionship in times of illness and adversity. Marriage, in short, has nothing to do with pleasure, though it certainly has its moments of joy. Would the world go on if everyone quit his job because he decided it was not totally pleasurable, or was not providing him with consistent satisfaction? Marriage is too important, too vital for us to burden it with such improbable demands as total sharing of all thoughts, complete empathy with the partner, constant evidence of validation of the partner's worth, and other irrelevant romanticisms. The proof of a good marriage is the work accomplished, the respect of partners for one another, and the undying commitment to the life they have chosen to share.

The development of oneself as a person at the expense of a loved one was once a privilege reluctantly accorded by society only to the most esteemed artists and other men of genius. Now, denly, it has become the inalienable right of any citizen to overthrow spouse, children, and obligations in a quixotic quest for some personal gratification and glory, which he can no more envision than one can imagine what a typical day in heaven is like from dawn to dusk. People speak in glowing terms of careers for which marriage should be readily sacrificed, although nearly all the work of the world is mere drudgery and not worth the missing of one smile from a child in terms of personal satisfaction.

The modern couple lives for the present, not the future, and values the dictates of "gut feeling" over cold logic, thus losing the prime advantages of millions of years of evolution whereby man became the only creature with a conception of the future and a logical intellect to plan for it. They disavow traditional patterns, losing the advantage of the human to profit from the experience of history instead of suffering the pain of his own errors. They advocate sexual freedom, returning to a primitive pattern that only the wily fox and industrious beaver have evaded, and forsake the security of the devotion of a single mate that causes the birds to sing. In short, they reject everything that is human, and then complain about the inhuman state of marriage.

Finally, let us not forget that marriage is for families, not couples. Although 95 per cent of couples have them at some point, children are shunted off-camera as husbands and wives attempt to preserve the image of carefree passion and adventure the media teach them to value. Our children are our breakwater against the tides of time, our link with immortality, and our commitment to a race and universe that transcend our brief hours of personal involvement.

Bishop Bridgenorth's sister-in-law, Lesbia, declares, "I'm afraid I think this rage for happiness rather vulgar."

Perhaps she is right. It certainly is not getting us anywhere, and maybe, as far as marriage is concerned, it's time we got back to business.